the Mixer bible Second Edition

Over 300 recipes for your stand mixer

Meredith Deeds & Carla Snyder

For complete cataloguing information, see page 418.

Disclaimer
The recipes in this book have been carefully tested by our kitchen and our tasters. To the best of our knowledge, they are safe and nutritious for ordinary use and users. For those people with food or other allergies, or who have special food requirements or health issues, please read the suggested contents of each recipe carefully and determine whether or not they may create a problem for you. All recipes are used at the risk of the consumer.

We cannot be responsible for any hazards, loss or damage that may occur as a result of any recipe use.

For those with special needs, allergies, requirements or health problems, in the event of any doubt, please contact your medical adviser prior to the use of any recipe.

Design & Production: Daniella Zanchetta/PageWave Graphics Inc.
Editor: Sue Sumeraj
Recipe Tester: Jennifer Mackenzie
Proofreader: Sheila Wawanash
Indexer: Gillian Watts
Photography: Colin Erricson
Food Styling: Kathryn Robertson and Kate Bush
Props Styling: Charlene Erricson

Cover image: Cranberry Maple Squares (see recipe, page 318)

We acknowledge the financial support of the Government of Canada through the Book Publishing Industry Development Program (BPIDP) for our publishing activities.

Published by Robert Rose Inc.
120 Eglinton Avenue East, Suite 800, Toronto, Ontario, Canada M4P 1E2
Tel: (416) 322-6552 Fax: (416) 322-6936

Printed in Canada

1 2 3 4 5 6 7 8 9 CPL 16 15 14 13 12 11 10 09 08

Contents

Introduction

As food professionals, we've had stand mixers in our kitchens for longer than we can remember. Because of their versatility, they are perhaps the most integral piece of culinary equipment we own. Certainly our cupboards are filled with all kinds of machines, tools and gadgets, but we can turn to no other one machine to knead dough, grind meat, slice vegetables, whip egg whites and make ice cream. Because of that, we have come to rely on our stand mixers as trusted culinary companions.

As cooking teachers, though, we are always surprised to find that so many of our students don't own a stand mixer — and if they do, they are often unaware of all of its capabilities. One student that stands out in our memories had had her own stand mixer for years, but had never used any attachment other than the whip. She had long ago put away her flat beater and dough hook, never stopping to consider how they might be used. Once we clued her in to the possibilities, she felt as though she had rediscovered an old friend.

There are many brands of stand mixers on the market, and more and more of them are developing attachments that will revolutionize the time you spend in the kitchen: pasta makers, food grinders, grain mills, juicers and ravioli makers all offer you the chance to be more creative and spend less time making dinner.

The stand mixer, with all of its available attachments, can now complete almost any culinary task. While the majority of handheld mixers have stood still in their evolution, holding fast to their limited power and functions, the stand mixer has blossomed into a culinary work center capable of saving you time and money. Who would have thought years ago that this machine we've always turned to for preparing lemon meringue pies and cinnamon rolls would be capable of producing perfect pasta or paper-thin mushroom slices or mountains of grated cheese, all so quickly and efficiently?

The evolution of the stand mixer makes a book like this necessary. Our goal is to help you understand the equipment and ease you into a comfortable working relationship with the machine and its attachments. We have provided you with an assortment of delicious recipes, everything from Hearty Harvest Roasted Vegetable Soup to Mocha Almond Ice Cream. Although many of the recipes require one or more of the additional attachments, the majority concentrate on the standard flat beater, whip and dough hook.

While you're whipping, kneading and slicing your way through this book, you'll also be gaining valuable insight into basic cooking techniques. Tips on how to achieve success in the kitchen accompany many of the recipes. Our years as culinary instructors have taught us the stumbling blocks that home cooks can experience. We have addressed these issues so that you can cook confidently even when under pressure.

The recipes cover the globe in flavors and textures, from Moroccan-Style Lamb Turnovers to New England Clam Chowder to Tomatillo Chicken Tamales to Ginger-Spiked Tuna Burgers with Asian Coleslaw. We loved testing every recipe in this book. From simple to spectacular, there is truly something for everyone in this bible of a cookbook.

So pull out your stand mixer, dust it off and dive into making Shrimp Bisque and French Baguettes. It's easier than you think.

Understanding the Equipment

If you already own a stand mixer, congratulations! If you are thinking about buying a stand mixer or upgrading to a more powerful model, there are some important issues to consider: What are your needs? Do you frequently double recipes when you cook or bake? Do you make bread often? Answering these questions can give you direction as to which of the many different varieties of stand mixers available will work best for you.

Since most stand mixers come with a bowl, flat beater, dough hook and wire whip, the variables among the different models seem to be power, speed, capacity, weight and available attachments. Let's cover the issue of power first.

In our society of "more is better," it's easy to buy a mixer that has more power than you actually need. But the power of your mixer does make a difference. If you are a bread or pasta maker at heart, you should look at machines with more than 300 watts of power. If you only bake cakes and cookies, the power might not be as important.

Speed settings are probably the biggest variable among the brands. Some mixers have as many as 12 speed settings, and some have as few as 3. The recipes in this book have been tested on stand mixers with 10 speeds, but you can adapt them. When the instructions say Stir or Speed 2, set to low; when they say Speed 4 or Speed 6, set to medium; and when they say Speed 8 or Speed 10, set to high.

The bowl capacity of most stand mixers ranges from 4½ quarts (4.5 L) to 8 quarts (8 L). Obviously, the larger the bowl, the larger the batches of bread or cookies you can make. The larger bowl sizes are great if you need the room ... but that extra space can turn out to be expensive real estate if it's not something you'll use. We've found that it can be difficult to work with small quantities of ingredients in bowls that hold 6 quarts (6 L) or more.

Weight can also be an issue if you must move the stand mixer from a cupboard to your kitchen countertop. Stand mixers can run anywhere from 12 to 30 lbs (6 to 15 kg), with heights of 8 to 16 inches (20 to 40 cm). Because our mixers are in use so much of the time, we've found that being able to store it in a corner of the kitchen counter, underneath the upper cupboards, makes the most sense. The 14-inch (35 cm) mixers fit under most cupboards. If this is important to you, measure that space before you go shopping. It's a real bonus not to have to pick up and transfer 30 lbs (15 kg) of machine every time you want to use it. And you will use it more often if you don't have to move it every time.

Attachments are important because they really expand the usefulness of your stand mixer. From ice cream makers to pasta makers to food slicers, attachments give you more options than ever before, so think about what you would like to be able to do with your stand mixer and buy a model for which the appropriate attachments are available.

Stand Mixer Equipment and Attachments

Mixer bowl: It's always helpful to have a second mixer bowl. That way, if a recipe directs you to mix batter and then whip egg whites, you won't have to transfer the batter to another container and clean the mixer bowl. (Our recipes, though, have assumed that you have only one mixer bowl.) Mixer bowls are dishwasher-safe.

Flat beater: Perhaps the most versatile of all the attachments, the flat beater is used to mix batters and combine ingredients in everything from pie dough to mashed potatoes. Flat beaters can be washed in a dishwasher or by hand.

Dough hook: This attachment is most often used to knead dough. On some machines it is a "C" hook; on others it is a spiral. Both work very well for everything from soft bread dough to stiff pasta dough. The hook is a real timesaver, much more efficient than kneading by hand. Dough that might take 10 minutes to knead by hand will take only 5 minutes with the dough hook. The hook can be washed in the dishwasher or by hand.

Wire whip: The whip is a powerful mechanical version of a handheld whisk. Although this attachment works well most of the time, we have experienced difficulty when whipping up small amounts. Also, because it's powerful, both egg whites and whipping (35%) cream can be easily overwhipped, so pay attention! The wire whip is dishwasher-safe.

Pouring shield: Pouring shields come in handy when you're adding ingredients to the mixer bowl while the mixer is running. They help prevent spatter and ensure that the ingredients end up in your cake instead of on your countertop. They are dishwasher-safe and come standard with many machines.

Rotor slicer/shredder: The slicer/shredder can be a real timesaver when you have lots of vegetables to chop or cheese to grate. It comes with four cones: a thick slicer, a thin slicer, a coarse shredder and a fine shredder. Useful at any time of year, it really comes in handy during canning season, when large quantities of vegetables and fruit need to be processed. Follow the manufacturer's instructions for cleaning.

Food grinder: One of our favorite attachments, with the food grinder you can grind your own meat, thereby creating homemade sausages, hamburgers and pâtés. You can also use it to purée soups and grind beans for falafel, among many other uses. Not only is it great on its own, it's also the base for several other attachments, such as the pasta maker, sausage stuffer and fruit/vegetable strainer. The grinder comes with coarse and fine plates, which determine the size of the grind, and a wooden food stomper, which helps push food down into the grinder. Be sure to follow the manufacturer's directions regarding speed, assembly and cleaning.

Fruit/vegetable strainer: We found this attachment to be indispensable when we were making soups and sauces. The strainer attaches to the food grinder and comes with a grind worm, strainer cone, strainer tray and splash shield. Soft foods will strain easily, but firmer foods such as apples and squash must be cooked until tender before straining. When you use this attachment, have an extra bowl ready to catch the solids that are strained from the purée and come out the tip of the strainer cone. Follow the manufacturer's instructions for cleaning.

Sausage stuffer: A must for the serious sausage maker, this handy tool comes with two tubes that enable you to easily form homemade sausage into large or small links. It is dishwasher-safe.

Pasta roller and cutters: Anyone who has ever made pasta using a hand-cranked pasta roller will love these attachments. The pasta roller rolls the dough into thin sheets, ready for cutting — it's fast, easy and fun!

Two pasta cutters, the wide fettuccine cutter and the thinner spaghetti/linguine cutter, make cutting your fresh pasta a breeze. A companion set is now available containing an angel hair pasta cutter and a thick noodle cutter. It's important to follow the manufacturer's instructions when cleaning the pasta roller and cutters. You should never wash these attachments in water, as they will rust.

Pasta maker: This attachment simulates an extrusion pasta machine. It has five interchangeable plates that allow you to make everything from thin spaghetti to lasagna noodles. Drier pasta dough works best with this attachment. You must fill the hopper slowly so that pasta does not compress in the food grinder. The pasta maker is dishwasher safe.

Ravioli maker: Although this attachment takes some mastery, once you get the hang of it, making ravioli is a snap. The trick is to roll out the sheets of pasta as wide as possible and to avoid overfilling the ravioli maker with filling. As with the pasta roller, be sure to follow the manufacturer's instructions for use and cleaning.

Citrus juicer: Whether you're making lemonade or lemon meringue pie, the citrus juicer makes short work of an otherwise tedious chore. It's designed to juice lemons, limes, oranges and grapefruit and is dishwasher-safe.

Ice cream maker: One of the newest attachments to be offered for the stand mixer, the ice cream maker will soon shoot to the top of your favorites list. It comes with a freezer bowl, which needs to be placed in the freezer for at least 15 hours before using; a dasher, which mixes the ice cream in the freezer bowl; and a drive assembly, which drives the dasher. Make a permanent space in your freezer for the bowl so that you can whip up a fresh batch of ice cream on a moment's notice. Your ice cream mixture must be well chilled before you pour it into the freezer bowl. If it's too warm, it will raise the temperature of the bowl and the ice cream won't set. Follow the manufacturer's instructions for use and cleaning.

Tips on Ingredients

Flour: Although there are a huge variety of flours on the market, in this book we will typically refer to the three most-used types of white flour: cake flour, unbleached all-purpose flour and bread flour. Each of these flours contains different amounts of protein that will directly affect the texture of the end product. Therefore, it is very important that you use the specific flour called for in the recipe. Most of our recipes were tested with unbleached all-purpose flour. For the most consistent results, read the recipe carefully and use only the flour specified.

Eggs: The recipes in this book were tested using large eggs. Use grade AA or A eggs. Always buy eggs from a reputable source and never use cracked or dirty eggs that may allow harmful bacteria to enter your food.

To break eggs cleanly, rap them gently on the counter and separate. Breaking eggs on the edge of a bowl drives the eggshell into the egg and often breaks the yolk. When separating eggs, we try to break the egg shell in half as cleanly as possible and use the shell to pass the yolk back and forth, allowing the whites to fall into a clean bowl.

When breaking lots of eggs for a soufflé or angel food cake, separate your eggs one at a time into a small bowl and transfer the clean whites to a larger bowl. That way, one broken yolk won't waste an entire bowl of egg whites.

Eggs separate more easily when cold, but beat up to a higher volume if they are brought to room temperature first. Let separated eggs sit at room temperature for 30 minutes before beating.

When whipping egg whites, it is very important to use clean metal or glass bowls. Plastic bowls may harbor trace amounts of fat, which will prevent your whites from whipping properly. Likewise, even a trace of egg yolk in your whites will interfere with the whipping process.

Anyone with concerns about using raw eggs — and particularly pregnant women, very young children, seniors and the immune-compromised — should use pasteurized eggs in recipes in which the eggs will not be fully cooked. Pasteurized eggs have gone through a heating process that kills harmful pathogens. In this book, every recipe in which the eggs are not fully cooked contains a note advising you of this fact. If pasteurized eggs are not available in your grocery store, you can substitute pasteurized liquid whole eggs or egg whites. Substitute 1/4 cup (50 mL) liquid whole eggs for each whole egg and 2 tbsp (25 mL) liquid egg whites for each egg white.

Citrus fruits: A medium lemon will yield about 3 tbsp (45 mL) juice and 2 to 3 tsp (10 to 15 mL) zest; a medium lime will yield 1 to 2 tbsp (15 to 25 mL) juice and 1 tsp (5 mL) zest; a medium orange will yield 1/3 to 1/2 cup (75 to 125 mL) juice and 1 1/2 tbsp (22 mL) zest.

Buy lemons, limes and oranges that yield to pressure and have thinner skins. Harder, thick-skinned fruit tends to have less juice.

Room-temperature citrus fruit yields more juice. You can microwave fruit for 20 to 30 seconds to warm it up.

Always read the recipe thoroughly before juicing in case you also need the zest. It is difficult to zest an already-juiced lemon, lime or orange.

Tips on Techniques

Grinding meat: When you're grinding meat in the food grinder, it should be partially frozen to facilitate grinding and keep fat from melting in the process, but it should not be frozen solid. Our recipes recommend freezing for 30 minutes, but since freezer temperatures vary, make sure meat can be pierced with the tip of a sharp knife to ensure that it won't damage the grinder.

Straining and grinding food: When using the fruit/vegetable strainer or food grinder, add food (especially hot liquids) gradually, so that an excessive amount of force isn't necessary to push ingredients through the feed tube. This will prevent both damage to the mixer and dangerous spattering.

Using the dough hook: When mixing bread and pasta dough with the dough hook, don't set the speed to anything higher than Speed 2.

Scraping down the mixer bowl: When mixing batters and dough, stop the mixer occasionally to scrape down the sides and bottom of the bowl with a rubber spatula. This will ensure that all the ingredients are properly incorporated into the batter.

Rotating pans: Most ovens have hot spots. Because of this, when you're baking cookies, cakes and pies, rotate the pans 180 degrees about halfway through to ensure even baking. If you're baking more than one pan at once, you should also switch the pans' positions on the oven racks halfway through.

Using an instant-read thermometer: Instant-read thermometers are indispensable when roasting meats or baking breads because they take the guesswork out of determining doneness. Make sure the probe is inserted close to the center of the meat or bread to ensure the most accurate read. When checking the temperature of meat, don't insert the thermometer next to a bone.

Appetizers

Pot Stickers with Spicy Sesame-Soy Dipping Sauce

FOOD GRINDER FLAT BEATER

Filling		
1 lb	boneless pork shoulder blade, cut into 1-inch (2.5 cm) cubes	500 g
2	cloves garlic	2
1/4 cup	fresh cilantro	50 mL
1 tbsp	peeled gingerroot	15 mL
1	can (5 oz/150 g) water chestnuts, drained and minced	1
1/4 cup	minced green onions	50 mL
1 1/2 tbsp	light soy sauce	22 mL
1/2 tsp	toasted sesame oil (see tip, page 25)	2 mL
60	wonton wrappers, thawed if frozen	60
1	egg, lightly beaten	1
2 tbsp	vegetable oil, divided	25 mL
Spicy Sesame-Soy Dipping Sauce		
1	clove garlic, minced	1
1/3 cup	light soy sauce	75 mL
3 tbsp	seasoned rice vinegar	45 mL
1 tbsp	chili-garlic sauce	15 mL
2 tsp	minced gingerroot	10 mL
2 tsp	toasted sesame oil	10 mL

1. *Prepare the filling:* Place pork in a shallow container in the freezer for 30 minutes to facilitate grinding. Attach the food grinder, with the fine plate, to the mixer. Set to Speed 4 and run pork, garlic, cilantro and ginger through the grinder into the mixer bowl. Stir in water chestnuts, green onions, soy sauce and sesame oil. Remove the grinder and attach the flat beater and mixer bowl. Set to Speed 2 and mix just until ingredients are combined.
2. Working with a few at a time, lay out wonton wrappers on a clean work surface. Place a scant tablespoon (15 mL) filling in the center of each wrapper. Brush beaten egg around the edges. Gather up the corners of the wrapper and pinch them together around the top to form a pouch, making sure all edges are sealed. Place dumplings on a baking sheet lined with parchment paper as they are made.
3. In a large nonstick skillet, heat 1 tbsp (15 mL) of the oil over medium-high heat. Place half the dumplings in the pan so they aren't touching and sauté until they are nicely browned on the bottom. Add 1/2 cup (125 mL) water, cover and steam until pork is no longer pink inside, about 5 minutes. Transfer to a serving platter and keep warm. Repeat with the remaining dumplings.
4. *Prepare the dipping sauce:* In a small bowl, combine garlic, soy sauce, vinegar, chili-garlic sauce, ginger and sesame oil.
5. Serve hot dumplings with sauce.

Makes about 60 pot stickers

Make ahead

Prepare through Step 2 and freeze in a single layer on baking sheet. Transfer to a freezer bag and freeze for up to 1 month. Cook directly from the freezer, adding 3 to 5 minutes to the steaming time.

Thai Beef Meatballs with Peanut Dipping Sauce

FOOD GROWNDER ◆ FLAT BEATER

◆ Large baking sheet, lined with parchment paper

Meatballs		
1 lb	boneless beef chuck or cross rib, cut into 1-inch (2.5 cm) cubes	500 g
2	cloves garlic, chopped	2
1⁄4 cup	chopped fresh mint	50 mL
1⁄4 cup	chopped fresh cilantro	50 mL
2 tbsp	fish sauce	25 mL
2 tsp	Thai red curry paste	10 mL
1	egg, lightly beaten	1
1 cup	fresh bread crumbs	250 mL
Peanut Dipping Sauce		
1 cup	coconut milk	250 mL
1 tbsp	lightly packed light brown sugar	15 mL
1 tbsp	Thai red curry paste	15 mL
1 tbsp	fish sauce	15 mL
1⁄2 cup	crunchy peanut butter	125 mL

Make ahead

Prepare through Step 2 and refrigerate, loosely covered, for up to 1 day.

1. *Prepare the meatballs:* Place beef in a shallow container in the freezer for 30 minutes to facilitate grinding. Attach the food grinder, with the coarse plate, to the mixer. Set to Speed 4 and run beef through the grinder into a large bowl. Stir in garlic, mint, cilantro, fish sauce and red curry paste. Cover and refrigerate for 30 minutes. Run through the food grinder again, this time into the mixer bowl. Add egg and bread crumbs. Remove the food grinder and attach the flat beater and mixer bowl. Set to Stir and mix just until ingredients are well combined.
2. Preheat oven to 450°F (230°C). Form level tablespoonfuls (15 mL) of the meat mixture into 1 1⁄4-inch (3 cm) meatballs and arrange on prepared baking sheet, at least 1⁄2 inch (1 cm) apart.
3. Bake in upper third of preheated oven for 8 to 10 minutes, or until golden and no longer pink inside.
4. *Meanwhile, prepare the sauce:* In a small saucepan, combine coconut milk, sugar, curry paste and fish sauce. Bring to a gentle boil over medium heat for 3 minutes, stirring occasionally. Add peanut butter and cook, stirring, until peanut butter is well blended.
5. Place meatballs on a serving platter and serve warm with sauce.

Makes about 25 meatballs

Cumin-Spiced Meatballs in Light Tomato Sauce

FOOD GRINDER

◆ Baking sheet

Meatballs		
1 lb	boneless beef chuck or cross rib	500 g
8 oz	boneless veal shoulder	250 g
8 oz	boneless pork shoulder blade	250 g
1 tsp	cumin seeds	5 mL
1 tsp	ground cumin	5 mL
1	egg, lightly beaten	1
1 tsp	salt	5 mL
1⁄4 tsp	freshly ground black pepper	1 mL
Pinch	ground nutmeg	Pinch
Light Tomato Sauce		
2 tbsp	olive oil	25 mL
3⁄4 cup	minced onion	175 mL
2	cloves garlic, minced	2
1⁄2 cup	dry vermouth or white wine	125 mL
1	can (14 oz/398 mL) diced tomatoes, with juice	1
2 tbsp	minced fresh parsley	25 mL
	Salt and freshly ground black pepper	

1. *Prepare the meatballs:* Cut beef, pork and veal into 2-inch (5 cm) cubes. Place in a shallow container in the freezer for 30 minutes to facilitate grinding.
2. Meanwhile, in a large skillet, over medium-high heat, toast cumin seeds, shaking pan often, until fragrant, about 2 minutes. Remove to a plate and let cool.
3. Attach the food grinder, with the coarse plate, to the mixer. Set to Speed 4 and run meat, cooled cumin seeds and ground cumin through the grinder into the mixer bowl. Add egg, salt, pepper and nutmeg. Remove the food grinder and attach the flat beater and mixer bowl. Set to Speed 2 and mix just until ingredients are well combined.
4. Heat the same skillet over medium-high heat and cook a teaspoon-size (5 mL) piece of the meatball mixture, turning to brown all over, until no longer pink inside. Taste and adjust seasoning as desired with salt and pepper.
5. Preheat oven to 375°F (190°C). Roll meat between your hands to form 2-inch (5 cm) meatballs and arrange on baking sheet, at least 1⁄2 inch (1 cm) apart. Bake in preheated oven for 15 minutes or until firm to the touch.
6. *Prepare the sauce:* In the same skillet, heat oil over medium-high heat. Add onion and cook, stirring, until translucent, about 4 minutes. Add garlic and cook, stirring, for another 2 minutes. Add wine and tomatoes, with juice. Boil until the liquid reduces by one-third.
7. Reduce heat to low and add cumin meatballs and minced parsley to tomato sauce. Cover and simmer for about 30 minutes, until meatballs are no longer pink inside. Transfer to a chafing dish and serve with toothpicks.

Makes 30 meatballs

Moroccan-Style Lamb Turnovers

FOOD GRINDER

- 2 large baking sheets, lined with parchment paper

1 tsp	salt	5 mL
1 tsp	ground cumin	5 mL
1/2 tsp	ground ginger	2 mL
1/2 tsp	ground allspice	2 mL
1/2 tsp	ground cinnamon	2 mL
1/4 tsp	freshly ground black pepper	1 mL
1 lb	boneless lamb shoulder, cut into 1-inch (2.5 cm) cubes	500 g
1 tbsp	olive oil	15 mL
1/2 cup	chopped onion	125 mL
2	cloves garlic, minced	2
1/3 cup	white wine	75 mL
1 tbsp	tomato paste	15 mL
2 tbsp	golden raisins	25 mL
2 tbsp	pine nuts, toasted	25 mL
2 tbsp	chopped fresh cilantro	25 mL
1	egg	1
1 tbsp	whipping (35%) cream	15 mL
1	recipe Puff Pastry (page 323)	1

Make ahead

Prepare through Step 5 and freeze turnovers in a single layer on baking sheets. Once frozen, transfer turnovers to a plastic freezer bag and freeze for up to 1 month. Bake directly from the freezer, adding 5 minutes to the baking time.

1. In a small bowl, combine salt, cumin, ginger, allspice, cinnamon and pepper.
2. Place lamb in a shallow dish and sprinkle with spices. Toss with your hands to coat the meat. Arrange in a single layer and place in the freezer for 30 minutes to facilitate grinding. Attach the food grinder, with the fine plate, to the mixer. Set to Speed 4 and run meat through the grinder into a large bowl.
3. In a large skillet, heat oil over medium heat. Add onion and sauté until tender, about 2 minutes. Add garlic and sauté for 1 minute. Add ground lamb and cook, breaking up lumps with the back of a wooden spoon, until no longer pink. Add wine and tomato paste and cook until most of the liquid has evaporated, about 4 minutes. Remove from heat and add raisins, pine nuts and cilantro. Taste for seasoning and let cool.
4. In a small bowl, using a fork, whisk together egg and cream. Set aside.
5. Preheat the oven to 375°F (190°C). Divide puff pastry in half. Work with one half at a time, keeping the other half chilled. On a lightly floured surface, roll each half into a 15- by 12-inch (38- by 30 cm) rectangle. Trim with a knife if uneven. Cut across long side into 5 strips and short side into 4 strips to make twenty 3-inch (7.5 cm) squares. Place a scant tablespoonful (15 mL) of the filling in the center of each square. Brush the edges lightly with the egg wash. Fold each pastry into a triangle, enclosing filling, and crimp edges with a fork. Cut 1 small steam vent in the top of each. Brush tops lightly with egg wash. Set on prepared baking sheets, at least 1 inch (2.5 cm) apart. Repeat with remaining dough and filling.
6. Bake in preheated oven for 15 to 20 minutes, or until golden brown. Serve warm.

Makes 40 small turnovers

Salmon Cakes

FOOD GRINDER · FLAT BEATER

8 oz	skinless salmon fillet	250 g
1	egg white	1
1/4 cup	dry bread crumbs	50 mL
2 tbsp	finely diced red bell pepper	25 mL
2 tbsp	finely diced celery	25 mL
1 tbsp	finely chopped green onion	15 mL
1 tbsp	chopped fresh flat-leaf parsley	15 mL
1 tbsp	mayonnaise	15 mL
2 tsp	chopped rinsed capers	10 mL
	Zest of 1 lemon	
1 tsp	freshly squeezed lemon juice	5 mL
1/2 tsp	salt	2 mL
Pinch	freshly ground black pepper	Pinch
Pinch	cayenne pepper	Pinch
	Unbleached all-purpose flour, for dredging	
1/2 cup	vegetable oil (approx.)	125 mL
	Garlic Aioli (see recipe, page 401) (optional)	
	Homemade Wasabi Mayonnaise (see recipe, page 401) (optional)	

1. Cut salmon into 1-inch (2.5 cm) pieces and place in a shallow container in the freezer for 30 minutes to facilitate grinding.
2. Attach the food grinder, with the fine plate, to the mixer. Set to Speed 4 and run salmon through the grinder into the mixer bowl. Add egg white, bread crumbs, red pepper, celery, green onion, parsley, mayonnaise, capers, lemon zest, lemon juice, salt, black pepper and cayenne. Remove the food grinder and attach the flat beater and mixer bowl. Set to Stir and mix until ingredients are incorporated, about 30 seconds. Form salmon mixture into eight 3-inch (7.5 cm) cakes and dredge them in flour to lightly coat.
3. In a large skillet, heat 1/4 cup (50 mL) of the vegetable oil over medium-high heat. Add 4 salmon cakes and fry, turning once, until browned and heated through, about 3 minutes on each side. Remove to a serving platter. Repeat with the remaining cakes, adding more oil as necessary.
4. Serve hot with Garlic Aioli or Wasabi Mayonnaise.

Makes 8 cakes

Sausage in Puff Pastry

- Preheat oven to 400°F (200°C)
- Large baking sheet, lined with parchment paper

6	5-inch (13 cm) long fresh sausage links (about 1 ½ lbs/750 g)	6
½	recipe Puff Pastry (page 323)	½
3 tbsp	whole-grain mustard	45 mL
1	egg, beaten with 1 tbsp/15 mL water	1
	Sesame seeds	

TIP
For the sausage, we suggest Merguez (see recipe, page 177), Lamb, Mustard and Rosemary Sausage (see recipe, page 176) or Italian Sausage (see recipe, page 164).

1. Bake sausage on prepared baking sheet in preheated oven for 20 minutes. Turn and bake for 5 to 10 minutes more, until no longer pink inside and juices run clear when pierced. Let cool to room temperature.
2. Roll out pastry to a 15- by 10-inch (38 by 25 cm) rectangle and brush with mustard. Cut into six 5-inch (13 cm) squares. For each square, place one piece of sausage on top of the mustard and roll tightly, overlapping the end by ½ inch (1 cm) and sealing by brushing the edge with water. Cut off any excess pastry.
3. Place the rolls, seam side down, on prepared baking sheet, at least 2 inches (5 cm) apart. Brush with egg wash and sprinkle with sesame seeds. Lightly score the pastry of each roll diagonally to make 7 equal pieces. Bake in preheated oven for 20 to 25 minutes, until puffed and browned. Slice at scored marks and serve immediately.

Makes 42 pieces

Mushroom Pinwheels

- 2 large baking sheets, lined with parchment paper

Mushroom Filling		
1/4 cup	olive oil	50 mL
2 tbsp	unsalted butter	25 mL
3	shallots, diced	3
2	cloves garlic, minced	2
2 lbs	mushrooms, coarsely chopped	1 kg
1/3 cup	dry white wine	75 mL
1/4 cup	soy sauce	50 mL
1/3 cup	whipping (35%) cream	75 mL
1/4 cup	chopped fresh parsley	50 mL
1/2 tsp	dried thyme	2 mL
	Salt and freshly ground black pepper	

1	recipe Puff Pastry (page 323)	1
1	egg, beaten	1
1/4 cup	mustard seeds	50 mL
3 tbsp	coarse cornmeal	45 mL

1. *Prepare the filling:* Heat a large skillet over medium-high heat. Add oil, butter, shallots and garlic; sauté for 1 minute. Add mushrooms and cook, stirring occasionally, until liquid has released and cooked off, about 15 minutes. Add white wine and soy sauce; cook until almost dry, about 10 minutes. Add whipping cream and boil until mixture is reduced and thick, about 5 minutes. Stir in parsley and thyme and season to taste with salt and pepper. Transfer mixture to a food processor fitted with the metal blade. Using the pulse button, chop the mixture coarsely (do not purée). Let cool.
2. Divide puff pastry in half. Work with one half at a time, keeping the other half chilled. On a lightly floured surface, roll each half into a 14- by 8-inch (35 by 20 cm) rectangle. Trim with a knife if uneven. Brush surface with egg wash. Sprinkle with mustard seeds and cornmeal. Flip over and spread top surface with half of the mushroom mixture. Starting at one long side, fold the edge of the pastry over and roll firmly and completely to the other long side, jelly-roll style. Pinch edge to seal and place seam side down on prepared baking sheet. Repeat with the remaining pastry and filling.
3. Freeze logs until firm, but not frozen solid. Preheat oven to 375°F (190°C). Remove logs from freezer and, using a sharp knife, cut each log into 1/4-inch (0.5 cm) thick slices. Place on prepared baking sheets, at least 1/2-inch (1 cm) apart. Bake in preheated oven for 20 to 25 minutes or until golden brown. Serve hot or at room temperature.

Makes 40 to 50 pinwheels

Pissaladière

- Preheat oven to 425°F (220°C)
- 2 large baking sheets, lined with parchment paper

1	recipe Puff Pastry (page 323)	1
3 tbsp	olive oil	45 mL
3	onions, thinly sliced	3
3/4 tsp	salt, divided	4 mL
1/4 tsp	freshly ground black pepper, divided	1 mL
2 tbsp	all purpose flour (approx.)	25 mL
2	tomatoes, thinly sliced	2
1/2 cup	pitted kalamata olives	125 mL
2 tbsp	chopped fresh parsley	25 mL
1/2 tsp	dried basil	2 mL

1. Cut pastry in half, wrap in plastic and refrigerate until ready to use.
2. In a large skillet, heat oil over medium-high heat. Add onions, 1/2 tsp (2 mL) of the salt and a pinch of pepper; cook, stirring occasionally, until translucent, about 10 minutes. Reduce heat to medium and cook, stirring occasionally, until golden brown and caramelized, about 15 minutes. Remove from heat and set aside.
3. Sprinkle flour on a work area and roll out one piece of the pastry, using more flour as necessary to keep the pastry from sticking, into a 12- by 7-inch (30 by 18 cm) rectangle. Place on prepared baking sheet and fold 1/2 inch (1 cm) of the sides over the pastry to form an edge. Press the edges with the tines of a fork for a finished look. Lay half the tomatoes on the pastry. Sprinkle with a pinch each of salt and pepper. Top with half of the caramelized onions. Scatter half the olives over the top, followed by half the parsley and basil. Repeat with remaining pastry and toppings.
4. Bake in preheated oven for 20 to 25 minutes or until the pastry is crisp and brown on the bottom and not soggy in the middle. Cut into slices and serve hot or at room temperature.

Makes 8 slices

Parmesan Cheese Straws

- Preheat oven to 400°F (200°C)
- 2 baking sheets, lined with parchment paper

1	recipe Puff Pastry (page 323)	1
1	egg, beaten with 1 tbsp (15 mL) water	1
1 1⁄2 cups	grated Parmesan cheese	375 mL

Make ahead

Prepare up to 2 days ahead and store at room temperature in an airtight container.

1. On a lightly floured surface, roll the puff pastry into a 30- by 10-inch (75 by 25 cm) rectangle. Cut in half crosswise, forming two 15- by 10-inch (38 by 25 cm) rectangles. Lightly brush one piece of the pastry with half of the egg wash and sprinkle evenly with cheese. Place the other half of the pastry on top and lightly brush with remaining egg wash. With a sharp knife or pizza cutter, cut crosswise into sticks 1⁄4 inch (0.5 cm) wide.
2. Place about 1 inch (2.5 cm) apart on prepared baking sheets, pressing ends onto sheets. Bake in batches in middle of oven until golden, about 10 minutes. Transfer to a rack and let cool.

Makes 60 straws

Fennel Straws

- Preheat oven to 400°F (200°C)
- 2 baking sheets, lined with parchment paper

1	recipe Puff Pastry (page 323)	1
1	egg, beaten with 1 tbsp (15 mL) water	1
2 tbsp	fennel seeds	25 mL

Make ahead

Prepare up to 2 days ahead and store at room temperature in an airtight container.

TIP

Caraway seeds, poppy seeds and sesame seeds all make for lovely variations to this easy party favorite.

1. On a lightly floured surface, roll the puff pastry into a 30- by 10-inch (75 by 25 cm) rectangle. Cut in half crosswise, forming two 15- by 10-inch (38 by 25 cm) rectangles. Lightly brush one piece of the pastry with half of the egg wash and sprinkle evenly with fennel seeds. Place the other half of the pastry on top and lightly brush with remaining egg wash. With a sharp knife or pizza cutter, cut crosswise into sticks 1⁄4-inch (0.5 cm) wide.
2. Place about 1 inch (2.5 cm) apart on prepared baking sheets, pressing ends onto sheets. Bake in batches in middle of oven until golden, about 10 minutes. Transfer to a rack and let cool.

Makes 60 straws

White Bean, Rosemary and Pancetta Bruschetta

FLAT BEATER

- Preheat broiler
- Baking sheet

3 oz	pancetta, chopped	90 g
2	cans (each 14 to 19 oz/ 398 to 540 mL) cannellini beans or white kidney beans, drained	2
1/4 cup	olive oil	50 mL
1 1/2 tbsp	finely chopped fresh rosemary	22 mL
2 tsp	minced garlic	10 mL
	Salt and freshly ground black pepper	
1	baguette, cut on the diagonal into 3/8-inch (0.75 cm) thick slices	1
	Extra-virgin olive oil	

TIP
Pancetta is a salt-cured pork product from Italy. It's made out of the same cut of meat as bacon, but it isn't smoked. If you have trouble finding pancetta in your grocery store, you can substitute bacon, or leave it out altogether.

1. Heat a medium skillet over medium heat. Add pancetta and sauté until crispy and golden brown, about 5 minutes. Remove with a slotted spoon to drain on a paper towel.
2. Place cooked pancetta, beans, olive oil, rosemary and garlic in the mixer bowl. Attach the flat beater and mixer bowl to the mixer. Set to Speed 2 and mix until beans begin to break up. Increase to Speed 4 and mix until beans are crushed and slightly creamy, about 2 minutes. Season to taste with salt and pepper.
3. Brush both sides of baguette slices with extra-virgin olive oil and place on baking sheet in a single layer. Place under broiler and lightly brown on one side.
4. Spread white bean mixture on the toasted side of the baguette slices. Drizzle a little more extra-virgin olive oil on top of each slice. Serve immediately.

Makes 30 bruschetta

Vermont Cheddar Shortbread Crackers

ROTOR SLICER/SHREDDER
FLAT BEATER

- 2 large baking sheets, lined with parchment paper

1 lb	extra-sharp Cheddar cheese	500 g
1 cup	pecan halves, toasted	250 mL
2 cups	unbleached all-purpose flour	500 mL
1 cup	unsalted butter, softened and cut into about 16 pieces	250 mL
1⁄4 cup	Dijon mustard	50 mL
1⁄2 tsp	cayenne pepper	2 mL

Make ahead

Prepare through Step 2, place crackers in a resealable plastic freezer bag and freeze for up to 2 months. Let thaw slightly in the refrigerator before slicing.

TIP
Vermont Cheddar is generally regarded as a high-quality cheese, but any sharp Cheddar will do.

1. Cut cheese into cubes and place in a shallow dish in the freezer until very cold and firm but not frozen, about 10 minutes. Attach the slicer/shredder, with the fine shredder, to the mixer. Set to Speed 4 and shred Cheddar cheese, then toasted pecans, into the mixer bowl. Add flour, butter, mustard and cayenne. Remove the slicer/shredder and attach the flat beater and mixer bowl to the mixer. Set to Speed 4 and mix just until the mixture forms a dough.
2. Divide dough in half. Roll each half into a log about 2 inches (5 cm) in diameter. Wrap in parchment paper and refrigerate for at least 8 hours, until well chilled, or for up to 3 days.
3. Preheat oven to 350°F (180°C). Working with one log at a time, cut with a sharp knife crosswise into slices 1⁄8 inch (0.25 cm) thick and arrange on prepared baking sheets, at least 1 inch (2.5 cm) apart. Bake in preheated oven for 10 to 13 minutes or until pale golden and crisp. Let cool slightly on baking sheet on a rack, then remove to a rack to continue cooling. Serve warm or at room temperature.

Makes 60 crackers

Lemon, Pepper and Asiago Crackers

FLAT BEATER ◆ PASTA ROLLER

- ◆ Preheat oven to 350°F (180°C)
- ◆ 3 baking sheets, lined with parchment paper

1	egg	1
	Grated zest of 1 lemon	
1 ½ cups	unbleached all-purpose flour	375 mL
⅓ cup	granulated sugar	75 mL
1 tsp	freshly ground black pepper	5 mL
½ tsp	salt	2 mL
½ tsp	baking powder	2 mL
½ cup	unsalted butter, cubed	125 mL
⅓ cup	shredded Asiago cheese, divided	75 mL
1 tbsp	freshly squeezed lemon juice	15 mL
1 tbsp	milk	15 mL

Make ahead

The crackers will lose their crunch if kept tightly sealed. They can be made 1 day ahead and kept uncovered on a baking sheet at room temperature.

1. In a medium bowl, whisk together egg and lemon zest.
2. Place flour, sugar, pepper, salt, baking powder, butter and cheese in the mixer bowl. Attach the flat beater and mixer bowl to the mixer. Set to Stir and mix until butter is incorporated and mixture resembles coarse meal, about 2 minutes. Add egg mixture and lemon juice; increase to Speed 2 and mix until dough comes together and cleans the sides of the bowl, about 2 minutes. Cover the bowl with plastic wrap and let dough rest for 15 minutes.
3. Roll dough into a log about 12 inches (30 cm) long and cut crosswise into 12 slices. Keep the dough covered.
4. Remove the flat beater and attach the pasta roller to the mixer. Turn the adjustment knob to setting 1. On a floured work surface, flatten out one piece of dough. Set mixer to Speed 2 and feed dough once through the roller. Lay out on a prepared baking sheet. Repeat until all the crackers have been rolled out. As one sheet fills up, refrigerate it while you continue to roll the crackers.
5. Brush the tops of the crackers with milk and sprinkle with salt. Bake for 20 to 25 minutes or until crackers are firm and golden brown. Let cool on baking sheets on wire racks. The crackers will crisp up as they cool.

Makes twelve 12- by 4-inch (30 by 10 cm) crackers

Everything Crackers

FLAT BEATER   PASTA ROLLER

- Preheat oven to 425°F (220°C)
- 2 large baking sheets, lined with parchment paper

2 cups	unbleached all-purpose flour	500 mL
1 tbsp	granulated sugar	15 mL
3/4 tsp	salt	4 mL
1/4 tsp	freshly ground black pepper	1 mL
2 tbsp	cold unsalted butter	25 mL
2/3 cup	milk	150 mL
3 tbsp	poppy seeds	45 mL
3 tbsp	sesame seeds	45 mL
2 tbsp	dried minced garlic	25 mL
1 tbsp	caraway seeds	15 mL
1 1/2 tsp	kosher salt	7 mL
1	egg, beaten with 1 tbsp (15 mL) water	1

1. Place flour, sugar, salt and pepper in the mixer bowl. Attach the flat beater and mixer bowl to the mixer. Set to Stir and mix together the dry ingredients. Add butter and mix until coarse crumbs form. Pour in milk and mix until just moistened. Using your hands, form dough into a ball, then cut it into quarters. Cover with plastic wrap and let rest for 5 minutes. Press each quarter into a rectangle.
2. Meanwhile, in a small bowl, combine poppy seeds, sesame seeds, garlic, caraway seeds and kosher salt. Set aside.
3. Remove the flat beater and attach the pasta roller to the mixer. Turn the adjustment knob to setting 1. Set to Speed 2 and, working with one piece at a time and keeping the remaining pieces covered, roll dough once through the roller. Turn the knob to setting 2 and run the dough through one more time. Place on a lightly floured work surface.
4. Brush dough lightly with egg wash and sprinkle liberally with seed mixture. Using a sharp knife or pizza cutter, cut dough crosswise into 1 1/2-inch (4 cm) strips. Place on prepared baking sheets and pierce with a fork. Bake in preheated oven for 8 minutes. Rotate pans and bake for 8 to 10 minutes or until crackers are golden brown and crisp. Let cool on baking sheets on wire racks. The crackers will continue to crisp up as they cool.

Makes about 35 crackers

Gorgonzola and Walnut Fallen Soufflés

WIRE WHIP

- Preheat oven to 400°F (200°C)
- Two 12-cup mini-muffin tins, buttered

6 tbsp	finely chopped walnuts	90 mL
1 cup	milk	250 mL
1/4 cup	unsalted butter	50 mL
1/2 cup	unbleached all-purpose flour	125 mL
2	egg yolks	2
6 oz	Gorgonzola cheese, crumbled	175 g
4	egg whites	4
	Grapes	
	Pears, cored and sliced thinly	

TIP

Don't be alarmed that the batter is much thicker than usual for these little fallen soufflés. Just whisk in the whipped egg whites, and they will puff up beautifully; once out of the oven, they will fall, making them a bit easier to handle when removing them from the muffin tins.

1. Coat the buttered muffin tins with walnuts, knocking out any excess. Set aside.
2. In a saucepan, over medium heat, heat the milk and butter until butter is melted, then bring to a boil. Add flour all at once and whisk vigorously until mixture returns to a boil. Transfer to the mixer bowl.
3. Attach the whip and mixer bowl to the mixer. Set to Speed 4 and whip for 2 minutes, until slightly cooled. Whip in egg yolks (mixture will be very stiff). Remove the mixer bowl and, with a rubber spatula, stir in Gorgonzola. Transfer the mixture to another bowl and thoroughly clean and dry the mixer bowl and the whip (see tip, page 24).
4. Attach the clean mixer bowl to the mixer, with whip attached. Set to Speed 6 and beat egg whites until they just hold stiff peaks. Add half the whites to the cheese mixture and gently whisk together to lighten. Add the remaining whites and whisk gently until incorporated (mixture will be dense).
5. Divide batter among muffin cups and bake in middle of preheated oven until puffed and golden brown, about 15 minutes. Run a thin knife around each soufflé to loosen it. Remove from tins and set on a serving platter with grapes and pears as garnish. Serve warm or at room temperature.

Makes 24 mini soufflés

Cheddar and Rosemary Fallen Soufflés

WIRE WHIP

- Preheat oven to 400°F (200°C)
- Two 12-cup mini-muffin tins, buttered

1 cup	milk	250 mL
1/4 cup	unsalted butter	50 mL
1 1/2 tbsp	finely chopped fresh rosemary	22 mL
1/2 cup	unbleached all-purpose flour	125 mL
2	egg yolks	2
4 oz	sharp Cheddar cheese, shredded	125 g
4	egg whites	4

TIP
Make sure you thoroughly clean and dry the mixer bowl and whip before beating egg whites. If any fat remains on the bowl or whip, the whites will not beat up to an adequate volume.

1. In a saucepan, over medium heat, heat the milk, butter and rosemary until butter is melted, then bring to a boil. Add flour all at once and whisk vigorously until mixture returns to a boil. Transfer to the mixer bowl.
2. Attach the whip and mixer bowl to the mixer. Set to Speed 4 and whip for 2 minutes, until slightly cooled. Whip in egg yolks (mixture will be very stiff). Remove the mixer bowl and, with a rubber spatula, stir in Cheddar. Transfer the mixture to another bowl and thoroughly clean and dry the mixer bowl and the whip (see tip, at left).
3. Attach the clean mixer bowl to the mixer, with whip attached. Set to Speed 6 and beat egg whites until they just hold stiff peaks. Add half the whites to the cheese mixture and gently whisk together to lighten. Add the remaining whites and whisk gently until incorporated (mixture will be dense).
4. Divide batter among muffin cups and bake soufflés in middle of preheated oven until puffed and golden brown, about 15 minutes. Run a thin knife around each soufflé to loosen it. Remove from tins and set on a serving platter. Serve warm or at room temperature.

Makes 24 mini soufflés

Scallion Pancakes

FLAT BEATER • DOUGH HOOK

2 cups	unbleached all-purpose flour	500 mL
1 tsp	salt	5 mL
1 cup	boiling water	250 mL
2 tsp	toasted sesame oil, divided (see tip, below)	10 mL
3/4 cup	sliced scallions (green onions)	175 mL
3 tbsp	vegetable oil, divided	45 mL
	Coarse salt	
Soy and Sesame Dipping Sauce		
1/4 cup	light soy sauce	50 mL
2 tbsp	rice vinegar	25 mL
1 tbsp	grated gingerroot	15 mL
1 tbsp	granulated sugar	15 mL
1 tbsp	toasted sesame oil	15 mL

TIP

Make sure to look for dark sesame oil. The lighter version will not be toasted and will not have the same flavor.

1. Place flour and salt in the mixer bowl. Attach the flat beater and mixer bowl to the mixer. Set to Speed 2 and slowly add boiling water in a steady stream, beating until a ball is formed. Remove the flat beater and attach the dough hook. Set to Speed 2 and knead until dough is smooth, about 1 minute. Remove the mixer bowl and cover with plastic wrap. Let rest for about 30 minutes.
2. *Meanwhile, prepare the dipping sauce:* In a small bowl, combine soy sauce, vinegar, ginger, sugar and sesame oil; stir to dissolve sugar. Taste to see if the flavor is too strong (it may be, depending on your soy sauce). If it is, add water, one teaspoon (5 mL) at a time, until the flavor mellows. Set aside.
3. Divide dough in half. Working with one piece at a time, on a floured surface, roll out dough into a circle about 1/4 inch (0.5 cm) thick. Brush on 1 tsp (5 mL) sesame oil and press half the scallions into the pancake. Repeat with remaining dough.
4. In a large skillet, heat 1 1/2 tbsp (22 mL) of the oil over medium heat. Add a pancake and brown on both sides, turning once, about 5 minutes in total. Transfer to a cutting board and keep warm. Repeat with the remaining pancake. Sprinkle lightly with coarse salt, cut into wedges and serve immediately with dipping sauce.

Makes 32 wedges

Carrot Fritters with Curried Sour Cream

ROTOR SLICER/SHREDDER

Curried Sour Cream		
1/2 cup	sour cream	125 mL
1 tbsp	chopped fresh cilantro	15 mL
1 tsp	freshly squeezed lemon juice	5 mL
3/4 tsp	curry powder	4 mL
Pinch	salt	Pinch
Carrot Fritters		
4	carrots, peeled and trimmed	4
2	eggs, lightly beaten	2
1/3 cup	finely chopped fresh cilantro	75 mL
1/3 cup	fine dry bread crumbs	75 mL
1/4 tsp	salt	1 mL
	Freshly ground black pepper	
	Vegetable oil	
	Coarse salt	

1. *Prepare the curried sour cream:* In a small bowl, combine sour cream, cilantro, lemon juice, curry powder and salt. Set aside.
2. *Prepare the fritters:* Attach the slicer/shredder, with the fine shredder, to the mixer. Set to Speed 4 and shred carrots into a medium bowl. Stir in eggs, cilantro, bread crumbs, salt and black pepper to taste.
3. In a large nonstick skillet, heat 1/4 inch (0.5 cm) oil over medium-high heat until very hot, but not smoking. In batches, drop carrot mixture into the oil by tablespoonfuls (15 mL), and fry, turning once, for 1 1/2 to 2 minutes or until golden. Transfer to paper towels to drain. Sprinkle with coarse salt while still hot. Add more oil to keep depth at 1/4 inch (0.5 cm) and reheat as necessary between batches.
4. Serve fritters hot, topped with a small dollop of curried sour cream.

Makes 14 fritters

Chickpea Fritters with Yogurt Mint Sauce

FLAT BEATER

Yogurt Mint Sauce		
1 cup	plain yogurt	250 mL
1/4 cup	chopped fresh mint	50 mL
2 tbsp	freshly squeezed lemon juice	25 mL
1/4 tsp	salt	1 mL
Pinch	cayenne pepper	Pinch
Chickpea Fritters		
1/4 cup	medium-grind bulgur or cracked wheat	50 mL
1/2 cup	boiling water	125 mL
4 cups	chickpeas, rinsed	1 L
1	egg	1
1/2 cup	finely chopped onion	125 mL
1/4 cup	finely chopped fresh flat-leaf parsley	50 mL
1/4 cup	finely chopped fresh cilantro	50 mL
2 tbsp	finely minced garlic	25 mL
1 tbsp	freshly squeezed lemon juice	15 mL
1 tsp	ground cumin	5 mL
1 tsp	ground coriander	5 mL
1 tsp	salt	5 mL
Pinch	cayenne pepper	Pinch
1/2 cup	vegetable oil (approx.)	125 mL

1. *Prepare the sauce:* In a small bowl, combine yogurt, mint, lemon juice, salt and cayenne. Cover and refrigerate for 30 minutes or until ready to serve.
2. *Prepare the fritters:* Place bulgur in a heatproof bowl and cover with boiling water. Let stand for 30 minutes, or until bulgur is tender, then drain any remaining water. Place bulgur, chickpeas, egg, onion, parsley, cilantro, garlic, lemon juice, cumin, coriander, salt and cayenne in the mixer bowl. Attach the flat beater and bowl to the mixer. Set to Speed 2 and mix until ingredients form a paste. Remove the mixer bowl and, using a 1/4-cup (50 mL) scoop and your hands, form the paste into 8 patties, each 4 by 1/2 inch (10 by 1 cm).
3. In a skillet, heat a thin layer of oil over medium heat until it sizzles when the edge of a patty is dipped into it. Fry patties a few at a time for 2 to 3 minutes per side, until golden on both sides. With a slotted spatula, remove from skillet carefully: they will be fragile. Add more oil and reheat as necessary between batches. Serve with Yogurt Mint Sauce.

Makes 8 fritters

TIPS

These fritters are delicate, but they will firm up as they cook. Try flipping with two spatulas, one on top and one underneath, if they are difficult to flip.

Fritters can be kept hot in a 300°F (150°C) oven for up to 30 minutes before serving.

Chickpeas are also called garbanzo beans or ceci beans.

Mediterranean Tart with Goat Cheese and Roasted Vegetables

- Preheat oven to 375°F (190°C)
- 9-inch (23 cm) tart shell with removable bottom or pie plate
- 2 large baking sheets

1	recipe Flaky Pastry (page 321)	1
1	zucchini, cut into 1/4-inch (0.5 cm) thick slices	1
1	red bell pepper, cut into 1/4-inch (0.5 cm) thick slices	1
1	small eggplant, diced	1
1/2 cup	thinly sliced red onion	125 mL
2 tbsp	olive oil	25 mL
1/2 tsp	herbes de Provence	2 mL
1/2 tsp	salt	2 mL
1/4 tsp	freshly ground black pepper	1 mL
1	egg	1
1/2 cup	crumbled goat cheese	125 mL
1/2 cup	shredded mozzarella cheese	125 mL
1/3 cup	ricotta cheese	75 mL
1/4 cup	sour cream	50 mL
3 tbsp	grated Parmesan cheese	45 mL
1/4 tsp	salt	1 mL
Pinch	freshly ground black pepper	Pinch

TIP
Herbes de Provence is a blend of dried herbs such as basil, thyme, sage, rosemary, lavender, summer savory, marjoram and fennel seeds. If you can't find it in your grocery store, use a mix of basil and thyme or rosemary and marjoram.

1. Roll out the pastry and fit it into the tart shell. Poke holes in the bottom with a fork. Refrigerate for 30 minutes.
2. Place zucchini, red pepper, eggplant and red onion on baking sheet and sprinkle with olive oil, herbes de Provence, salt and pepper. Toss vegetables to coat with oil and spread out to a single layer. Bake in preheated oven until softened and beginning to brown around the edges, about 25 minutes. Let cool on baking sheet.
3. Line pastry shell with a sheet of parchment paper with a 4-inch (10 cm) overhang and fill with dried beans, rice or pie weights. Place on another baking sheet and bake for 20 minutes or until bottom of shell is set. Remove from the oven and, using the overhang as handles, remove pie weights and place them on a heatproof plate or baking sheet to cool. Let shell cool on a rack for 20 minutes before filling. Set baking sheet aside.
4. In a small bowl, combine egg, goat cheese, mozzarella, ricotta, sour cream and Parmesan. Mix well and season with salt and pepper.
5. Spread half of the cheese mixture evenly over the bottom of the tart shell. Top the cheese with the roasted vegetables, and dot the top of the vegetables with the remaining cheese mixture.
6. Return the tart to the baking sheet and bake in the lower third of the oven for 35 to 40 minutes or until golden brown around the edges and filling is set. Let cool in the pan for 5 minutes, remove the sides of the pan and then slide the tart off the pan and onto a serving plate. Serve hot, warm or at room temperature.

Makes 16 wedges

Mushroom Tart with Cheddar Crust

ROTOR SLICER/SHREDDER ◆ FLAT BEATER

◆ Preheat oven to 425°F (220°C)
◆ 9-inch (2.5 L) square baking pan

Cheddar Pastry		
2 oz	sharp Cheddar cheese	60 g
1 1/3 cups	unbleached all-purpose flour	325 mL
1/4 tsp	salt	1 mL
1/2 cup	cold unsalted butter, cut into small cubes	125 mL
1	egg yolk, beaten	1
2 tbsp	cold water	25 mL
Filling		
3 tbsp	unsalted butter	45 mL
1/2 cup	diced shallot	125 mL
8 oz	white button mushrooms, chopped	250 g
4 oz	shiitake mushrooms (stems discarded), chopped	125 g
1/2 tsp	salt, divided	2 mL
1/4 tsp	freshly ground black pepper, divided	1 mL
1/4 cup	dry white wine	50 mL
1 tbsp	balsamic vinegar	15 mL
2 tsp	Worcestershire sauce	10 mL
1/4 cup	chopped fresh flat-leaf parsley	50 mL
1/3 cup	whipping (35%) cream	75 mL
1	egg, beaten	1
Pinch	ground nutmeg	Pinch

1. *Prepare the pastry:* Place cheese in the freezer until very cold and firm but not frozen, about 10 minutes. Attach the slicer/shredder, with the coarse shredder, to the mixer. Set to Speed 4 and shred cheese into a bowl. Remove the slicer/shredder.
2. Place flour and salt in the mixer bowl. Attach the flat beater and bowl to the mixer. Set to Stir and mix briefly. Add butter and shredded cheese. Set to Speed 2 and mix until flour resembles coarse meal. Add egg yolk and water and mix until a dough forms. Remove dough from the bowl, pat into a disk and wrap in plastic. Refrigerate for 30 minutes, until firm. On a lightly floured surface, roll out dough and fit it into the baking pan so that the pastry is 1 inch (2.5 cm) up the sides of the pan. Refrigerate for 30 minutes.
3. *Meanwhile, prepare the filling:* In a large skillet, melt butter over medium-high heat. Add shallot and sauté until translucent, about 2 minutes. Add button and shiitake mushrooms, 1/4 tsp (1 mL) of the salt and a pinch of pepper. Sauté until mushroom juices evaporate, about 10 minutes. Add white wine, vinegar and Worcestershire; cook until pan is almost dry, about 4 minutes. Stir in parsley. Let cool.
4. In a small bowl, beat the egg into the cream. Add nutmeg, the remaining 1/4 tsp (1 mL) salt and a pinch of pepper. Stir into the cooled mushrooms.
5. Spread the mushroom mixture evenly over the chilled pastry. Bake in the lower third of the preheated oven for 25 minutes or until pastry is crisp and filling is set. Slice into 25 squares and serve hot, warm or at room temperature.

Makes 25 squares

Sausage and Cheddar Quiche

- Preheat oven to 375°F (190°C)
- 9-inch (2.5 L) square baking pan
- Baking sheet

1	recipe Flaky Pastry (page 321)	1
1 lb	spicy Italian sausage (store-bought or see recipe, page 164)	500 g
3	eggs	3
1/2 cup	whipping (35%) cream	125 mL
1/2 tsp	salt	2 mL
Pinch	freshly ground nutmeg	Pinch
1 cup	shredded sharp Cheddar cheese	250 mL
1	large tomato, thinly sliced	1
Pinch	freshly ground black pepper	Pinch

1. On a lightly floured surface, roll out pastry and fit into the baking pan, lining the pan up the sides and trimming edges. Refrigerate for 15 minutes. Lay a piece of parchment with a 4-inch (10 cm) overhang on top of the pastry and fill the shell with dried beans, rice or pie weights. Do not overfill. Bake the tart in the preheated oven for about 20 minutes or until the dough has set. Using the overhang as handles, carefully remove the parchment paper and the hot weights to a heatproof plate and return the tart to the oven to bake for another 5 minutes, until pastry is set. Let cool in pan on a rack.
2. Meanwhile, heat a large skillet over medium-high heat. Add sausage and cook, breaking it up into small chunks, until no longer pink. Drain off fat and set aside.
3. In a medium bowl, beat eggs and whipping cream until blended. Season with salt and nutmeg.
4. Place the tomato slices in a single layer in the bottom of the cooled pie shell and sprinkle with pepper and a pinch of salt. Top with sausage and Cheddar cheese. Pour in egg mixture.
5. Place baking pan on the baking sheet and bake in preheated oven for 5 minutes. Reduce temperature to 350°F (180°C) and bake for an additional 25 minutes, or until custard is set in the middle. Let stand for 5 minutes to set.
6. Slice quiche into 25 squares and serve hot, warm or at room temperature.

Makes 25 squares

Mini Ham and Asparagus Quiche Cups

- Preheat oven to 400°F (200°C)
- Two 12-cup mini-muffin tins, buttered

2	recipes Flaky Pastry (page 321)	2
1 cup	chopped asparagus (1/2-inch/1 cm pieces), tough ends discarded	250 mL
3/4 cup	finely chopped ham (about 4 oz/125 g)	175 mL
2	eggs	2
3/4 cup	whipping (35%) cream	175 mL
1/2 tsp	dried tarragon	2 mL
1/4 tsp	salt	1 mL
Pinch	freshly ground black pepper	Pinch
Pinch	cayenne pepper	Pinch
Pinch	ground nutmeg	Pinch
3/4 cup	shredded Swiss cheese	175 mL

TIP
Substitute equal amounts of finely chopped broccoli and red bell pepper, zucchini and carrot or yellow squash and green onion for the asparagus. Experiment with different cheeses such as Cheddar, Colby, Monterey Jack and goat cheese.

1. On a lightly floured surface, roll out pastry to 1/8 inch (0.25 cm) and cut out circles with a 2 1/2-inch (6 cm) round cutter. Press pastry rounds into mini-muffin tins. Refrigerate for 20 minutes.
2. Meanwhile, blanch asparagus in a saucepan of boiling salted water for 1 minute. Drain in a colander and rinse under running cold water to stop the cooking. Lay asparagus out on a clean towel to dry.
3. In a small bowl, combine asparagus and ham; mix well.
4. In another small bowl, beat eggs, whipping cream, tarragon, salt, pepper, cayenne and nutmeg until blended.
5. Divide the asparagus-ham mixture evenly among each pastry-lined cup. Top evenly with Swiss cheese, then with egg mixture.
6. Bake in preheated oven for 25 minutes or until the pastry is crisp and custard is set. Serve hot or at room temperature.

Makes 24 quiche cups

Spinach Roulade with Tomatoes, Ricotta and Basil

WIRE WHIP

- Preheat oven to 400°F (200°C)
- 15- by 10-inch (38 by 25 cm) rimmed baking sheet, lined with buttered and floured parchment paper

Roulade Batter		
1/4 cup	unsalted butter	50 mL
1/3 cup	unbleached all-purpose flour	75 mL
1 1/4 cups	milk	300 mL
1/2 tsp	salt	2 mL
Dash	freshly ground black pepper	Dash
Pinch	cayenne pepper	Pinch
Pinch	ground nutmeg	Pinch
5	eggs, separated	5
1	package (10 oz/300 g) frozen chopped spinach, thawed and squeezed dry	1
1/2 cup	grated Parmesan cheese	125 mL
Filling		
1 cup	ricotta cheese	250 mL
1/2 cup	plain yogurt	125 mL
	Salt and freshly ground black pepper	
4	tomatoes, thinly sliced	4
1/2 cup	fresh basil leaves	125 mL

TIP
Spinach Roulade is an attractive addition to the buffet table. Serve for brunch with a green salad and a fruit salad.

1. *Prepare the batter:* In a medium saucepan, melt butter over medium heat. Add flour and cook, stirring constantly, for 1 minute. Gradually whisk in milk and cook, stirring, until mixture thickens, about 5 minutes. Season with salt, black pepper, cayenne and nutmeg. Let cool for 5 minutes, then vigorously whisk in 1 egg yolk. Whisk in the remaining yolks, one at a time. Add spinach and Parmesan cheese, stirring to incorporate evenly.
2. Place egg whites in the mixer bowl. Attach the whip and bowl to the mixer. Set to Speed 8 and beat until egg whites form firm peaks. Fold 1/4 of the whites into the roulade batter to lighten it and then add the rest of the whites to the base in 2 additions. Do not overmix.
3. Spread batter in prepared pan, smoothing top. Bake in middle of preheated oven until top is puffed and lightly golden, about 15 minutes. Let cool in pan on a rack for 10 minutes. Run a knife around the edge of the baking sheet. Place a sheet of parchment paper the same size as the baking sheet on a work surface and turn out the roulade upside down onto it. Remove the paper that was used in the baking pan if it is attached to the top of the roulade.
4. In a small bowl, combine ricotta, yogurt, 1/4 tsp (1 mL) salt and a pinch of pepper. Spread over roulade. Place tomatoes on top in a single layer and season with more salt and pepper. Top with basil.
5. Starting at one long side, roll the roulade jelly-roll style, using the parchment paper as a guide. Cover with parchment and place on a baking sheet. Refrigerate for up to 2 hours or slice into 1 1/2-inch (4 cm) thick slices and serve immediately.

Makes 10 slices

Hot Spinach and Garlic Dip

FLAT BEATER

- Preheat oven to 400°F (200°C)
- Large baking sheet

1	package (10 oz/300 g) frozen spinach, thawed	1
1 tbsp	olive oil	15 mL
3	cloves garlic, minced	3
1¾ cups	chopped onion	425 mL
1	can (14 oz/398 g) artichoke bottoms or hearts, drained and chopped	1
6 oz	cream cheese, softened	175 g
1 cup	grated Parmesan cheese	250 mL
¼ cup	sour cream	50 mL
¼ cup	mayonnaise	50 mL
½ tsp	cayenne pepper	2 mL
Pinch	ground nutmeg	Pinch
	Salt and freshly ground black pepper	
1	loaf (1½ lbs/750 g) round sheepherder's or pumpernickel bread, unsliced	1
	Crudités	

1. Squeeze as much liquid as possible out of the spinach, chop finely and set aside.
2. In a skillet, heat oil over medium heat. Add garlic and onion; sauté until onion is tender, about 6 minutes. Let cool.
3. Transfer to the mixer bowl and add spinach, artichokes, cream cheese, Parmesan cheese, sour cream, mayonnaise, cayenne and nutmeg. Attach the flat beater and bowl to the mixer. Set to Stir and beat until ingredients are well combined. Season to taste with salt and pepper.
4. Slice top 2 inches (5 cm) off bread. Cut out insides of bread, leaving a 1-inch (2.5 cm) thick shell. (Tear the top and insides of bread into hunks and reserve to use for dipping.) Fill the bread shell with spinach mixture. Place on a baking sheet and bake in preheated oven until filling is very hot and lightly browned, about 20 minutes. Place on a large serving tray. Serve with reserved bread hunks and crudités.

Makes 4 cups (1 L)

Hummus

FLAT BEATER

2	cans (each 16 to 19 oz/454 to 540 mL) chickpeas, rinsed and drained	2
1	clove garlic, minced	1
1/4 cup	olive oil	50 mL
2 tbsp	tahini	25 mL
1 1/2 tbsp	freshly squeezed lemon juice	22 mL
1/4 tsp	salt (approx.)	1 mL
	Pita toasts or crudités	

1. Place chickpeas in the mixer bowl. Attach the flat beater and bowl to the mixer. Set to Speed 2 and mix until chickpeas begin to break up. Set to Speed 4 and add garlic, olive oil, tahini, lemon juice, 1 tbsp (15 mL) water and salt. Mix for 4 minutes, until slightly lumpy, but creamy, adding 1 tbsp (15 mL) more water if necessary. Season to taste with salt. Serve with pita toasts or crudités.

Makes 3 cups (750 mL)

TIP

This recipe is a great base for other flavors. Try adding chopped roasted red peppers or kalamata olives. The variations are endless.

Roasted Garlic Hummus

FLAT BEATER

◆ Preheat oven to 350°F (180°C)

1	head garlic	1
1 tsp	olive oil	5 mL
2	cans (each 16 to 19 oz/454 to 540 mL) chickpeas, rinsed and drained	2
1/4 cup	olive oil	50 mL
2 tbsp	tahini	25 mL
1 1/2 tbsp	freshly squeezed lemon juice	22 mL
1/4 tsp	salt (approx.)	1 mL

1. Cut 1/2 inch (1 cm) off the top of the garlic. Place garlic in a large square of foil, drizzle with the 1 tsp (5 mL) olive oil and enclose in the foil. Place the garlic packet in preheated oven and roast for 45 minutes, or until soft and golden brown. When cool enough to handle, squeeze the soft cloves into a small bowl and mash with the back of a fork. Set aside.
2. Place chickpeas in the mixer bowl. Attach the flat beater and bowl to the mixer. Set to Speed 2 and mix until chickpeas begin to break up. Set to Speed 4 and add roasted garlic, the 1/4 cup (50 mL) olive oil, tahini, lemon juice, 1 tbsp (15 mL) water and salt. Mix for 2 minutes, until slightly lumpy, but creamy, adding 1 tbsp (15 mL) more water if necessary. Season to taste with salt.

Makes 3 cups (750 mL)

Herbed Goat Cheese Spread

FLAT BEATER

8 oz	fresh goat cheese (such as Montrachet), softened	250 g
4 oz	cream cheese, softened	125 g
1/3 cup	minced fresh chives, divided	75 mL
8	fresh basil leaves, chopped	8
1	clove garlic, finely minced	1
	Salt and freshly ground black pepper	
	Baguette slices or crackers	

1. Place goat cheese, cream cheese, 2 tbsp (25 mL) of the chives, basil and garlic in the mixer bowl. Attach the flat beater and bowl to the mixer. Set to Speed 4 and mix until well blended. Season to taste with salt and pepper.
2. Place a large piece of plastic wrap on a work surface. Spoon cheese mixture into an 8-inch (20 cm) row in the center of the plastic. Roll into a log, twisting the ends of the plastic wrap so that it tightens around the cheese. Refrigerate for at least 4 hours, until firm, or for up to 2 days. Remove plastic wrap and roll the cheese in the remaining 1/4 cup (50 mL) chives. Serve with baguette slices or crackers.

Makes 2 cups (500 mL)

Lemon Crab Dip

FLAT BEATER

8 oz	crab meat, picked over for shells and cartilage	250 g
4 oz	cream cheese, softened	125 g
4 oz	goat cheese, softened	125 g
1/2 cup	mayonnaise	125 mL
2 tbsp	minced fresh parsley	25 mL
	Zest of 2 lemons	
2 tbsp	freshly squeezed lemon juice	25 mL
	Salt and freshly ground black pepper	
	Crackers, pita chips or toasted baguette slices	

1. Squeeze excess moisture out of crab meat and pick through to remove any shell or cartilage; set aside.
2. Place cream cheese, goat cheese, mayonnaise, parsley, lemon zest and lemon juice in the mixer bowl. Attach the flat beater and bowl to the mixer. Set to Speed 4 and mix until ingredients are well combined. Remove the bowl from the mixer and, using a rubber spatula, lightly fold in crab. Season to taste with salt and pepper. Serve with crackers, pita chips or toasted baguette slices.

Makes 2 1/2 cups (625 mL)

Spinach Terrine

ROTOR SLICER/SHREDDER (OPTIONAL) ◆ WIRE WHIP

- ◆ Preheat oven to 350°F (180°C)
- ◆ 9- by 5-inch (2 L) loaf pan
- ◆ 13- by 9-inch (3 L) baking pan, lined with a kitchen towel

2 tbsp	vegetable oil	25 mL
1 cup	dry bread crumbs, divided	250 mL
1/2 cup	unsalted butter, divided	125 mL
3/4 cup	finely chopped onions	175 mL
1 tsp	salt, divided	5 mL
1/4 tsp	freshly ground black pepper, divided	1 mL
2	packages (each 10 oz/300 g) frozen chopped spinach, thawed and squeezed dry	2
Pinch	ground nutmeg	Pinch
1 cup	milk	250 mL
2 oz	Swiss cheese	60 g
5	eggs, separated	5
Pinch	freshly ground white pepper	Pinch

Easy Cream Sauce

1 cup	whipping (35%) cream	250 mL
1/2 cup	grated Parmesan cheese	125 mL
1/4 tsp	salt	1 mL
Pinch	cayenne pepper	Pinch

1. Grease loaf pan with oil and roll 1/4 cup (50 mL) of the bread crumbs around the inside to coat. Knock out excess crumbs.
2. In a large skillet, melt 3 tbsp (45 mL) of the butter over medium-high heat. Add onions and a pinch of salt and black pepper; sauté until tender, about 4 minutes. Add spinach and 2 tbsp (25 mL) of the butter and cook, stirring, until spinach is dry and sticks somewhat to the bottom of the pan. Season with nutmeg, 1/2 tsp (2 mL) salt and a pinch of black pepper. Set aside.
3. In a small saucepan, over medium-high, bring milk and the remaining 1/4 cup (50 mL) butter to a boil. Remove from heat; set aside.
4. Attach the slicer/shredder, with the fine shredder, to the mixer. Set to Speed 4 and shred the Swiss cheese into a bowl. (Or shred by hand with a box grater.)
5. In a large bowl, combine onion-spinach mixture, shredded cheese, egg yolks, the remaining 3/4 cup (175 mL) bread crumbs, the remaining 1/4 tsp (1 mL) salt and white pepper. Slowly beat in the hot milk mixture.
6. Place egg whites in the mixer bowl. Remove the slicer/shredder and attach the whip and bowl to the mixer. Set to Speed 8 and beat egg whites until stiff peaks form. Fold into egg mixture and gently pour into prepared loaf pan.

7. Place loaf pan in center of baking pan lined with towel. Pour in boiling water to reach halfway up the sides of the loaf pan. Place in the lower half of preheated oven and bake for 35 to 40 minutes or until a knife inserted in center comes out clean. Remove loaf pan from water bath and let cool on a rack for 5 to 10 minutes to firm up.
8. *Meanwhile, prepare the sauce:* In a skillet, over medium heat, bring whipping cream to a boil. Boil until cream thickens somewhat and becomes saucy, about 5 minutes. Remove from heat and add Parmesan cheese, salt and cayenne. Stir to mix.
9. Unmold the terrine to a warm serving plate and serve with hot Easy Cream Sauce.

Makes 1 loaf

TIP

Spinach terrine can also be served as a luncheon entrée. Just serve larger slices, garnished with halved grape tomatoes for an eye-popping presentation.

Variation

Other cheeses used could be Gruyère, Cheddar, fontina or Asiago. Or try a blend of your favorites.

Chicken and Ham Terrine

FOOD GRINDER • FLAT BEATER

- 9- by 5-inch (2 L) loaf pan
- 13- by 9-inch (3 L) baking pan, lined with a kitchen towel
- 8- by 4-inch (20 by 10 cm) piece of wood or cardboard, wrapped in foil
- 4-lb (2 kg) weight

1/3 cup	cognac, divided	75 mL
1 tbsp	minced shallot	15 mL
	Dried tarragon	
	Salt and freshly ground black pepper	
12 oz	boneless skinless chicken, dark and light meat	375 g
4 oz	boneless skinless chicken breast, cut into thin strips	125 g
3 tbsp	unsalted butter	45 mL
3/4 cup	finely minced onion	175 mL
3	cloves garlic, minced	3
1/2 cup	port or Madeira	125 mL
8	slices bacon	8
12 oz	trimmed boneless pork shoulder blade	375 g
12 oz	boneless veal shoulder	375 g
12 oz	salt pork	375 g
2	eggs	2
1/4 tsp	dried thyme	1 mL
4 oz	ham, cut into 9-inch (23 cm) strips	125 g
1/2 cup	shelled natural pistachios	125 mL
	Rustic bread, mustard and cornichons (small French pickles)	

1. In a small bowl, whisk together 3 tbsp (45 mL) of the cognac, shallot, and a pinch each of tarragon, salt and pepper.
2. Place chicken and chicken breast strips in a shallow dish and brush with shallot mixture, coating evenly. Cover and refrigerate while preparing the remaining ingredients.
3. In a skillet, melt butter over medium heat. Add onion and a pinch of salt; sauté until tender, about 10 minutes. Add garlic and sauté for 2 minutes. Add port and cook until liquid is reduced by half. Remove from heat and let cool.
4. In a saucepan, bring 2 cups (500 mL) water to a boil. Add bacon and cook for about 5 minutes to remove some of the smoky flavor. Drain off water and pat bacon dry on paper towels. Set aside.
5. Cut the pork, veal, salt pork and 12 oz (375 g) of marinated chicken into 1-inch (2.5 cm) cubes. Place in a shallow container in the freezer for 30 minutes to facilitate grinding. Attach the food grinder, with the fine plate, to the mixer. Set to Speed 4 and run meat cubes through the grinder into a large bowl. Return to the freezer for 30 minutes. Run through the grinder again into the mixer bowl. Remove the food grinder.
6. Remove the chicken breast strips from the marinade and set aside. Add marinade, onion mixture, eggs, the remaining 2 tbsp (25 mL) cognac, 2 tsp (10 mL) salt, 1 tsp (5 mL) tarragon, 1/4 tsp (1 mL) pepper and thyme to the ground meat in the mixer bowl. Attach the flat beater and bowl to the mixer. Set to Stir, and mix until well combined, about 1 minute. In a skillet, over medium-high heat, sauté a small amount of the mixture, until no longer pink. Taste and adjust seasoning as desired.

7. Preheat oven to 350°F (180°C). Line the bottom and sides of loaf pan crosswise with the bacon, leaving a 2- to 3-inch (5 to 7.5 cm) overhang. Divide stuffing mixture into 4 portions and pack one portion in the bottom of the pan in an even layer. Place one-third each of the chicken breast strips, ham and pistachios on top of the stuffing. Top with another portion of stuffing. Repeat the layers of chicken breast, ham, pistachios and stuffing, ending with a layer of stuffing, smoothing top. Flip the overhanging bacon over the top.
8. Cover loaf pan with foil and set in center of baking pan lined with towel. Pour in boiling water to reach halfway up the sides of the loaf pan. Bake in preheated oven for 90 minutes or until terrine reaches an internal temperature of 170°F (75°C). The terrine will have shrunk from the sides of the pan and will be full of liquid fat
9. Carefully remove loaf pan from the water bath. Fit wood or cardboard inside pan on top of terrine and top with the 4-lb (2 kg) weight. (This compacts the terrine and creates a better texture). Let cool to room temperature in pan on a rack. Refrigerate, weighted, for at least 8 hours or overnight.
10. Unmold the terrine and serve sliced on a platter, accompanied by rustic bread, mustard and cornichons.

Makes 1 loaf

TIPS

Pork shoulder blade used to be known as pork shoulder butt.

In its pan, covered with its fat, the terrine will keep for up to 1 week. Once it is removed from the pan and the fat is disturbed, it will keep for 3 to 4 days. The terrine may be frozen, but the texture will become a bit grainy.

Veal and Ham Pâté

FOOD GRINDER ◆ FLAT BEATER

- ◆ 9- by 5-inch (2 L) loaf pan
- ◆ 13- by 9-inch (3 L) baking pan, lined with a kitchen towel
- ◆ 8- by 4-inch (20 by 10 cm) piece of wood or cardboard, wrapped in foil
- ◆ 4-lb (2 kg) weight

12 oz	trimmed boneless pork shoulder blade	375 g
12 oz	boneless veal shoulder	375 g
12 oz	pork fat	375 g
3 tbsp	unsalted butter	45 mL
3/4 cup	finely minced onion	175 mL
	Salt	
3	cloves garlic, minced	3
1/2 cup	port or Madeira	125 mL
8	slices bacon	8
2	carrots, trimmed into strips 5 inches (13 cm) long, 1/4 inch (0.5 cm) wide	2
2	eggs	2
2 tbsp	cognac	25 mL
1 tbsp	minced fresh chives	15 mL
1 tsp	dried marjoram	5 mL
1/4 tsp	freshly ground black pepper	1 mL
1/4 tsp	five-spice powder	1 mL
4 oz	ham, sliced into 9 thin strips 5 inches (13 cm) long, 1/4 inch (0.5 cm) wide	125 g
1/2 cup	shelled natural pistachios	125 mL
	Rustic bread, mustard and cornichons (small French pickles)	

1. Cut pork, veal and pork fat into 1-inch (2.5 cm) cubes. Place in a shallow container in the freezer for 30 minutes to facilitate grinding. Attach the food grinder, with the fine plate, to the mixer. Set to Speed 4 and run meat cubes through the grinder into a large bowl. Return to freezer for 30 minutes. Run through the grinder again into the mixer bowl. Remove the food grinder.
2. Meanwhile, in a skillet, melt butter over medium heat. Add onion and a pinch of salt; sauté until tender, about 10 minutes. Add garlic and sauté for another 2 minutes. Add port and cook until liquid is reduced by half. Let cool.
3. In a medium saucepan, bring 2 cups (500 mL) water to a boil. Add carrots and boil until tender-crisp, about 2 minutes. Remove carrots with a slotted spoon and pat dry on paper towels; set aside. Add bacon to the boiling water and cook for about 5 minutes to remove some of the smoky flavor. Drain off water and pat bacon dry on paper towels. Set aside.
4. Add onion mixture, eggs, cognac, chives, 2 tsp (10 mL) salt, marjoram, pepper and five-spice powder to the ground meat in the mixer bowl. Attach the flat beater and the bowl to the mixer. Set to Stir and mix until well combined, about 1 minute. In a skillet, over medium-high heat, sauté a small amount of the stuffing until no longer pink. Taste and adjust seasoning as desired.

5. Preheat oven to 350°F (180°C). Line the bottom and sides of loaf pan crosswise with the bacon, leaving a 2- to 3-inch (5 to 7.5 cm) overhang. Divide the stuffing mixture into 3 portions and pack one portion in the bottom of the pan in an even layer. Place 3 lengths of ham and 3 lengths of carrot, alternating, on top of stuffing. Arrange pistachios between the rows. Top with another layer of stuffing. Repeat the layers of ham, carrots and pistachios and stuffing, ending with a layer of stuffing. Flip the overhanging bacon over the top.
6. Cover loaf pan with foil and set in center of baking pan lined with towel. Pour in boiling water to reach halfway up the sides of the loaf pan. Bake in preheated oven for 90 minutes or until pâté reaches an internal temperature of 160°F (71°C). The pâté will have shrunk from the sides of the pan and will be full of liquid fat.
7. Carefully remove loaf pan from the water bath. Fit wood or cardboard inside pan on top of pâté and top with the 4-lb (2 kg) weight. (This compacts the pâté and creates a better texture.) Let cool to room temperature in pan on a rack. Refrigerate, weighted, for at least 8 hours or overnight.
8. Unmold the pâté from its pan and serve sliced on a platter, accompanied by rustic bread, mustard and cornichons.

Makes 1 loaf

TIP

In its pan, covered with its fat, the pâté will keep for up to 1 week. Once it is removed from the pan and the fat is disturbed, it will keep for 3 to 4 days. The pâté may be frozen, but the texture will become a bit grainy.

Duck Pâté

FOOD GRINDER ◆ FLAT BEATER

- ◆ 9- by 5-inch (2 L) loaf pan
- ◆ 13- by 9-inch (3 L) baking pan, lined with a kitchen towel
- ◆ 8- by 4-inch (20 by 10 cm) piece of wood or cardboard, wrapped in foil
- ◆ 4-lb (2 kg) weight

1⁄3 cup	cognac, divided	75 mL
1 tbsp	minced shallot	15 mL
	Dried thyme	
	Salt and freshly ground black pepper	
12 oz	boneless skinless duck leg and breast	375 g
4 oz	boneless skinless duck breast, cut into thin strips	125 g
3 tbsp	unsalted butter	45 mL
3⁄4 cup	finely minced onion	175 mL
3	cloves garlic, minced	3
1⁄2 cup	port or Madeira	125 mL
8	slices bacon	8
12 oz	trimmed boneless pork shoulder blade	375 g
12 oz	boneless veal shoulder	375 g
12 oz	pork fat	375 g
2	eggs	2
1⁄4 tsp	five-spice powder	1 mL
	Rustic bread, mustard and cornichons (little French pickles)	

1. In a small bowl, whisk together 3 tbsp (45 mL) of the cognac, shallot, and a pinch each of thyme, salt and pepper.
2. Place duck and duck breast strips in a shallow dish and brush with marinade, coating evenly. Cover and refrigerate while preparing the remaining ingredients.
3. In a skillet, melt butter over medium heat. Add onion and a pinch of salt; sauté until tender, about 10 minutes. Add garlic and sauté for 2 minutes. Add port and cook until liquid is reduced by half. Let cool.
4. In a saucepan, bring 2 cups (500 mL) water to a boil. Add bacon and cook for about 5 minutes to remove some of the smoky flavor. Drain off water and pat bacon dry on paper towels. Set aside.
5. Cut pork, veal, pork fat and the 12 oz (375 g) of duck into 1-inch (2.5 cm) cubes. Place in a shallow container in the freezer for 30 minutes to facilitate grinding. Attach the food grinder, with the fine plate, to the mixer. Set to Speed 4 and run meat cubes through the grinder into a large bowl. Return to the freezer for 30 minutes. Run through the grinder again into the mixer bowl. Remove the food grinder.
6. Remove the duck breast strips from the marinade and set aside. Add marinade, onion mixture, eggs, the remaining 2 tbsp (25 mL) cognac, 2 tsp (10 mL) salt, 1 tsp (5 mL) thyme, 1⁄4 tsp (1 mL) pepper and five-spice powder to the ground meat in the mixer bowl. Attach the flat beater and bowl to the mixer. Set to Stir and mix until well combined, about 1 minute. In a skillet, over medium-high heat, sauté a small amount of the stuffing until no longer pink. Taste and adjust seasoning as desired.

7. Preheat oven to 350°F (180°C). Line the bottom and sides of loaf pan crosswise with the bacon, leaving a 2- to 3-inch (5 to 7.5 cm) overhang. Divide the stuffing mixture into 4 portions and pack one portion in the bottom of the pan in an even layer. Place one-third of the duck breast strips on top. Top with another layer of stuffing. Repeat the layers of duck breast strips and stuffing, ending with a layer of stuffing. Flip the overhanging bacon over the top.
8. Cover the loaf pan with foil and set in center of baking pan lined with towel. Pour in boiling water to reach halfway up the sides of the loaf pan. Bake in preheated oven for 90 minutes or until pâté reaches an internal temperature of 160°F (71°C). The pâté will have shrunk from the sides of the pan and will be full of liquid fat.
9. Carefully remove loaf pan from the water bath. Fit wood or cardboard inside pan on top of pâté and top with the 4-lb (2 kg) weight. (This compacts the pâté and creates a better texture.) Let cool to room temperature. Refrigerate, weighted, for at least 8 hours or overnight.
10. Unmold the pâté from its pan and serve sliced on a platter, accompanied by rustic bread, mustard and cornichons.

Makes 1 loaf

TIP

In its pan, covered with its fat, the pâté will keep for up to 1 week. Once it is removed from the pan and the fat is disturbed, it will keep for 3 to 4 days. The pâté may be frozen, but the texture will become a bit grainy.

Game Pâté

FOOD GRINDER ◆ FLAT BEATER

- 9- by 5-inch (2 L) loaf pan
- 13- by 9-inch (3 L) baking pan, lined with a kitchen towel
- 8- by 4-inch (20 by 10 cm) piece of wood or cardboard, wrapped in foil
- 4-lb (2 kg) weight

1/3 cup	cognac, divided	75 mL
1 tbsp	minced shallot	15 mL
Pinch	dried thyme	Pinch
	Salt and freshly ground black pepper	
12 oz	boneless skinless game, such as quail, pheasant or partridge	375 g
4 oz	skinless breast meat of game, such as quail, pheasant or partridge, cut into strips	125 g
3 tbsp	unsalted butter	45 mL
3/4 cup	finely minced onion	175 mL
3	cloves garlic, minced	3
1/2 cup	port or Madeira	125 mL
8	slices bacon	8
6	green onions, trimmed to 9 inches (23 cm) long	6
12 oz	trimmed boneless pork shoulder blade	375 g
12 oz	boneless veal shoulder	375 g
12 oz	pork fat	375 g
2	eggs	2
1 tsp	herbes de Provence	5 mL
1/4 tsp	five-spice powder	1 mL
1/2 cup	shelled natural pistachios	125 mL
	Rustic bread, mustard and cornichons (little French pickles)	

1. In a small bowl, whisk together 3 tbsp (45 mL) of the cognac, shallot, thyme and a pinch each of salt and pepper.
2. Place game and game breast strips in a shallow dish and brush with marinade, coating evenly. Cover and refrigerate for at least 30 minutes while preparing the remaining ingredients.
3. In a skillet, melt butter over medium heat. Add onion and a pinch of salt; sauté until tender, about 10 minutes. Add garlic and sauté for 2 minutes. Add port and cook until liquid is reduced by half. Let cool.
4. In a saucepan, bring 2 cups (500 mL) water to a boil. Add bacon and cook for about 5 minutes to remove some of the smoky flavor. Remove bacon from the pan with tongs and pat dry on paper towels; set aside. Add green onions to the boiling water and cook until tender, about 2 minutes. Drain off water and pat onions dry on paper towels. Set aside.
5. Cut pork, veal, pork fat and the 12 oz (375 g) of game meat into 1-inch (2.5 cm) cubes. Place in a shallow container in the freezer for 30 minutes to facilitate grinding. Attach the food grinder, with the fine plate, to the mixer. Run meat cubes through the grinder into a large bowl. Return to the freezer for 30 minutes. Run through grinder again into the mixer bowl. Remove the food grinder.

6. Remove the game breast strips from the marinade and set aside. Add marinade, onion mixture, eggs, the remaining 2 tbsp (25 mL) cognac, 2 tsp (10 mL) salt, herbes de Provence, 1/4 tsp (1 mL) pepper and five-spice powder to the ground meat in the mixer bowl. Attach the flat beater and bowl to the mixer. Set to Stir and mix until well combined, about 1 minute. In a skillet, over medium-high heat, sauté a small amount of the stuffing until no longer pink. Taste and adjust seasoning as desired.
7. Preheat oven to 350°F (180°C). Line the bottom and sides of loaf pan crosswise with the bacon, leaving a 2- to 3-inch (5 to 7.5 cm) overhang. Divide the stuffing mixture into 4 portions and pack one portion in the bottom of the pan in an even layer. Place 2 of the green onions lengthwise on top and arrange some of the pistachios in between. Top with one-third of the game breast strips and another layer of stuffing. Repeat the layers of game breast strips and stuffing, ending with a layer of stuffing. Flip the overhanging bacon over the top.
8. Cover loaf pan with foil and set in center of baking pan lined with towel. Pour in boiling water to reach halfway up the sides of the loaf pan. Place in preheated oven and bake for 90 minutes or until pâté reaches an internal temperature of 160°F (71°C). The pâté will have shrunk from the sides of the pan and will be full of liquid fat.
9. Carefully remove loaf pan from the water bath. Fit wood or cardboard inside pan on top of pâté and top with the 4-lb (2 kg) weight. (This compacts the pâté and creates a better texture.) Let cool to room temperature in pan on a rack. Refrigerate, weighted, for at least 8 hours or overnight.
10. Unmold the pâté from its pan and serve sliced on a platter, accompanied by rustic bread, mustard and cornichons.

Makes 1 loaf

TIP

In its pan, covered with its fat, the pâté will keep for up to 1 week. Once it is removed from the pan and the fat is disturbed, it will keep for 3 to 4 days. The pâté may be frozen, but the texture will become a bit grainy.

Rabbit Pâté

FOOD GRINDER ◆ FLAT BEATER

- 9- by 5-inch (2 L) loaf pan
- 13- by 9-inch (3 L) baking pan, lined with a kitchen towel
- 8- by 4-inch (20 by 10 cm) piece of wood or cardboard, wrapped in foil
- 4-lb (2 kg) weight

1/3 cup	cognac, divided	75 mL
1 tbsp	minced shallot	15 mL
	Dried thyme	
	Salt and freshly ground black pepper	
1 lb	boneless skinless rabbit meat (about 1 rabbit, boned), cut into thin strips	500 g
3 tbsp	unsalted butter	45 mL
3/4 cup	finely minced onion	175 mL
3	cloves garlic, minced	3
1/2 cup	port or Madeira	125 mL
2	carrots, peeled and trimmed into strips 5 inches (13 cm) long, 1/4 inch (0.5 cm) wide	2
8	slices bacon	8
6	green onions, trimmed to 9 inches (23 cm) long	6
12 oz	trimmed boneless pork shoulder blade	375 g
12 oz	boneless veal shoulder	375 g
12 oz	pork fat	375 g
2	eggs	2
1/4 tsp	five-spice powder	1 mL
1/2 cup	shelled natural pistachios	125 mL
	Rustic bread, mustard and cornichons (little French pickles)	

1. In a small bowl, whisk together 3 tbsp (45 mL) of the cognac, shallot, and a pinch each of thyme, salt and pepper.
2. Place rabbit meat in a shallow dish and brush with marinade, coating evenly. Cover and refrigerate while preparing the remaining ingredients.
3. In a skillet, melt butter over medium heat. Add onion and a pinch of salt; sauté until tender, about 10 minutes. Add garlic and sauté for 2 minutes. Add port and cook until liquid is reduced by half. Let cool.
4. In a saucepan, bring 2 cups (500 mL) water to a boil. Add carrots and cook until tender-crisp, about 2 minutes. Remove carrots with a slotted spoon and pat dry on paper towels; set aside. Add bacon to the boiling water and cook for about 5 minutes to remove some of the smoky flavor. Remove bacon with tongs and pat dry on paper towels; set aside. Add green onions to the boiling water and cook until tender, about 4 minutes. Drain off water and pat onions dry on paper towels. Set aside.
5. Cut pork, veal and pork fat into 1-inch (2.5 cm) cubes. Place meat cubes and half of the marinated rabbit meat in a shallow container in the freezer for 30 minutes to facilitate grinding. Attach the food grinder, with the fine plate, to the mixer. Run the meat through the grinder into a large bowl. Return to the freezer for 30 minutes. Run through the grinder again into the mixer bowl. Remove the food grinder.

6. Remove the remaining rabbit meat from the marinade and set aside. Add marinade, onion mixture, eggs, the remaining 2 tbsp (25 mL) cognac, 2 tsp (10 mL) salt, 1 tsp (5 mL) thyme, 1/4 tsp (1 mL) pepper and five-spice powder to the ground meat in the mixer bowl. Attach the flat beater and bowl to the mixer. Set to Stir and mix until well combined, about 1 minute. In a skillet, over medium-high heat, sauté a small amount of the stuffing until no longer pink. Taste and adjust seasoning as desired.
7. Preheat oven to 350°F (180°C). Line the bottom and sides of loaf pan crosswise with the bacon, leaving a 2- to 3-inch (5 to 7.5 cm) overhang. Divide the stuffing into 4 portions and pack one portion into the bottom of the pan in an even layer. Place 3 of the green onions lengthwise and arrange some of the pistachios in between. Top with one-third of the rabbit meat strips and another layer of stuffing. Repeat the process, using carrots in the second layer and green onions in the third layer, and ending with a layer of stuffing. Flip the overhanging bacon over the top.
8. Cover loaf pan with foil and set in center of baking pan lined with towel. Pour in boiling water to reach halfway up the sides of the loaf pan. Place in preheated oven and bake for 90 minutes or until pâté reaches an internal temperature of 160°F (71°C). The pâté will have shrunk from the sides of the pan and will be full of liquid fat.
9. Carefully remove loaf pan from the water bath. Fit wood or cardboard inside pan on top of pâté and top with the 4-lb (2 kg) weight. (This compacts the pâté and creates a better texture.) Let cool to room temperature in pan on a rack. Refrigerate, weighted, for at least 8 hours or overnight.
10. Unmold the pâté from its pan and serve sliced on a platter, accompanied by rustic bread, mustard and cornichons.

Makes 1 loaf

TIP

In its pan, covered with its fat, the pâté will keep for up to 1 week. Once it is removed from the pan and the fat is disturbed, it will keep for 3 to 4 days. The pâté may be frozen, but the texture will become a bit grainy.

Spicy Ham Spread

ROTOR SLICER/SHREDDER
FOOD GRINDER

- Preheat broiler
- Baking sheet

6 tbsp	unsalted butter, divided	90 mL
3 tbsp	unbleached all-purpose flour	45 mL
1 cup	half-and-half (10%) cream	250 mL
1/2 tsp	salt	2 mL
1/4 tsp	cayenne pepper	1 mL
Pinch	freshly ground black pepper	Pinch
Pinch	ground nutmeg	Pinch
1	egg yolk	1
1 oz	Swiss cheese	30 g
1 oz	Parmesan cheese	30 g
8 oz	ham, cut into chunks	250 g
1/4 cup	sliced green onions, white and green parts	50 mL
1	baguette, sliced and toasted	1

1. In a saucepan, melt 3 tbsp (45 mL) of the butter over medium-high heat. Stir in flour and cook, stirring, until roux is foamy, about 2 minutes.
2. In a small microwave-safe bowl, microwave cream on Medium until hot, about 1 minute. Whisk rapidly into the hot roux. The sauce will thicken quickly. Stir in salt, cayenne pepper, black pepper and nutmeg. Remove from heat and whisk in egg yolk. Set aside.
3. Attach the slicer/shredder, with the fine shredder, to the mixer. Set to Speed 4 and shred Swiss and Parmesan cheeses into a bowl. Add shredded cheese to the sauce and stir to combine.
4. Remove the slicer/shredder and attach the food grinder, with the fine plate, to the mixer. Set to Speed 4 and run ham through the grinder into a bowl.
5. In a skillet, melt the remaining 3 tbsp (45 mL) butter over medium heat. Add ground ham and green onions; cook, stirring, until ham is heated and onion is slightly cooked, about 3 minutes. Stir into the cheese sauce.
6. Spread on toasted baguette slices and place on baking sheet. Broil for 1 to 2 minutes or until lightly browned. Serve warm.

Makes 2 cups (500 mL)

Soups

Spicy Black Bean Soup

FRUIT/VEGETABLE STRAINER

2 cups	dried black beans	500 mL
3	slices bacon, chopped	3
1	onion, chopped	1
3	cloves garlic, chopped	3
2	bay leaves	2
2	chipotle chilies in adobo sauce, chopped	2
1	large carrot, chopped	1
1 1/4 tsp	ground cumin	6 mL
2 cups	chicken stock (approx.)	500 mL
1/4 cup	chopped fresh cilantro	50 mL
	Salt and freshly ground black pepper	
	Sour cream	
	Additional chopped fresh cilantro, for garnish	

TIP

Chipotle chilies are dried and smoked jalapeños. There are most often found canned in adobo sauce, a vinegary, tomato-based sauce. They are quite hot and should be used sparingly if you like your food on the mild side.

Use homemade chicken stock for this soup if you have it. If using canned stock, use the low-sodium type.

1. Place beans in a large bowl. Add enough cold water to cover beans by 2 inches (5 cm). Cover and soak overnight at room temperature or quick-soak them (see tip, page 72). Rinse and drain.
2. In a large saucepan, over medium heat, cook bacon until browned and crispy. Remove bacon with a slotted spoon and set aside. Drain all but 1 tablespoon (15 mL) fat from the pan. Add onion and sauté until tender, about 5 minutes. Add garlic and sauté for 2 minutes. Add 4 1/2 cups (1.125 L) water, beans, bay leaves, chilies, carrot and cumin; bring to a boil. Reduce heat, cover and simmer, stirring occasionally, until beans are very tender, about 70 minutes.
3. Attach the fruit/vegetable strainer to the mixer. Set to Speed 4 and run soup, 1 ladleful at a time, through the strainer into a large bowl, with another bowl to catch the solids. Run the solids through the strainer one more time into the large bowl.
4. Discard leftover solids and return soup to the saucepan. Add stock and bring to a simmer over medium heat, thinning with additional stock if necessary. Stir in cilantro and season to taste with salt and pepper.
5. Ladle into bowls and garnish with sour cream, cilantro and reserved bacon. Serve hot.

Serves 4

Make ahead

Can be prepared through Step 4 up to 2 days ahead. Let cool, cover and refrigerate. Bring to a simmer over medium heat before garnishing, thinning with additional stock if necessary.

Cream of Cauliflower Soup

FRUIT/VEGETABLE STRAINER

1 1/2 lbs	cauliflower (1 small)	750 g
9 tbsp	unsalted butter, divided	135 mL
3	slices bacon, diced	3
1 cup	diced onion	250 mL
1/3 cup	unbleached all-purpose flour	75 mL
4 cups	chicken or vegetable stock	1 L
1 1/2 cups	milk	375 mL
1 1/2 tsp	salt	7 mL
1/4 tsp	freshly ground white pepper	1 mL
1/4 tsp	ground nutmeg	1 mL
2	egg yolks	2
1/2 tsp	freshly squeezed lemon juice	2 mL
Pinch	cayenne pepper (optional)	Pinch
1/4 cup	minced fresh parsley or chives (optional)	50 mL

Make ahead

Can be prepared through Step 4 up to 1 day ahead. Let cool, cover and refrigerate. Bring to a simmer over medium heat before continuing.

1. Cut off the thick stem base of the cauliflower and trim off the leaves from the florets. Wash florets under cold water and chop into 1-inch (2.5 cm) pieces.
2. In a large saucepan, melt butter over medium-high heat. Add bacon and onion and sauté until onion is translucent, about 4 minutes. Reduce heat to medium; add flour and cook, stirring, for 2 minutes. Whisk in stock and 1 cup (250 mL) water; bring to a boil over high heat. Reduce heat to medium-low, add cauliflower and simmer until cauliflower is tender, about 20 minutes. Remove from heat and let cool for about 10 minutes.
3. Attach the fruit/vegetable strainer to the mixer. Set to Speed 4 and run half the soup, 1 ladleful at a time, through the strainer into a large bowl, with another bowl to catch the solids.
4. Return soup and solids to the saucepan. Add milk, salt, white pepper and nutmeg; bring to a simmer over medium heat.
5. Ladle 1 cup (250 mL) of the liquid into a heatproof bowl. Quickly whisk in egg yolks, then stir back into soup. Cook, stirring, for about 3 minutes. Do not let boil or the eggs will curdle. Stir in lemon juice. Taste and adjust seasoning as desired with salt, pepper and nutmeg. Add cayenne, if desired.
6. Ladle into bowls and garnish with minced parsley, if desired. Serve hot.

Serves 6

Lentil Soup

ROTOR SLICER/SHREDDER ◆
FRUIT/VEGETABLE STRAINER

2	carrots, cut into thirds	2
1	parsnip, cut into thirds	1
1	smoked ham hock (about 12 oz/375 g)	1
6 cups	chicken stock	1.5 L
1 cup	lentils, rinsed and drained	250 mL
½ tsp	salt	2 mL
Pinch	freshly ground black pepper	Pinch
2 tbsp	olive oil	25 mL
1 cup	chopped onion	250 mL
8 oz	spicy sausage, such as Chorizo (see recipe, page 167) or Italian (see recipe, page 164), in bulk form	250 g
3	cloves garlic, minced	3
2 cups	mixed spring greens (mesclun mix)	500 mL
½ cup	chopped fresh cilantro	125 mL
2 tbsp	freshly squeezed lemon juice	25 mL

Make ahead

Can be prepared through Step 5 up to 1 day ahead. Let cool, cover and refrigerate. Bring to a simmer over medium heat before continuing.

1. Attach the slicer/shredder, with the thick slicer, to the mixer. Set to Speed 4 and slice carrots and parsnip.
2. In a large saucepan, over medium-high heat, bring carrots, parsnip, ham, stock, lentils, salt and pepper to a simmer. Reduce heat, cover and simmer until lentils are tender, about 45 minutes.
3. Transfer ham to a plate and let cool slightly. Remove the meat from the ham hock and cut into bite-size pieces, discarding bones, fat and skin. Set aside.
4. Remove the slicer/shredder and attach the fruit/vegetable strainer. Set to Speed 4 and run soup, one ladleful at a time, through the strainer into a large bowl, with another bowl to catch the solids. Set soup and solids aside. Clean the saucepan.
5. In clean saucepan, heat oil over medium-high heat. Add onion and sauté until tender, about 3 minutes. Reduce heat to medium, add sausage and cook, breaking it up into small chunks, until no longer pink, about 5 minutes. Add garlic and cook, stirring, for 1 minute. Add the reserved soup, solids and ham; bring to a simmer.
6. Add spring greens, cilantro and lemon juice; cook, stirring, until greens have wilted, about 2 minutes. Taste and adjust seasoning as desired with salt and pepper.
7. Ladle into bowls and serve hot.

Serves 6

Creamy Mushroom Soup

ROTOR SLICER/SHREDDER

1 1/2 lbs	button mushrooms	750 g
3 tbsp	unsalted butter	45 mL
2 tbsp	olive oil	25 mL
3	cloves garlic, minced	3
1	onion, chopped	1
4 oz	shiitake mushrooms, stems removed and thinly sliced	125 g
1/4 cup	unbleached all-purpose flour	50 mL
3	sprigs fresh thyme	3
5 cups	chicken stock	1.25 L
1/4 cup	Madeira	50 mL
1/2 cup	whipping (35%) cream	125 mL
	Salt and freshly ground black pepper	

1. Attach the slicer/shredder, with the thin slicer, to the mixer. Set to Speed 4 and slice button mushrooms.
2. In a large saucepan, heat butter and oil over medium-high heat. Add garlic and onion; sauté for 2 minutes. Add button and shiitake mushrooms; sauté until all moisture from mushrooms has evaporated, about 4 minutes. Add flour and cook, stirring, for 2 minutes. Add thyme, stock and Madeira. Reduce heat and simmer, uncovered, until slightly thickened, about 10 minutes. Add whipping cream and simmer, uncovered, for 10 minutes. Season to taste with salt and pepper.
3. Ladle into bowls and serve hot.

Serves 4 to 6

Make ahead

Can be prepared up to 1 day ahead. Let cool slightly, cover and refrigerate. Bring to a simmer over medium heat before serving, thinning with additional stock if necessary.

Split Pea Soup

FRUIT/VEGETABLE STRAINER

1 tbsp	olive oil	15 mL
2	cloves garlic, minced	2
1	small onion, chopped	1
1	large carrot, chopped	1
2	bay leaves	2
1	smoked ham hock (about 12 oz/375 g)	1
5 cups	chicken stock	1.25 L
1 1/2 cups	green split peas, rinsed	375 mL
	Salt and freshly ground black pepper	

Make ahead

Can be prepared up to 2 days ahead. Let cool, cover and refrigerate. Bring to a simmer over medium heat before serving, thinning with additional stock if necessary.

1. In a large saucepan, heat oil over medium-high heat. Add garlic, onion and carrot; sauté until vegetables begin to soften, about 6 minutes. Add bay leaves, ham, stock and peas; bring to a boil. Reduce heat to medium-low, cover and simmer, stirring occasionally, until peas are tender, about 1 hour. Discard bay leaves.
2. Transfer ham to a plate and let cool slightly. Remove the meat from the ham hock and cut into bite-size pieces, discarding bones, fat and skin. Set aside.
3. Attach the fruit/vegetable strainer to the mixer. Set to Speed 4 and run soup, 1 ladleful at a time, through the strainer into a large bowl, with another bowl to catch the solids. Run the solids through the strainer one more time into the large bowl.
4. Discard leftover solids and return soup to the saucepan. Add reserved meat and bring to simmer over medium heat. Simmer until heated through, about 5 minutes. Season to taste with salt and pepper.
5. Ladle into bowls and serve hot.

Serves 4 to 6

Potato and Leek Soup

ROTOR SLICER/SHREDDER
FRUIT/VEGETABLE STRAINER

2 lbs	potatoes, peeled and cut into quarters	1 kg
2	leeks, sliced (white and light green parts only)	2
6 cups	chicken stock	1.5 L
Pinch	ground nutmeg	Pinch
Pinch	cayenne pepper	Pinch
	Salt and freshly ground black pepper	
1 cup	whipping (35%) cream	250 mL

TIP
This soup is also good chilled. To chill, allow soup to cool to room temperature, cover and refrigerate for at least 4 hours.

1. Attach the slicer/shredder, with the thick slicer, to the mixer. Set to Speed 4 and slice potatoes into a large saucepan. Add leeks and stock and bring to a simmer over medium heat. Reduce heat and simmer, uncovered, until potatoes are tender, about 20 minutes. Remove from heat and let cool for 20 minutes.
2. Remove the slicer/shredder and attach the fruit/vegetable strainer. Set to Speed 4 and run soup, 1 ladleful at a time, through the strainer into a large bowl, with another bowl to catch the solids.
3. Return soup and solids to the saucepan and bring to a simmer over medium heat. Season with nutmeg, cayenne, salt and pepper. Add whipping cream, taste and adjust seasoning as desired with salt and pepper.
4. Ladle into bowls and serve hot.

Serves 6

Make ahead
Can be prepared up to 2 days ahead. Let cool, cover and refrigerate. Bring to a simmer over medium heat before serving.

Butternut Squash Soup with Nutmeg Cream

WIRE WHIP FRUIT/VEGETABLE STRAINER

Nutmeg Cream		
1/2 cup	cold whipping (35%) cream	125 mL
1/4 tsp	ground nutmeg	1 mL
Soup		
1/4 cup	unsalted butter	50 mL
1	butternut squash (about 2 lbs/1 kg), peeled and chopped into 1-inch (2.5 cm) pieces	1
1	clove garlic, minced	1
1 cup	diced onion	250 mL
1 tsp	salt	5 mL
1/2 tsp	ground coriander	2 mL
1/2 tsp	dried thyme	2 mL
Pinch	freshly ground black pepper	Pinch
5 cups	chicken or vegetable stock	1.25 L
1/2 cup	orange juice	125 mL
1/2 cup	cold whipping (35%) cream	125 mL
Pinch	ground nutmeg	Pinch
	Cayenne pepper	
1/4 cup	chopped fresh cilantro	50 mL

Make ahead

Soup can be prepared through Step 4 up to 2 days ahead. Let cool, cover and refrigerate. Prepare the nutmeg cream up to 3 hours before you plan to serve the soup, and bring soup to a simmer over medium heat before topping with cream and garnishing.

1. *Prepare the nutmeg cream:* Place whipping cream in the mixer bowl. Attach the whip and mixer bowl to the mixer. Set to Speed 8 and beat until soft peaks form. Add nutmeg and beat to combine well. Cover and refrigerate for up to 3 hours, until ready to use.
2. *Prepare the soup:* In a large saucepan, melt butter over medium-high heat. Add squash, garlic and onion; sauté until onion is tender, about 3 minutes. Reduce heat to medium and add salt, coriander, thyme and pepper. Sauté, stirring occasionally, until squash begins to soften, about 5 minutes. Add stock and orange juice. Reduce heat, cover and simmer until squash is tender, about 30 minutes. Remove from heat and let cool for 10 minutes.
3. Remove the whip and attach the fruit/vegetable strainer. Set to Speed 4 and run soup, 1 ladleful at a time, through the strainer into a large bowl, with another bowl to catch the solids.
4. Return soup and solids to the saucepan. Add whipping cream, nutmeg and cayenne; bring to a simmer over medium heat. Taste and adjust seasoning as desired with salt and pepper.
5. Ladle into bowls, top with a dollop of nutmeg cream and garnish with cilantro. Serve hot.

Serves 6

Roasted Winter Squash and Apple Soup

FRUIT/VEGETABLE STRAINER

- Preheat oven to 425°F (220°C)
- 2 large rimmed baking sheets, lined with foil

4	acorn squash, halved and seeds removed	4
2 tbsp	unsalted butter	25 mL
1	large onion, chopped	1
4½ cups	chicken stock (approx.)	1.125 L
1	Granny Smith apple, cored and diced	1
1	bay leaf	1
¼ tsp	ground nutmeg	1 mL
½ cup	whipping (35%) cream	125 mL
	Salt and freshly ground black pepper	
	Sour cream	
	Chopped fresh chives	

Variation

Any winter squash — especially butternut — will work well in this soup. Have fun experimenting with different varieties! Use about 2½ lbs (1.25 kg) in total.

Make ahead

Can be prepared through Step 4 up to 2 days ahead. Let cool, cover and refrigerate. Bring to a simmer over medium heat before garnishing.

1. Place squash halves, cut side down, on prepared baking sheets. Roast in preheated oven until tender, about 45 minutes. Let cool, then scoop out flesh and discard shells.
2. In a large saucepan, melt butter over medium-high heat. Add onion and sauté until beginning to brown, about 5 minutes. Add squash, stock, apple, bay leaf and nutmeg; bring to a boil. Reduce heat and simmer, uncovered, until squash and apple are tender, about 30 minutes. Discard bay leaf.
3. Attach the fruit/vegetable strainer to the mixer. Set to Speed 4 and run soup, 1 ladleful at a time, through the strainer into a large bowl, with another bowl to catch the solids. Run the solids through the strainer one more time into the large bowl.
4. Discard leftover solids and return soup to the saucepan. Add whipping cream and bring to a simmer over medium heat, thinning with more stock if desired. Season to taste with salt and pepper.
5. Ladle into bowls and garnish with sour cream and chives. Serve hot.

Serves 8

Sweet Potato, Coconut and Ginger Soup

FRUIT/VEGETABLE STRAINER

1	can (14 oz/398 mL) coconut milk	1
1	2-inch (5 cm) piece gingerroot, peeled and cut into matchsticks	1
2 lbs	orange-fleshed sweet potatoes, peeled and cut into 1-inch (2.5 cm) cubes	1 kg
3 cups	chicken stock	750 mL
1/2 tsp	salt	2 mL
Pinch	cayenne pepper	Pinch
	Freshly ground black pepper	
1 tbsp	freshly squeezed lime juice	15 mL

1. In a large saucepan, bring coconut milk, ginger, sweet potatoes, stock, salt, cayenne and black pepper to a simmer over medium heat. Cook until sweet potatoes are tender, about 20 minutes.
2. Attach the fruit/vegetable strainer to the mixer. Set to Speed 4 and run soup, 1 ladleful at a time, through the strainer into a large bowl, with another bowl to catch the solids. Run the solids through the strainer one more time into the large bowl.
3. Discard leftover solids and return soup to the saucepan. Add lime juice and bring to a simmer over medium heat. Taste and adjust seasoning as desired with salt, cayenne and black pepper.
4. Ladle into bowls and serve hot.

Serves 4 to 6

Variation

For a spicier version, add 1 tbsp (15 mL) Thai red curry paste.

Make ahead

Can be prepared up to 2 days ahead. Let cool, cover and refrigerate. Bring to a simmer over medium heat before serving.

Tomato and Rice Soup with Basil

FRUIT/VEGETABLE STRAINER

3 tbsp	unsalted butter	45 mL
1/2 cup	chopped onion	125 mL
1/4 cup	chopped celery	50 mL
1 tsp	dried basil	5 mL
2	cans (each 14 oz/398 mL) diced tomatoes, with juice	2
2 tbsp	tomato paste	25 mL
3 cups	chicken or vegetable stock	500 mL
1/2 cup	long-grain rice	125 mL
1/2 tsp	salt	2 mL
1/4 tsp	freshly ground black pepper	1 mL
Pinch	cayenne pepper (optional)	Pinch
1 cup	milk (approx.)	250 mL
1/2 cup	freshly grated Parmesan cheese	125 mL
1/2 cup	finely sliced fresh basil	125 mL

1. In a large saucepan, melt butter over medium-high heat. Add onion and celery; sauté until tender, about 2 minutes. Add dried basil and sauté until the basil is fragrant, about 1 minute. Add canned tomatoes, with juice, and tomato paste. Stir to incorporate paste, breaking up tomatoes. Reduce heat and simmer, uncovered, until liquid is reduced by about one-quarter, about 20 minutes. Add stock and bring back to a simmer. Add rice and simmer, uncovered, for 15 to 20 minutes, or until rice is tender.
2. Attach the fruit/vegetable strainer to the mixer. Set to Speed 4 and run half the soup, 1 ladleful at a time, through the strainer into a large bowl, with another bowl to catch the solids.
3. Return soup and solids to the saucepan and bring to a simmer over medium heat. Season with salt, black pepper and cayenne, if using. Add enough milk to thin to desired consistency.
4. Ladle into bowls and garnish with Parmesan cheese and fresh basil. Serve hot.

Serves 4

Make ahead

Can be prepared through Step 3 up to 2 days ahead. Let cool, cover and refrigerate. Bring to a simmer over medium heat before garnishing.

Hearty Harvest Roasted Vegetable Soup

ROTOR SLICER/SHREDDER

- Preheat oven to 400°F (200°C)
- 2 large rimmed baking sheets

3	carrots, cut into thirds	3
2	parsnips, cut into thirds	2
2	zucchini, cut into thirds	2
1	head fennel, trimmed, cored and quartered	1
3	onions, sliced into 1-inch (2.5 cm) wide slices	3
2	stalks celery, sliced	2
1 cup	cubed peeled winter squash (1-inch/2.5 cm cubes)	250 mL
1⁄4 cup	olive oil	50 mL
1 tbsp	dried basil	15 mL
1 tsp	dried oregano	5 mL
1⁄2 tsp	salt	2 mL
1⁄2 tsp	freshly ground black pepper	2 mL
8 cups	vegetable stock	2 L
1	can (14 oz/398 mL) diced tomatoes, with juice	1
2 oz	Parmesan cheese	60 g
1⁄2 cup	chopped fresh flat-leaf parsley	125 mL
1 tbsp	balsamic vinegar	15 mL
Pinch	cayenne pepper (optional)	Pinch
	Additional grated Parmesan cheese (optional)	

1. Attach the slicer/shredder, with the thick slicer, to the mixer. Set to Speed 4 and slice carrots, parsnips, zucchini and fennel into a large bowl. Add onions, celery, squash, oil, basil, oregano, salt and pepper and toss to evenly coat vegetables with oil and seasonings.
2. Divide vegetables between baking sheets and roast in preheated oven for 20 to 25 minutes, or until tender and lightly browned.
3. In a large saucepan, bring roasted vegetables, stock and tomatoes with juice to a simmer over medium heat. Simmer, uncovered, for 30 minutes to allow flavors to blend.
4. Remove the thick slicer from the slicer/shredder and attach the coarse shredder. Set to Speed 4 and grate Parmesan cheese into a bowl. Add cheese, parsley, vinegar and cayenne (if using) to the soup. Taste and adjust seasoning as desired with salt and pepper.
5. Ladle into bowls and serve hot, with additional Parmesan cheese to sprinkle over individual servings, if desired.

Serves 6

Variation

Replace vegetable stock with chicken stock and add 3 to 4 diced boneless skinless chicken breast halves in Step 3.

Make ahead

Can be prepared through Step 3 up to 2 days ahead. Let cool, cover and refrigerate. Bring to a simmer over medium heat before serving.

Minestrone

FRUIT/VEGETABLE STRAINER
ROTOR SLICER/SHREDDER

2	cans (each 14 to 19 oz/ 398 to 540 mL) Great Northern or navy beans, rinsed and drained	2
7 cups	chicken stock, divided	1.75 L
2	carrots, cut into thirds	2
2	zucchini, cut into thirds	2
1/4 cup	olive oil	50 mL
1 cup	diced onion	250 mL
3	cloves garlic, minced	3
1	stalk celery, sliced	1
2 tsp	dried oregano	10 mL
1 tsp	salt	5 mL
1/2 tsp	freshly ground black pepper	2 mL
1	can (14 oz/398 mL) diced tomatoes, with juice	1
4 oz	prosciutto, diced	125 g
2 cups	thinly sliced napa or savoy cabbage	500 mL
1 cup	elbow macaroni	250 mL
1/4 cup	chopped fresh parsley	50 mL
	Juice of 1 lemon	
2 oz	Parmesan cheese	60 g

Make ahead

Can be prepared through Step 4 up to 2 days ahead. Let cool, cover and refrigerate. Bring to a simmer over medium heat before serving, thinning with additional stock if necessary.

1. In a medium saucepan, bring beans and 3 cups (750 mL) of the stock to a simmer over medium heat. Reduce heat and simmer, uncovered, for 5 minutes.
2. Attach the fruit/vegetable strainer to the mixer. Set to Speed 4 and run half the beans and their liquid, 1 ladleful at a time, through the strainer into a large bowl, with another bowl to catch the solids. Return liquid and solids to the saucepan and set aside.
3. Remove the strainer and attach the slicer/shredder, with the thick slicer. Set to Speed 4 and slice carrots and zucchini into a bowl.
4. In a large saucepan, heat oil over medium-high heat. Add onion and sauté until tender, about 2 minutes. Add carrot, zucchini, garlic, celery, oregano, salt and pepper; sauté until tender, about 5 minutes, reducing heat if vegetables begin to burn. Add the remaining 4 cups (1 L) stock, tomatoes with juice, prosciutto and cabbage. Reduce heat and simmer, uncovered, for 10 minutes. Add beans and their liquid and cook for 10 minutes. Add elbow macaroni and cook until tender, about 10 minutes. Add parsley and lemon juice. Taste and adjust seasoning as desired with salt and pepper.
5. Meanwhile, remove the thick slicer from the slicer/shredder and attach the coarse shredder. Grate Parmesan cheese into a bowl.
6. Ladle soup into bowls and sprinkle with cheese. Serve hot.

Serves 6 to 8

Curried Pear Soup

FRUIT/VEGETABLE STRAINER

Soup		
1/3 cup	unsalted butter	75 mL
6 cups	diced peeled pears (about 6)	1.5 L
2 cups	chopped onions	500 mL
2 cups	sliced leeks (white and light green parts only)	500 mL
1 tsp	minced garlic	5 mL
3 tbsp	unbleached all-purpose flour	45 mL
2 tbsp	curry powder (store-bought or see recipe, opposite)	25 mL
6 cups	chicken stock	1.5 L
1/2 cup	dry white wine	125 mL
1/4 tsp	salt	1 mL
Pinch	freshly ground black pepper	Pinch
Garnish		
1 tbsp	unsalted butter	15 mL
1/4 cup	sliced green onions	50 mL
1 tbsp	liquid honey	15 mL
1 tsp	toasted sesame oil	5 mL
1/3 cup	plain yogurt	75 mL
	Salt and freshly ground black pepper	

TIP

Because leeks are grown in sandy soil, dirt can hide in their many layers. To wash, trim the bottoms and the dark green tops and slice down the middle lengthwise. Run under cold water, flushing the layers free of sand and grit.

1. *Prepare the soup:* In a large saucepan, melt butter over medium-high heat. Add pears, onions, leeks and garlic; sauté for 2 minutes. Reduce heat to medium and sauté for 1 minute. Add flour and curry powder; sauté until pears are soft, about 5 minutes. Stir in stock and wine; reduce heat and simmer until soup is velvety and lightly thickened, about 15 minutes. Taste and adjust seasoning as desired with salt and pepper.
2. Attach the fruit/vegetable strainer to the mixer. Set to Speed 4 and run soup, 1 ladleful at a time, through the strainer into a large bowl, with another bowl to catch the solids.
3. Return soup and solids to the saucepan and bring to a simmer over low heat.
4. *Prepare the garnish:* In a skillet, melt butter over medium-high heat. Add green onions and sauté until tender, about 2 minutes. Add honey and sesame oil; cook for 1 minute. Remove from heat and stir in yogurt. Season to taste with salt and pepper.
5. Ladle soup into bowls and top with garnish. Draw a chopstick or a knife through the yogurt to create a decorative swirl. Serve hot.

Serves 6

Make ahead

Can be prepared through Step 3 up to 2 days ahead. Let cool, cover and refrigerate. Bring soup to a simmer over medium heat before garnishing.

Curry Powder

- Preheat oven to 375°F (190°C)
- Rimmed baking sheet

1	dried ancho or pasilla chili	1
1	stick cinnamon (about 4 inches/10 cm long)	1
1 tbsp	coriander seeds	15 mL
1 tbsp	cumin seeds	15 mL
1 tbsp	cardamom seeds	15 mL
1 tbsp	fenugreek seeds	15 mL
1 tsp	mustard seeds	5 mL
1 tbsp	ground turmeric	15 mL
1 tsp	ground ginger	5 mL

Homemade curry powder adds a fresh, lively character to your dishes.

1. On baking sheet, toss chili, cinnamon, coriander seeds, cumin seeds, cardamom seeds, fenugreek seeds and mustard seeds. Toast in preheated oven until fragrant, about 5 minutes. Let cool and grind with a mortar and pestle or in a spice mill. Stir in turmeric and ginger.

Makes about 1/2 cup (125 mL)

Make ahead

Store at room temperature in an airtight container and use within a few weeks.

Chilled Minted Melon Soup

FRUIT/VEGETABLE STRAINER

1	large ripe honeydew melon, cut into 1-inch (2.5 cm) cubes	1
1/2 cup	loosely packed chopped fresh mint	125 mL
3 tbsp	freshly squeezed lime juice (approx.)	45 mL
1 tbsp	granulated sugar (approx.)	15 mL
Pinch	salt	Pinch
4	sprigs fresh mint (optional)	4

Chilled melon soup can be very refreshing on a hot summer day when the last thing you want to do is heat up your kitchen.

1. In a large bowl, combine melon, mint, lime juice, sugar and salt. Let stand for 15 minutes.
2. Attach the fruit/vegetable strainer to the mixer. Set to Speed 4 and run melon mixture, 1 tablespoonful (15 mL) at a time, through the strainer into a large bowl, with another bowl to catch the solids. Run the solids through the strainer one more time into the large bowl. Discard leftover solids, cover soup and refrigerate for at least 1 hour or for up to 2 days.
3. Ladle into bowls and garnish each with a sprig of mint, if desired.

Serves 4

Shrimp Bisque

FOOD GRINDER

1 lb	raw shrimp, shell on	500 g
2 tbsp	unsalted butter	25 mL
½ cup	diced onion	125 mL
2	tomatoes, halved and seeded	2
1	clove garlic, crushed	1
½ cup	diced carrot	125 mL
½ cup	diced parsnip	125 mL
½ cup	diced celery	125 mL
1 tbsp	unbleached all-purpose flour	15 mL
¼ tsp	dried thyme	1 mL
Pinch	salt	Pinch
Pinch	freshly ground black pepper	Pinch
5 cups	chicken stock	1.25 L
½ cup	whipping (35%) cream	125 mL
Pinch	cayenne pepper	Pinch
Pinch	ground nutmeg	Pinch
2 tbsp	minced fresh chives	25 mL

Make ahead

Can be prepared through Step 6 up to 2 days ahead. Let cool, cover and refrigerate.

TIP

It may seem odd to cook the shells and grind them up, but the process imparts a more pronounced shrimp taste to the bisque. Be sure to use a strainer with a very fine mesh to remove all the shells and solids from the soup.

1. Devein and shell shrimp. Refrigerate shrimp and shells separately until needed.
2. In a large saucepan, melt butter over medium-high heat. Add onion and sauté until tender, about 1 minute. Add tomatoes, garlic, carrot, parsnip, celery, flour, thyme, salt and pepper; sauté until vegetables are tender, about 4 minutes. Add shrimp shells and sauté until shells turn pink, about 1 minute. Add stock, reduce heat and simmer, uncovered, for about 20 minutes to let flavors develop.
3. Attach the food grinder, with the coarse plate, to the mixer. Set to Speed 4 and run soup, 1 ladleful at a time, through the grinder into a large bowl, being careful not to overfill the tube with liquid.
4. Strain soup through a handheld fine-mesh strainer lined with wet cheesecloth into a clean saucepan. Discard shells and vegetable solids. Clean the food grinder and reattach it.
5. Bring soup to a simmer over medium heat. Add shrimp and simmer, uncovered, until shrimp are firm and opaque, about 3 minutes.
6. Set mixer to Speed 4 and run soup and shrimp, 1 ladleful at a time, through the clean grinder into the large bowl. Transfer back to the saucepan.
7. Bring back to a simmer over low heat and add whipping cream, cayenne and nutmeg. Taste and adjust seasoning as desired with salt and pepper.
8. Ladle into bowls and garnish with chives. Serve hot.

Serves 4

New England Clam Chowder

FRUIT/VEGETABLE STRAINER

3	slices bacon, chopped	3
1 tbsp	unsalted butter	15 mL
2	cloves garlic, finely chopped	2
2	stalks celery, chopped	2
2	bay leaves	2
1 cup	chopped onion	250 mL
2 tsp	chopped fresh thyme	2
2 lbs	Yukon gold or other all-purpose potatoes, peeled and cut into $\frac{1}{2}$-inch (1 cm) cubes	1 kg
3 cups	clam juice	750 mL
3	cans (each 6.5 oz/190 g) minced clams	3
1 $\frac{1}{2}$ cups	whipping (35%) cream	375 mL
	Salt and freshly ground black pepper	
2 tbsp	chopped fresh parsley	25 mL

Make ahead

Can be prepared through Step 4 up to 1 day ahead. Let cool, then refrigerate. Cover once chowder is completely chilled. Bring to a simmer over medium heat before serving. Refrigerate bacon separately and crisp in a skillet before garnishing.

1. Heat a large, heavy saucepan over medium heat. Add bacon and cook, stirring occasionally, until crisp and golden brown, about 3 minutes. Remove bacon from the pan with a slotted spoon and set aside.
2. To the fat remaining in the saucepan, add butter, garlic, celery, bay leaves, onion and thyme. Sauté until onion is tender but not browned, about 5 minutes. Add potatoes, clam juice and 2 cups (500 mL) water. (The liquid should barely cover the potatoes; if it doesn't, add enough water to cover them.) Increase heat to medium-high and bring to a boil. Reduce heat, cover and simmer until potatoes are just tender, about 20 minutes. Discard bay leaves.
3. Attach the fruit/vegetable strainer to the mixer. Set to Speed 4 and run half the soup, 1 ladleful at a time, through the strainer into a large bowl, with another bowl to catch the solids.
4. Return soup and solids to the saucepan, stir and bring to a simmer over low heat. Simmer until slightly thickened, about 5 minutes. Remove from heat, and stir in clams and whipping cream. Season to taste with salt and pepper.
5. Ladle into bowls and sprinkle with parsley and reserved bacon. Serve hot.

Serves 6 to 8

Corn Chowder with Ham

FRUIT/VEGETABLE STRAINER

6	ears of corn, shucked	6
4 cups	vegetable or chicken stock	1 L
2 cups	milk	500 mL
3 tbsp	unsalted butter	45 mL
1 cup	diced red onion	250 mL
2 tbsp	unbleached all-purpose flour	25 mL
2	potatoes, peeled and diced	2
1 tsp	dried basil	5 mL
1 tsp	salt	5 mL
1/4 tsp	freshly ground black pepper	1 mL
1/4 tsp	hot pepper flakes	1 mL
Pinch	ground nutmeg	Pinch
8 oz	ham, diced	250 g
1/4 cup	minced fresh flat-leaf parsley	50 mL

Make ahead

Can be prepared through Step 5 up to 2 days ahead. Let cool, cover and refrigerate. Bring to a simmer over medium heat before garnishing.

TIP

Running soup through the strainer helps to thicken it, without adding extra fat.

1. Cut corn kernels from the cobs into a bowl. Using the back of a knife, scrape down the cobs, releasing the corn milk into the bowl. Set aside.
2. In a large saucepan, bring stock and corn cobs to a simmer over medium heat. Cook for about 30 minutes to extract the flavor from the cobs. Remove cobs and discard. Add milk to the stock.
3. In another large saucepan, melt butter over medium-high heat. Add onion and sauté until soft and translucent, about 4 minutes. Add flour and sauté until foamy, about 3 minutes. Stir in milk-stock mixture. Add potatoes, half of the corn, basil, salt, black pepper, hot pepper flakes and nutmeg. Reduce heat and simmer, uncovered, until potatoes are tender, about 25 minutes.
4. Attach the fruit/vegetable strainer to the mixer. Set to Speed 4 and run soup, 1 ladleful at a time, through the strainer into a large bowl, with another bowl to catch the solids.
5. Return soup and solids to the saucepan. Add ham and the remaining corn; bring to a simmer over medium heat. Simmer for 20 minutes to allow flavors to blend. Taste and adjust seasoning as desired with salt and pepper.
6. Ladle into bowls and garnish with parsley. Serve hot.

Serves 6

Old-Fashioned Chicken and Noodle Soup

PASTA ROLLER

- Large baking sheet

16 cups	chicken stock	4 L
1	whole chicken (about 3½ lbs/1.75 kg), cut into 8 pieces	1
2	sprigs fresh thyme	2
2	carrots, thinly sliced	2
2	stalks celery, sliced	2
½ cup	chopped onion	125 mL
1 lb	Basic Egg Pasta dough (see recipe, page 192)	500 g
	Unbleached all-purpose flour	
½ cup	finely chopped fresh parsley	125 mL
1 tbsp	freshly squeezed lemon juice	15 mL
	Salt and freshly ground black pepper	

This classic soup is sure to alleviate the common cold, or whatever else may ail you. Adding lemon juice may seem strange, but it really heightens the other flavors.

TIP

Use homemade chicken stock for this soup if you have it. If using canned stock, use the low-sodium type.

1. In a large saucepan, bring stock and chicken to a boil over medium-high heat. Reduce heat, cover partially and simmer until chicken is no longer pink inside, about 20 minutes. Remove from heat. Transfer chicken to a large bowl and let cool slightly. Remove the meat from the bones and cut into bite-size pieces, discarding skin and bones. Set aside.
2. Spoon fat off the top of the stock and return stock to a simmer over medium heat. Add thyme, carrots, celery and onion; simmer until vegetables are tender, about 15 minutes.
3. Meanwhile, roll pasta to setting 4 (see Pasta Basics, page 190, for instructions on rolling pasta). With a knife, cut pasta crosswise into ½-inch (1 cm) strips to create short, thick noodles. Toss lightly with flour and spread out on large baking sheet as they are made.
4. Remove thyme and stir in noodles. Simmer until noodles are tender, about 5 minutes. Add chicken, parsley and lemon juice. Season to taste with salt and pepper.
5. Ladle into bowls and serve hot.

Serves 10

Make ahead

Can be prepared through Step 2 up to 1 day ahead. Cover chicken meat and broth separately and refrigerate. Bring broth to a boil over medium-high heat before continuing.

Amish Beef and Noodle Soup

PASTA ROLLER

- Large baking sheet

2 lbs	boneless beef chuck or cross rib	1 kg
	Salt and freshly ground black pepper	
2 tbsp	vegetable oil	25 mL
1	onion, diced	1
5 cups	beef stock	1.25 L
8 oz	Basic Egg Pasta dough (see recipe, page 192)	250 g
	Unbleached all-purpose flour	
4	potatoes (about 1 1/4 lbs/ 625 g), cut into 1/2-inch (1 cm) cubes	4
3	carrots, cut into 1/2-inch (1 cm) cubes	3
2	stalks celery, sliced crosswise into 1/2-inch (1 cm) slices	2

1. Trim beef, cut into 2-inch (5 cm) chunks and season lightly with salt and pepper.
2. In a large Dutch oven, heat oil over medium-high heat. In 2 batches, brown the beef. Transfer to a plate and add onion to the Dutch oven; sauté until tender, about 5 minutes. Transfer beef back to the Dutch oven and add stock. Reduce heat, cover and simmer until beef is tender and pulls apart easily, about 2 hours.
3. Meanwhile, roll pasta to setting 4 (see Pasta Basics, page 190, for instructions on rolling pasta). With a knife, cut pasta crosswise into 1/4-inch (0.5 cm) strips to create short, thick noodles. Toss lightly with flour and spread out on large baking sheet as they are made.
4. Transfer beef to a plate and, using two forks, pull apart into bite-size shreds. Add back to the soup. Add potatoes, carrots, celery and 3 cups (750 mL) water; cook until potatoes are tender, about 25 minutes. Add noodles and cook until noodles are just tender, about 4 minutes. Season to taste with salt and pepper.
5. Ladle into bowls and serve hot.

Serves 6 to 8

Make ahead

Can be prepared through Step 2 up to 2 days ahead. Let cool, cover and refrigerate. Bring to a boil over medium-high heat before continuing.

Zucchini, Cheese and Sausage Soup

ROTOR SLICER/SHREDDER

3	medium zucchini, cut in half lengthwise	3
8 oz	extra-sharp Cheddar cheese	250 g
1 tbsp	cornstarch	15 mL
2 tbsp	unsalted butter	25 mL
1 lb	sausage, such as Country Pork (see recipe, page 161) or Italian (see recipe, page 164), in bulk form	500 g
2	cloves garlic, minced	2
1	onion, chopped	1
3 tbsp	unbleached all-purpose flour	45 mL
6 cups	chicken stock	1.5 L
½ cup	whipping (35%) cream	125 mL
1 tbsp	freshly squeezed lemon juice	15 mL
	Freshly ground black pepper	

TIP
Use homemade chicken stock for this soup if you have it. If using canned stock, use the low-sodium type.

1. Attach the slicer/shredder, with the thick slicer, to the mixer. Set to Speed 4 and slice the zucchini into a bowl. Set aside.
2. Remove the thick slicer and attach the coarse shredder. Set to Speed 4 and shred cheese into another bowl. Add cornstarch and toss to coat. Set aside.
3. In a large saucepan, melt butter over medium-high heat. Add sausage and sauté, breaking it up into small chunks, until no longer pink, about 5 minutes. Add garlic and onion; sauté for 1 minute. Add flour and cook, stirring, for 2 minutes. Whisk in stock and bring to a boil. Add zucchini, reduce heat and simmer, uncovered, until tender, about 15 minutes. Stir in whipping cream. Add cheese a handful at a time, stirring to incorporate each handful completely. Add lemon juice and pepper to taste.
4. Ladle into bowls and serve hot.

Serves 6

Variation

For an Oktoberfest twist, replace 1½ cups (375 mL) of the chicken stock with a 12-oz (341 mL) bottle of a good-quality lager and the sausage with diced smoked Kielbasa (see recipe, page 174).

Pork and Scallion Wonton Soup

FOOD GRINDER

- Baking sheet, lined with parchment paper

Broth		
2 lbs	chicken necks and backs	1 kg
8 cups	chicken stock	2 L
5	whole peppercorns	5
5	quarter-sized slices fresh gingerroot	5
1	onion, quartered	1
1	carrot, sliced	1
1	stalk celery, sliced	1
1	bay leaf	1
1	stick cinnamon	1
	Salt and freshly ground black pepper (optional)	
Wontons		
8 oz	boneless pork shoulder blade	250 g
2 tbsp	chopped scallions (green onions)	25 mL
½ tsp	five-spice powder	2 mL
½ tsp	salt	2 mL
¼ tsp	freshly ground black pepper	1 mL
24	wonton wrappers	24
	Finely chopped scallion (green onion)	

1. *Prepare the broth:* Rinse the chicken necks and backs under cold water. Place in a large saucepan with stock, peppercorns, ginger, onion, carrot, celery, bay leaf and cinnamon. Bring to a simmer over medium heat. Reduce heat and simmer, uncovered, skimming and discarding scum as it rises to the surface, for 1 hour to allow flavors to develop. Strain all solids from the broth and return broth to the saucepan, discarding solids. Skim fat from the surface and bring broth back to a simmer. Add salt and pepper to taste, if desired.
2. *Meanwhile, prepare the wontons:* Cut pork into 1-inch (2.5 cm) cubes, place in a shallow container and freeze for 30 minutes to facilitate grinding. Attach the food grinder, with the fine plate, to the mixer. Set to Speed 4 and run pork through the grinder into a medium bowl. Using your hands, thoroughly mix in scallions, five-spice powder, salt and pepper. In a small skillet, over medium heat, cook 1 tablespoon (15 mL) of the meat mixture until no longer pink inside. Taste and adjust seasoning as desired with salt and pepper.
3. Working with a few at a time, place wonton wrappers on a work surface, keeping remaining wrappers covered with plastic. Moisten the edges of each wrapper with a brush or your fingertip dipped in water. Drop 1 tablespoon (15 mL) of the meat mixture into the center of each wrapper, flattening it out slightly but keeping a ½-inch (1 cm) border around it. Lay another wrapper on top (like ravioli). Press from the center of the meat to the edges of the wonton, pressing out the air and sealing the edges. Repeat with the remaining wrappers and meat mixture. Arrange wontons on prepared baking sheet and refrigerate until ready to use.

4. Add wontons 4 at a time to the broth. Cook, stirring, to keep wontons from sticking to the bottom of the pan, until fully cooked, about 5 minutes. Remove wontons with a slotted spoon and set aside in a covered dish. Repeat until all of the wontons are cooked.
5. Ladle broth into bowls, add 2 wontons to each serving and garnish with chopped scallion. Serve hot.

Serves 6

Variation

You could also use western-style or country-style ribs, with bones removed, in place of the pork shoulder blade in the wontons.

Make ahead

Broth can be prepared up to 2 days ahead. Let cool, cover and refrigerate. Bring to a simmer over medium heat before adding wontons. Wontons can be prepared through Step 3 up to 2 weeks ahead. Place baking sheet in the freezer. Once wontons are frozen, transfer them to a freezer bag. They can be added frozen to the broth, but increase cooking time by 3 minutes.

TIP

Cooking chicken parts and vegetables in chicken stock may seem like an unnecessary extra step, but it creates an intensely flavored broth that really makes this soup stand out.

Creamy Navy Bean and Ham Soup

FRUIT/VEGETABLE STRAINER

1 lb	navy (white pea) beans, picked over, rinsed and drained	500 g
2	large smoked ham hocks (about $1\frac{3}{4}$ lbs/875 g)	2
2	sprigs fresh thyme	2
1	bay leaf	1
1	onion, coarsely chopped	1
1	carrot, coarsely chopped	1
1	clove garlic, coarsely chopped	1
8 cups	cold water	2 L
	Salt and freshly ground black pepper	

Make ahead

Can be prepared up to 2 days ahead. Let cool, cover and refrigerate. Bring to a simmer over medium heat before serving, thinning with additional stock if necessary.

TIP

To quick-soak dried beans: In a colander, rinse beans under cold water. Discard any discolored ones. Place beans in a large saucepan and add enough cold water to cover beans by 2 inches (5 cm). Bring to a boil over high heat, then reduce heat and simmer, uncovered, for 5 minutes. Remove from heat, cover and let stand for 1 hour.

1. Place beans in a large bowl. Add enough cold water to cover beans by 2 inches (5 cm). Cover and soak overnight at room temperature or quick-soak them (see tip, at left). Rinse and drain.
2. In the same saucepan, bring beans, ham, thyme, bay leaf, onion, carrot, garlic and water to a boil. Reduce heat, cover and simmer until beans and ham are tender, about $1\frac{1}{2}$ hours. Remove from heat and discard thyme and bay leaf.
3. Transfer ham to a plate and let cool slightly. Remove the meat from the hocks and cut into bite-size pieces, discarding bones, fat and skin. Set aside.
4. Attach the fruit/vegetable strainer to the mixer. Set to Speed 4 and run half the soup, 1 ladleful at a time, through the strainer into a large bowl, with another bowl to catch the solids. Run the solids through the strainer one more time into the large bowl.
5. Discard leftover solids and return soup to the saucepan. Add ham and bring to a simmer over medium heat. Season to taste with salt and pepper.
6. Ladle into soup bowls and serve hot.

Serves 6 to 8

Chorizo Chili Soup

FRUIT/VEGETABLE STRAINER

1 lb	Chorizo (see recipe, page 167), in bulk form	500 g
1 tbsp	olive oil	15 mL
6	cloves garlic, minced	6
1	red bell pepper, diced	1
1	bay leaf	1
1 cup	diced onion	250 mL
2 tbsp	chili powder	25 mL
1 tsp	ground cumin	5 mL
1/2 tsp	cayenne pepper	2 mL
4	cans (each 14 to 19 oz/ 398 to 540 mL) red kidney beans, drained and rinsed	4
1	can (14 oz/398 mL) crushed tomatoes	1
4 cups	chicken stock (approx.)	1 L
	Salt and freshly ground black pepper	
	Shredded Cheddar cheese	
	Sour cream	

Make ahead

Can be prepared through step 4 up to 1 day ahead. Let cool, cover and refrigerate. Bring to a simmer over medium heat before garnishing, thinning with additional stock if necessary.

1. In a large saucepan, over medium-high heat, sauté chorizo, breaking it up into small chunks, until drippings come to a simmer, about 5 minutes. Drain off fat and set sausage aside.
2. In a large Dutch oven, heat oil over medium heat. Add garlic, red pepper, bay leaf and onion; stir to coat with oil. Cover and cook, stirring occasionally, until vegetables are tender and light golden, about 10 minutes. Add chili powder, cumin and cayenne; sauté for 1 minute. Add beans, tomatoes and stock; bring to a boil. Reduce heat, cover and simmer for about 30 minutes to allow flavors to blend. Discard bay leaf.
3. Attach the fruit/vegetable strainer to the mixer. Set to Speed 4 and run soup, 1 ladleful at a time, through the strainer into a large bowl, with another bowl to catch the solids. Run the solids through the strainer one more time into the large bowl.
4. Discard leftover solids and return soup to the Dutch oven. Add chorizo and bring to a simmer over medium heat, thinning with more stock, if desired. Simmer until heated through, about 10 minutes. Season to taste with salt and pepper.
5. Ladle into bowls and garnish with cheese and sour cream. Serve hot.

Serves 4 to 6

Red Bean and Sausage Soup

FRUIT/VEGETABLE STRAINER

1 lb	dried red kidney beans	500 g
3	slices bacon, chopped	3
8 oz	Spiced Habanero Sausage (see recipe, page 166), in bulk form	250 g
2	cloves garlic, chopped	2
1 ½ cups	finely chopped onions	375 mL
1 ½ cups	chopped celery	375 mL
1 ½ cups	chopped carrots	375 mL
1	small smoked ham hock (about 8 oz/250 g)	1
1	bay leaf	1
6 cups	chicken stock (approx.)	1.5 L
½ tsp	dried oregano	2 mL
½ tsp	dried thyme	2 mL
3 tbsp	dry sherry	45 mL
	Salt and freshly ground black pepper	
	Chopped scallion (green onion) greens	
	Sour cream	

Make ahead

Can be prepared through Step 6 up to 2 days ahead. Let cool, cover and refrigerate. Bring to a simmer over medium heat before garnishing, thinning with additional stock if necessary.

1. Place beans in a large bowl. Add enough cold water to cover beans by 2 inches (5 cm). Cover and soak overnight at room temperature or quick-soak them (see tip, page 72). Rinse and drain.
2. In a large saucepan, over medium-low heat, cook bacon, stirring occasionally, for 3 minutes. Add sausage and cook, breaking it up into small chunks, until lightly browned, about 5 minutes. Using a slotted spoon, transfer bacon and sausage to a bowl and set aside. Pour off all but ¼ cup (50 mL) of the fat.
3. To the fat in the saucepan, add garlic, onions, celery and carrots; sauté over medium heat until tender, about 5 minutes. Add beans, ham, bay leaf, stock, oregano and thyme; cover and simmer for 1 to 1½ hours, or until beans are tender. Discard bay leaf.
4. Transfer ham to a plate and let cool slightly. Remove the meat from the hocks and cut into bite-size pieces, discarding bones, fat and skin. Set aside.
5. Attach the fruit/vegetable strainer to the mixer. Set to Speed 4 and run soup, 1 ladleful at a time, through the strainer into a large bowl, with another bowl to catch the solids. Run the solids through the strainer one more time into the large bowl.
6. Discard leftover solids and return soup to the saucepan. Stir in bacon, sausage, ham, sherry, and salt and pepper to taste. Thin with additional stock, if necessary, and bring to a simmer over medium heat. Simmer until heated through, about 5 minutes.
7. Ladle into bowls and garnish with scallion greens and sour cream.

Serves 6 to 8

Main Dishes

Sausage Shepherd's Pie

- Preheat oven to 425°F (220°C)
- 10-cup (2.5 L) baking dish, greased

2 lbs	Merguez (see recipe, page 177) or Italian Sausage (see recipe, page 164), in bulk form	1 kg
2 cups	chopped onions	500 mL
1 tbsp	minced garlic	15 mL
3 tbsp	unbleached all-purpose flour	45 mL
2	sprigs fresh thyme	2
2 cups	beef stock	500 mL
1 ½ tbsp	tomato paste	22 mL
3	carrots, cut diagonally into ¼-inch (0.5 cm) slices	3
¾ cup	frozen peas	175 mL
⅓ cup	whipping (35%) cream	75 mL
	Salt and freshly ground black pepper	
1	recipe Smashed Potatoes (page 146)	1

TIP

Use homemade beef stock for this dish if you have it. If using canned stock, use the low-sodium type.

1. In a large skillet, over medium-high heat, cook sausage, breaking it up into small chunks, until no longer pink. With a slotted spoon, transfer sausage to a large bowl. Drain off all but 2 tbsp (25 mL) of the fat.
2. Add onions and garlic to fat in skillet and sauté until tender and golden, about 7 minutes. Sprinkle with flour and sauté for 2 minutes. Add sausage, thyme, stock and tomato paste; reduce heat and simmer, uncovered, for 15 minutes to allow flavors to blend. Add carrots and cook until tender, about 10 minutes. Remove from heat and mix in peas and whipping cream. Season to taste with salt and pepper. Remove thyme.
3. Transfer to prepared baking dish and spoon mashed potatoes around the edge, leaving the center of the sausage mixture uncovered. Bake in preheated oven until heated through and potatoes begin to brown around edges, about 45 minutes. Let cool for 5 minutes before serving.

Serves 6

Make ahead

Can be prepared through Step 2 up to 1 day ahead. Let cool, cover and refrigerate. Add 15 minutes to the baking time.

Deep-Dish Chicken and Sausage Pie with Biscuit Crust

3 cups	chicken stock	750 mL
4	whole chicken legs (thighs and drumsticks) (about 2 lbs/1 kg)	4
2	carrots, sliced	2
1	stalk celery, sliced	1
1	onion, sliced	1
1	bay leaf	1
1/2 tsp	dried thyme	2 mL
1 lb	Italian Sausage (see recipe, page 164), or 1 lb (500 g) spicy store-bought sausage, in bulk form or casings removed	500 g
3 tbsp	unsalted butter	45 mL
1/3 cup	unbleached all-purpose flour	75 mL
2 tbsp	minced fresh parsley	25 mL
	Salt and freshly ground black pepper (optional)	
1	recipe Lemon-Thyme Biscuit dough (page 256)	1

1. In a large saucepan, over medium-high heat, bring stock, chicken, carrots, celery, onion, bay leaf and thyme to a simmer. Reduce heat to low, cover and simmer until chicken is no longer pink inside, about 40 minutes. Transfer chicken to a plate and strain vegetables, removing the bay leaf and reserving the chicken stock. When chicken is cool enough to handle, remove the meat from the bones, discarding bones and skin, and set aside with the vegetables. Preheat oven to 400°F (200°C).
2. Meanwhile, in a skillet, over medium-high heat, cook sausage, breaking it up into small chunks, until no longer pink, about 5 minutes. Drain off fat and set aside.
3. In a Dutch oven, melt butter over medium-high heat. Add flour and cook, stirring, until roux becomes foamy, about 2 minutes. Add reserved stock and cook, stirring, until sauce thickens, about 2 minutes. Add reserved vegetables, chicken, sausage and parsley. Taste for seasoning and add salt and pepper, if desired.
4. Use a scoop to drop dough on top of the chicken-sausage mixture, evenly covering the surface. Bake in preheated oven until biscuits are firm, about 25 minutes. Serve hot.

Serves 6

Chicken and Fennel Pot Pie

◆ Large ovenproof skillet

3 cups	chicken stock	750 mL
1	fryer chicken (about 2 lbs/ 1 kg), cut up	1
2	carrots, chopped	2
2	potatoes, peeled and diced	2
1	parsnip, chopped	1
1	stalk celery, chopped	1
1	onion, chopped	1
1	head fennel, trimmed, cored and chopped	1
1	bay leaf	1
1/2 tsp	dried thyme	2 mL
3 tbsp	unsalted butter	45 mL
1/4 cup	unbleached all-purpose flour	50 mL
1/4 tsp	salt	1 mL
1 tbsp	freshly squeezed lemon juice	15 mL
1/4 cup	chopped fresh flat-leaf parsley	50 mL
	Freshly ground black pepper	
1	recipe Flaky Pastry (page 321)	1

1. In a large saucepan, over medium heat, bring stock, chicken, carrots, potatoes, parsnip, celery, onion, fennel, bay leaf and thyme to a simmer. Reduce heat and simmer, uncovered, until chicken is no longer pink inside, about 45 minutes. Transfer chicken to a plate and skim some of the fat from the stock. Discard the bay leaf. Remove chicken from the bones, discarding bones and skin, and cut into bite-size pieces. Set aside. Preheat oven to 400°F (200°C).
2. In a large ovenproof skillet, melt butter over medium-high heat. Add flour and salt; cook, stirring, until roux becomes foamy, about 2 minutes. Add hot stock and vegetables; cook, stirring, until thickened, about 3 minutes. Add reserved chicken, lemon juice and parsley. Taste and adjust seasoning as desired with salt and pepper.
3. On a floured work surface, roll out pastry and fit it over the skillet. Seal the edges over rim of skillet and make a few slits in the pastry to allow steam to vent. Bake in preheated oven until pastry is golden brown, about 30 minutes. Serve hot.

Serves 6

Variation

Instead of covering the skillet with pastry, cover the surface of the pot pie evenly with Cheddar Cheese Biscuit dough (see recipe, page 255), Buttermilk Biscuit dough (see recipe, page 253) or Lemon-Thyme Biscuit dough (see recipe, page 256).

Turkey Pot Pie with Herbed Crust

FLAT BEATER

- 13- by 9-inch (3 L) glass baking pan
- Baking sheet

Crust		
1 ½ cups	unbleached all-purpose flour	375 mL
½ cup	chilled unsalted butter, cut into ¼-inch (0.5 cm) pieces	125 mL
¼ cup	chilled vegetable shortening	50 mL
2 tsp	finely chopped fresh thyme	10 mL
½ tsp	salt	2 mL
2 tbsp	ice-cold water (approx.)	25 mL
Filling		
⅓ cup	unsalted butter	75 mL
3	carrots, cut into ¼-inch (0.5 cm) slices	3
2	small stalks celery, cut into ¼-inch (0.5 cm) slices	2
1	large onion, finely chopped	1
⅓ cup	unbleached all-purpose flour	75 mL
2¼ cups	chicken stock	550 mL
1 cup	milk	250 mL
5 cups	chopped boneless skinless cooked turkey	1.25 L
1 cup	frozen green peas	250 mL
2 tbsp	chopped fresh parsley	25 mL
2 tsp	chopped fresh thyme	10 mL
1¾ tsp	salt	8 mL
½ tsp	freshly ground black pepper	2 mL
1	egg, beaten with 1 tbsp (15 mL) water	1

1. *Prepare the crust:* Place flour, butter, shortening, thyme and salt in the mixer bowl. Attach the flat beater and mixer bowl to the mixer. Set to Stir and mix until butter and shortening form pea-size pieces in the flour. Sprinkle with 1 tbsp (5 mL) of the cold water. Continue mixing on Stir until all the particles are just moistened. Press dough with your fingers to see if it will hold together; add the remaining 1 tbsp (5 mL) cold water if necessary. Shape dough into a ball, then flatten it into a 4-inch (10 cm) disk. Wrap in plastic and refrigerate for at least 30 minutes.
2. Place rack in the lower third of the oven. Preheat oven to 400°F (200°C).
3. *Prepare the filling:* In a large saucepan, melt butter over medium-high heat. Add carrots, celery and onion; sauté until tender, about 5 minutes. Add flour and cook, stirring, for 1 minute. Add stock and milk; cook, stirring constantly, for 2 to 3 minutes, or until thick and bubbly. Stir in turkey, peas, parsley, thyme, salt and pepper. Transfer to baking pan and place on a rack to cool slightly, about 5 minutes.
4. On a floured work surface, roll out dough to a 15- by 11-inch (38 by 28 cm) rectangle, about ⅛ inch (0.25 cm) thick. Carefully roll the dough over the rolling pin and roll out over the pot pie. Tuck overhanging dough down into the pan. Brush with egg wash and make a few slits in the dough to allow steam to vent.
5. Place on baking sheet and bake in preheated oven for 30 to 40 minutes or until crust is golden brown and filling is bubbly. Let cool for 10 minutes before serving.

Serves 6 to 8

Beef Pot Pie with Cheddar Biscuit Crust

◆ 13- by 9-inch (3 L) glass baking pan

3 lbs	lean stewing beef	1.5 kg
	Salt and freshly ground black pepper	
6	slices lean bacon, chopped	6
1	onion, minced	1
1⁄3 cup	unsalted butter	75 mL
1⁄3 cup	unbleached all-purpose flour	75 mL
6 cups	beef stock	1.5 L
1 cup	dry red wine	250 mL
3 tbsp	tomato paste	45 mL
2	cloves garlic, minced	2
2	bay leaves	2
3	carrots, cut into 1⁄2-inch (1 cm) cubes	3
2	large Yukon gold potatoes, peeled and cut into 1⁄2-inch (1 cm) cubes	2
1⁄2 cup	frozen green peas	125 mL
1	recipe Cheddar Cheese Biscuit dough (page 255)	1
1	egg, beaten with 1 tbsp (15 mL) water	1

TIP
Use homemade beef stock for this dish if you have it. If using canned stock, use the low-sodium type.

1. Cut beef into 3⁄4-inch (2 cm) cubes, dry thoroughly with a paper towel and season with salt and pepper.
2. In a large saucepan, over medium heat, cook bacon until browned. Transfer to a plate with a slotted spoon. Increase heat to medium-high. Working in small batches, brown beef in bacon fat. Transfer to a plate with a slotted spoon. Reduce heat to medium. Add onions to the remaining fat and sauté until tender, about 3 minutes. Add butter and flour; cook, stirring constantly, until flour is foamy, about 3 minutes. Return bacon and beef to the saucepan and stir to coat with browned flour. Stir in stock, wine, tomato paste, garlic and bay leaves. Reduce heat and simmer, partially covered, for 2 hours, stirring occasionally and skimming fat if necessary. Add carrots and potatoes and simmer for 20 to 30 minutes, or until just tender. Add peas. Taste and adjust seasoning as desired with salt and pepper. Preheat oven to 400°F (200°C).
3. Transfer to baking pan and let cool for 5 minutes. Use a scoop to drop dough on top, evenly covering the surface. Brush dough with egg wash. Bake in preheated oven until biscuits are lightly browned and filling is bubbly, about 20 minutes. Let cool for 5 minutes before serving.

Serves 6 to 8

Salmon Pot Pie

- Preheat oven to 400°F (200°C)
- Large ovenproof skillet

3 cups	chicken stock	750 mL
2	carrots, sliced	2
2	heads fennel, trimmed, cored and thinly sliced	2
1	onion, sliced	1
1	stalk celery, sliced	1
1 tsp	dried tarragon	5 mL
3 tbsp	unsalted butter	45 mL
1/4 cup	unbleached all-purpose flour	50 mL
	Grated zest of 1 lemon	
2 tbsp	freshly squeezed lemon juice	25 mL
2 tbsp	minced fresh flat-leaf parsley	25 mL
2 tbsp	minced fresh chives	25 mL
1/2 tsp	salt	2 mL
1/4 tsp	freshly ground black pepper	1 mL
2 lbs	salmon fillet, skinned and cut into 1-inch (2.5 cm) pieces	1 kg
1	recipe Flaky Pastry (page 321), chilled	1

1. In a large saucepan, over medium-high heat, bring stock, carrots, fennel, onion, celery and tarragon to a simmer. Reduce heat, cover and simmer until vegetables are tender, about 20 minutes. Set aside.
2. In a large ovenproof skillet, melt butter over medium-high heat. Add flour and cook, stirring, until roux becomes foamy, about 2 minutes. Add hot stock and vegetables; cook, stirring, until sauce thickens, about 5 minutes. Add lemon zest, lemon juice, parsley, chives, salt and pepper. Remove from heat. Taste and adjust seasoning as desired with salt and pepper. Stir in salmon.
3. On a floured work surface, roll out pastry and fit it over the skillet. Seal the edges over the rim of the skillet and make a few slits in the pastry to allow steam to vent. Bake in preheated oven until the crust is brown and crisp, about 35 minutes. Serve hot.

Serves 6

Ham and Pork Loaf with Apricot Glaze

FOOD GRINDER · FLAT BEATER

- Preheat oven to 350°F (180°C)
- Large shallow baking pan

1 lb	boneless pork shoulder blade, cut into 1-inch (2.5 cm) cubes	500 g
1 lb	smoked ham, cut into 1-inch (2.5 cm) cubes	500 g
2 tbsp	unsalted butter	25 mL
1 cup	finely chopped onion	250 mL
3⁄4 cup	finely chopped red bell pepper	175 mL
2	eggs, lightly beaten	2
1 cup	finely crushed saltine crackers (about 28)	250 mL
1⁄2 cup	milk	125 mL
2 tbsp	Dijon mustard	25 mL
1⁄2 tsp	salt	2 mL
1⁄2 tsp	freshly ground black pepper	2 mL
1⁄2 cup	apricot jam	125 mL
1⁄4 cup	lightly packed light brown sugar	50 mL
2 tbsp	Dijon mustard	25 mL

1. Place pork and ham in a shallow container in the freezer for 30 minutes to facilitate grinding.
2. Meanwhile, in a skillet with a lid, melt butter over medium-low heat. Add onion and red pepper; cover and cook, stirring occasionally, until vegetables are tender, about 10 minutes. Let cool completely.
3. Attach the food grinder, with the fine plate, to the mixer. Set to Speed 4 and run pork and ham through the grinder into the mixer bowl. Add onion mixture, eggs, crackers, milk, mustard, salt and pepper to bowl. Remove the food grinder and attach the flat beater and mixer bowl to the mixer. Set to Stir and mix until just combined.
4. Transfer to baking pan and shape mixture into a 9- by 4-inch (23 by 10 cm) loaf. With a long knife, make a shallow crisscross (diamond) pattern in the top of the loaf. Bake in preheated oven for 30 minutes.
5. Meanwhile, in a small bowl, combine jam, brown sugar and mustard. Brush loaf with 1⁄3 cup (75 mL) glaze and bake for 15 minutes. Brush with another 1⁄3 cup (75 mL) glaze and bake for 15 minutes. Brush with remaining glaze and bake until loaf reaches an internal temperature of 170°F (75°C), about 20 minutes. Transfer to a serving platter and let cool for 10 minutes. Cut crosswise into 3⁄4-inch (1.75 cm) thick slices and serve.

Serves 8

BBQ Meatloaf

FOOD GRINDER ◆ FLAT BEATER

- ◆ Preheat oven to 350°F (180°C)
- ◆ Large shallow baking pan

1 lb	boneless beef chuck or cross rib, cut into 1-inch (2.5 cm) cubes	500 g
1 lb	boneless skinless turkey breast, cut into 1-inch (2.5 cm) cubes	500 g
1	slice homestyle white bread	1
1/3 cup	milk	75 mL
2 tsp	olive oil	10 mL
1	stalk celery, finely chopped	1
1	carrot, finely chopped	1
1 1/2 cups	finely chopped onions	375 mL
1 tbsp	minced garlic	15 mL
1/2 cup	barbecue sauce (store-bought or see recipe, page 406), divided	125 mL
2 tsp	Worcestershire sauce	10 mL
1 1/2 tsp	salt	7 mL
1 tsp	freshly ground black pepper	5 mL
1	egg, lightly beaten	1
1/3 cup	minced fresh parsley	75 mL

1. Place beef and turkey in a shallow container in the freezer for 30 minutes to facilitate grinding.
2. In a small bowl, soak bread in milk until milk is absorbed. Set aside.
3. Attach the food grinder, with the fine plate, to the mixer. Set to Speed 4 and run beef and turkey through the grinder into the mixer bowl.
4. In a skillet, heat oil over medium heat. Add celery, carrot, onions and garlic; sauté until softened, about 5 minutes. Stir in 1/4 cup (50 mL) of the barbecue sauce, Worcestershire sauce, salt and pepper; cook, stirring, for 1 minute.
5. Add soaked bread, cooked vegetables, egg and parsley to the meat in the mixer bowl. Remove the food grinder and attach the flat beater and mixer bowl to the mixer. Set to Speed 2 and mix just until combined.
6. Transfer to baking pan and shape mixture into a 10- by 5-inch (25 by 13 cm) oval loaf. Spread with the remaining 1/4 cup (50 mL) barbecue sauce. Bake in preheated oven until loaf reaches an internal temperature of 170°F (75°C), about 1 hour.

Serves 6 to 8

Ultimate Steak Burgers

FOOD GRINDER

1 $\frac{1}{2}$ lbs	boneless beef chuck or cross rib, cut into 1-inch (2.5 cm) cubes	750 g
$\frac{1}{4}$ cup	steak sauce	50 mL
1 tsp	salt	5 mL
$\frac{1}{4}$ tsp	freshly ground black pepper	1 mL
6	Sandwich Buns (see recipe, page 238), split	6
	Desired toppings	

Make ahead

Can be prepared through Step 1 and stored in an airtight container in the refrigerator for up to 1 day or in the freezer for up to 6 weeks.

1. Place beef in a shallow container in the freezer for 30 minutes to facilitate grinding. Attach the food grinder, with the coarse plate, to the mixer. Set to Speed 4 and run beef through the grinder into a large bowl. Add steak sauce, salt and pepper; mix together with your hands. Freeze for 30 minutes, then run through the grinder one more time into a bowl. Form into 6 patties, each about 1 $\frac{1}{2}$ inches (4 cm) thick, creating a slight depression in the middle of each one to ensure even cooking.
2. Preheat the grill to medium-high. Grill patties, uncovered, without pressing down on them, until well seared on bottom, about 5 minutes. Flip with a metal barbecue spatula and grill until no longer pink inside, about 5 minutes.
3. Serve immediately on buns, with desired toppings.

Serves 6

Lemon-Thyme Turkey Burgers

FOOD GRINDER

1 lb	boneless turkey breast, with skin, cut into 1-inch (2.5 cm) cubes	500 g
1 lb	boneless turkey thigh, with skin, cut into 1-inch (2.5 cm) cubes	500g
	Grated zest of 1 lemon	
3 tbsp	freshly squeezed lemon juice	45 mL
2 tsp	dried thyme	10 mL
1 1/4 tsp	salt	6 mL
1/2 tsp	freshly ground black pepper	2 mL
1/3 cup	fresh bread crumbs	75 mL
	Vegetable oil	
	Sliced Monterey Jack cheese (optional)	
8	hamburger buns (store-bought or see recipe, page 238)	8
	Mayonnaise	
	Sliced red onion	
	Romaine lettuce	

1. Place turkey breast and thigh in a shallow container in the freezer for 30 minutes to facilitate grinding. Attach the food grinder, with the coarse plate, to the grinder. Set to Speed 4 and run turkey through the grinder into a large bowl. Sprinkle with lemon zest, lemon juice, thyme, salt and pepper; mix together with your hands. Freeze for 30 minutes, then run through the grinder one more time into a bowl. Add bread crumbs and mix together with your hands. Form into 8 patties, each about 1 inch (2.5 cm) thick, creating a slight depression in the middle of each one to ensure even cooking.
2. In a large skillet with a lid, heat a thin layer of oil over medium heat. Add 4 of the patties. Cover and cook, flipping once, until no longer pink inside, about 4 minutes per side. Top each patty with cheese, if desired. Cover and cook until just melted. Transfer to a plate and keep warm. Repeat with remaining patties.
3. Serve on buns, topped with mayonnaise, red onion and lettuce.

Serves 8

Deviled Roast Chicken with Roasted Vegetables

ROTOR SLICER/SHREDDER

- Baking sheet, lined with parchment paper

1	fryer chicken, cut up and breasts halved (about 3½ lbs/1.75 kg)	1
½ cup	grainy Dijon mustard	125 mL
3	carrots, cut into thirds	3
2	zucchini, cut into thirds	2
2	stalks celery, sliced	2
1	head fennel, trimmed, cored and thinly sliced	1
½ tsp	dried oregano	2 mL
½ tsp	salt	2 mL
¼ tsp	freshly ground black pepper	1 mL

This is an easy dish for a busy weeknight. The chicken and vegetables can be prepared the night before and kept tightly covered in the refrigerator. When you get home from work, all you need to do is preheat the oven and arrange everything on the baking sheet. Dinner is done in 1 hour.

1. In a large bowl, toss chicken and mustard. Cover with plastic and refrigerate for at least 1 hour or overnight. Preheat oven to 375°F (190°C).
2. Attach the slicer/shredder, with the thick slicer, to the mixer. Set to Speed 4 and slice carrots and zucchini into a large bowl. Add celery, fennel, oregano, salt and pepper; toss to combine.
3. Mound vegetables on prepared baking sheet, laying them no thicker than 3 inches (7.5 cm) deep. Top with chicken. (Do not lay chicken pieces on top of each other or they will not cook properly.) Roast in preheated oven until chicken reaches an internal temperature of 170°F (75°C), about 1 hour. Serve hot.

Serves 4

Rolled Chicken Breasts with Vegetable Stuffing

ROTOR SLICER/SHREDDER

1	carrot, cut into thirds	1
1	zucchini, cut into thirds	1
1	small onion, halved	1
2	cloves garlic, minced	2
1 cup	thinly sliced napa cabbage	250 mL
3 tbsp	olive oil	45 mL
1/2 tsp	dried thyme	2 mL
1/4 tsp	salt	1 mL
Pinch	freshly ground black pepper	Pinch
1/4 cup	dry white wine	50 mL
3 oz	goat cheese or cream cheese	90 g
1/4 cup	chopped fresh flat-leaf parsley	50 mL
6	boneless skinless chicken breasts (about 2 1/4 lbs/ 1.125 kg), pounded to 1/4 inch (0.5 cm) thick	6
1 cup	chicken stock	250 mL
1/4 cup	minced fresh flat-leaf parsley	50 mL

1. Attach the slicer/shredder, with the thick slicer, to the mixer. Set to Speed 4 and slice carrot, zucchini and onion into the mixer bowl. Add garlic and cabbage; toss to combine.
2. In a large skillet, heat oil over medium-high heat. Add vegetables, thyme, salt and pepper; sauté for 5 minutes, reducing heat if vegetables begin to over-brown. Add wine and cook, stirring, until wine has evaporated and vegetables are tender, about 4 minutes. Remove from heat and stir in goat cheese and parsley. Taste and adjust seasoning as desired with salt and pepper. Set aside.
3. Lay chicken breasts, smooth side down, on a cutting board. Sprinkle lightly with salt and pepper. Spread 1/6 of the vegetable mixture over each breast. Roll up jelly-roll style, starting at the thinner tail end, and secure with toothpicks, if necessary.
4. In a large skillet with a lid, bring stock to a simmer over medium heat. Add chicken rolls, spacing evenly. Reduce heat, cover and simmer until chicken is no longer pink inside and reaches an internal temperature of 170°F (75°C), about 30 minutes. Transfer chicken rolls to a heated serving plate and tent with foil to keep warm. Increase heat to high and cook stock, uncovered, until reduced by half.
5. Top chicken with sauce and garnish with parsley. Serve hot.

Serves 6

Amish Pot Roast with Egg Noodles

PASTA ROLLER • FETTUCCINE CUTTER

- Preheat oven to 350°F (180°C)
- Large Dutch oven or roasting pan with a lid

2 tbsp	vegetable oil	25 mL
4	slices bacon, chopped	4
4 to 5 lbs	boneless beef chuck or cross rib roast, tied	2 to 2.5 kg
1 tsp	salt	5 mL
1/4 tsp	freshly ground black pepper	1 mL
2	carrots, chopped	2
1	onion, sliced	1
1	stalk celery, chopped	1
1 1/2 cups	unsweetened apple cider or apple juice	375 mL
3 tbsp	lightly packed light brown sugar	45 mL
2 tbsp	prepared mustard	25 mL
1	recipe Basic Egg Pasta (page 192)	1
1/4 cup	unsalted butter	50 mL
2 tbsp	chopped fresh flat-leaf parsley	25 mL
1/4 cup	sour cream	50 mL

1. In Dutch oven, heat oil over medium-high heat. Add the bacon and sauté until still limp, but cooked, about 3 minutes. Transfer to a plate with a slotted spoon and set aside.
2. Season beef with salt and pepper and add to the bacon fat. Brown on all sides, about 3 minutes per side. Add carrots, onion and celery; cook, stirring, until vegetables begin to soften, about 2 minutes. (Reduce heat to medium if roast and vegetables are browning too fast.)
3. In a small bowl, combine apple cider, brown sugar and mustard. Pour over beef. Add bacon and cover. Bake in preheated oven until roast is fork tender, about 3 hours. Remove from oven and let stand, covered.
4. Meanwhile, roll pasta to setting 5 and cut with the fettuccine cutter (see Pasta Basics, page 190, for instructions on rolling and cutting pasta).
5. Bring a large pot of salted water to a boil over medium-high heat. Add noodles and cook, stirring for the first minute to keep them from sticking together, until al dente (tender to the bite), about 3 minutes. Drain and toss with butter and parsley.
6. Remove roast to a cutting board and skim fat from the cooking juices. Taste the vegetables and juices in the pan and adjust seasoning as desired with salt and pepper. Stir in sour cream, taste and adjust seasoning again as desired. Slice the beef.
7. Serve sliced beef with noodles, topped with pan sauce and vegetables.

Serves 6

Cowboy Beef Skillet

FOOD GRINDER • FLAT BEATER

◆ Large ovenproof skillet

1 1/2 lbs	boneless beef chuck or cross rib, cut into 1-inch (2.5 cm) cubes	750 g
1 tbsp	olive oil	15 mL
3	cloves garlic, minced	3
1	onion, chopped	1
1/2 cup	chopped red bell pepper	125 mL
3 tbsp	chili powder	45 mL
1/4 tsp	cayenne pepper	1 mL
1 tsp	salt	5 mL
1	can (14 to 19 oz/398 to 540 mL) kidney beans, rinsed and drained	1
1/2 cup	fresh or frozen corn kernels	125 mL
1	can (8 oz/250 mL) tomato sauce	1
Chili-Cheddar Cornbread Topping		
1/2 cup	unbleached all-purpose flour	125 mL
1/2 cup	cornmeal	125 mL
1/2 cup	shredded Cheddar cheese	125 mL
1 tbsp	chili powder	15 mL
1 tsp	baking powder	5 mL
1/4 tsp	salt	1 mL
1	egg	1
1/2 cup	milk	125 mL
2 tbsp	unsalted butter, melted	25 mL

1. Place beef in a shallow container in the freezer for 30 minutes to facilitate grinding. Attach the food grinder, with the fine plate, to the mixer. Set to Speed 4 and run beef through the grinder into a bowl. Preheat oven to 375°F (190°C).
2. In large ovenproof skillet, heat oil over medium heat. Add beef and sauté, breaking it up into small chunks, until browned, about 5 minutes. Drain off fat and add garlic, onion, red pepper, chili powder, cayenne and salt; sauté until tender, about 5 minutes. Add beans, corn, tomato sauce and 1/4 cup (50 mL) water; simmer until sauce thickens, about 5 minutes.
3. *Meanwhile, prepare the topping:* In the mixer bowl, combine flour, cornmeal, cheese, chili powder, baking powder and salt. Add egg, milk and butter. Remove the food grinder and attach the flat beater and mixer bowl to the mixer. Set to Speed 2 and beat until just combined.
4. Spoon cornbread topping into the skillet, spreading it to make a thin layer that completely covers the beef mixture. Bake in preheated oven for 20 to 25 minutes, or until cornbread is golden brown.

Serves 6

Beef Wellington

ROTOR SLICER/SHREDDER

- Preheat oven to 425°F (220°C)
- Baking sheet, lined with parchment paper

1 lb	button mushrooms	500 g
¼ cup	unsalted butter	50 mL
¼ cup	minced green onions	50 mL
½ tsp	salt	2 mL
Pinch	freshly ground black pepper	Pinch
2 lbs	center-cut beef tenderloin	1 kg
2 tbsp	vegetable oil	25 mL
1	recipe Puff Pastry (page 323)	1
1	egg, beaten with 1 tbsp (15 mL) water	1

TIP
Use the trimmed pastry to create decorative leaves or flowers. Stick them to the egg-washed pastry and brush decorations with egg wash.

1. Attach the slicer/shredder, with the thin slicer, to the mixer. Set to Speed 4 and slice mushrooms into a bowl.
2. In a skillet, melt butter over medium-high heat. Add green onions and sauté for 2 minutes. Add mushrooms, salt and pepper; sauté until mushrooms have given off all their water and are dry and soft, about 10 minutes. Remove from heat and let cool.
3. Season beef lightly with salt and pepper. In another skillet, heat oil over medium-high heat. Add beef and brown on all sides, about 5 minutes per side. Transfer to a plate and let cool to room temperature.
4. On a floured work surface, roll out pastry to a 12-inch (30 cm) square. Spread mushroom mixture over the entire surface of the beef. Working quickly, lay beef on one side of the pastry and roll to encase it. The crease should be on the bottom. Cut excess pastry from the bottom of the open ends. Fold the top piece of pastry down and tuck under the beef to encase the ends. Brush pastry with egg wash.
5. Transfer to prepared baking sheet and bake in preheated oven for 20 minutes. Reduce heat to 375°F (190°C) and bake until meat juices begin to escape the pastry at the bottom and beef reaches an internal temperature of 130°F (50°C) for medium-rare, about 20 minutes. (The meat will continue to cook for a few minutes after it is removed from the oven, and the temperature will rise to about 137°F/55°C.) Let stand for 10 minutes to allow juices to settle and redistribute through the meat. Slice into 6 servings and serve hot.

Serves 6

Chicken and Andouille Gumbo

2 tbsp	olive oil	25 mL
1 lb	Andouille sausage (see recipe, page 165), sliced into 1⁄4-inch (0.5 cm) rounds	500 g
2	cloves garlic	2
1 tsp	salt	5 mL
1 tsp	paprika	5 mL
1 tsp	dried oregano	5 mL
1⁄4 tsp	freshly ground black pepper	1 mL
Pinch	cayenne pepper	Pinch
1	fryer chicken, cut up and breasts cut into 4 pieces (about 3 1⁄2 lbs/1.75 kg)	1
1 cup	diced onion	250 mL
1⁄2 cup	diced red bell pepper	125 mL
1⁄2 cup	diced green bell pepper	125 mL
1	can (14 oz/398 mL) diced tomatoes, with juice	1
3 cups	chicken stock	750 mL
1 cup	long-grain white rice	250 mL
1	package (10 oz/300 g) frozen okra, thawed	1
1⁄4 cup	chopped fresh flat-leaf parsley	50 mL
2 tbsp	sherry vinegar or balsamic vinegar (optional)	25 mL

TIP

To make for more carefree dining, remove chicken from the gumbo and pick the meat from the bones, then stir meat back into the pot.

1. In a Dutch oven, heat oil over medium heat. Add sausage and sauté for 4 to 5 minutes, or until browned. Transfer to a plate with a slotted spoon and set aside. Reserve fat in pan; set aside.
2. With a mortar and pestle, mash the garlic, salt, paprika, oregano, black pepper and cayenne pepper to make a paste (or finely mince garlic and mash together with the back of a spoon). Smear chicken with paste. Return Dutch oven to medium heat and reheat fat. Add half the chicken to the pan. Cook for 6 to 8 minutes, or until golden on one side; turn and cook the other side for 6 to 8 minutes, or until golden. Transfer to a plate and repeat with remaining chicken.
3. Pour off all but 2 tbsp (25 mL) fat. Add onion and cook for 3 minutes. Add red and green peppers; cook for 3 minutes. Add tomatoes with juice and stock; bring to a boil. Return chicken and sausage to the pan, tucking them down into the liquid. Reduce heat, cover and simmer until chicken is tender, about 40 minutes. Stir in rice, cover and simmer until rice is tender, about 20 minutes. Stir in okra, parsley and vinegar, if using. Cook, uncovered, until okra is heated through. Taste and adjust seasoning as desired with salt and pepper. Serve hot.

Serves 6

Corn Fritters with Sausage

WIRE WHIP

8 oz	Country Pork Sausage (see recipe, page 161), in bulk form	250 g
1 1/2 cups	unbleached all-purpose flour	375 mL
1/2 cup	stone-ground cornmeal	125 mL
2 tsp	baking powder	10 mL
1/2 tsp	baking soda	2 mL
1/4 tsp	salt	1 mL
3	eggs, separated	3
1 cup	buttermilk	250 mL
1/4 cup	unsalted butter, melted	50 mL
1 cup	frozen corn kernels	250 mL
1 cup	vegetable oil, divided	250 mL
	Maple syrup or liquid honey	

TIP

Fritters can be kept warm in a 200°F (100°C) oven for 30 minutes.

1. In a skillet, over medium-high heat, cook sausage, breaking it up into small chunks, until no longer pink, about 5 minutes. Drain off fat and set aside.
2. In a large bowl, combine flour, cornmeal, baking powder, baking soda and salt.
3. Place egg whites in the mixer bowl. Attach the whip and mixer bowl to the mixer. Set to Speed 10 and whip until whites hold stiff peaks. Set aside.
4. In a small bowl, whisk together egg yolks, buttermilk and butter. Add to the flour mixture and mix with a large spatula until combined. Using the spatula, carefully fold in half the egg whites. Add sausage and corn; mix lightly. Gently fold in the rest of the egg whites.
5. In a large skillet, heat 1/4 cup (50 mL) of the oil over medium heat. When oil begins to smoke, pour in 1/4 cup (50 mL) batter for each fritter. Cook 4 or 5 at a time until bottom is browned, about 2 minutes; flip and cook until bottom is browned, about 2 minutes. Reduce heat if fritters begin to cook too fast on the outside and are still raw on the inside. Remove to a plate and keep warm. Repeat with the remaining batter, adding and heating oil as necessary between batches.
6. Serve with maple syrup or honey.

Serves 6

Tomatillo Chicken Tamales

FLAT BEATER

Filling		
4 cups	packed coarsely shredded cooked chicken (from a $3\frac{1}{2}$-lb/875 mL chicken)	1 L
2 cups	Tomatillo Salsa (see recipe, page 407)	500 mL
1	package (8 oz/250 g) dried corn husks	1
Dough		
$1\frac{1}{3}$ cups	lard or vegetable shortening	325 mL
$1\frac{1}{2}$ tsp	salt	7 mL
$1\frac{1}{2}$ tsp	baking powder	7 mL
4 cups	freshly ground masa (see tip, page 95)	1 L
$1\frac{1}{4}$ to 2 cups	low-sodium chicken stock (approx.)	300 to 500 mL

1. *Prepare the filling:* In a bowl, gently toss together chicken and salsa. Set aside.
2. Place corn husks in a large pot or bowl and add enough hot water to cover. Place a heavy plate on husks to keep them submerged. Let stand, turning occasionally, until husks soften, about 20 minutes.
3. *Meanwhile, prepare the dough:* Place lard, salt and baking powder in the mixer bowl. Attach the flat beater and mixer bowl to the mixer. Set to Speed 6 and beat until fluffy. Reduce to Speed 2 and beat in masa a handful at a time. Gradually beat in $\frac{1}{2}$ cup (125 mL) of the stock. Continue to beat in stock as needed until dough resembles thick cake batter. Test dough by dropping a small spoonful in a cup of cold water. The dough should float to the surface. If it sinks, continue beating for a minute, adding more stock, and retest.
4. Fill bottom of a large stock pot fitted with a vegetable steamer insert with enough water to reach bottom of insert (about 2 inches/5 cm). Line bottom of insert with some of the softened corn husks. Tear 4 or 5 large husks into $\frac{1}{4}$-inch (0.5 cm) wide strips to use as ties and set aside. On a clean work surface, open 2 large husks. Spread $\frac{1}{4}$ cup (50 mL) dough in 4-inch (10 cm) square in the center of each husk, leaving a 2-inch (5 cm) border at the pointed end. Spoon 2 tbsp (25 mL) filling in the center of each dough square. Using long sides of husk to lift dough, bring dough up over filling, meeting in the middle so that the dough completely encompasses the filling. Press to make sure dough covers filling. Then wrap both sides of husk around dough, overlapping at edges. Fold up narrow end of husk. Tie folded portion with strip of husk to secure, leaving wide end of tamale open. Stand tamales open-end up in the steamer basket. (If necessary, to keep tamales upright in steamer, insert pieces of crumpled foil between them.) Repeat until all filling has been used. Bring water in pot to a boil. Cover and steam tamales, adding more water as necessary, until dough is firm to the touch and separates easily from husks, about 1 hour. Let cool for 10 minutes before serving.

Makes about 30 tamales

Make ahead

Can be prepared up to 2 days ahead. Let cool for 1 hour, cover and refrigerate. Before serving, resteam tamales until hot, about 35 minutes.

Black Bean Tamales

FLAT BEATER

Filling		
2 tbsp	lard or olive oil	25 mL
1	large white onion, chopped	1
2	cloves garlic, chopped	2
1 lb	dried black beans, picked over, rinsed and soaked overnight	500 g
2	chipotle peppers in adobo sauce, chopped	2
1 tsp	salt	5 mL
1	package (8 oz/250 g) dried corn husks	1
Dough		
1 1/3 cups	lard or vegetable shortening	325 mL
1 1/2 tsp	salt	7 mL
1 1/2 tsp	baking powder	7 mL
4 cups	freshly ground masa (see tip, opposite)	1 L
1 1/4 to 2 cups	warm low-sodium chicken stock (approx.)	300 to 500 mL

1. *Prepare the filling:* In a large saucepan, melt lard over medium heat. Add onion and sauté for 10 to 15 minutes, or until golden brown. Add garlic and sauté for 2 minutes. Add beans, chipotle peppers and 10 cups (2.5 L) water. Reduce heat and simmer, uncovered, until beans are tender, about 1 1/4 hours. Add salt and simmer until enough water has evaporated that liquid reaches just below level of beans and beans are quite tender, about 30 minutes. Remove from heat and let cool for 30 minutes.
2. Transfer to the mixer bowl. Attach the flat beater and mixer bowl to the mixer. Set to Speed 2 and mix until beans are partially crushed and creamy. Transfer to a large bowl and set aside. Clean the mixer bowl and flat beater.
3. Place corn husks in a large pot or bowl and add enough hot water to cover. Place a heavy plate on husks to keep them submerged. Let stand, turning occasionally, until husks soften, about 20 minutes.
4. *Meanwhile, prepare the dough:* Place lard, salt and baking powder in clean mixer bowl. Attach the mixer bowl to the mixer (the flat beater should still be attached). Set to Speed 6 and beat until fluffy. Reduce to Speed 2 and beat in masa a handful at a time. Gradually beat in 1/2 cup (125 mL) of the stock. Continue to beat in stock as needed until dough resembles thick cake batter. Test dough by dropping a small spoonful in a cup of cold water. The dough should float to the surface. If it sinks, continue beating for a minute and retest.

5. Fill bottom of a large stock pot fitted with a vegetable steamer insert with enough water to reach bottom of insert (about 2 inches/ 5 cm). Line bottom of insert with some of the softened corn husks. Tear 4 or 5 large husks into 1/4-inch (0.5 cm) wide strips to use as ties and set aside. On a clean work surface, open 2 large husks. Spread 1/4 cup (50 mL) dough in a 4-inch (10 cm) square in the center of each husk, leaving a 2-inch (5 cm) border at the pointed end. Spoon 2 tbsp (25 mL) filling in the center of each dough square. Using long sides of husk to lift dough, bring dough up over filling, meeting in the middle so that the dough completely encompasses the filling. Press to make sure dough covers filling. Then wrap both sides of husk around dough, overlapping at edges. Fold up narrow end of husk. Tie folded portion with strip of husk to secure, leaving wide end of tamale open. Stand tamales open-end up in the steamer basket. (If necessary, to keep tamales upright in steamer, insert pieces of crumpled foil between them.) Repeat until all dough and filling has been used. Bring water in pot to a boil. Cover and steam tamales, adding more water as necessary, until dough is firm to the touch and separates easily from husks, about 1 hour. Let cool for 10 minutes before serving.

Makes about 30 tamales

Make ahead

Can be prepared up to 2 days ahead. Let cool for 1 hour, cover and refrigerate. Before serving, re-steam tamales until hot, about 35 minutes.

TIP

Freshly ground masa is used to make corn tortillas. It can sometimes be purchased at a Latin grocery store or, if you are lucky enough to live near a tortilleria, where fresh tortillas are made, you can often buy your masa there. Fresh masa must be used the day you purchase it, or it may become sour tasting. If you cannot find fresh masa, you can make a masa dough using masa harina, which is a dry corn tortilla mix that needs to be reconstituted with water. To make masa dough, mix 3 1/2 cups (875 mL) masa harina with 2 1/4 cups (550 mL) warm water. Omit the salt and baking powder from the dough if the masa harina already contains them.

Chorizo and Potato Tortilla

- Preheat broiler
- Large ovenproof skillet

2	large potatoes, peeled and cut into 1/2-inch (1 cm) cubes	2
2 tbsp	olive oil	25 mL
8 oz	Chorizo sausage (see recipe, page 167), cut into 1/2-inch (1 cm) slices	250 g
1/2 cup	diced onion	125 mL
1/2 cup	diced zucchini	125 mL
2	cloves garlic, minced	2
1/2 cup	diced red bell pepper	125 mL
6	large eggs	6
1/4 cup	chopped fresh flat-leaf parsley	50 mL
1/2 tsp	salt	2 mL
1/4 tsp	freshly ground black pepper	1 mL
1/2 cup	shredded Cheddar cheese	125 mL

1. In a medium saucepan, over medium-high heat, bring 4 cups (1 L) salted water and potatoes to a boil. Reduce heat to medium-low and cook until tender, about 10 minutes. Drain and set aside.
2. In large ovenproof skillet, heat oil over medium heat. Add sausage and sauté for 3 minutes. Add onion and sauté for 2 minutes. Add zucchini and sauté for 3 minutes. Add garlic and red pepper; sauté for 3 to 4 minutes, or until sausage is browned and vegetables are tender. Stir in potatoes and spread vegetables and sausage evenly in the skillet.
3. In a medium bowl, beat eggs, parsley, salt and pepper. Pour over sausage mixture and reduce heat to medium-low. Cook for 3 minutes, then transfer skillet to the highest rack in the preheated oven and broil until tortilla is set, about 5 minutes. Remove from oven and sprinkle with cheese. Broil until cheese is melted, about 1 minute. Let cool for a few minutes before cutting into servings. Serve hot or at room temperature.

Serves 6

Thai Beef Meatballs with Peanut Dipping Sauce (page 11)

White Bean, Rosemary and Pancetta Bruschetta (page 19)

Hearty Harvest Roasted Vegetable Soup (page 60)

Sausage Shepherd's Pie (page 76)
made with Italian Sausage (page 164)

Lentil and Wild Rice Salad with Game Sausages

9 cups	chicken stock, divided	2.25 L
1 cup	wild rice, rinsed	250 mL
3/4 tsp	salt, divided	3 mL
2 cups	green or brown lentils, rinsed	500 mL
1/2 cup	dried cranberries	125 mL
1 cup	boiling water	250 mL
6 tbsp	olive oil, divided	90 mL
1	recipe game sausage (pages 184–85 and 187)	1
1/2 cup	chopped walnuts	125 mL
1 cup	sliced green onions, white and green parts	250 mL
Pinch	freshly ground black pepper	Pinch
1/4 cup	chopped fresh flat-leaf parsley	50 mL
2 tbsp	chopped fresh tarragon	25 mL
2	Granny Smith apples, peeled and sliced	2
2 tbsp	freshly squeezed lemon juice	25 mL

1. In a medium saucepan, over medium heat, bring 3 cups (750 mL) of the stock, wild rice and 1/4 tsp (1 mL) salt to a boil. Reduce heat, cover and simmer for 40 to 50 minutes, or until grains are tender but still have a little resistance when you bite down on them. Pour off any extra stock, cover and let stand for 10 minutes. Fluff with a fork and set aside.
2. Meanwhile, in another medium saucepan, over medium-high heat, bring 4 cups (1 L) of the stock, lentils and 1/2 tsp (2 mL) salt to a boil. Reduce heat, cover and simmer until tender, about 25 minutes. Pour off any extra stock, cover and let stand for 10 minutes. Set aside.
3. Place dried cranberries in a small heatproof bowl and cover with boiling water. Let stand for 20 minutes, until softened; drain and set aside.
4. In a large skillet, heat 2 tbsp (25 mL) of the olive oil over medium heat. Add sausage and cook until browned on all sides. Add the remaining 2 cups (500 mL) stock and bring to a simmer. Cook for 10 to 15 minutes, or until sausage is no longer pink in the middle and reaches an internal temperature of 160°F (71°C). Remove from heat and set aside.
5. In clean skillet, heat 2 tbsp (25 mL) of the olive oil over medium heat. Add walnuts and cook, stirring, until they begin to sizzle, about 2 minutes. Add green onions, pepper and a pinch of salt; cook, stirring, until onions soften, about 2 minutes. Remove from heat.
6. In a large bowl, toss wild rice, lentils, cranberries, walnut mixture, parsley and tarragon. Add apples, lemon juice and the remaining 2 tbsp (25 mL) olive oil; toss to combine. Taste and adjust seasoning as desired with salt and pepper.
7. Serve warm on a large platter surrounded by sausages.

Serves 6

Falafel Pita Sandwiches

FOOD GRINDER ◆ FLAT BEATER

2 cups	dried chickpeas, picked through and rinsed	500 mL
6	cloves garlic, minced	6
1/2 cup	chopped onion	125 mL
1/4 cup	coarsely chopped fresh flat-leaf parsley	50 mL
1/4 cup	coarsely chopped fresh cilantro	50 mL
2 tsp	cumin seeds, toasted and ground	10 mL
2 tsp	coriander seeds, toasted and ground	10 mL
1 1/2 tsp	salt	7 mL
1 tsp	baking powder	5 mL
1/4 tsp	cayenne pepper	1 mL
1/4 tsp	freshly ground black pepper	1 mL
	Vegetable oil	
8	warm pita breads, halved	8
	Tahini Sauce and/or Yogurt Mint Sauce (see recipes, opposite)	
	Shredded lettuce, sliced tomatoes and chopped cucumbers	

TIP

Whole spices are much more fragrant and flavorful after they have been toasted. To toast dry spices, heat a skillet over medium heat and add spices once the pan is hot. Stir or toss the spices until you begin to smell their fragrance, about 30 seconds. Spices have a tendency to burn easily. Remove them from the hot pan to a heatproof plate immediately, as they will continue to cook in the hot pan.

1. Place chickpeas in a large bowl and cover with 2 inches (5 cm) cool water. Place in the refrigerator and let soak for at least 18 hours or for up to 1 day. (The chickpeas will swell to triple their original size.) Drain and rinse thoroughly.
2. Attach the food grinder, with the fine plate, to the mixer. Set to Speed 4 and run chickpeas, by small handfuls, through the grinder into a large bowl. (Be careful not to run too many chickpeas through at once, or they may jam the grinder.) Stir in garlic, onion, parsley and cilantro. Run mixture through the grinder into the mixer bowl. Add cumin, coriander, salt, baking powder, cayenne pepper and black pepper. Remove the grinder and attach the flat beater and mixer bowl to the mixer. Set to Speed 2 and mix until well incorporated. Refrigerate for 15 minutes.
3. In a deep-fryer or a deep heavy saucepan, heat 3 inches (7.5 cm) oil to 375°F (190°C). Roll the falafel mixture into balls just smaller than ping-pong balls. Carefully slip 4 to 5 at a time into the hot oil, making sure they don't stick to the bottom. Fry until falafel are a crusty dark brown on all sides, turning as needed, about 3 to 5 minutes per batch. Remove with a slotted spoon to drain on a platter lined with paper towels. Add oil and reheat as necessary between batches.
4. Open the pita bread halves to make pockets (don't split all the way) and put 3 to 4 falafels in each. Drizzle with tahini sauce and/or yogurt mint sauce and layer with lettuce, tomatoes and cucumbers. Serve immediately.

Serves 8

Tahini Sauce

WIRE WHIP

1	clove garlic, minced	1
1/2 cup	tahini (sesame seed paste)	125 mL
1/2 cup	water	125 mL
2 tbsp	freshly squeezed lemon juice	25 mL
Pinch	salt	Pinch

1. Place garlic, tahini, water, lemon juice and salt in the mixer bowl. Attach the whip and mixer bowl to the mixer. Set to Speed 4 and whip for 1 to 2 minutes, or until smooth and creamy. Taste and adjust seasoning as desired with salt.

Makes about 1 cup (250 mL)

Yogurt Mint Sauce

1 cup	plain yogurt	250 mL
1/4 cup	chopped fresh mint	50 mL
2 tbsp	freshly squeezed lemon juice	25 mL
1/4 tsp	salt	1 mL
Pinch	cayenne pepper	Pinch

1. In a small bowl, combine yogurt, mint, lemon juice, salt and cayenne. Cover and refrigerate for 30 minutes or until ready to serve.

Makes about 1 cup (250 mL)

Broccoli and Swiss Cheese Quiche

- 9-inch (23 cm) tart pan with removable bottom or pie plate
- Large baking sheet

1	recipe Flaky Pastry (page 321)	1
6	slices lean bacon	6
1/4 cup	thinly sliced onion	50 mL
2	heads broccoli, stems removed and florets chopped into 1-inch (2.5 cm) pieces	2
4	eggs	4
3/4 cup	half-and-half (10%) cream	175 mL
1/2 tsp	salt	2 mL
Pinch	freshly ground black pepper	Pinch
Pinch	ground nutmeg	Pinch
Pinch	cayenne pepper	Pinch
3/4 cup	shredded Swiss or Gruyère cheese	175 mL

TIP
Reserve broccoli stems for another use, such as for soup.

1. On a floured work surface, roll out pastry and fit it into the tart shell. Poke holes in the bottom with a fork. Refrigerate for 30 minutes. Preheat oven to 375°F (190°C). Line pastry shell with a sheet of parchment paper, leaving a 4-inch (10 cm) overhang around the edges. Cover the bottom with dried beans, rice or pie weights. Place on baking sheet and bake in preheated oven until the bottom of the shell is set, about 20 minutes. Remove from oven and, using the edges of the parchment paper, remove the pie weights from the shell and place them on a heatproof plate or baking sheet to cool. Cool the tart shell for 20 minutes before filling.
2. Meanwhile, heat a skillet over medium-high heat and fry bacon until crisp and brown. Remove bacon to a plate and blot with paper towels.
3. Add onion to the bacon fat in the skillet and sauté until tender and translucent, about 3 minutes. Set aside.
4. In a large saucepan, bring 4 cups (1 L) salted water to a boil. Add broccoli and blanch for 1 minute. Drain and stop the cooking by immersing broccoli under cold water for 2 minutes. Blot dry on paper towels.
5. In a medium bowl, whisk together eggs, cream, salt, black pepper, nutmeg and cayenne.
6. Crumble bacon in the bottom of the tart shell. Lay onions and broccoli on top and sprinkle evenly with cheese. Pour in egg mixture. Place on baking sheet and bake in preheated oven until center is set, about 25 minutes. Remove from oven and let cool for 10 minutes before cutting. Serve hot or at room temperature.

Serves 6

Classic Cheese Soufflé

WIRE WHIP

- Preheat oven to 400°F (200°C)
- 8-inch (20 cm) soufflé dish, buttered

2 tbsp	freshly grated Parmesan cheese	25 mL
2½ tbsp	unsalted butter	32 mL
3 tbsp	unbleached all-purpose flour	45 mL
1 cup	hot milk	250 mL
½ tsp	salt	2 mL
¼ tsp	cayenne pepper	1 mL
Pinch	ground nutmeg	Pinch
	Freshly ground black pepper	
4	egg yolks	4
5	egg whites	5
1 cup	coarsely shredded Swiss cheese	250 mL

1. Cover the bottom and sides of the buttered soufflé dish with grated Parmesan. Use a double thickness of buttered foil to make a collar that rises about 3 inches (7.5 cm) over the rim of the dish. Secure the collar with a metal paper clip.
2. In a medium saucepan, melt butter over medium heat. Add flour and cook, stirring, for 2 to 3 minutes, or until roux becomes foamy. Remove from heat, add hot milk and whisk vigorously to blend. Return to heat and cook, stirring with a wooden spoon, until thickened, about 3 minutes. Whisk in salt, cayenne, nutmeg and black pepper. Remove from heat. One by one, whisk in egg yolks. Transfer to a large bowl.
3. Place egg whites in the mixer bowl. Attach the whip and mixer bowl to the mixer. Set to Speed 6 and whip to stiff, shining peaks. Scoop ¼ of the egg whites on top of the egg yolk mixture and stir with a wooden spoon to lighten. Using a rubber spatula, rapidly, yet gently, fold in the remaining egg whites, alternating scoops with sprinkles of Swiss cheese, making 3 additions of egg whites and 2 of cheese.
4. Pour into prepared dish and place in preheated oven. Reduce heat to 375°F (190°C) and bake for 25 to 30 minutes, or until soufflé has puffed and is golden brown and a tester inserted in the center comes out clean. Carefully remove the collar and serve immediately.

Serves 4

Ham and Vermont Cheddar Soufflé

WIRE WHIP

- Preheat oven to 400°F (200°C)
- 8-inch (20 cm) soufflé dish, buttered

2 tbsp	freshly grated Parmesan cheese	25 mL
2½ tbsp	unsalted butter	32 mL
3 tbsp	unbleached all-purpose flour	45 mL
1 cup	hot milk	250 mL
½ tsp	salt	2 mL
¼ tsp	cayenne pepper	1 mL
	Freshly ground black pepper	
4	egg yolks	4
5	egg whites	5
1 cup	coarsely shredded Vermont sharp Cheddar cheese	250 mL
½ cup	finely chopped ham (about 2 oz/60 g)	125 mL

1. Cover the bottom and sides of the buttered soufflé dish with grated Parmesan. Use a double thickness of buttered foil to make a collar that rises about 3 inches (7.5 cm) over the rim of the dish. Secure the collar with a metal paper clip.
2. In a medium saucepan, melt butter over medium heat. Add flour and cook, stirring, for 2 to 3 minutes, or until roux becomes foamy. Remove from heat, add hot milk and whisk vigorously to blend. Return to heat and cook, stirring with a wooden spoon, until thickened, about 3 minutes. Whisk in salt, cayenne and black pepper. Remove from heat. One by one, whisk in egg yolks. Transfer to a large bowl.
3. Place egg whites in the mixer bowl. Attach the whip and mixer bowl to the mixer. Set to Speed 6 and whip to stiff, shining peaks. Scoop ¼ of the egg whites on top of the egg yolk mixture and stir with a wooden spoon to lighten. Using a rubber spatula, rapidly, yet gently, fold in the remaining egg whites, alternating scoops with sprinkles of Cheddar cheese and ham, making 3 additions of egg whites and 1 each of cheese and ham.
4. Pour into prepared dish and place in preheated oven. Reduce heat to 375°F (190°C) and bake for 25 to 30 minutes, or until soufflé has puffed and is golden brown and a tester inserted in the center comes out clean. Carefully remove the collar and serve immediately.

Serves 4

Porcini Mushroom and Fontina Soufflé

WIRE WHIP

- Preheat oven to 400°F (200°C)
- 8-inch (20 cm) soufflé dish, buttered

1/2 oz	dried porcini mushrooms	15 g
1/2 cup	hot water	125 mL
2 tbsp	freshly grated Parmesan cheese	25 mL
2 1/2 tbsp	unsalted butter	32 mL
3 tbsp	unbleached all-purpose flour	45 mL
1 cup	hot milk	250 mL
1/2 tsp	salt	2 mL
	Freshly ground black pepper	
4	egg yolks	4
5	egg whites	5
1 cup	coarsely shredded fontina cheese	250 mL

1. Soak mushrooms in hot water for 20 minutes, or until softened. Gently lift from water with a slotted spoon, trying not to disturb the sediment at the bottom. Transfer to a cutting board and finely chop. Strain water through two layers of cheesecloth or a coffee filter. Set aside mushrooms and liquid.
2. Cover bottom and sides of soufflé dish with Parmesan. Use a double thickness of buttered foil to make a collar that rises about 3 inches (7.5 cm) over the rim of the dish. Secure with a metal paper clip.
3. In a medium saucepan, melt butter over medium heat. Add flour and cook, stirring, for 2 to 3 minutes, or until roux becomes foamy. Remove from heat and add hot milk and mushroom liquid; whisk vigorously to blend. Return to heat and cook, stirring with a wooden spoon, until thickened, about 3 minutes. Whisk in mushrooms, salt and pepper. Remove from heat. One by one, whisk in egg yolks. Transfer to a large bowl.
4. Place egg whites in the mixer bowl. Attach the whip and mixer bowl to the mixer. Set to Speed 6 and whip to stiff, shining peaks. Scoop 1/4 of the egg whites on top of the egg yolk mixture and stir with a wooden spoon to lighten. Using a rubber spatula, rapidly, yet gently, fold in the remaining egg whites, alternating scoops with sprinkles of fontina cheese, making 3 additions of egg whites and 2 of cheese.
5. Pour into prepared dish and place in preheated oven. Reduce heat to 375°F (190°C) and bake for 25 to 30 minutes, or until soufflé has puffed and is golden brown and a tester inserted in the center comes out clean. Carefully remove the collar and serve immediately.

Serves 4

Gruyère Soufflé Roll with Sautéed Spinach

Soufflé Layer		
1/3 cup	unsalted butter	75 mL
1/3 cup	unbleached all-purpose flour	75 mL
1 tsp	salt	5 mL
1/2 tsp	dried tarragon	2 mL
1 3/4 cups	hot milk	425 mL
1/4 tsp	ground nutmeg	1 mL
Pinch	freshly ground black pepper	Pinch
6	eggs, separated	6
2 tbsp	finely minced fresh flat-leaf parsley	25 mL
1/2 cup	shredded Gruyère cheese	125 mL
Spinach Filling		
2 tbsp	olive oil	25 mL
1 cup	sliced onion	250 mL
2	cloves garlic, minced	2
1 tsp	dried tarragon	5 mL
1 lb	fresh spinach, trimmed	500 g
1/4 tsp	salt	1 mL
Pinch	freshly ground black pepper	Pinch
1 tbsp	balsamic vinegar	15 mL
3/4 cup	shredded Gruyère cheese	175 mL
1/2 cup	freshly grated Parmesan cheese	125 mL
Roasted Red Bell Pepper Sauce		
3	red bell peppers, halved and seeded	3
2	cloves garlic, minced	2
1 tsp	cider vinegar	5 mL
1/4 tsp	salt	1 mL
Pinch	freshly ground black pepper	Pinch

WIRE WHIP • FRUIT/VEGETABLE STRAINER

- Preheat oven to 400°F (200°C)
- Baking sheet, lined with greased and floured parchment paper

1. *Prepare the soufflé layer:* In a medium saucepan, melt butter over medium-high heat. Add flour, salt and tarragon; cook, stirring, until roux becomes foamy, about 2 minutes. Remove from heat, add hot milk and whisk vigorously to blend. Return to heat and cook, stirring with a wooden spoon, until thickened, about 3 minutes. Whisk in nutmeg and pepper. Remove from heat. One by one, whisk in egg yolks. Stir in parsley. Transfer to a large bowl.
2. Place egg whites in the mixer bowl. Attach the whip and mixer bowl to the mixer. Set to Speed 6 and whip to stiff, shining peaks. Scoop 1/4 of the egg whites on top of the egg yolk mixture and stir with a wooden spoon to lighten. Using a rubber spatula, rapidly, yet gently, fold in the remaining egg whites, making 3 additions.
3. Pour into prepared baking sheet, smoothing to edges and top with Gruyère cheese. Bake in preheated oven until soufflé has puffed and is golden brown, about 15 minutes. Remove to a rack and let cool for 5 minutes. Invert onto a sheet of clean parchment paper and peel off baked parchment paper. Roll up, starting at one of the long sides, rolling clean paper with the soufflé.

4. *Prepare the spinach filling:* In a skillet with a lid, heat oil over medium-high heat. Add onions and sauté until tender, about 5 minutes. Reduce heat to medium and add garlic and tarragon; sauté for 3 minutes. Add 1/4 cup (50 mL) water, cover and cook for 5 minutes. Add spinach a handful at a time, adding more as it wilts and fits in the pan. Add salt and pepper; cook until spinach is wilted, about 2 minutes. Remove vegetables with a slotted spoon and strain out any excess liquid. Transfer to a large bowl and stir in vinegar. Taste and adjust seasoning as desired with salt and pepper. Let cool and mix in Gruyère and Parmesan cheeses. Set aside.
5. *Prepare the sauce:* Preheat the broiler. Lay peppers skin side up on a baking sheet and broil until skins char and blacken. Using tongs, transfer to a bowl, cover with plastic wrap and let steam for about 15 minutes. When cool enough to handle, remove and discard the skins. The peppers should be soft and pliable.
6. Attach the fruit/vegetable strainer to the mixer. Set to Speed 4 and run the peppers through the strainer into a large bowl, with another bowl to catch the solids.
7. Discard solids and transfer liquid to a small saucepan. Add garlic, vinegar, salt and pepper; cook over medium heat until heated through.
8. *To assemble:* Preheat oven to 350°F (180°C). Unroll soufflé and spread spinach filling evenly (it will look sparse) over the surface, leaving a 1-inch (2.5 cm) edge on the far long side. Roll up from the long side closest to you, using the parchment paper as a guide. Place on a baking sheet and bake in preheated oven for 15 to 20 minutes, or until hot in the center. Slice and serve with roasted red bell pepper sauce.

Serves 6

Variations

Try an assortment of different greens in place of spinach, such as Swiss chard, dandelion greens and escarole.

Gruyère is a semi-hard Swiss cheese. Regular Swiss cheese can be substituted. Other cheese combinations could be feta and Parmesan or smoked Gouda and Romano.

Substitute prepared salsa for the Roasted Red Bell Pepper Sauce.

Make ahead

Soufflé roll can be prepared through Step 4, covered and refrigerated overnight. Spinach filling can be prepared, covered and refrigerated for up to 1 day. You may need to add about 10 minutes to the baking time.

Potato Gnocchi with Bolognese Sauce

- Preheat oven to 400°F (200°C)
- Baking sheet, lightly floured

2 lbs	baking potatoes, preferably russets (about 4)	1 kg
1	egg	1
1 1/2 cups	unbleached all-purpose flour (approx.)	375 mL
1 tsp	salt	5 mL
1/2 tsp	baking powder	2 mL
2 1/2 cups	Bolognese Sauce (see recipe, page 410)	625 mL
	Freshly grated Parmesan cheese	

Make ahead

Can be prepared through Step 3 up to 12 hours ahead. Cover with plastic wrap and refrigerate.

TIP

Make sure you don't overwork the dough with the dough hook. It should be kneaded only until it has just become smooth. Overworked gnocchi dough makes dense, leaden gnocchi.

1. Prick potatoes all over with a fork. Bake in preheated oven until fork tender, about 1 hour. Peel while still hot and press through a potato ricer or food mill.
2. Place potatoes, egg, flour, salt and baking powder in the mixer bowl. Attach the flat beater and mixer bowl to the mixer. Set to Speed 2 and mix until a dough forms. Remove the flat beater and attach the dough hook. Set to Speed 2 and knead until smooth, about 1 minute, adding a little more flour, if necessary, to keep dough from sticking to the sides of bowl.
3. Divide dough into 4 pieces. Working with one piece at a time, roll it back and forth into a rope about the thickness of your index finger. Cut rope into 1-inch (2.5 cm) pieces. Gently roll each piece down the back of a floured fork while pressing a small dimple with your finger. The gnocchi should be slightly curved and marked with ridges. This will allow the pillows to hold sauce when served. Place gnocchi on prepared baking sheet.
4. In a large skillet, heat Bolognese sauce over medium heat and keep warm while you are cooking the gnocchi.
5. Bring a large pot of salted water to a boil over high heat. Add half the gnocchi and cook until they float to the surface, then continue cooking for 2 minutes longer. Remove with a slotted spoon, place in the skillet with the sauce and toss to coat. Repeat with remaining gnocchi.
6. Serve hot with Parmesan cheese.

Serves 6

Italian Spaghetti and Meatballs

FOOD GRINDER ◆ FLAT BEATER

Meatballs		
1 lb	boneless beef chuck or cross rib, cut into 1-inch (2.5 cm) cubes	500 g
2	slices homestyle white bread	2
3/4 cup	milk	175 mL
2	eggs	2
2	cloves garlic, minced	2
1 lb	Italian Sausage (see recipe, page 164), in bulk form	500 g
1/4 cup	packed freshly grated Parmesan cheese	50 mL
3 tbsp	minced fresh flat-leaf parsley	45 mL
1 tsp	salt	5 mL
1/2 tsp	freshly ground black pepper	2 mL
2 1/2 cups	Marinara Sauce (see recipe, page 409)	625 mL
1 lb	spaghetti	500 g
	Freshly grated Parmesan cheese	

Make ahead

Prepare meatballs through Step 3, place on a baking sheet, cover with plastic wrap and refrigerate for up to 1 day.

1. Place beef in a shallow container in the freezer for 30 minutes to facilitate grinding.
2. Place bread in the mixer bowl and cover with milk. Let stand until bread is soft, about 10 minutes.
3. Attach the food grinder, with the fine plate, to the mixer. Set to Speed 4 and run beef through the grinder onto the bread and milk in the mixer bowl. Add eggs, garlic, sausage, Parmesan, parsley, salt and pepper. Remove the food grinder and attach the flat beater to the mixer. Set to Stir and mix until well combined, about 30 seconds. With wet hands, form meatballs slightly smaller than golf balls.
4. In a medium saucepan, bring marinara sauce to a simmer over medium-low heat. Add meatballs and simmer until no longer pink inside, about 20 minutes.
5. Meanwhile, bring a large pot of salted water to a boil over high heat. Add spaghetti and cook, stirring for the first minute to keep noodles from sticking together, until al dente (tender to the bite), about 8 minutes. Drain.
6. Add about 1 1/2 cups (375 mL) of the sauce to the pasta pot. Return pasta and cook, stirring with the sauce, for about 30 seconds to let the flavors blend.
7. Transfer pasta to a large serving bowl. Top with meatballs and 1 cup (250 mL) sauce. Serve with additional sauce and Parmesan cheese on the side.

Serves 4

Summer Pasta with Fresh Tomatoes and Basil

PASTA ROLLER ◆ FETTUCCINE CUTTER

- ◆ Preheat oven to 375°F (190°C)
- ◆ Baking sheet

Croutons		
1/4 cup	unsalted butter, melted	50 mL
1	clove garlic, minced	1
2 cups	cubed French or Italian bread (1-inch/2.5 cm cubes)	500 mL
Pasta		
1	recipe Basic Egg Pasta (page 192)	1
3	large tomatoes, diced	3
3	cloves garlic, minced	3
1/4 cup	extra-virgin olive oil	50 mL
1/2 tsp	balsamic vinegar	2 mL
1/2 tsp	salt	2 mL
1/4 tsp	hot pepper flakes	1 mL
1/4 tsp	freshly ground black pepper	1 mL
1/3 cup	thinly sliced fresh basil	75 mL

This dish is best made in August and September, when tomatoes are at their peak. If you want to make it in the winter, use 6 to 9 plum tomatoes.

1. *Prepare the croutons:* In a small saucepan, melt butter over medium-high heat. Add garlic and sauté until fragrant, about 30 seconds. Remove from heat.
2. Place bread on baking sheet. Pour garlic butter over bread, tossing with a spatula to distribute butter evenly. Spread out bread cubes. Bake in preheated oven until crispy and lightly browned, about 10 minutes. Remove from oven and let cool.
3. *Prepare the pasta:* Roll pasta to setting 5 and cut with the fettuccine cutter (see Pasta Basics, page 190, for instructions on rolling and cutting pasta). Set aside on a floured baking sheet.
4. In a large bowl, toss tomatoes, garlic, oil, vinegar, salt, hot pepper flakes and black pepper. Taste and adjust seasoning as desired with salt, hot pepper flakes and vinegar. Set aside.
5. Bring a large pot of salted water to a boil over high heat. Add pasta and cook, stirring for the first minute to keep noodles from sticking together, until al dente (tender to the bite), about 3 minutes. Drain, reserving about 1/2 cup (125 mL) of the cooking water.
6. Add pasta to the bowl of tomatoes. Toss and add enough of the cooking water to moisten. Add croutons and basil and toss again. Serve immediately.

Serves 4

Pasta with Gorgonzola, Prosciutto and Hazelnuts

PASTA ROLLER ◆ PASTA CUTTER OF CHOICE ◆ FLAT BEATER

1	recipe Basic Egg Pasta (page 192) or Whole Wheat Pasta (page 193)	1
3 oz	Gorgonzola cheese, crumbled, at room temperature	90 g
6 tbsp	unsalted butter, softened	90 mL
½ tsp	minced garlic	2 mL
½ cup	chopped hazelnuts, toasted and husked (see tip, below)	125 mL
3 oz	prosciutto, minced	90 g
¼ tsp	freshly ground black pepper	1 mL
	Freshly grated Parmesan cheese	

TIP

To husk hazelnuts, spread nuts out on a baking sheet and bake in a 350°F (180°C) oven for about 10 minutes. Dump nuts into a clean, dry kitchen towel. Fold the towel over to cover the nuts and let cool for about 5 minutes. Rub vigorously to remove the husks from the nuts.

1. Roll pasta to setting 5 (see Pasta Basics, page 190, for instructions on rolling pasta). Let pasta sheets rest until slightly dry but still pliable, 15 to 20 minutes. Attach the pasta cutter to the mixer. Set to Speed 2 and, working with one sheet at a time, cut to the desired length. Using floured hands, toss strands to separate; spread out on towels.
2. Place Gorgonzola, butter and garlic in the mixer bowl. Remove the pasta cutter and attach the flat beater and mixer bowl to the mixer. Set to Speed 2 and mix until well combined. Add hazelnuts and prosciutto and pepper; mix until just combined. Transfer to a large serving bowl.
3. Bring a large pot of salted water to a boil over high heat. Add pasta and cook, stirring occasionally, for 3 to 5 minutes, or until just tender and no longer rubbery. Drain, reserving ½ cup (125 mL) of the cooking water.
4. Add pasta to the Gorgonzola mixture and toss to coat, adding enough of the cooking water to moisten, if necessary. Serve immediately, with Parmesan on the side.

Serves 4 to 6

Linguine with Zucchini, Sun-Dried Tomatoes and Lemon

PASTA ROLLER • LINGUINE CUTTER OR PASTA CUTTER OF CHOICE

1	recipe Basic Egg Pasta (page 192)	1
3 tbsp	extra-virgin olive oil	45 mL
1	large onion, sliced	1
1/2 tsp	dried thyme	2 mL
2	cloves garlic, minced	2
2	large zucchini (or 4 small), cut into matchsticks	2
1/2 cup	oil-packed sun-dried tomatoes, drained and slivered	125 mL
1/4 cup	torn fresh basil	50 mL
1/2 tsp	kosher salt	2 mL
1/4 tsp	freshly ground black pepper	1 mL
	Grated zest and juice of 1 lemon	
1/2 cup	chopped walnuts, toasted (see tip, below)	125 mL
1/2 cup	freshly grated Parmesan cheese	125 mL

TIP
To toast nuts, spread them on a baking sheet and toast in a 350°F (180°C) oven for 7 to 8 minutes, or until lightly browned.

1. Roll pasta to setting 5 and cut into linguine (see Pasta Basics, page 190, for instructions on rolling and cutting pasta). Set aside on a floured baking sheet.
2. In a large skillet, heat oil over medium heat. Add onion and thyme; sauté until softened, about 6 minutes. Add garlic and zucchini; sauté until zucchini is tender, about 5 minutes. Stir in sun-dried tomatoes, basil, salt and pepper. Add lemon zest and juice. Taste and adjust seasoning with salt and pepper, if necessary.
3. Meanwhile, bring a large pot of salted water to a boil over medium-high heat. Add linguine and cook, stirring for the first minute to keep noodles from sticking together, until al dente (tender to the bite), about 3 minutes. Drain, reserving 1 cup (250 mL) of the cooking water.
4. Toss the linguine with the vegetables in the skillet, adding enough of the cooking water to moisten. Serve sprinkled with walnuts and Parmesan.

Serves 6

Linguine with Roasted Asparagus and Lemon Cream Sauce

PASTA ROLLER ◆
SPAGHETTI/LINGUINE CUTTER

- ◆ Preheat oven to 425°F (220°C)
- ◆ Large baking sheet

1	recipe Basic Egg Pasta (page 192)	1
1 1/2 lbs	asparagus	1.5 kg
1 1/2 tbsp	olive oil	22 mL
1/4 tsp	salt	1 mL
1/4 tsp	freshly ground black pepper	1 mL
1 cup	whipping (35%) cream	250 mL
1/4 cup	unsalted butter	50 mL
	Grated zest of 1 lemon	
2 tbsp	freshly squeezed lemon juice	25 mL
1/4 cup	freshly grated Parmesan cheese	50 mL

1. Roll pasta to setting 5 and cut into linguine with the spaghetti/linguine cutter (see Pasta Basics, page 190, for instructions on rolling and cutting pasta). Set aside on a floured baking sheet.
2. Snap tough ends off asparagus and cut spears on the diagonal into 1 1/2-inch (4 cm) pieces. Drizzle olive oil on the baking sheet. Add asparagus, salt and pepper; toss until asparagus is well coated. Arrange in a single layer and roast in preheated oven until tender, about 12 minutes.
3. In a large skillet, bring whipping cream, butter and lemon juice to a boil over medium heat. Cook until liquid has reduced to a sauce consistency, about 3 minutes. Stir in lemon zest and Parmesan cheese. Season to taste with salt and pepper.
4. Meanwhile, bring a large pot of salted water to a boil over high heat. Add linguine and cook, stirring for the first minute to keep noodles from sticking together, until al dente (tender to the bite), about 3 minutes. Drain and return to the pot. Add asparagus and sauce; cook for 1 minute over medium heat. Taste and adjust seasoning as desired with salt and pepper. Serve hot.

Serves 4

Fettuccine Alfredo

PASTA ROLLER ◆ FETTUCCINE CUTTER

1	recipe Basic Egg Pasta (page 192)	1
½ cup	unsalted butter	125 mL
2 cups	whipping (35%) cream	500 mL
1 cup	finely grated Parmigiano-Reggiano cheese, divided	250 mL
2 tbsp	freshly squeezed lemon juice	25 mL
½ tsp	salt	2 mL
¼ tsp	freshly ground black pepper	1 mL
Pinch	ground nutmeg	Pinch
	Chopped fresh parsley (optional)	

1. Roll pasta to setting 5 and cut into fettuccine (see Pasta Basics, page 190, for instructions on rolling and cutting pasta). Set aside on a floured baking sheet.
2. Bring a large pot of salted water to a boil over high heat. Add pasta and cook, stirring occasionally, for 3 to 5 minutes, or until just tender and no longer rubbery. Drain.
3. Meanwhile, in a large skillet, melt butter over medium heat. Add cream, bring to a boil and cook until slightly reduced, about 3 minutes. Add pasta, half the Parmesan, lemon juice, salt, pepper and nutmeg; toss to combine. Serve immediately, sprinkled with the remaining Parmesan and parsley, if desired.

Serves 4 to 6

Pasta "Handkerchiefs" with Roasted Tomatoes and Lemon

PASTA ROLLER

- Preheat oven to 425°F (220°C)
- Rimmed baking sheet
- 8-cup (2 L) casserole dish

1	recipe Basic Egg Pasta (page 192)	1
10	plum (Roma) tomatoes, quartered and seeded	10
1/4 cup	olive oil, divided	50 mL
3	cloves garlic, chopped	3
1/2 tsp	salt, divided	2 mL
1/4 tsp	freshly ground black pepper, divided	1 mL
1/2 cup	reduced-sodium chicken or vegetable stock	125 mL
1	container (15 oz/425 g) ricotta cheese	1
1 cup	shredded mozzarella cheese, divided	250 mL
1/2 cup	freshly grated Parmesan cheese, divided	125 mL
1/2 cup	shredded Asiago cheese, divided	125 mL
1	bunch fresh basil, finely sliced (about 1 cup/250 mL), divided	1
1	egg	1
	Grated zest of 1 lemon	
Pinch	ground nutmeg	Pinch
Pinch	cayenne pepper	Pinch

1. Roll pasta to setting 5 (see Pasta Basics, page 190, for instructions on rolling pasta). Cut into 4-inch (10 cm) squares and set aside on a floured baking sheet.
2. Arrange tomatoes on baking sheet, drizzle with 3 tbsp (45 mL) of the oil and sprinkle with garlic, 1/4 tsp (1 mL) of the salt and a pinch of black pepper; toss to coat and spread in a single layer. Roast in preheated oven for 30 minutes, or until tomatoes have dried and colored slightly. Remove from oven, and pour stock over the tomatoes, scraping up any brown bits from the bottom of the pan with a spatula. (It may seem strange to add chicken stock after roasting tomatoes, but most of this flavorful stock will be absorbed by the pasta as it bakes.) Set aside. Reduce oven temperature to 350°F (180°C).
3. In a medium bowl, combine ricotta, half each of the mozzarella, Parmesan and Asiago, half the basil, egg, lemon zest, 1/4 tsp (1 mL) salt, a pinch of black pepper, nutmeg and cayenne.
4. Meanwhile, bring a large pot of salted water to a boil over high heat. Add pasta and cook, stirring frequently to keep it from sticking together, for 2 minutes, or until tender. Drain and rinse under cold running water until cool. Separate the pasta sheets and lay out on a towel to dry (not terrycloth, as it will stick.)
5. Add the remaining oil to the casserole dish and swirl to coat. Lay a square of pasta on a work surface and place a large tablespoon (15 mL) of filling in the center. Fold the pasta in half, slightly off-center, to form an open V, enclosing the filling. Fold again, corner to corner, slightly off-center, to create the shape of a folded handkerchief. Repeat with the remaining pasta and filling and lay the pasta "handkerchiefs," slightly overlapping, in the dish. Top with the tomato mixture and remaining basil, mozzarella, Parmesan and Asiago. Bake for 20 minutes, or until pasta is heated through and cheeses are melted.

Serves 4 to 6

Make ahead

The dish can be assembled up to 1 day ahead and kept covered in the refrigerator. Add 10 minutes to the baking time.

Pasta Roulades with Spinach and Cheese

FLAT BEATER ◆ PASTA ROLLER

◆ Preheat oven to 375°F (190°C)
◆ 8-cup (2 L) casserole dish

1	recipe Basic Egg Pasta (page 192)	1
10 oz	spinach, trimmed	300 g
1	egg	1
1 ½ cups	ricotta cheese	375 mL
¾ cup	freshly grated Parmesan cheese	175 mL
½ tsp	ground nutmeg	2 mL
½ tsp	salt	2 mL
Pinch	cayenne pepper	Pinch
	Freshly ground black pepper	
1	recipe Marinara Sauce (page 409)	1
	Additional freshly grated Parmesan cheese (optional)	

1. Roll pasta to setting 5 (see Pasta Basics, page 190, for instructions on rolling pasta). Cut into 4-inch (10 cm) squares. In a large pot of boiling water, cook pasta, stirring frequently to keep it from sticking together, for about 3 minutes, or until pliable and almost cooked. Remove with a slotted spoon and plunge into cold water to stop the cooking. Lay out on a towel to dry.
2. In the same pot of boiling water, blanch spinach for 30 seconds. Drain and plunge into cold water to stop the cooking. Drain, let cool, squeeze out as much water as possible and finely chop.
3. In a large bowl, combine spinach, egg, ricotta, Parmesan, nutmeg, salt, cayenne and black pepper to taste.
4. Divide filling among pasta sheets, spreading evenly, and roll up pasta jelly-roll style. Spread a thin layer of marinara sauce on bottom of casserole dish. Place rolls in dish and cover with more sauce. Sprinkle with additional Parmesan, if desired. Bake in preheated oven for about 25 minutes, or until top is bubbly and lightly browned. Let cool for 5 minutes before serving.

Serves 6

Butternut Squash Ravioli with Brown Butter Pecan Sauce

PASTA ROLLER

- Preheat oven to 425°F (220°C)
- Baking sheet

Ravioli		
2 lbs	butternut squash, halved lengthwise and seeded	1 kg
1 tbsp	unsalted butter	15 mL
1 ½ cups	finely chopped onion	375 mL
2 tbsp	finely chopped fresh sage	25 mL
	Salt and freshly ground black pepper	
Pinch	ground nutmeg	Pinch
1	recipe Basic Egg Pasta (page 192) or flavored pasta of choice	1
Brown Butter Pecan Sauce		
½ cup	unsalted butter	125 mL
⅓ cup	pecan halves, coarsely chopped	75 mL
	Salt and freshly ground black pepper	

Roasting the squash brings out its natural sweetness and reduces the liquid in the filling, making the ravioli easier to fill.

1. *Prepare the ravioli:* Put squash halves cut side down on baking sheet and roast in middle of preheated oven until flesh is very tender, about 30 minutes.
2. Meanwhile, in a skillet, melt butter over medium heat. Add onion, sage and salt and pepper to taste; sauté until onion is golden brown, about 5 minutes.
3. When squash is cool enough to handle, scoop out the flesh into the bowl of a food processor. Add onions and pulse several times until smooth.
4. Roll pasta to setting 5 (see Pasta Basics, page 190, for instructions on rolling pasta). Cut a single sheet at a time into 2- by 1-inch (5 by 2.5 cm) rectangles. Place ½ tbsp (7 mL) squash mixture in the center of each rectangle, brush the edges lightly with water, fold down like a piece of notebook paper and seal to form a 1-inch (2.5 cm) square. Repeat with remaining pasta and squash.
5. Bring a large pot of salted water to a gentle boil over medium-high heat. Add half of the ravioli and cook, being careful not to let water come to a rolling boil, for 6 to 8 minutes, or until al dente (tender to the bite). Remove with a slotted spoon and drain well. Repeat with remaining ravioli.
6. *Meanwhile, prepare the sauce:* In a skillet, melt butter over medium heat. Add pecans and cook, stirring, until butter begins to brown, about 3 minutes. Remove from heat (nuts will continue to cook). Season to taste with salt and pepper, cover and keep warm.
7. Serve ravioli with brown butter pecan sauce.

Serves 6 as a first course, 4 as a main course

Herbed Cheese Ravioli

FLAT BEATER · PASTA ROLLER

2	eggs	2
2 cups	drained ricotta cheese	500 mL
1/2 cup	shredded mozzarella cheese	125 mL
1/2 cup	freshly grated Parmesan cheese	125 mL
1/4 cup	finely chopped fresh parsley	50 mL
1/4 cup	finely chopped fresh basil	50 mL
1 tbsp	dry bread crumbs (approx.)	15 mL
1/2 tsp	salt	2 mL
1/4 tsp	freshly ground black pepper	1 mL
1	recipe Basic Egg Pasta (page 192) or flavored pasta of choice	1
	Pasta sauce	

TIP
Marinara Sauce (see recipe, page 409) works well with this recipe.

1. Place eggs, ricotta cheese, mozzarella cheese, Parmesan cheese, parsley, basil, bread crumbs, salt and pepper in the mixer bowl. Attach the flat beater and mixer bowl to the mixer. Set to Speed 2 and beat until well combined. Add more bread crumbs if the mixture appears too loose.
2. Roll pasta to setting 5 (see Pasta Basics, page 190, for instructions on rolling pasta). Cut a single sheet at a time into 2- by 1-inch (5 by 2.5 cm) rectangles. Place 1/2 tbsp (7 mL) cheese mixture in the center of each rectangle, brush the edges lightly with water, fold down like a piece of notebook paper and seal to form a 1-inch (2.5 cm) square. Repeat with remaining pasta and cheese mixture.
3. Bring a large pot of salted water to a gentle boil over medium-high heat. Add half of the ravioli and cook, being careful not to let water come to a rolling boil, for 6 to 8 minutes, or until al dente (tender to the bite). Remove with a slotted spoon and drain well. Repeat with remaining ravioli.
4. Serve ravioli with pasta sauce of your choice.

Serves 4

Meat Ravioli

FOOD GRINDER ◆ PASTA ROLLER

8 oz	boneless beef chuck or cross rib, cut into 1-inch (2.5 cm) cubes	250 g
8 oz	boneless pork shoulder blade, cut into 1-inch (2.5 cm) cubes	250 g
2 oz	ham, cut into 1-inch (2.5 cm) cubes	60 g
2 tbsp	olive oil	25 mL
1 cup	red wine or beef stock	250 mL
	Salt and freshly ground black pepper	
2	cloves garlic, minced	2
1	egg	1
1/2 cup	minced fresh parsley	125 mL
1/2 cup	freshly grated Parmesan cheese	125 mL
	Dry bread crumbs (if needed)	
1	recipe Basic Egg Pasta (page 192) or flavored pasta of choice	1
	Pasta sauce	

TIP
Marinara Sauce (see recipe, page 409) works well with this recipe.

1. Place beef, pork and ham in a shallow container in the freezer for 30 minutes. Attach the food grinder, with the fine plate, to the mixer. Set to Speed 4 and run meat twice through the grinder into a large bowl.
2. In a large, deep skillet, heat oil over medium heat. Add meat and cook, breaking up any clumps, until no longer pink, about 5 minutes. Add wine and salt and pepper to taste. Reduce heat and simmer, uncovered, stirring occasionally, until meat is tender, about 45 minutes. Add garlic and cook for 5 minutes. Remove from heat, let cool slightly, then add egg, parsley and Parmesan. Add bread crumbs, 1 tbsp (15 mL) at a time, if mixture is too liquid. Set aside and let cool.
3. Roll pasta to setting 5 (see Pasta Basics, page 190, for instructions on rolling pasta). Cut a single sheet at a time into 2- by 1-inch (5 by 2.5 cm) rectangles. Place 1/2 tbsp (7 mL) meat mixture in the center of each rectangle, brush the edges lightly with water, fold down like a piece of notebook paper and seal to form a 1-inch (2.5 cm) square. Repeat with remaining pasta and meat mixture.
4. Bring a large pot of salted water to a gentle boil over medium-high heat. Add half of the ravioli and cook, being careful not to let water come to a rolling boil, for 6 to 8 minutes, or until al dente (tender to the bite). Remove with a slotted spoon and drain well. Repeat with remaining ravioli.
5. Serve ravioli with pasta sauce of your choice.

Serves 4

Roasted Vegetable Lasagna

PASTA ROLLER

- Preheat oven to 400°F (200°C)
- 3 rimmed baking sheets
- 8-cup (2 L) baking dish or casserole dish

1	recipe Basic Egg Pasta (page 192)	1
1	eggplant, cut lengthwise into 1/2-inch (1 cm) slices	1
1	zucchini, cut lengthwise into 1/4-inch (0.5 cm) slices	1
1	yellow summer squash, cut lengthwise into 1/4-inch (0.5 cm) slices	1
1	red bell pepper, cut into 1-inch (2.5 cm) slices	1
2 cups	grape tomatoes	500 mL
1/3 cup	extra-virgin olive oil, divided	75 mL
	Salt and freshly ground black pepper	
1	large sweet onion, thinly sliced	1
2	cloves garlic, minced	2
1 lb	ricotta cheese	500 g
2	eggs, beaten, divided	2
1 cup	freshly grated Parmigiano-Reggiano cheese, divided	250 mL
1/4 tsp	ground nutmeg, divided	1 mL
1/4 tsp	cayenne pepper, divided	1 mL
2 cups	shredded mozzarella cheese	500 mL
2 cups	shredded Asiago cheese	500 mL
3 tbsp	unsalted butter	45 mL
3 tbsp	unbleached all-purpose flour	45 mL
2 cups	milk, heated	500 mL

1. Roll pasta to setting 5 (see Pasta Basics, page 190, for instructions on rolling pasta). Cut into 5 sheets that will fit snugly in the baking dish and set aside on a floured baking sheet.
2. Arrange eggplant, zucchini, squash, red pepper and tomatoes on baking sheets, drizzle with 3 tbsp (45 mL) of the oil and sprinkle with salt and black pepper to taste; toss to coat and spread out in a single layer. Roast in preheated oven (in batches if necessary) for about 20 minutes, or until tender and golden. Let cool. Reduce oven temperature to 350°F (180°C).
3. In a large skillet, heat 2 tbsp (25 mL) of the oil over medium heat. Add onion and salt and pepper to taste; sauté until browned and tender, about 15 minutes. Add garlic and sauté until fragrant, about 1 minute. Set aside.
4. In a large bowl, combine ricotta, half the eggs, 1/4 cup (50 mL) of the Parmesan, a pinch each of the nutmeg and cayenne, and salt and black pepper to taste. Set aside.
5. In another bowl, combine mozzarella, Asiago and the remaining Parmesan. Set aside.
6. In a medium saucepan, melt butter over medium heat. Sprinkle with flour and cook, stirring, until foamy, about 2 minutes. Add heated milk in a steady stream, whisking until well blended. Cook, whisking constantly, until mixture boils and thickens, 3 to 4 minutes. Season with the remaining nutmeg and cayenne, and salt and black pepper to taste. Transfer to a large bowl and whisk in the remaining egg. Set aside.

7. Meanwhile, bring a large pot of salted water to a boil over medium-high heat. Add pasta and cook, stirring frequently to keep it from sticking together, for 2 minutes, or until tender. Drain and plunge into a cold water bath to stop the cooking. Separate the pasta sheets and lay out on a towel to dry (not terrycloth, as it will stick).
8. Add the remaining oil to the baking dish and swirl to coat. Add one-fifth of the white sauce and spread to the edges. Top with one sheet of pasta, the eggplant, one-quarter of ricotta mixture, half of the caramelized onion and one-fifth of the cheese mixture. Top with layers of pasta, zucchini, white sauce, ricotta and cheese. Top with layers of pasta, summer squash and red pepper, white sauce, ricotta and cheese. Top with layers of pasta, tomatoes, remaining caramelized onions, white sauce, ricotta and cheese. Top with the remaining pasta, drizzle with the remaining white sauce and sprinkle with the remaining cheese.
9. Butter a sheet of foil and lay it buttered side down on top of the lasagna; seal the edges. Bake for about 1 hour, or until heated through. Carefully remove foil and bake for 15 minutes, or until top is lightly browned. Let cool for 15 minutes before cutting.

Serves 6 to 8

Make ahead

The lasagna can be assembled, wrapped and frozen for up to 2 weeks. Thaw overnight in the refrigerator before baking. Or it can be wrapped and refrigerated for up to 1 day. In either case, add 10 minutes to the baking time.

Sausage and Cheese Lasagna

PASTA ROLLER

- Preheat oven to 350°F (180°C)
- Lasagna pan or 13- by 9-inch (3 L) baking pan

1	recipe Basic Egg Pasta (page 192) or Spinach Pasta (page 205)	1
3 lbs	ricotta cheese	1.5 kg
3	eggs, beaten	3
½ cup	finely chopped fresh parsley	125 mL
1½ tsp	salt	7 mL
Pinch	ground nutmeg	Pinch
	Freshly ground black pepper	
2 cups	shredded mozzarella cheese	500 mL
1 cup	shredded fontina cheese	250 mL
1 cup	shredded Asiago cheese	250 mL
1 cup	freshly grated Parmesan cheese	250 mL
1	recipe Marinara Sauce (page 409)	1
2 lbs	Italian sausage (store-bought or see recipe, page 164), crumbled	1 kg

1. Bring a large pot of salted water to a boil over medium-high heat. Meanwhile, roll pasta to setting 5 (see Pasta Basics, page 190, for instructions on rolling pasta). Cut into 9-inch (23 cm) strips (you will have leftover pieces; go ahead and cook them, as you may need them to piece a layer together). Set up an ice bath next to the stovetop. Add the pasta to the boiling water and cook, stirring frequently to keep it from sticking together, for 1 minute. Drain and plunge into the ice bath to stop the cooking. Remove with a slotted spoon and lay out on damp towels.
2. In a large bowl, combine ricotta, eggs, parsley, salt, nutmeg and pepper to taste. Set aside.
3. In another large bowl, combine mozzarella, fontina, Asiago and Parmesan. Set aside.
4. In a large pot, warm marinara sauce over medium-low heat.
5. In a large skillet, sauté sausage over medium-high heat until no longer pink, about 5 minutes. Add to the marinara sauce and bring to a simmer over medium heat.
6. Spread a ladleful of sauce over the bottom of the lasagna pan. Cover with a layer of pasta. Spread one-third of the ricotta mixture over the pasta and sprinkle with 1 cup (250 mL) of the shredded cheese mixture. Top with a layer of pasta, another third of the ricotta, 2 cups (500 mL) sauce and 1 cup (250 mL) cheese. Top with a layer of pasta, the remaining ricotta and 1 cup (250 mL) cheese. Top with the remaining pasta, sauce and cheese.
7. Butter a sheet of foil and lay it buttered side down on top of the lasagna; seal the edges. Bake in preheated oven for 1 hour, or until heated through. Carefully remove foil and bake for 15 to 20 minutes, or until top is lightly browned. Let cool for 10 minutes before cutting.

Serves 8 to 10

Make ahead

The lasagna can be assembled, wrapped and frozen for up to 4 weeks. Thaw overnight in the refrigerator before baking. Or it can be covered and refrigerated for up to 1 day. In either case, add 10 minutes to the baking time.

Chicken Paprikash and Spaetzle

FLAT BEATER

Chicken		
4 to 5 lbs	whole chicken, cut into 8 pieces	2 to 2.5 kg
	Salt and freshly ground black pepper	
2 tbsp	vegetable oil	25 mL
1	onion, chopped	1
2 tbsp	Hungarian sweet paprika	25 mL
2 cups	chicken stock	500 mL
1/2 cup	sour cream	125 mL
2 tbsp	unbleached all-purpose flour	25 mL
Spaetzle		
2 3/4 cups	unbleached all-purpose flour	675 mL
1 1/4 tsp	salt	6 mL
4	eggs	4
3/4 cup	milk	175 mL
1/4 cup	unsalted butter	50 mL
	Freshly ground black pepper	

Make ahead

Spaetzle can be prepared through Step 4 up to 2 hours ahead. Let stand at room temperature.

1. *Prepare the chicken:* Rinse and dry chicken and season lightly with salt and pepper. In a large skillet, heat oil over medium-high heat. Working in 2 batches, add chicken and cook, flipping once, until browned on both sides, about 3 minutes per side. Transfer chicken to a plate. Reduce heat to medium and add onion to the skillet. Sauté until tender, about 3 minutes. Add paprika and sauté for 1 minute. Return chicken to the skillet and pour in stock. Reduce heat and simmer, partly covered, until chicken is no longer pink inside, about 40 minutes.
2. In a small bowl, whisk together sour cream and flour until smooth. Add to the skillet and bring back to a simmer. Cook until sauce is slightly thickened, about 5 minutes. Season with salt and pepper.
3. *Meanwhile, prepare the spaetzle:* Place flour and salt in the mixer bowl. Attach the flat beater and the mixer bowl to the mixer. Set to Speed 2 and beat in eggs, one at a time, and milk until a smooth, thick batter forms, about 2 minutes.
4. Bring a large pot of salted water to a boil over high heat. Working in batches, pour batter through a spaetzle maker, potato ricer or slotted spoon held above boiling water, pressing with a spatula to form strands that drop into the water. Stir gently to prevent sticking. Simmer until spaetzle float to the surface, then continue cooking for 1 minute longer. Using a slotted spoon, transfer spaetzle to a buttered baking dish. Repeat with remaining batter.
5. In a large skillet, melt butter over medium heat. Add spaetzle and cook, tossing, until heated through. Season to taste with salt and pepper. Divide spaetzle among 4 plates, top each with 2 pieces of chicken and cover with sauce.

Serves 4

Braised Pork with Sauerkraut and Sausages

1/4 cup	finely diced salt pork	50 mL
1 cup	diced onion	250 mL
1/2 tsp	salt, divided	2 mL
2	cloves garlic, chopped	2
10 oz	bone-in pork shoulder blade	300 g
3/4 tsp	freshly ground black pepper, divided	3 mL
1 lb	sauerkraut	500 g
1 tsp	ground coriander	5 mL
1/2 tsp	ground cumin	2 mL
1	bottle (750 mL) Riesling wine	1
6	small Kielbasa sausages (see recipe, page 174)	6
6	Bratwurst sausages (see recipe, page 173)	6
6	Chicken Bockwurst sausages (see recipe, page 181)	6
	Variety of mustards, as an accompaniment	

1. Heat a large saucepan over medium-high heat until hot. Add salt pork and cook until it renders its fat, about 3 minutes. Add onion and 1/4 tsp (1 mL) of the salt; sauté until translucent, about 4 minutes. Add garlic and reduce heat to medium. Add pork shoulder seasoned with 1/4 tsp (1 mL) salt and 1/4 tsp (1 mL) pepper. Lay sauerkraut over and around the pork shoulder and sprinkle with coriander, 1/2 tsp (2 mL) pepper and cumin. Pour in wine and 1 cup (250 mL) water. Reduce heat, cover and simmer until pork is tender, about 90 minutes. Add kielbasa, bratwurst and bockwurst and push down into the liquid. Cover and simmer until sausages are no longer pink inside, about 30 minutes. Remove from heat.
2. Transfer sauerkraut to a large warmed serving platter. Slice pork and sausages and arrange around the sauerkraut. Serve with a variety of mustards.

Serves 6

Swedish Meatballs

FOOD GRINDER • FLAT BEATER

1 lb	boneless beef chuck or cross rib, cut into 1-inch (2.5 cm) cubes	500 g
8 oz	boneless veal shoulder, cut into 1-inch (2.5 cm) cubes	250 g
1/3 cup	unsalted butter, divided	75 mL
1/2 cup	minced onion	125 mL
1	egg, lightly beaten	1
1/2 cup	dry bread crumbs	125 mL
1/2 tsp	ground cardamom	2 mL
1/2 tsp	ground coriander	2 mL
1/2 tsp	salt	2 mL
1/4 tsp	freshly ground black pepper	1 mL
2 tbsp	unbleached all-purpose flour	25 mL
1 1/2 cups	chicken or beef stock	375 mL
	Cooked rice or noodles	
1/4 cup	minced fresh flat-leaf parsley	50 mL

TIP

Meatballs can be turned into an appetizer by rolling them smaller into one-bite morsels. Serve in the sauce in a chafing dish with toothpicks.

1. Place beef and veal in a shallow container in the freezer for 30 minutes to facilitate grinding.
2. In a large skillet, melt 1 tbsp (15 mL) of the butter over medium-high heat. Add onion and sauté until tender, about 4 minutes. Remove from heat and let cool.
3. Attach the food grinder, with the coarse plate, to the mixer. Set to Speed 4 and run beef and veal through the grinder into a large bowl. Return to the freezer for 30 minutes. Run through the grinder again, this time into the mixer bowl. Add onion, egg, bread crumbs, cardamom, coriander, salt and pepper. Remove the food grinder and attach the flat beater and mixer bowl. Set to Stir and mix until well combined. In skillet, over medium heat, sauté 1 tbsp (15 mL) of the mixture until no longer pink. Taste and adjust seasoning as desired with salt and pepper. Roll meat mixture into 1-inch (2.5 cm) balls.
4. In skillet, melt 2 tbsp (25 mL) of the butter over medium heat. Add meatballs and sauté until browned. Transfer to a bowl or platter. Melt the remaining 2 tbsp (25 mL) butter. Add flour and cook, stirring, for 2 to 3 minutes, or until roux becomes foamy. Add stock and cook, scraping up any cooked bits stuck to bottom, until thickened, about 5 minutes. Return meatballs to the skillet, reduce heat, cover and simmer for 30 minutes to allow flavors to blend.
5. Serve meatballs on top of rice or noodles and garnish with parsley.

Serves 4

Potato and Cheese Pierogi

FLAT BEATER ◆ DOUGH HOOK

◆ Large baking sheet, very well floured

Filling		
1 1/2 lbs	baking potatoes, unpeeled (about 3)	750 g
1/3 cup	buttermilk	75 mL
1 1/2 cups	shredded Cheddar cheese	375 mL
	Salt and freshly ground black pepper	
Dough		
4	eggs	4
1 cup	sour cream	250 mL
1 tsp	salt	5 mL
4 1/4 cups	unbleached all-purpose flour	1.05 L

1. *Prepare the filling:* Place potatoes in a large pot and cover with cold water. Bring to a boil and cook for 20 to 30 minutes, or until potatoes are tender. Drain and let cool just enough that you can handle them. Peel, cut into small pieces and place in the mixer bowl. Attach the flat beater and mixer bowl to the mixer. Set to Speed 2 and beat just until mashed. *Do not overbeat.* Add buttermilk, cheese and salt and pepper to taste; beat just until mixed. Taste and adjust seasoning as desired with salt and pepper. Transfer to a large bowl and set aside. Clean the mixer bowl and flat beater.
2. *Prepare the dough:* Place eggs, sour cream and salt in the mixer bowl. Attach the flat beater and mixer bowl to the mixer. Set to Speed 2 and mix until well combined. Gradually add flour and mix until a dough forms. Remove the flat beater and attach the dough hook. Set to Speed 4 and knead for about 2 minutes. Dough should be silky and fairly soft, but should not stick to the sides of the bowl. Add a little more flour if dough sticks. Let dough rest, loosely covered, for 10 minutes.
3. Divide dough into 2 pieces. Work with one piece at a time, keeping the other covered to prevent drying out. On a well-floured work surface, roll dough out to 1/8-inch (0.25 cm) thickness. Cut into 2-inch (5 cm) rounds. Place 1/2 tbsp (7 mL) filling in the center of each circle and fold into a half-moon shape, pinching the edges to seal the pierogi. Place pierogi on prepared baking sheet as they are filled. Make sure they don't touch one another or they will stick together.

4. Bring a large pot of salted water to a gentle boil over medium-high heat. Add pierogi, in batches of 15, and cook, being careful not to let water come to a rolling boil, until the filling is heated through and dough is just tender to the bite, about 8 minutes. With a slotted spoon, carefully transfer to a warm serving platter. Repeat with remaining pierogi.

Serves 10

Make ahead

Pierogi can be prepared through Step 3 and frozen for up to 2 months. Place baking sheet in the freezer. Once pierogi are frozen, transfer them to a freezer bag. Cook from frozen, increasing boiling time to 10 minutes.

TIPS

Boiling the potatoes in their skins eliminates excess moisture in the filling. A firmer filling makes it easier to form the pierogi.

Don't cook pierogi at a rolling boil or they will burst (not a pretty sight!).

Serving pierogi is a matter of taste. Most people prefer to serve them with onions that have been sautéed in butter to a nice brown color. You can carefully toss pierogi with the onions just to warm them, or you can sauté pierogi until crispy. To gild the lily, serve with some sour cream on the side.

Sweet Cabbage Pierogi

FLAT BEATER DOUGH HOOK

- Large baking sheet, very well floured

Filling		
2 tbsp	unsalted butter	25 mL
1 tbsp	vegetable oil	15 mL
1	onion, finely chopped	1
5 cups	finely chopped green cabbage	1.25 L
2 tbsp	cider vinegar	25 mL
3 tbsp	chopped fresh dill (or 1 tbsp/15 mL dried dillweed)	45 mL
4 oz	cream cheese, softened	125 g
	Salt and freshly ground black pepper	
Dough		
4	eggs	4
1 cup	sour cream	250 mL
1 tsp	salt	5 mL
$4\frac{1}{4}$ cups	unbleached all-purpose flour	1.05 L

1. *Prepare the filling:* In a large skillet, heat butter and oil over medium heat. Add onion and sauté until lightly browned, about 5 minutes. Add cabbage and sauté, stirring often, until tender and any liquid has evaporated, about 20 minutes. Remove from heat and add vinegar and dill. Let cool slightly.
2. Place cabbage mixture and cream cheese in the mixer bowl. Attach the flat beater and mixer bowl to the mixer. Set to Speed 2 and mix until well combined. Season to taste with salt and pepper. Transfer to a large bowl and set aside. Clean the mixer bowl and flat beater.
3. *Prepare the dough:* Place eggs, sour cream and salt in the mixer bowl. Attach the flat beater and mixer bowl to the mixer. Set to Speed 2 and mix until well combined. Gradually add flour and mix until a dough forms. Remove the flat beater and attach the dough hook. Set to Speed 4 and knead for about 2 minutes. Dough should be silky and fairly soft, but should not stick to the sides of the bowl. Add a little more flour if dough sticks. Let dough rest, loosely covered, for 10 minutes.

4. Divide dough into 2 pieces. Work with one piece at a time, keeping the other half covered to prevent drying out. On a well-floured work surface, roll out dough to 1⁄8-inch (0.25 cm) thickness. Cut into 2-inch (5 cm) rounds. Place 1⁄2 tbsp (7 mL) filling in the center of each circle and fold into a half-moon shape, pinching the edges to seal the pierogi. Place pierogi on prepared baking sheet as they are filled. Make sure they don't touch one another or they will stick together.
5. Bring a large pot of salted water to a gentle boil over medium-high heat. Add pierogi and cook, being careful not to let water come to a rolling boil, until filling is heated and the dough is tender to the bite, about 8 minutes. With a slotted spoon, carefully transfer to a warm serving platter. Repeat with remaining pierogi.

Serves 10

Make ahead

Pierogi can be prepared through Step 3 and frozen for up to 2 months. Place baking sheet in the freezer. Once pierogi are frozen, transfer them to a freezer bag. Cook from frozen, increasing boiling time to 10 minutes.

TIP

One of the keys to making successful pierogi is to adequately season your filling. Be sure to taste the filling and season fairly aggressively. You don't want to oversalt it, but keep in mind that there will be only a bite or two of filling wedged into the dough, so it has to taste good!

Don't cook pierogi at a rolling boil or they will burst (not a pretty sight!).

Serving pierogi is a matter of taste. Most people prefer to serve them with onions that have been sautéed in butter to a nice brown color. You can carefully toss pierogi with the onions just to warm them, or you can sauté pierogi until crispy. To gild the lily, serve with some sour cream on the side.

Beef and Rice–Stuffed Cabbage Rolls

FOOD GRINDER • FLAT BEATER

12 oz	boneless pork shoulder blade, cut into 1-inch (2.5 cm) cubes	375 g
12 oz	boneless beef chuck or cross rib, cut into 1-inch (2.5 cm) cubes	375 g
1	large head napa or savoy cabbage	1
2	cloves garlic, minced	2
1	egg	1
1⁄2	small onion, finely chopped	1⁄2
1 cup	cooked long-grain white rice	250 mL
1⁄4 cup	chopped fresh flat-leaf parsley	50 mL
2 tbsp	Hungarian paprika (see tip, opposite)	25 mL
2 tsp	salt, divided	10 mL
1⁄2 tsp	dried thyme	2 mL
1⁄4 tsp	freshly ground black pepper	1 mL
Pinch	ground nutmeg	Pinch
6	slices lean bacon, chopped	6
1⁄2	small onion, sliced	1⁄2
1	can (28 oz/796 mL) diced tomatoes, with juice	1
1 cup	dry white wine	250 mL
2 tbsp	tomato paste	25 mL
1 cup	sour cream	250 mL

1. Place pork and beef in a shallow container in the freezer for 30 minutes to facilitate grinding.
2. Meanwhile, bring a large saucepan of salted water to a boil over high heat. Fill a large bowl with cold water. Tear 12 to 14 large leaves from the cabbage and drop half of them into the boiling water. Push them down to immerse them and cook until soft and pliable, about 4 minutes. Remove with a slotted spoon and drop into the cold water to stop the cooking. Repeat with the rest of the cabbage leaves. Remove from water and lay out on a towel to dry. Coarsely chop the remaining cabbage and set aside.
3. Attach the food grinder, with the coarse plate, to the mixer. Set to Speed 4 and run pork and beef through the grinder into the mixer bowl. Add garlic, egg, chopped onion, rice, parsley, paprika, 1 1⁄2 tsp (7 mL) of the salt, thyme, pepper and nutmeg. Remove the food grinder and attach the flat beater. Set to Stir and mix until well combined.
4. Place 1⁄4 cup (50 mL) of the meat mixture at the thick base of each cooked cabbage leaf and roll to enclose the meat (the sides will be open). Secure with toothpicks, if necessary.

5. In a large saucepan, over medium-high heat, cook bacon until almost crisp. Add chopped cabbage and sliced onion; cook, stirring, until cabbage begins to wilt, about 4 minutes. Add tomatoes, wine and tomato paste, stirring to dissolve paste. Bring to a boil, add cabbage rolls and season with 1/2 tsp (2 mL) salt and a pinch of pepper. Reduce heat, cover and simmer until filling is cooked and cabbage is tender, about 45 minutes. With a slotted spoon, transfer cabbage rolls to a plate and keep warm. Add sour cream to the tomato-cabbage mixture and mix well. Taste and adjust seasoning as desired with salt and pepper.
6. With a slotted spoon, transfer tomato-cabbage mixture to a large serving platter. Top with cabbage rolls and the remaining sauce. Serve hot.

Serves 6

Make ahead

Can be prepared up to 1 day ahead. Let cool at room temperature for 1 hour, cover and refrigerate. Reheat, covered, over medium-low heat until heated through.

TIPS

These cabbage rolls taste even better when you reheat them the next day!

Pork shoulder blade used to be known as pork shoulder butt.

For the best flavor, use a good-quality sweet Hungarian paprika, as opposed to the generic paprika brands found on the spice shelf at the grocery store. For a spicier version, look for hot Hungarian paprika.

Ginger-Spiked Tuna Burgers with Asian Coleslaw

FOOD GRINDER • FLAT BEATER

1 lb	fresh tuna steak	500 g
2	egg whites	2
1	clove garlic, finely minced	1
1⁄3 cup	dry bread crumbs	75 mL
1⁄4 cup	finely diced celery	50 mL
1⁄4 cup	finely diced red bell pepper	50 mL
2 tbsp	grated gingerroot	25 mL
1 tsp	finely grated lemon zest	5 mL
2 tsp	freshly squeezed lemon juice	10 mL
1 tsp	salt	5 mL
1⁄4 tsp	freshly ground black pepper	1 mL
1 cup	additional dry bread crumbs, for dredging	250 mL
1⁄4 cup	vegetable oil	50 mL
4	hamburger buns, toasted if desired	4
	Asian Coleslaw (see recipe, opposite)	

TIP
To serve this recipe as an appetizer or a first course, form smaller tuna burgers and top with Asian Coleslaw. For appetizers, make them small enough to be eaten in one or two bites. Make them slightly larger if you're serving them as a sit-down first course.

1. Cut out the blood line on the tuna steak, then cut tuna into 2-inch (5 cm) cubes. Place in a shallow container in the freezer for 30 minutes to facilitate grinding. Attach the food grinder, with the coarse plate, to the mixer. Set to Speed 4 and run tuna though the grinder into the mixer bowl. Add egg whites, garlic, the 1⁄3 cup (75 mL) bread crumbs, celery, red pepper, ginger, lemon zest, lemon juice, salt and pepper to bowl. Remove the food grinder and attach the flat beater and mixer bowl. Set to Stir and mix just until ingredients are well combined. Form into 4 patties no more than 1 inch (2.5 cm) thick. Cover and refrigerate for at least 1 hour or for up to 3 hours.
2. Pour additional bread crumbs onto a plate and gently press tuna patties into the crumbs so that they adhere. In a skillet, heat oil over high heat. Add patties and cook, flipping once, for 3 to 4 minutes per side, or until crispy and browned on both sides.
3. Serve burgers on buns with a topping of Asian coleslaw, or serve coleslaw on the side.

Serves 4

Asian Coleslaw

ROTOR SLICER/SHREDDER

1	carrot, cut into thirds	1
1	serrano or jalapeño pepper, finely diced	1
2 cups	very thinly sliced napa, Chinese or snow cabbage	500 mL
1/2 cup	thinly sliced red bell pepper	125 mL
1/3 cup	thinly sliced red onion	75 mL
1/4 cup	finely chopped fresh cilantro	50 mL
2 tbsp	rice wine vinegar or cider vinegar	25 mL
2 tbsp	vegetable oil	25 mL
1 tsp	liquid honey	5 mL
1 tsp	toasted sesame oil	5 mL
1/2 tsp	salt	2 mL
1/4 tsp	freshly ground black pepper	1 mL

1. Remove the flat beater and attach the slicer/shredder, with the coarse shredder, to the mixer. Set to Speed 4 and grate carrot into a medium bowl. Add serrano pepper, cabbage, red pepper, red onion, cilantro, vinegar, vegetable oil, honey, sesame oil, salt and pepper; toss. Refrigerate for at least 1 hour or for up to 3 hours.

Makes about 2 1/2 cups (625 mL)

Scallops and Asian Noodle Salad

PASTA ROLLER ◆
SPAGHETTI/LINGUINE CUTTER

◆ Large baking sheet

1	clove garlic, minced	1
2 tbsp	soy sauce	25 mL
2 tbsp	rice vinegar	25 mL
1 tbsp	sesame oil	15 mL
2 tsp	grated gingerroot	10 mL
1	recipe Basic Egg Pasta (page 192)	1
	Unbleached all-purpose flour	
1	carrot, sliced into matchstick-size pieces	1
1	red bell pepper, sliced into matchstick-size pieces	1
4 oz	snow peas, thinly sliced on the diagonal	125 g
1 tbsp	sesame seeds	15 mL
1 lb	large sea scallops	500 g
	Salt and freshly ground black pepper	
1 tbsp	vegetable oil	15 mL

TIP

If you crowd the scallops in the skillet while you're sautéing them, they will become tough and will not brown properly. Scallops are at their best slightly undercooked, when their sweetness and natural tenderness shine. Overcooked scallops tend to resemble hockey pucks.

1. In a small bowl, combine garlic, soy sauce, vinegar, sesame oil and ginger. Set aside.
2. Roll pasta to setting 3 and cut into linguine with the spaghetti/linguine cutter (see Pasta Basics, page 190, for instructions on rolling and cutting pasta).
3. Bring a large pot of salted water to a boil over high heat. Add linguine and cook, stirring for the first minute to keep noodles from sticking together, until al dente (tender to the bite), about 3 minutes. Drain and rinse under cold water.
4. In a large bowl, gently toss together linguine, soy sauce mixture, carrot, red pepper, snow peas and sesame seeds. Set aside.
5. Dry scallops with paper towels and season lightly with salt and pepper. In a large skillet, heat oil over medium-high heat. Add scallops in a single layer (you may need to cook them in 2 batches so they aren't too crowded) and cook, flipping once, for 1 to 2 minutes per side, or until lightly browned on both sides and just done in the middle.
6. Divide noodle salad among 4 plates and top with scallops. Serve immediately.

Serves 4

Side Dishes

Carrots with Cilantro and Cumin

ROTOR SLICER/SHREDDER

2 lbs	carrots, quartered	1 kg
	Salt	
1	clove garlic, minced	1
3 tbsp	fresh lemon juice	45 mL
3 tbsp	olive oil	45 mL
1 tbsp	liquid honey	15 mL
1 tbsp	ground cumin	15 mL
1⁄4 cup	chopped fresh cilantro	50 mL
	Freshly ground black pepper	

Partner this North African–inspired side with the Moroccan Merguez sausage (see recipe, page 177) and couscous.

Make ahead

Can be prepared up to 2 hours ahead. Let stand at room temperature.

1. Attach the slicer/shredder, with the thick slicer, to the mixer. Set to Speed 4 and slice carrots into a large bowl.
2. In a large saucepan, cover carrots with water and add salt to taste. Bring to a simmer over medium heat. Cover and cook, stirring occasionally, for 5 to 8 minutes, or until carrots are tender-crisp. Drain.
3. In a large shallow bowl, mix garlic, lemon juice, oil, honey and cumin. Add carrots and cilantro; gently toss together. Season to taste with salt and pepper. Let cool to room temperature.

Serves 8

Variation

For something a little different, substitute 2 tbsp (25 mL) chopped fresh mint for the cumin and cilantro.

Gingered Carrots with Dates

ROTOR SLICER/SHREDDER

1 lb	carrots, quartered	500 g
1⁄4 tsp	salt	1 mL
5	quarter-sized pieces gingerroot, minced	5
3 tbsp	lightly packed light brown sugar	45 mL
2 tbsp	unsalted butter	25 mL
1⁄3 cup	chopped pitted dates	75 mL
	Freshly ground black pepper	

1. Attach the slicer/shredder, with the thick slicer, to the mixer. Set to Speed 4 and slice carrots into a large bowl.
2. Transfer carrots to a large saucepan, cover with water and bring to a simmer over medium heat. Add salt, reduce heat and cook, uncovered, until tender, about 10 minutes. Drain off water and add ginger, brown sugar and butter to pan. Increase heat to medium and cook, stirring, for 3 minutes. Add dates and toss to mix. Cook for 2 minutes to heat the dates. Season to taste with salt and pepper. Serve hot.

Serves 4

Carrot and Zucchini Sauté with Sesame Oil

ROTOR SLICER/SHREDDER

2	carrots, quartered	2
2	large zucchini, quartered crosswise	2
2 tsp	vegetable oil	10 mL
1 tsp	toasted sesame oil (see tip, below)	5 mL
	Salt and freshly ground black pepper	

This dish would pair well with Lemon-Thyme Turkey Burgers (see recipe, page 85) or Ham and Pork Loaf with Apricot Glaze (see recipe, page 82).

TIP
Make sure to look for dark sesame oil. The lighter version will not be toasted and will not have the same flavor.

1. Attach the slicer/shredder, with the thick slicer, to the mixer. Set to Speed 4 and slice carrots into a bowl. Slice zucchini into another bowl.
2. In a large skillet, heat vegetable oil over medium-high heat. Add carrots and sauté for 2 minutes. Add zucchini and sauté until vegetables are tender-crisp, about 2 minutes. Remove from heat and add sesame oil. Season to taste with salt and pepper. Serve hot.

Serves 4

Variation

Try this recipe with blanched sugar snap peas instead of sliced carrots and zucchini for an easy and flavorful side dish.

Fried Zucchini

ROTOR SLICER/SHREDDER

- Preheat oven to 200°F (100°C)
- Deep fryer or heavy saucepan
- Candy/deep-fry thermometer
- Baking sheet, lined with paper towels

2 lbs	zucchini, quartered crosswise	1 kg
2 cups	unbleached all-purpose flour	500 mL
1/2 tsp	salt	2 mL
1 cup	chilled beer (not dark or ale) (approx.)	250 mL
	Vegetable oil	
	Coarse salt	

TIP
For crisp zucchini, make sure the oil is at the correct temperature before you begin frying. Don't crowd the pan with too many zucchini pieces at once — this will lower the heat of the oil and make your zucchini seem oily and soggy.

1. Attach the slicer/shredder, with the thick slicer, to the mixer. Set to Speed 4 and slice zucchini into a large bowl.
2. In another large bowl, whisk together flour and salt. Whisk in beer until smooth. Let stand for 10 minutes. If necessary, thin batter with more beer until it reaches the consistency of crêpe batter.
3. In deep-fryer or heavy saucepan, heat 2 inches (5 cm) of oil to 375°F (190°C). Working in batches, dip zucchini in batter, shaking off excess. Fry until golden brown. With a slotted spoon, transfer to prepared baking sheet to drain. Sprinkle with coarse salt and keep warm in preheated oven. Reheat oil as necessary between batches.

Serves 6 to 8

Zucchini and Fresh Herb Fritters

ROTOR SLICER/SHREDDER

- Preheat oven to 200°F (100°C)
- Baking sheet

2 lbs	zucchini, quartered crosswise	1 kg
1⁄4 tsp	salt	1 mL
Pinch	freshly ground black pepper	Pinch
2	eggs, lightly beaten	2
2	cloves garlic, minced	2
1 cup	thinly sliced green onions	250 mL
1 cup	fresh bread crumbs (see tip, at right)	250 mL
1 tbsp	lightly chopped fresh basil	15 mL
1⁄2 cup	chopped fresh flat-leaf parsley	125 mL
1⁄3 cup	olive oil, divided	75 mL

Serve these fritters with Amish Pot Roast with Egg Noodles (see recipe, page 88) or Rolled Chicken Breasts with Vegetable Stuffing (see recipe, page 87).

1. Attach the slicer/shredder, with the coarse shredder, to the mixer. Set to Speed 4 and shred zucchini into a large colander. Toss with salt and pepper and let stand for 30 minutes to drain. Place colander over a bowl or in the sink and press down on the zucchini to squeeze out as much liquid as possible. Transfer to a large bowl and add eggs, garlic, green onions, bread crumbs, basil and parsley; toss to combine well.
2. In a large nonstick skillet, heat 2 tbsp (25 mL) oil over medium-high heat. When bubbles form around a wooden spoon dipped in the oil, pour in 1⁄4 cup (50 mL) batter for each fritter, making 4 mounds. Flatten with a fork into 4-inch (10 cm) rounds. Cook until bottoms are browned and crusted, about 3 minutes; flip and brown the other sides, about 3 minutes. Reduce heat to medium if fritters are browning too fast. Transfer to baking sheet and keep warm in preheated oven. Repeat with remaining batter, adding and reheating oil as necessary between batches.

Serves 4

TIPS

Fresh bread crumbs bind these fritters together and make them a little easier to flip. To make 1 cup (250 mL) fresh bread crumbs, place about 4 slices day-old bread in a food processor and pulse to fine crumbs.

These fritters are fragile. When flipping them, use the thinnest spatula possible for the best results.

Roasted Root Vegetables with Balsamic Vinaigrette

ROTOR SLICER/SHREDDER

- Preheat oven to 400°F (200°C)
- 2 large baking sheets, lined with parchment paper

2	zucchini, quartered crosswise	2
2	carrots, quartered	2
2	parsnips, cut into thirds	2
2	yellow squash, cut into thirds	2
1	head fennel, cut into quarters	1
2	red bell peppers, each cut into 8 pieces	2
1	red onion, cut into 8 pieces	1
1/4 cup	olive oil	50 mL
1/2 tsp	salt	2 mL
Pinch	freshly ground black pepper	Pinch
1/4 cup	chopped fresh flat-leaf parsley	50 mL
2 tbsp	chopped fresh thyme	25 mL
1 tbsp	chopped fresh chives	15 mL
2 tbsp	balsamic vinegar	25 mL

Any assortment of vegetables can be substituted. Try a mixture of turnips, kohlrabi and celery root.

1. Attach the slicer/shredder, with the thick slicer, to the mixer. Set to Speed 4 and slice zucchini, carrots, parsnips, squash and fennel into a large bowl.
2. Divide sliced vegetables between baking sheets and add bell peppers and onion. Drizzle with olive oil and season with salt and pepper; toss to distribute oil and seasonings. Roast in preheated oven for 25 minutes. Stir with a spatula and roast until tender and golden brown, about 5 minutes.
3. Transfer to a large bowl and toss with parsley, thyme, chives and balsamic vinegar. Taste and adjust seasoning as desired with salt and pepper. Serve hot.

Serves 6

Winter Vegetable Gratin

ROTOR SLICER/SHREDDER

- Preheat oven to 375°F (190°C)
- 10-cup (2.5 L) baking dish, greased

1	head garlic	1
1 tbsp	olive oil	15 mL
1 lb	Yukon gold or red-skinned potatoes, peeled and quartered	500 g
1 lb	parsnips, cut into thirds	500 g
8 oz	turnips, quartered	250 g
2½ cups	whipping (35%) cream	625 mL
1	bay leaf	1
2 tsp	salt	10 mL
¼ tsp	dried thyme	1 mL
¼ tsp	freshly ground black pepper	1 mL
Pinch	ground nutmeg	Pinch
Pinch	cayenne pepper	Pinch
2 cups	shredded Gruyère or Swiss cheese	500 mL
3 tbsp	unsalted butter	45 mL

The richness of this dish is a nice foil to simply roasted meats.

1. Cut the top ¼ inch (0.5 cm) off the garlic. Drizzle with olive oil and wrap in foil. Roast in preheated oven until tender and golden brown, about 40 minutes. Remove from oven and let cool, unwrapped. When garlic is cool enough to handle, squeeze from the bottom to eject soft cloves into a small bowl. (Don't worry if some of them are mashed.) Set aside.
2. Attach the slicer/shredder, with the thick slicer, to the mixer. Set to Speed 4 and slice potatoes, parsnips and turnips into a large bowl. Layer sliced vegetables and roasted garlic in prepared baking dish.
3. In a medium saucepan, bring whipping cream, bay leaf, salt, thyme, pepper, nutmeg and cayenne to a boil over medium-high heat. Reduce heat and simmer, uncovered, for 10 minutes to allow flavors to blend. Discard bay leaf and pour cream mixture over potato mixture. Top with cheese and dot with butter. Bake until vegetables have absorbed most of the cream and the top is browned and crusty, about 1 hour. Let stand for 10 minutes before serving.

Serves 6

Butternut Squash Gratin

ROTOR SLICER/SHREDDER

- Preheat oven to 400°F (200°C)
- Large baking sheet, lined with parchment paper
- 8-cup (2 L) shallow baking dish, lightly greased

2½ lbs	butternut squash	1.25 kg
3 tbsp	vegetable oil, divided	45 mL
2¾ tsp	salt, divided (approx.)	13 mL
Pinch	freshly ground black pepper	Pinch
2 tbsp	unsalted butter	25 mL
4 cups	thinly sliced onions	1 L
3	eggs	3
1½ cups	whipping (35%) cream	375 mL
1 tbsp	minced fresh thyme	15 mL
¼ tsp	ground nutmeg	1 mL

Try this dish at your next Thanksgiving meal as an alternative to sweet potatoes.

Variation

This dish works equally well with other fall squash, such as acorn or Hubbard.

1. Halve squash lengthwise, then cut crosswise into quarters. Scrape out seeds with a large spoon and peel with a vegetable peeler. Attach the slicer/shredder, with the thick slicer, to the mixer. Set to Speed 4 and slice squash into a large bowl. Transfer to baking sheet, drizzle with 1 tbsp (15 mL) of the oil, and season with ¼ tsp (1 mL) salt and pepper. Roast in preheated oven until slightly tender when pierced with a knife, about 20 minutes. Let cool completely. Reduce oven temperature to 350°F (180°C).
2. Meanwhile, in a large skillet, heat butter and the remaining 2 tbsp (25 mL) oil over medium-high heat. Add onions and sauté until tender, about 5 minutes. Reduce heat to low, add ½ tsp (2 mL) salt and cook, stirring occasionally, until onions caramelize to a golden brown, about 20 minutes. Remove from heat.
3. Place half the squash in bottom of prepared baking dish. Sprinkle with salt and pepper to taste, then top with half the onions. Repeat with another layer of squash, salt and pepper and onions.
4. In a medium bowl, whisk together eggs, whipping cream, thyme, 2 tsp (10 mL) salt, nutmeg and pepper to taste. Pour into baking dish and rearrange squash and onions to distribute the custard mixture evenly. Cover loosely with foil. Bake until custard is set and a knife inserted in the center comes out clean, about 55 minutes. Let stand for 10 minutes before serving.

Serves 6

Potato and Red Bell Pepper Gratin

ROTOR SLICER/SHREDDER

- Preheat oven to 375°F (190°C)
- 8-cup (2 L) shallow baking dish, generously greased

1 1/2 lbs	Yukon gold or red-skinned potatoes, peeled and quartered	750 g
2	red bell peppers, halved and seeded	2
3 tbsp	unsalted butter or olive oil	45 mL
1	large onion, thinly sliced	1
1 cup	diced ham	250 mL
1 tsp	salt	5 mL
1/2 tsp	dried thyme	2 mL
1/4 tsp	freshly ground black pepper	1 mL
2 cups	chicken stock	500 mL
1 cup	shredded Asiago cheese	250 mL

This gratin is lower-fat and, with the addition of more ham, it could serve as an entrée.

1. Attach the slicer/shredder, with the thick slicer, to the mixer. Set to Speed 4 and slice potatoes into a large bowl. Slice red pepper into the same bowl.
2. In a skillet, melt butter over medium-high heat. Add onion and sauté until tender, about 4 minutes. Add to potato-pepper mixture and toss. Add ham, salt, thyme and pepper; toss to combine.
3. Transfer to prepared baking dish. Pour in stock and top with cheese. Bake in preheated oven until most of the stock is absorbed, about 45 minutes. Let stand for 10 minutes before serving.

Serves 6

Warm Potato and Sausage Salad

ROTOR SLICER/SHREDDER

2 lbs	Yukon gold potatoes, peeled and quartered	1 kg
1 tbsp	unsalted butter	15 mL
1 lb	sausage, in bulk form	500 g
1 cup	diced onion	250 mL
2 tbsp	unbleached all-purpose flour	25 mL
1/2 cup	cider vinegar	125 mL
2 tbsp	granulated sugar	25 mL
1 tbsp	whole-grain mustard	15 mL
2 tsp	salt	10 mL
1/2 tsp	freshly ground black pepper	2 mL
2 tbsp	chopped fresh parsley	25 mL

This dish is a very hearty side that goes well with simple roasted meat and a green salad.

TIP

For the sausage, try Country Pork (see recipe, page 161) or Hungarian (see recipe, page 172).

1. Attach the slicer/shredder, with the thick slicer, to the mixer. Set to Speed 4 and slice potatoes into a steamer basket. Fit steamer basket over a saucepan of boiling water, cover and steam for 5 to 7 minutes, or until potatoes are just tender. Transfer to a large bowl.
2. In a large skillet, melt butter over medium-high heat. Add sausage and sauté, breaking it up into small chunks, until no longer pink, about 5 minutes. Transfer to a plate with a slotted spoon. Add onion and flour to the fat in the skillet and sauté for 3 minutes. Stir in vinegar, 1/2 cup (125 mL) water, sugar, mustard, salt and pepper; cook until slightly thickened, about 3 minutes.
3. Add onion mixture, sausage and parsley to the potatoes. Mix carefully to avoid mashing the potatoes. Let cool slightly and serve warm.

Serves 8

Scalloped Potatoes with Caramelized Onions

ROTOR SLICER/SHREDDER

- Preheat oven to 375°F (190°C)
- 10-cup (2.5 L) baking dish

1	clove garlic, halved	1
1 tbsp	unsalted butter, softened	15 mL
3 lbs	Yukon gold potatoes, peeled and quartered	1.5 kg
2 cups	milk	500 mL
1 cup	whipping (35%) cream	250 mL
1	bay leaf	1
1⁄4 tsp	dried thyme	1 mL
1 1⁄4 tsp	salt, divided	6 mL
7 tbsp	unsalted butter, divided	105 mL
3	large onions, thinly sliced	3
3	cloves garlic, finely chopped	3
	Freshly ground black pepper	
Pinch	ground nutmeg	Pinch
2 cups	shredded Gruyère or Swiss cheese	500 mL

1. Rub halved garlic clove over inner surface of baking dish, then coat with softened butter. Finely chop garlic clove to use with the others in Step 3.
2. Attach the slicer/shredder, with the thick slicer, to the mixer. Set to Speed 4 and slice potatoes into a large saucepan. Add milk, whipping cream, bay leaf, thyme and 1⁄2 tsp (2 mL) salt; bring to a boil over medium heat. Reduce heat and simmer, uncovered, until potatoes are just tender but not falling apart, about 15 minutes. Discard bay leaf and drain, reserving liquid.
3. Meanwhile, in a large skillet, melt 1⁄4 cup (50 mL) of the butter over medium-high heat. Add onions and 1⁄4 tsp (1 mL) salt; sauté until tender, about 4 minutes. Reduce heat to medium-low and add garlic. Cook, stirring occasionally, until onions are browned and caramelized, about 20 minutes. Remove from heat.
4. Place half the potatoes in prepared baking dish and season with 1⁄4 tsp (1 mL) salt and a pinch of pepper. Top with onions. Add the remaining potatoes and season with 1⁄4 tsp (1 mL) salt and a pinch of pepper. Season the reserved milk with nutmeg and pour just enough over potatoes to reach the second layer. Top with cheese and dot with the remaining 3 tbsp (45 mL) butter. Bake in preheated oven until potatoes have absorbed most of the milk and the top is browned and crusty, about 1 hour. Let stand for 10 minutes before serving.

Serves 6

Potato Latkes

ROTOR SLICER/SHREDDER

- Preheat oven to 250°F (120°C)
- Shallow baking pan fitted with wire rack

1 lb	russet potatoes, peeled and quartered	500 g
1/2	onion, halved	1/2
1	egg, lightly beaten	1
1 tbsp	unbleached all-purpose flour	15 mL
1/2 tsp	salt	2 mL
	Freshly ground black pepper	
1/4 cup	vegetable oil (approx.)	50 mL
	Sour cream (optional)	
	Applesauce (optional)	

These pancakes go well with any of the sausages or meatloaves.

Make ahead

Can be prepared up to 2 hours ahead. Keep at room temperature on a baking sheet lined with paper towels. Reheat on a wire rack set in a shallow baking pan in a 350°F (180°C) oven for about 5 minutes.

1. Attach the slicer/shredder, with the coarse shredder, to the mixer. Set to Speed 4 and shred potatoes into a large bowl. Shred onion into another bowl.
2. Spread shredded potatoes on a kitchen towel and roll up jelly-roll style. Twist tightly to wring out as much liquid as possible. Transfer potatoes back to the large bowl and stir in onion, egg, flour, salt and black pepper to taste.
3. In a nonstick skillet, heat oil over medium-high heat until hot but not smoking. Spoon in 2 tbsp (25 mL) potato mixture for each latke, making 4 mounds. Flatten with a fork into 3-inch (7.5 cm) rounds. Reduce heat to medium and cook until bottoms are browned, about 2 minutes; flip and brown the other sides, about 2 minutes. Transfer to paper towels to drain. Repeat with remaining potato mixture, adding and reheating more oil as needed. Keep warm in preheated oven on a wire rack set in a shallow baking pan. Serve with sour cream and applesauce, if desired.

Serves 4 to 6

Variation

For a sophisticated alternative, try garnishing these crispy cakes with smoked salmon or caviar instead of applesauce.

Rösti Potato Cakes

ROTOR SLICER/SHREDDER

- Preheat oven to 200°F (100°C)
- Large baking sheet

2 lbs	Yukon gold or red-skinned potatoes, peeled and quartered	1 kg
2 tbsp	chopped fresh flat-leaf parsley	25 mL
2 tbsp	chopped fresh chives	25 mL
$\frac{1}{2}$ tsp	salt	2 mL
$\frac{1}{4}$ cup	olive oil (approx.)	50 mL
	Freshly ground black pepper	

Rösti goes well with any grilled or roasted meats.

TIP
Serve rösti as a base for cooked asparagus or roasted meat.

1. Attach the slicer/shredder, with the coarse shredder, to the mixer. Set to Speed 4 and shred potatoes into a large bowl. Toss with parsley, chives and salt.
2. In a large nonstick skillet, heat 2 tbsp (25 mL) of the oil over medium-high heat until hot but not smoking. Spoon in $\frac{1}{3}$ cup (75 mL) potato mixture for each rösti, making 3 mounds. Flatten with a fork into 4-inch (10 cm) rounds and straighten the sides. Season with salt and pepper to taste. Reduce heat to medium and cook until bottoms are browned, about 3 minutes; flip carefully and brown the other sides, about 3 minutes. Transfer to baking sheet and keep warm in preheated oven. Repeat with remaining potato mixture, adding and reheating oil as necessary.

Serves 6

Make ahead

Can be prepared up to 2 hours ahead. Cover and refrigerate. Reheat on a wire rack set in a shallow pan in a 375°F (190°C) oven for about 10 minutes.

Smashed Potatoes

FLAT BEATER

1¾ lbs	Yukon gold potatoes, peeled and quartered	875 g
1¾ tsp	salt, divided	8 mL
1 cup	whipping (35%) cream	250 mL
¼ cup	unsalted butter	50 mL
¼ tsp	freshly ground black pepper	1 mL

Variation

These potatoes lend themselves to a million variations. It's easy to give this standby a complete makeover by adding Parmesan cheese, pesto or tapenade.

1. Place potatoes in a large saucepan and cover with water. Season with 1 tsp (5 mL) salt and bring to boil over medium-high heat. Reduce heat and simmer, uncovered, until tender, about 20 minutes. Drain and return potatoes to the pan over medium heat for a moment to dry them out.
2. Meanwhile, in a small saucepan, heat whipping cream and butter over medium heat until butter is melted and cream is steaming. Keep warm.
3. Transfer potatoes to the mixer bowl. Attach the flat beater and mixer bowl to the mixer. Set to Speed 2 and mix until potatoes are just mashed. Slowly add cream mixture, ¾ tsp (3 mL) salt and pepper; mix until just creamy. Do not overmix: the potatoes should be creamy but still lumpy, and may seem loose. Return to the pan to warm and stiffen over low heat. Serve hot.

Serves 4 to 6

Roasted Garlic Mashed Potatoes

FLAT BEATER

◆ Preheat oven to 350°F (180°C)

2	heads garlic	2
1 tbsp	olive oil	15 mL
1¾ lbs	Yukon gold potatoes, peeled and quartered	875 g
1¾ tsp	salt, divided	8 mL
1 cup	whipping (35%) cream	250 mL
¼ cup	unsalted butter	50 mL
¼ tsp	freshly ground black pepper	1 mL

TIP
Roast more garlic then you need for this recipe. It makes a wonderful spread on toasted Italian or French bread, or an interesting addition to soups and stews.

1. Cut the top ¼ inch (0.5 cm) off the garlic. Drizzle with oil and wrap in foil. Roast in preheated oven until tender and golden brown, about 45 minutes. Remove from oven and let cool, unwrapped. When garlic is cool enough to handle, squeeze from the bottom to eject soft cloves into a small bowl. (Don't worry if some of them are mashed.) Set aside.
2. Place potatoes in a large saucepan and cover with water. Season with 1 tsp (5 mL) salt and bring to boil over medium-high heat. Reduce heat and simmer, uncovered, until tender, about 20 minutes. Drain and return potatoes to the pan over medium heat for a moment to dry them out.
3. Meanwhile, in a small saucepan, heat whipping cream, butter and roasted garlic over medium heat until butter is melted and cream is steaming. Keep warm.
4. Transfer potatoes to the mixer bowl. Attach the flat beater and mixer bowl to the mixer. Set to Speed 2 and mix until potatoes are just mashed. Slowly add cream mixture, ¾ tsp (3 mL) salt and pepper; mix until just creamy. Do not overmix: the potatoes should be creamy but still lumpy, and may seem loose. Return to the pan to warm and stiffen over low heat. Serve hot.

Serves 4 to 6

Yukon Gold Mashed Potatoes with Buttermilk

FLAT BEATER

2¼ lbs	Yukon gold potatoes, peeled and quartered	1.125 kg
2 tsp	salt, divided	10 mL
1 cup	buttermilk, warmed	250 mL
3 tbsp	unsalted butter, softened	45 mL
¼ tsp	freshly ground black pepper	1 mL

This recipe is perfect when you're trying to cut out the fat, but not the flavor.

1. Place potatoes in a large saucepan and cover with water. Add 1 tsp (5 mL) salt and bring to a boil over medium-high heat. Reduce heat and simmer, uncovered, until tender, about 20 minutes. Drain and return potatoes to the pan over medium heat for a moment to dry them out.
2. Transfer potatoes to the mixer bowl. Attach the flat beater and mixer bowl to the mixer. Set to Speed 2 and mix until potatoes are just mashed. Slowly add buttermilk, butter, 1 tsp (5 mL) salt and pepper; mix until just creamy. Do not overmix: the potatoes should be creamy but still lumpy, and may seem loose. Return to the pan to warm and stiffen over low heat. Serve hot.

Serves 6 to 8

Mashed Potatoes with Parsnips

FLAT BEATER

1 1/2 lbs	russet or Yukon gold potatoes, peeled and quartered	750 g
8 oz	parsnips, cut into 2-inch (5 cm) pieces	250 g
	Salt	
1/2 cup	whipping (35%) cream or half-and-half (10%) cream (approx.)	125 mL
1/4 cup	unsalted butter (approx.)	50 mL
	Freshly ground black pepper	
	Ground nutmeg	
	Cayenne pepper	
2 tbsp	chopped fresh flat-leaf parsley	25 mL

This dish goes very well with roasted meats or chicken.

1. Place potatoes and parsnips in a large saucepan and cover with water. Add 1 tsp (5 mL) salt and bring to a boil over medium heat. Reduce heat and simmer, uncovered, until tender, about 20 minutes. Drain and return vegetables to the pan over medium heat for a moment to dry them out.
2. Meanwhile, in a small saucepan, heat whipping cream and butter over medium heat until butter is melted and cream is steaming.
3. Transfer vegetables to the mixer bowl. Attach the flat beater and mixer bowl to the mixer. Set to Stir and slowly add cream mixture. When cream is incorporated, increase to Speed 6 and beat for 1 minute. Don't overbeat or potatoes will become gluey. Taste and adjust seasoning as desired with salt, black pepper, nutmeg and cayenne. Add more butter or cream to taste. Garnish with chopped parsley. Serve hot.

Serves 6

Porcini Mashed Potatoes with Truffle Oil

FLAT BEATER

2½ lbs	red-skinned or Yukon gold potatoes, each peeled and quartered	1.25 kg
	Salt	
⅓ oz	dried porcini or boletus mushrooms	10 g
½ cup	whipping (35%) cream	125 mL
½ cup	unsalted butter	125 mL
	Freshly ground black pepper	
¼ cup	milk, heated (optional)	50 mL
2 tbsp	truffle oil, or to taste	25 mL

Any dried mushroom will work in this recipe. Try dried chanterelles or shiitake mushrooms for a different ethnic twist to your menu.

1. Place potatoes in a large saucepan and cover with cold water. Add 1 tsp (5 mL) salt and bring to a boil over medium-high heat. Reduce heat and simmer, uncovered, until tender, about 20 minutes. Drain and return potatoes to the pan over medium heat for a moment to dry them out.
2. Meanwhile, in a spice grinder, grind mushrooms to a powder. Set aside.
3. In a small saucepan, heat whipping cream and butter over medium heat until butter is melted and cream is steaming.
4. Transfer potatoes to the mixer bowl. Attach the flat beater and mixer bowl to the mixer. Set to Stir and slowly add cream mixture. When cream is incorporated, increase to Speed 4 and beat for 30 seconds. Decrease to Stir, add mushroom powder and mix until incorporated. Season to taste with salt and pepper. (The potatoes will become stiff after the addition of the mushroom powder. Add hot milk to taste if you want them to be lighter.)
5. Transfer to a serving bowl and drizzle with truffle oil. Serve hot.

Serves 6

Maple-Mashed Sweet Potatoes with Toasted Pecans

FLAT BEATER

- Preheat oven to 350°F (180°C)
- 2 baking sheets, one lined with parchment paper

1 1/2 lbs	orange-fleshed sweet potatoes (about 2)	750 g
1 tbsp	vegetable oil	15 mL
1/3 cup	pecan halves, chopped	75 mL
1/4 cup	unsalted butter	50 mL
1/4 cup	pure maple syrup	50 mL
1/4 tsp	salt	1 mL
Pinch	ground nutmeg	Pinch
Pinch	cayenne pepper	Pinch

1. Scrub sweet potatoes; dry and coat with vegetable oil. Pierce in several places with a fork and lay on lined baking sheet. Bake in preheated oven for 45 to 60 minutes, or until tender when pierced with a fork. Let cool slightly, then peel, discarding skins.
2. Meanwhile, spread pecans on unlined baking sheet and bake for about 8 minutes, giving pan a toss halfway through, until toasted. Let cool.
3. Place sweet potatoes, butter, maple syrup, salt, nutmeg and cayenne in the mixer bowl. Attach the flat beater and mixer bowl to the mixer. Set to Stir and mix for 30 seconds. Increase to Speed 4 and beat for 1 minute, until smooth.
4. Transfer to a heated serving dish and top with pecans. Serve hot.

Serves 4

Baked Citrus Sweet Potatoes

FLAT BEATER WIRE WHIP

- Preheat oven to 400°F (200°C)
- Baking sheet
- 13- by 9-inch (3 L) baking dish, greased

6 lbs	orange-fleshed sweet potatoes (about 7 or 8)	3 kg
2	eggs	2
1/2 cup	half-and-half (10%) cream	125 mL
1/3 cup	lightly packed light brown sugar	75 mL
	Grated zest of 1 orange	
1/4 cup	freshly squeezed orange juice	50 mL
1/4 cup	unsalted butter, softened	50 mL
1 tbsp	freshly squeezed lemon juice	15 mL
	Salt and freshly ground black pepper	
1 1/2 cups	pecan halves, coarsely chopped (optional)	375 mL

1. Pierce sweet potatoes in several places with a fork. Place on baking sheet and bake in preheated oven until tender when pierced with a fork, about 55 minutes. Let cool slightly, then peel, discarding skins. Reduce oven temperature to 350°F (180°C).
2. Place sweet potatoes in the mixer bowl. Attach the flat beater and mixer bowl to the mixer. Set to Stir and mix for 30 seconds. Increase to Speed 4 and beat until mashed. Slowly add eggs, cream, brown sugar, orange zest and juice, butter, lemon juice and salt and pepper to taste. Remove the flat beater and attach the whip. Set to Speed 6 and whip until smooth.
3. Transfer to prepared baking dish and sprinkle with pecans, if desired. Bake for 30 to 40 minutes, or until a bit puffy and hot in the center. Serve hot.

Serves 8 to 10

Mushrooms and Wild Rice

ROTOR SLICER/SHREDDER

10 oz	white button or cremini mushrooms	300 g
3 tbsp	unsalted butter	45 mL
½ cup	diced onion	125 mL
3	cloves garlic, minced	3
1 cup	wild rice blend (see tip, at right)	250 mL
½ tsp	salt (approx.)	2 mL
½ tsp	dried thyme	2 mL
¼ tsp	freshly ground black pepper (approx.)	1 mL
1¾ cups	chicken stock	425 mL
1 cup	pecan halves, toasted (see tip, page 155) and chopped	250 mL
¼ cup	chopped fresh flat-leaf parsley	50 mL
3 tbsp	whipping (35%) cream	45 mL
1 tsp	freshly squeezed lemon juice	5 mL

1. Attach the slicer/shredder, with the thick slicer, to the mixer. Set to Speed 4 and slice mushrooms into a bowl.
2. In a large saucepan, melt butter over medium-high heat. Add onion and sauté for 1 minute. Add mushrooms, garlic, rice, salt, thyme and pepper; cook, stirring, until mushrooms begin to give off liquid, about 4 minutes. Add chicken stock and bring to a boil. Reduce heat, cover and simmer for 40 minutes, until rice is tender. Check to see if most of the liquid has evaporated. If rice is still too juicy, simmer uncovered over medium heat to reduce the liquid. Increase heat to medium and stir in pecans, parsley, whipping cream and lemon juice; cook, stirring, until hot. Taste and adjust seasoning as desired with salt and pepper. Serve hot.

Serves 4

TIP

For the wild rice blend, try a mix of wild, black and mahogany rice.

Cornbread and Sausage Stuffing

FLAT BEATER

- Preheat oven to 400°F (200°C)
- 2 large baking sheets
- 13- by 9-inch (3 L) baking pan, greased

Cornbread

2 cups	yellow cornmeal	500 mL
1 cup	unbleached all-purpose flour	250 mL
2 tbsp	granulated sugar	25 mL
1 tbsp	baking powder	15 mL
1 tsp	salt	5 mL
3/4 tsp	baking soda	4 mL
2	eggs	2
1 1/2 cups	buttermilk	375 mL
1/2 cup	unsalted butter, melted	125 mL

4 cups	cubed homestyle white bread (1-inch/2.5 cm cubes)	1 L
1 tbsp	unsalted butter	15 mL
1 1/2 lbs	sausage, in bulk form	750 g
1	large onion, diced	1
2	stalks celery, diced	2
2	eggs, lightly beaten	2
1 cup	pecan halves, toasted (see tip, opposite) and coarsely chopped	250 mL
3/4 cup	dried cranberries	175 mL
1/4 cup	unsalted butter, melted	50 mL
2 tsp	dried thyme	10 mL
2 tsp	dried sage	10 mL
3 1/4 to 4 1/2 cups	low-sodium chicken stock	800 mL to 1.125 L
	Salt and freshly ground black pepper	

1. *Prepare the cornbread:* In a medium bowl, combine cornmeal, flour, sugar, baking powder, salt and baking soda. Place eggs, buttermilk and butter in the mixer bowl. Attach the flat beater and mixer bowl to the mixer. Set to Speed 2 and mix until combined. Reduce to Stir and gradually add dry ingredients; mix until just combined. Transfer to prepared pan, smoothing top. Bake for 20 to 30 minutes, or until edges are lightly browned and a tester inserted in center comes out clean. Let cool completely in pan on a rack. Reduce oven temperature to 350°F (180°C).
2. Cut cornbread into 1-inch (2.5 cm) cubes. Spread on baking sheets with cubed homestyle bread. Bake until dry but not firm, about 25 minutes. Let cool.
3. Meanwhile, in a large skillet, melt the 1 tbsp (15 mL) butter over medium heat. Add sausage and sauté, breaking it up into small chunks, until no longer pink, about 5 minutes. Add onion and celery; sauté until tender, about 2 minutes.
4. In a large bowl, combine dried bread cubes, sausage mixture, eggs, pecans, cranberries, melted butter, thyme and sage. Stir in enough stock to thoroughly moisten but not drench the stuffing. Season to taste with salt and pepper.
5. Transfer to prepared baking dish and cover with buttered foil, buttered side down. Bake until heated through, about 30 minutes. Uncover and bake until top is crisp and golden, about 20 minutes. Serve hot.

Serves 8 to 10

Variations

Substitute an equal amount of dried cherries for the cranberries.

Add 1 cup (250 mL) chopped apples or walnut halves.

Make ahead

Cornbread can be prepared up to 2 days ahead. Wrap tightly in foil and store at room temperature.

TIPS

You could use Farmhouse White Bread (see recipe, page 210) for the homestyle bread if you like.

For the sausage, we suggest Country Pork (see recipe, page 161), Chicken and Apple (see recipe, page 178), Pork and Ham (see recipe, page 163) or Breakfast (see recipe, page 160).

To toast pecan halves, spread out on a baking sheet and bake at 350°F (180°C) for about 8 minutes, giving pan a toss halfway through. Let cool.

Brown Sugar Cinnamon Apples

ROTOR SLICER/SHREDDER

4	Granny Smith apples (about 1 1/2 lbs/750 g), peeled and quartered	4
2 tbsp	unsalted butter	25 mL
1/4 cup	lightly packed light brown sugar	50 mL
1 tsp	freshly squeezed lemon juice	5 mL
1/4 tsp	ground cinnamon	1 mL
Pinch	salt	Pinch

This dish is great with country or breakfast sausage and potato cakes.

1. Attach the slicer/shredder, with the thick slicer, to the mixer. Set to Speed 4 and slice apples into a bowl.
2. In a heavy skillet, heat butter over medium-high heat until foam subsides. Add apples and sauté until liquid has evaporated and apples are tender, about 10 minutes. Stir in brown sugar, lemon juice, cinnamon and salt; cook, stirring, until sugar is dissolved and apples are well coated. Serve hot.

Serves 4

Noodles and Cabbage

PASTA ROLLER • FETTUCCINE CUTTER

2 tbsp	unsalted butter	25 mL
1 cup	sliced onion	250 mL
4 cups	thinly sliced cabbage	1 L
	Salt and freshly ground black pepper	
1/2 cup	whipping (35%) cream	125 mL
1/4 cup	freshly grated Parmesan cheese	50 mL
1 tbsp	poppy seeds	15 mL
1	recipe Basic Egg Pasta (page 192)	1

This dish is a winner paired with Swedish Meatballs (see recipe, page 123) or Ham and Pork Loaf with Apricot Glaze (see recipe, page 82).

TIP
To lower the fat in this dish, substitute an equal amount of chicken stock for the whipping (35%) cream.

1. In a large skillet, melt butter over medium-high heat. Add onion and sauté until tender, about 4 minutes. Add cabbage, 1/2 tsp (2 mL) salt and a pinch of pepper. Reduce heat, cover and simmer, stirring occasionally, until cabbage is tender, about 40 minutes. Add whipping cream and cook until cream has thickened slightly, about 7 minutes. Stir in Parmesan cheese and poppy seeds. Remove from heat. Taste and adjust seasoning as desired with salt and pepper.
2. Roll pasta to setting 5 and cut with the fettuccine cutter (see Pasta Basics, page 190, for instructions on rolling and cutting pasta).
3. Bring a large saucepan of salted water to a boil over high heat. Add pasta and cook until al dente (tender to the bite), about 3 minutes. Drain, add to cabbage mixture and toss to mix. Serve hot.

Serves 6

Sausages

Sausage Basics

There are a million different varieties of sausage. You'll find people enjoying this delicacy in almost every country in the world. With so many varieties available in your local grocery store, why should you bother to make it yourself? One of the most important reasons is control. When you buy sausage in a grocery store, it can be anywhere from 30% to 50% fat and full of preservatives, binders, sugar and salt. And once the meat is ground, it's impossible to determine the quality of the meat products used. By making your own sausage, you can control the level of fat and additives and the quality of meat used.

It's also fun to be able to play with the seasonings. If you like your food spicy, you can add extra heat to your sausage. If you don't, you can tone it down. And if you're trying to cut back on sodium, you can bump up the other flavorings to compensate. You have the ability to alter it to your own taste.

Many of the sausages in this book incorporate fresh herbs. They add a bright note that's often difficult to find in store-bought sausage.

Now that many stand mixers offer food grinder attachments, making your own sausage has never been easier.

Preparing and Storing Bulk Sausage

Many of the sausages in this chapter can be used in bulk form (before the mixture is stuffed into casings). Once you've prepared the bulk sausage, you can feel free to cook it right away, either alone or as part of another recipe. But if you cover and refrigerate it overnight, the flavors will blend and develop, and you'll end up with even better-tasting sausage! Unless the recipe says otherwise, you can store uncooked bulk sausage in the refrigerator for up to 3 days or in the freezer for up to 2 months.

Casings

There are two types of casings: natural and synthetic. Natural casings are made from the intestines of hogs, lambs or cows. These are thoroughly cleaned, dried and packed in salt. They can often be purchased from your local butcher, or can be ordered online from sausage supply companies. They last for several years in the refrigerator. Collagen casings are made from edible protein derived from animal connective tissues. They are not packed in salt. They tend to be smaller in diameter than the natural casings and are often used for breakfast links. Collagen casings will not stretch as natural casings do, so it's important not to over-fill them. They should not be rinsed or soaked prior to filling.

For the beginning sausage maker who is looking to purchase only one type of casing, medium hog casings make the most sense. Because they're easy to work with and their size is versatile, they can be used for most of the sausage recipes in this book.

Preparing the Casing

If you are using salt-packed natural casing, it must be rinsed under cold running water, then soaked for 30 minutes in cool water. Rinse again, holding one end open under the water to remove any salt from the inside, and soak for another 30 minutes in clean cool water.

Stuffing Sausage

The sausage stuffer attachment works with the food grinder. Both must be attached to the mixer following the manufacturer's instructions. Grease the outside funnel of the stuffer with vegetable shortening and slide the full length of the casing onto the funnel. Tie a knot at the end of the casing. Slowly and steadily feed the chilled sausage into the food grinder, tamping down with the stomper as you go. Hold the tied end of the casing in one hand to guide the sausage into the casing. Prick the casing every couple of inches to allow air to escape and the casing to fill evenly. Once the casing is completely filled, twist off the links in alternating directions and tie the open end.

Once you have formed the sausage into links, place the links on a rack over a baking sheet, uncovered, in the refrigerator to dry overnight. This allows the flavors to blend.

Storing Uncooked Links

Unless the recipe indicates otherwise, you can store uncooked links in an airtight container in the refrigerator for up to 3 days or in the freezer for up to 2 months. Frozen sausages should be thawed overnight in the refrigerator before they are cooked.

Cooking Sausage

There are several different ways to cook sausage. Some sausages are traditionally done one way, and some another, but any of the following methods can be used for most of the sausages in this chapter. First cut links apart, then choose your cooking method:

- *Pan-fry* over medium heat.
- *Grill* over medium heat.
- *Roast* in a 425°F (220°C) oven.
- *Poach* in simmering water or chicken stock. (Sausages may be browned in a skillet after they are poached.)
- *Hot- or cold-smoke* sausages following the manufacturer's directions for your smoker.

Whatever the cooking method, pork and beef sausage must be cooked to an internal temperature of 170°F (75°C) and chicken sausage to an internal temperature of 175°F (80°C). To get an accurate reading, insert an instant-read thermometer into the end of the sausage and push it at least 3 inches (7.5 cm) in.

Food Safety and Sanitation

Purchase meat from a reputable butcher and use it the same day. Since ground meat spoils faster than whole cuts, it should always be kept cold. While you're making the sausage, the mixture should never reach a temperature above 50°F (10°C). After you've ground the meat and fat, refrigerate the mixture until you are ready to use it in bulk form or stuff it into casing.

The food grinder has lots of nooks and crannies in which bacteria can grow. This makes the cleaning of your grinder extremely important, so read the manufacturer's instructions carefully. And, of course, always clean your cutting boards and knives well with hot soapy water after each use.

Breakfast Sausage

FOOD GRINDER • FLAT BEATER • SAUSAGE STUFFER (OPTIONAL)

2½ lbs	boneless pork shoulder blade	1.25 kg
8 oz	pork fat	250 g
¼ cup	pure maple syrup	50 mL
1 tsp	salt	5 mL
¼ tsp	dried sage leaves	1 mL
¼ tsp	dried thyme	1 mL
¼ tsp	freshly ground black pepper	1 mL
Pinch	ground allspice	Pinch
4 feet	small hog casing (optional)	120 cm

Prepare Bulk Sausage

1. Cut pork and pork fat into 1-inch (2.5 cm) cubes. Place in a shallow container in the freezer for 30 minutes to facilitate grinding. Attach the food grinder, with the coarse plate, to the mixer. Set to Speed 4 and run pork and fat through the grinder into the mixer bowl.
2. Add maple syrup, salt, sage, thyme, pepper and allspice to the mixer bowl. Remove the food grinder and attach the flat beater and mixer bowl to the mixer. Set to Stir and mix until seasonings are evenly incorporated, about 1 minute.
3. In a skillet, over medium-high heat, sauté a small amount of the sausage mixture until no longer pink. Taste and adjust seasoning as desired.

To Make Links (Optional)

1. Prepare hog casing as directed on page 158.
2. Stuff sausage into casing as directed on pages 158–59 and twist into 3-inch (7.5 cm) links. Coil links and dry overnight, uncovered, on a rack over a baking sheet in the refrigerator.

Makes 3 lbs (1.5 kg)

Lemon-Thyme Turkey Burgers (page 85)

Summer Pasta with Fresh Tomatoes and Basil (page 108)

Maple-Mashed Sweet Potatoes
with Toasted Pecans (page 151)

Focaccia with Caramelized Onions (page 220)

Country Pork Sausage

FOOD GRINDER ◆ FLAT BEATER ◆ SAUSAGE STUFFER (OPTIONAL)

2½ lbs	boneless pork shoulder blade	1.25 kg
8 oz	pork fat	250 g
1 cup	unsweetened apple cider or apple juice	250 mL
2 tbsp	vegetable oil	25 mL
½ cup	diced onion	125 mL
2 tsp	salt	10 mL
1 tsp	crumbled herbes de Provence	5 mL
¾ tsp	freshly ground black pepper	3 mL
½ tsp	dried sage leaves	2 mL
4 feet	small hog casing (optional)	120 cm

Prepare Bulk Sausage

1. Cut pork and pork fat into 1-inch (2.5 cm) cubes. Place in a shallow container in the freezer for 30 minutes to facilitate grinding.
2. Meanwhile, in a medium saucepan, heat cider over medium-high heat and boil until it is reduced to a few tablespoons and liquid looks syrupy, about 15 to 20 minutes. Let cool.
3. In a skillet, heat oil over medium-high heat. Add onion and sauté until tender, about 3 minutes. Set aside.
4. Attach the food grinder, with the coarse plate, to the mixer. Set to Speed 4 and run pork and fat through the grinder into the mixer bowl.
5. Add reduced cider, onion, salt, herbes de Provence, pepper and sage to the mixer bowl. Remove the food grinder and attach the flat beater and mixer bowl to the mixer. Set to Stir and mix until seasonings are evenly incorporated, about 1 minute.
6. In skillet, over medium-high heat, sauté a small amount of the sausage mixture until no longer pink. Taste and adjust seasoning as desired.

To Make Links (Optional)

1. Prepare hog casing as directed on page 158.
2. Stuff sausage into casing as directed on pages 158–59 and twist into 12-inch (30 cm) links. Coil links and dry overnight, uncovered, on a rack over a baking sheet in the refrigerator.

Makes 3 lbs (1.5 kg)

Garlic Fennel Sausage

FOOD GRINDER ◆ SAUSAGE STUFFER (OPTIONAL)

6	cloves garlic, chopped	6
1 tbsp	fennel seeds	15 mL
2 tsp	salt	10 mL
1 tsp	ground sage	5 mL
1/2 tsp	cayenne pepper	2 mL
1/2 tsp	dried thyme	2 mL
1/4 tsp	freshly ground black pepper	1 mL
2 lbs	boneless pork shoulder blade	1 kg
8 oz	pork fat	250 g
1/2 cup	dry red wine	125 mL
3 feet	medium hog casing (optional)	90 cm

Prepare Bulk Sausage

1. Cut pork and pork fat into 1-inch (2.5 cm) cubes and place in a shallow container. In a small bowl, combine garlic, fennel, salt, sage, cayenne pepper, thyme and black pepper; sprinkle over pork. Place in the freezer for 30 minutes to facilitate grinding. Attach the food grinder, with the coarse plate, to the mixer. Set to Speed 4 and run pork and fat through the grinder into a large bowl. Return to the freezer for 15 minutes. Run through the grinder again into a bowl. Using your hands, mix in red wine.
2. In a skillet, over medium-high heat, sauté a small amount of the sausage mixture until no longer pink. Taste and adjust seasoning as desired.

To Make Links (Optional)

1. Prepare hog casing as directed on page 158.
2. Stuff sausage into casing as directed on pages 158–59 and twist into 6-inch (15 cm) links. Coil links and dry overnight, uncovered, on a rack over a baking sheet in the refrigerator.

Makes 2 1/2 lbs (1.25 kg)

Pork and Ham Sausage

FOOD GRINDER ◆ FLAT BEATER ◆ SAUSAGE STUFFER (OPTIONAL)

1 lb	boneless pork shoulder blade	500 g
12 oz	smoked ham	375 g
6 oz	salt pork	175 g
3	cloves garlic, minced	3
1⁄4 cup	minced fresh parsley	50 mL
1 tbsp	liquid honey	15 mL
1 tsp	dried thyme	5 mL
1 tsp	freshly ground black pepper	5 mL
1 tsp	dry mustard	5 mL
1⁄2 tsp	salt	2 mL
1⁄4 tsp	ground allspice	1 mL
1⁄4 tsp	ground cinnamon	1 mL
1⁄4 tsp	ground nutmeg	1 mL
Pinch	cayenne pepper	Pinch
3 feet	medium hog casing (optional)	90 cm

TIP
These sausages are traditionally poached, then browned in a skillet.

Prepare Bulk Sausage

1. Cut pork, ham and salt pork into 1-inch (2.5 cm) cubes. Place in a shallow container in the freezer for 30 minutes to facilitate grinding. Attach the food grinder, with the coarse plate, to the mixer. Set to Speed 4 and run meat through the grinder into the mixer bowl.
2. Add garlic, parsley, honey, thyme, black pepper, dry mustard, salt, allspice, cinnamon, nutmeg and cayenne pepper to the mixer bowl. Remove the food grinder and attach the flat beater and mixer bowl to the mixer. Set to Stir and mix until seasonings are evenly distributed, about 1 minute.
3. In a skillet, over medium-high heat, sauté a small amount of the sausage mixture until no longer pink. Taste and adjust seasoning as desired.

To Make Links (Optional)

1. Prepare hog casing as directed on page 158.
2. Stuff sausage into casing as directed on pages 158–59 and twist into 6-inch (15 cm) links. Coil links and dry overnight, uncovered, on a rack over a baking sheet in the refrigerator.

Makes 2 lbs (1 kg)

Italian Sausage

FOOD GRINDER ◆ SAUSAGE STUFFER (OPTIONAL)

3 lbs	boneless pork shoulder blade	1.5 kg
8 oz	pork fat	250 g
1 ½ tbsp	fennel seeds	22 mL
4 tsp	salt	20 mL
3	cloves garlic, chopped	3
1 tsp	hot pepper flakes	5 mL
½ tsp	cayenne pepper	2 mL
¼ tsp	freshly ground black pepper	1 mL

4 feet	medium hog casing (optional)	120 cm

Prepare Bulk Sausage

1. Cut pork and pork fat into 1-inch (2.5 cm) cubes and place in a shallow container. In a small bowl, combine fennel, salt, garlic, hot pepper flakes, cayenne pepper and black pepper; sprinkle over pork. Place in the freezer for 30 minutes to facilitate grinding. Attach the food grinder, with the coarse plate, to the mixer. Set to Speed 4 and run pork and fat through the grinder into a large bowl. Return to the freezer for 15 minutes. Run through the grinder again into a bowl.

2. In a skillet, over medium-high heat, sauté a small amount of the sausage mixture until no longer pink. Taste and adjust seasoning as desired.

To Make Links (Optional)

1. Prepare hog casing as directed on page 158.

2. Stuff sausage into casing as directed on pages 158–59 and twist into 6-inch (15 cm) links. Coil links and dry overnight, uncovered, on a rack over a baking sheet in the refrigerator.

Makes 3½ lbs (1.75 kg)

Andouille

FOOD GRINDER ◆ FLAT BEATER ◆ SAUSAGE STUFFER (OPTIONAL)

2½ lbs	boneless pork shoulder blade	1.25 kg
8 oz	pork fat	250 g
4	cloves garlic, minced	4
1 tbsp	salt	15 mL
2 tsp	coarsely ground black pepper	10 mL
1½ tsp	dried thyme	7 mL
1 tsp	cayenne pepper	5 mL
4 feet	large hog casing (optional)	120 cm

A Cajun favorite, no gumbo or jambalaya would be complete without andouille (pronounced ond-wee). This spicy sausage is typically smoked, but it's also wonderful when used in bulk form in soups, stews and casseroles.

TIPS

These sausages are traditionally hot-smoked, which can take anywhere from 2½ to 4 hours (see your manufacturer's instructions). Smoked sausages can be stored in an airtight container in the refrigerator for up to 1 week or in the freezer for up to 2 months.

Use andouille as bulk sausage in stuffing for hot peppers and in jambalaya and pasta dishes.

Prepare Bulk Sausage

1. Cut pork and pork fat into 1-inch (2.5 cm) cubes. Place in a shallow container in the freezer for 30 minutes to facilitate grinding. Attach the food grinder, with the coarse plate, to the mixer. Set to Speed 4 and run pork and fat through the grinder into the mixer bowl.
2. Add garlic, salt, black pepper, thyme and cayenne pepper to the mixer bowl. Remove the food grinder and attach the flat beater and mixer bowl to the mixer. Set to Stir and mix until seasonings are evenly distributed, about 1 minute.
3. In a skillet, over medium-high heat, sauté a small amount of the sausage mixture until no longer pink. Taste and adjust seasoning as desired.

To Make Links (Optional)

1. Prepare hog casing as directed on page 158.
2. Stuff sausage into casing as directed on pages 158–59 and twist into 12-inch (30 cm) links. Coil links and dry overnight, uncovered, on a rack over a baking sheet in the refrigerator.

Makes 3 lbs (1.5 kg)

Spiced Habanero Sausage

FOOD GRINDER • FLAT BEATER • SAUSAGE STUFFER (OPTIONAL)

2 lbs	boneless pork shoulder blade	1 kg
8 oz	pork fat	250 g
2	cloves garlic, minced	2
1 to 2	habanero chilies, finely minced (see tip, below)	1 to 2
2½ tbsp	cold water	32 mL
2 tsp	paprika	10 mL
1½ tsp	granulated sugar	7 mL
1½ tsp	salt	7 mL
1 tsp	freshly ground black pepper	5 mL
½ tsp	ground bay leaf	2 mL
½ tsp	ground allspice	2 mL
4 feet	medium hog casing (optional)	120 cm

TIP
Make sure you protect your hands with rubber gloves while handling chilies. And don't rub your eyes!

Prepare Bulk Sausage

1. Cut pork and pork fat into 1-inch (2.5 cm) cubes. Place in a shallow container in the freezer for 30 minutes to facilitate grinding. Attach the food grinder, with the coarse plate, to the mixer. Set to Speed 4 and run pork and fat through the grinder into the mixer bowl.
2. Add garlic, chilies, water, paprika, sugar, salt, pepper, bay leaf and allspice to the mixer bowl. Remove the food grinder and attach the flat beater and mixer bowl to the mixer. Set to Stir and mix until seasonings are evenly distributed, about 1 minute.
3. In a skillet, over medium-high heat, sauté a small amount of the sausage mixture until no longer pink. Taste and adjust seasoning as desired.

To Make Links (Optional)

1. Prepare hog casing as directed on page 158.
2. Stuff sausage into casing as directed on pages 158–59 and twist into 6-inch (15 cm) links. Coil links and dry overnight, uncovered, on a rack over a baking sheet in the refrigerator.

Makes 2¾ lbs (1.375 kg)

Chorizo

FOOD GRINDER • SAUSAGE STUFFER (OPTIONAL)

2 lbs	boneless pork shoulder blade	1 kg
8 oz	pork fat	250 g
8	dried ancho chilies	8
2	cloves garlic, minced	2
1⁄4 cup	cider vinegar	50 mL
2 1⁄2 tbsp	cold water	32 mL
2 tsp	dried oregano	10 mL
1 1⁄2 tsp	granulated sugar	7 mL
1 1⁄2 tsp	ground cumin	7 mL
1 1⁄2 tsp	salt	7 mL
1 tsp	freshly ground black pepper	5 mL
1 tsp	ground cinnamon	5 mL
1⁄4 tsp	ground cloves	1 mL

4 feet	medium hog casing (optional)	120 cm

Chorizo is a spicy sausage made in Spain, Portugal, Mexico and South America. There are a million variations of this recipe; ours is the fresh variety typically used in Mexican dishes. Try frying it up in bulk form and adding it to scrambled eggs. Serve with your favorite salsa and warm flour tortillas for a memorable Sunday brunch.

Prepare Bulk Sausage

1. Cut pork and pork fat into 1-inch (2.5 cm) cubes. Place in a shallow container in the freezer for 30 minutes to facilitate grinding.
2. Meanwhile, remove stem and seeds from dried chilies. Open chilies up so they lie flat. Heat a skillet over medium-high heat and toast chilies for about 20 seconds, pressing them down with a spatula so they make good contact with the pan. Let cool and grind to a fine powder in a food processor or spice grinder.
3. Attach the food grinder, with the coarse plate, to the mixer. Set to Speed 4 and run pork and fat through the grinder into a large bowl. Add ancho chili powder, garlic, vinegar, water, oregano, sugar, cumin, salt, pepper, cinnamon and cloves to the bowl; mix together with your hands. Cover and place in the freezer for 15 minutes. Run through the grinder again into a bowl.
4. In a skillet, over medium-high heat, sauté a small amount of the sausage mixture until no longer pink. Taste and adjust seasoning as desired.

To Make Links (Optional)

1. Prepare hog casing as directed on page 158.
2. Stuff sausage into casing as directed on pages 158–59 and twist into 6-inch (15 cm) links. Coil links and dry overnight, uncovered, on a rack over a baking sheet in the refrigerator.

Makes 2 3⁄4 lbs (1.375 kg)

Spicy Chinese Pork Sausage

FOOD GRINDER • FLAT BEATER • SAUSAGE STUFFER (OPTIONAL)

2 lbs	boneless pork shoulder blade	1 kg
8 oz	pork fat	250 g
2 tbsp	rice wine	25 mL
2 tbsp	chopped green onions	25 mL
2 tbsp	chopped fresh cilantro	25 mL
2 tsp	minced garlic	10 mL
1 tsp	freshly ground Szechuan peppercorns	5 mL
1 tsp	freshly ground black pepper	5 mL
1 tsp	five-spice powder	5 mL
Pinch	ground cinnamon	Pinch

4 feet	small hog casing (optional)	120 cm

Use spicy Chinese sausage to flavor stir-fries and rice dishes. Traditionally, these are stuffed into links and baked until dry, but feel free to use them in bulk form.

Make ahead

Store cooked sausages in an airtight container in the refrigerator for up to 1 week or in the freezer for up to 2 months.

Prepare Bulk Sausage

1. Cut pork and pork fat into 1-inch (2.5 cm) cubes. Place in a shallow container in the freezer for 30 minutes to facilitate grinding. Attach the food grinder, with the fine plate, to the mixer. Set to Speed 4 and run pork and fat through grinder into the mixer bowl.
2. Add rice wine, green onions, cilantro, garlic, Szechuan pepper, black pepper, five-spice powder and cinnamon to the mixer bowl. Remove the food grinder and attach the flat beater and mixer bowl to the mixer. Set to Stir and mix until seasonings are evenly distributed, about 1 minute.
3. In a skillet, over medium-high heat, sauté a small amount of the sausage mixture until no longer pink. Taste and adjust seasoning as desired.

To Make Links (Optional)

1. Prepare hog casing as directed on page 158.
2. Stuff sausage into casing as directed on pages 158–59 and twist into 6-inch (15 cm) links. Coil links and dry overnight, uncovered, on a rack over a baking sheet in the refrigerator.

To Cook

1. Preheat oven to 200°F (100°C.) Cut links apart and arrange on a rack on a baking sheet so that they do not touch. Bake until firm and dry, about 5 hours. Turn off oven and let sausages cool very slowly in oven, about 2 hours. Discard fat.

Makes 2 lbs (1 kg)

Chinese Pork Sausage with Five-Spice Powder

FOOD GRINDER ◆ FLAT BEATER ◆ SAUSAGE STUFFER (OPTIONAL)

2 lbs	boneless pork shoulder blade	1 kg
8 oz	pork fat	250 g
1/4 cup	sweet sherry	50 mL
2 tbsp	lightly packed light brown sugar	25 mL
2 tbsp	soy sauce	25 mL
2 tsp	five-spice powder	10 mL
1 3/4 tsp	salt	8 mL
1/2 tsp	hot pepper flakes	2 mL
4 feet	small hog casing (optional)	120 cm

Chinese sausage is delicious in stir-fries, noodle dishes and rice dishes.

Prepare Bulk Sausage

1. Cut pork and pork fat into 1-inch (2.5 cm) cubes. Place in a shallow container in the freezer for 30 minutes to facilitate grinding. Attach the food grinder, with the fine plate, to the mixer. Set to Speed 4 and run pork and fat through the grinder into the mixer bowl.
2. Add sherry, brown sugar, soy sauce, five-spice powder, salt and hot pepper flakes to the mixer bowl. Remove the food grinder and attach the flat beater and mixer bowl to the mixer. Set to Stir and mix until seasonings are evenly distributed, about 1 minute.
3. In a skillet, over medium-high heat, sauté a small amount of the sausage mixture until no longer pink. Taste and adjust seasoning as desired.

To Make Links (Optional)

1. Prepare hog casing as directed on page 158.
2. Stuff sausage into casing as directed on pages 158–59 and twist into 12-inch (30 cm) links. Coil links and dry overnight, uncovered, on a rack over a baking sheet in the refrigerator.

Makes 2 1/2 lbs (1.25 kg)

Thai Sausage

FOOD GRINDER • SAUSAGE STUFFER (OPTIONAL)

3 lbs	boneless pork shoulder blade	1.5 kg
8 oz	pork fat	250 g
3/4 cup	chopped fresh cilantro	175 mL
3 tbsp	chopped fresh mint	45 mL
3 tbsp	freshly squeezed lime juice	45 mL
2 tbsp	Thai red curry paste (see tip, below)	25 mL
2 tbsp	Southeast Asian fish sauce	25 mL
1 tbsp	chopped garlic	15 mL
1 tbsp	minced gingerroot	15 mL
2 tsp	salt	10 mL
1/2 tsp	hot pepper flakes	2 mL
1/4 tsp	freshly ground black pepper	1 mL
4 feet	medium hog casing (optional)	120 cm

Try using this sausage, in bulk form, in place of the meat in Thai Beef Meatballs with Peanut Dipping Sauce (see recipe, page 11).

TIP

Use as much or as little Thai red curry paste as you like, depending on how hot you like your sausage.

Prepare Bulk Sausage

1. Cut pork and pork fat into 1-inch (2.5 cm) cubes. In a large bowl, combine cilantro, mint, lime juice, curry paste, fish sauce, garlic, ginger, salt, hot pepper flakes and black pepper. Add pork and fat; toss to coat evenly. Place in a shallow container in the freezer for 30 minutes to facilitate grinding. Attach the food grinder, with the fine plate, to the mixer. Set to Speed 4 and run pork and fat through the grinder into a large bowl.
2. In a skillet, over medium-high heat, sauté a small amount of the sausage mixture until no longer pink. Taste and adjust seasoning as desired.

To Make Links (Optional)

1. Prepare hog casing as directed on page 158.
2. Stuff sausage into casing as directed on pages 158–59 and twist into 6-inch (15 cm) links. Coil links and dry overnight, uncovered, on a rack over a baking sheet in the refrigerator.

Makes 3 1/2 lbs (1.75 kg)

Swedish Potato Sausage

FOOD GRINDER • FLAT BEATER • SAUSAGE STUFFER (OPTIONAL)

2 lbs	Yukon gold potatoes, peeled and chopped	1 kg
1 tbsp	freshly squeezed lemon juice	15 mL
1 lb	boneless pork shoulder blade	500 g
1 lb	boneless beef chuck or cross rib	500 g
8 oz	pork fat	250 g
1	clove garlic, minced	1
4 tsp	salt	20 mL
2 tsp	ground caraway seeds	10 mL
1 tsp	dry mustard	5 mL
1/2 tsp	ground allspice	2 mL
1/4 tsp	ground nutmeg	1 mL
1/4 tsp	freshly ground black pepper	1 mL
1	onion, chopped	1
4 feet	medium hog casing (optional)	120 cm

This sausage is a popular breakfast dish in Sweden, but you will also find it on many diner menus in the upper Midwest. Although it's not traditional, in bulk form this sausage also makes a nice hash. Brown in a skillet, breaking it up into small chunks, and serve with poached or fried eggs.

TIP
These sausages are traditionally poached.

Prepare Bulk Sausage

1. Place potatoes in a large bowl and cover with water. Add lemon juice to prevent browning.
2. Cut pork, beef and pork fat into 1-inch (2.5) cubes and place in a shallow container. In a small bowl, combine garlic, salt, caraway, mustard, allspice, nutmeg and pepper; sprinkle over meat mixture. Place in the freezer for 30 minutes to facilitate grinding. Attach the food grinder, with the coarse plate, to the mixer. Set to Speed 4 and run meat mixture, potatoes and onion through the grinder into the mixer bowl.
3. Remove the food grinder and attach the flat beater and mixer bowl to the mixer. Set to Stir and mix until well combined, about 30 seconds.
4. In a skillet, over medium-high heat, sauté a small amount of the sausage mixture until no longer pink. Taste and adjust seasoning as desired.

To Make Links (Optional)

1. Prepare hog casing as directed on page 158.
2. Stuff sausage into casing as directed on pages 158–59 and twist into 5- or 6-inch (13 or 15 cm) links. Coil links and dry overnight, uncovered, on a rack over a baking sheet in the refrigerator.

Makes 3 1/2 lbs (1.75 kg)

Hungarian Sausage

FOOD GRINDER ◆ SAUSAGE STUFFER (OPTIONAL)

1 1/2 lbs	boneless pork shoulder blade	750 g
12 oz	boneless beef chuck or cross rib	375 g
8 oz	pork fat	250 g
3	cloves garlic, minced	3
2 1/2 tbsp	Hungarian sweet paprika	32 mL
1 tbsp	salt	15 mL
1/2 tsp	ground allspice	2 mL
1/4 tsp	ground cloves	1 mL
1/4 tsp	freshly ground black pepper	1 mL
1/2 cup	cold water	125 mL
3 feet	medium hog casing (optional)	90 cm

The hallmark of this sausage is lots of good-quality sweet Hungarian paprika and garlic. Try it in your favorite goulash recipe. It's also great in stuffed peppers and cabbage rolls.

Prepare Bulk Sausage

1. Cut pork, beef and pork fat into 1-inch (2.5 cm) cubes and place in a shallow container. In a small bowl, combine garlic, paprika, salt, allspice, cloves and pepper; sprinkle over meat mixture. Place in the freezer for 30 minutes to facilitate grinding. Attach the food grinder, with the coarse plate, to the mixer. Set to Speed 4 and run meat mixture through the grinder into a large bowl. Stir in water.
2. In a skillet, over medium-high heat, sauté a small amount of the sausage mixture until no longer pink. Taste and adjust seasoning as desired.

To Make Links (Optional)

1. Prepare hog casing as directed on page 158.
2. Stuff sausage into casing as directed on pages 158–59 and twist into 6-inch (15 cm) links. Coil links and dry overnight, uncovered, on a rack over a baking sheet in the refrigerator.

Makes 2 lbs (1 kg)

Bratwurst

FOOD GRINDER ◆ SAUSAGE STUFFER

3½ feet	medium hog casing	105 cm
1½ lbs	boneless pork shoulder blade	750 g
1 lb	boneless veal shoulder	500 g
8 oz	pork fat	250 g
½ cup	milk	125 mL
2 tsp	salt	10 mL
1 tsp	granulated sugar	5 mL
1 tsp	ground caraway seeds	5 mL
¾ tsp	finely ground black pepper	3 mL
½ tsp	ground allspice	2 mL
½ tsp	ground nutmeg	2 mL
½ tsp	dried marjoram	2 mL

1. Prepare hog casing as directed on page 158.
2. Cut pork, veal and pork fat into 1-inch (2.5 cm) cubes. Place in a shallow container in the freezer for 30 minutes to facilitate grinding. Attach the food grinder, with the fine plate, to the mixer. Set to Speed 4 and run meat and fat through grinder into a large bowl. Add milk, salt, sugar, caraway, pepper, allspice, nutmeg and marjoram; mix together with your hands. Cover and place in the freezer for 15 minutes. Run through the grinder again into a bowl.
3. In a skillet, over medium-high heat, sauté a small amount of the sausage mixture until no longer pink. Taste and adjust seasoning as desired.
4. Stuff sausage into casing as directed on pages 158–59 and twist into 6-inch (15 cm) links. Coil links and dry overnight, uncovered, on a rack over a baking sheet in the refrigerator.

Makes 3 lbs (1.5 kg)

Kielbasa

FOOD GRINDER ◆ FLAT BEATER ◆ SAUSAGE STUFFER

4 feet	medium hog casing	120 cm
1 lb	boneless pork shoulder blade	500 g
8 oz	boneless beef chuck or cross rib	250 g
8 oz	boneless veal shoulder	250 g
8 oz	pork fat	250 g
2	cloves garlic, minced	2
1 tbsp	paprika	15 mL
1¾ tsp	salt	8 mL
1 tsp	ground coriander	5 mL
½ tsp	freshly ground black pepper	2 mL
¼ tsp	dried thyme	1 mL
¼ tsp	cayenne pepper	1 mL
¼ tsp	dried marjoram	1 mL

Kielbasa is the Polish word for sausage. It can be used in any dish that calls for a mild country sausage.

1. Prepare hog casing as directed on page 158.
2. Cut pork, beef, veal and pork fat into 1-inch (2.5 cm) cubes. Place in a shallow container in the freezer for 30 minutes to facilitate grinding. Attach the food grinder, with the coarse plate, to the mixer. Set to Speed 4 and run meat and fat through the grinder into the mixer bowl.
3. Add garlic, paprika, salt, coriander, black pepper, thyme, cayenne pepper and marjoram to the mixer bowl. Remove the food grinder and attach the flat beater and mixer bowl to the mixer. Set to Stir and mix until seasonings are evenly incorporated, about 1 minute.
4. In a skillet, over medium-high heat, sauté a small amount of the sausage mixture until no longer pink. Taste and adjust seasoning as desired.
5. Stuff sausage into casing as directed on pages 158–59 and twist into 12-inch (30 cm) links. Coil links and dry overnight, uncovered, on a rack over a baking sheet in the refrigerator.

Makes 2½ lbs (1.25 kg)

Garlic Kielbasa

FOOD GRINDER ◆ FLAT BEATER ◆ SAUSAGE STUFFER

4 feet	large hog casing	120 cm
1 1/2 lbs	boneless pork shoulder blade	750 g
8 oz	boneless beef chuck or cross rib	250 g
8 oz	boneless veal shoulder	250 g
8 oz	pork fat	250 g
6	cloves garlic, minced	6
1 1/2 tbsp	paprika	22 mL
2 tsp	freshly ground black pepper	10 mL
2 tsp	salt	10 mL
2 tsp	ground coriander	10 mL
2 tsp	dried marjoram	10 mL
1/2 tsp	ground allspice	2 mL

TIP
These sausages are traditionally hot- or cold-smoked. They take anywhere from 2 to 4 hours to hot-smoke and about 12 hours to cold-smoke (see your manufacturer's instructions). Smoked sausages can be stored in an airtight container in the refrigerator for up to 1 week or in the freezer for up to 2 months.

1. Prepare hog casing as directed on page 158.
2. Cut pork, beef, veal and pork fat into 1-inch (2.5 cm) cubes. Place in a shallow container in the freezer for 30 minutes to facilitate grinding. Attach the food grinder, with the coarse plate, to the mixer. Set to Speed 4 and run meat and fat through the grinder into the mixer bowl.
3. Add garlic, paprika, pepper, salt, coriander, marjoram and allspice to the mixer bowl. Remove the food grinder and attach the flat beater and mixer bowl to the mixer. Set to Stir and mix until seasonings are evenly incorporated, about 1 minute.
4. In a skillet, over medium-high heat, sauté a small amount of the sausage mixture until no longer pink. Taste and adjust seasoning as desired.
5. Stuff sausage into casing as directed on pages 158–59 and twist into 12-inch (30 cm) links. Coil links and dry overnight, uncovered, on a rack over a baking sheet in the refrigerator.

Makes 3 lbs (1.5 kg)

Lamb, Mustard and Rosemary Sausage

FOOD GRINDER ◆ FLAT BEATER ◆ SAUSAGE STUFFER (OPTIONAL)

2 lbs	trimmed boneless lamb shoulder or leg	1 kg
8 oz	lamb fat (reserved from trimming, plus more if necessary)	250 g
4	cloves garlic, minced	4
1⁄2 cup	cold water	125 mL
2 1⁄2 tbsp	Dijon mustard	32 mL
2 tbsp	chopped fresh rosemary	25 mL
2 tsp	salt	10 mL
1 1⁄2 tsp	granulated sugar	7 mL
1 tsp	freshly ground black pepper	5 mL
4 feet	medium hog casing (optional)	120 cm

Prepare Bulk Sausage

1. Cut lamb and lamb fat into 1-inch (2.5 cm) cubes. Place in a shallow container in the freezer for 30 minutes to facilitate grinding. Attach the food grinder, with the coarse plate, to the mixer. Set to Speed 4 and run lamb and fat through the grinder into the mixer bowl.
2. Add garlic, water, mustard, rosemary, salt, sugar and pepper to the mixer bowl. Remove the food grinder and attach the flat beater and mixer bowl to the mixer. Set to Stir and mix until seasonings are evenly incorporated, about 1 minute.
3. In a skillet, over medium-high heat, sauté a small amount of the sausage mixture until no longer pink. Taste and adjust seasoning as desired.

To Make Links (Optional)

1. Prepare hog casing as directed on page 158.
2. Stuff sausage into casing as directed on pages 158–59 and twist into 6-inch (15 cm) links. Coil links and dry overnight, uncovered, on a rack over a baking sheet in the refrigerator.

Makes 2 3⁄4 lbs (1.375 kg)

Merguez

FOOD GRINDER • SAUSAGE STUFFER (OPTIONAL)

2 lbs	trimmed boneless lamb shoulder or leg	1 kg
8 oz	lamb fat (reserved from trimming, plus more if necessary)	250 g
4	cloves garlic, minced	4
1/2 cup	cold water	125 mL
2 tbsp	paprika	25 mL
2 tsp	salt	10 mL
1 1/2 tsp	granulated sugar	7 mL
1 1/2 tsp	ground cumin	7 mL
1 tsp	freshly ground black pepper	5 mL
1 tsp	ground fennel seeds	5 mL
1 tsp	ground coriander	5 mL
1 tsp	cayenne pepper	5 mL
1/2 tsp	ground allspice	2 mL
4 feet	medium hog casing (optional)	120 cm

This spicy North African lamb sausage is great with couscous or lentils or slow-cooked with hearty greens.

Prepare Bulk Sausage

1. Cut lamb and lamb fat into 1-inch (2.5 cm) cubes. Place in a shallow container in the freezer for 30 minutes to facilitate grinding. Attach the food grinder, with the coarse plate, to the mixer. Set to Speed 4 and run lamb and fat through the grinder into a large bowl. Add garlic, water, paprika, salt, sugar, cumin, black pepper, fennel, coriander, cayenne pepper and allspice to the bowl; mix together with your hands. Cover and place in the freezer for 15 minutes. Run through the grinder again into a bowl.
2. In a skillet, over medium-high heat, sauté a small amount of the sausage mixture until no longer pink. Taste and adjust seasoning as desired.

To Make Links (Optional)

1. Prepare hog casing as directed on page 158.
2. Stuff sausage into casing as directed on pages 158–59 and twist into 6-inch (15 cm) links. Coil links and dry overnight, uncovered, on a rack over a baking sheet in the refrigerator.

Makes 2 3/4 lbs (1.375 kg)

Chicken and Apple Sausage

FOOD GRINDER • FLAT BEATER • SAUSAGE STUFFER (OPTIONAL)

2 lbs	boneless chicken thighs, cut into 1-inch (2.5 cm) cubes (see tip, below)	1 kg
¾ cup	unsweetened apple cider	175 mL
1	Granny Smith apple, peeled and grated	1
2 tsp	salt	10 mL
1 tsp	dried sage leaves	5 mL
½ tsp	finely ground black pepper	2 mL
½ tsp	ground allspice	2 mL
¼ tsp	ground ginger	1 mL
Pinch	ground cinnamon	Pinch
Pinch	ground nutmeg	Pinch
3 feet	medium hog casing (optional)	90 cm

TIP
Don't trim away the fat or skin from the chicken thighs when you are cutting them into cubes. If purchasing bone-in thighs, you'll need about 2¾ lbs (1.375 kg).

Prepare Bulk Sausage

1. Place chicken in a shallow container in the freezer for 1 hour to facilitate grinding.
2. Meanwhile, in a medium saucepan, heat cider over medium-high heat and boil for 10 to 15 minutes, or until reduced to 2 tbsp (15 mL) and liquid looks syrupy. Let cool.
3. Attach the food grinder, with the fine plate, to the mixer. Set to Speed 4 and run chicken through the grinder into the mixer bowl.
4. Add reduced cider, apple, salt, sage, pepper, allspice, ginger, cinnamon and nutmeg to the mixer bowl. Remove the food grinder and attach the flat beater and mixer bowl to the mixer. Set to Stir and mix until seasonings are evenly incorporated, about 1 minute.
5. In a skillet, over medium-high heat, sauté a small amount of the sausage mixture until no longer pink. Taste and adjust seasoning as desired.

To Make Links (Optional)

1. Prepare hog casing as directed on page 158.
2. Stuff sausage into casing as directed on pages 158–59 and twist into 3-inch (7.5 cm) links. Coil links and dry overnight, uncovered, on a rack over a baking sheet in the refrigerator.

Makes 2¼ lbs (1.125 kg)

Chicken and Thyme Sausage

FOOD GRINDER • FLAT BEATER • SAUSAGE STUFFER (OPTIONAL)

2½ lbs	boneless chicken thighs, cut into 1-inch (2.5 cm) cubes (see tip, below)	1.25 kg
1 tbsp	unsalted butter	15 mL
1 cup	finely chopped onion	250 mL
½ cup	dry white wine	125 mL
1½ tbsp	finely chopped fresh thyme (or 2½ tsp/12 mL dried)	22 mL
2½ tsp	salt	12 mL
½ tsp	freshly ground black pepper	2 mL
3 feet	medium hog casing (optional)	90 cm

TIP

Don't trim away the fat or skin from the chicken thighs when you are cutting them into cubes. If purchasing bone-in thighs, you'll need about 3½ lbs (1.75 kg).

Prepare Bulk Sausage

1. Place chicken in a shallow container in the freezer for 1 hour to facilitate grinding.
2. Meanwhile, in a skillet, melt butter over medium heat. Add onion and sauté until tender and lightly browned, about 5 minutes. Let cool.
3. Attach the food grinder, with the fine plate, to the mixer. Set to Speed 4 and run chicken through the grinder into the mixer bowl.
4. Add onion, wine, thyme, salt and pepper to the mixer bowl. Remove the food grinder and attach the flat beater and mixer bowl to the mixer. Set to Stir and mix until seasonings are evenly incorporated, about 1 minute.
5. In a skillet, over medium-high heat, sauté a small amount of the sausage mixture until no longer pink. Taste and adjust seasoning as desired.

To Make Links (Optional)

1. Prepare hog casing as directed on page 158.
2. Stuff sausage into casing as directed on pages 158–59 and twist into 6-inch (15 cm) links. Coil links and dry overnight, uncovered, on a rack over a baking sheet in the refrigerator.

Makes 2¾ lbs (1.375 kg)

Chicken Bratwurst

FOOD GRINDER ◆ SAUSAGE STUFFER

3 feet	medium hog casing	90 cm
2½ lbs	boneless chicken thighs, cut into 1-inch (2.5 cm) cubes (see tip, below)	1.25 kg
½ cup	milk	125 mL
2½ tsp	salt	12 mL
1 tsp	ground caraway seeds	5 mL
½ tsp	freshly ground black pepper	2 mL
½ tsp	ground allspice	2 mL
¼ tsp	ground ginger	1 mL
Pinch	ground nutmeg	Pinch

TIP
Don't trim away the fat or skin from the chicken thighs when you are cutting them into cubes. If purchasing bone-in thighs, you'll need about 3½ lbs (1.75 kg).

1. Prepare hog casing as directed on page 158.
2. Place chicken in a shallow container in the freezer for 1 hour to facilitate grinding. Attach the food grinder, with the fine plate, to the mixer. Set to Speed 4 and run chicken through the grinder into a large bowl. Add milk, salt, caraway, pepper, allspice, ginger and nutmeg; mix together with your hands. Cover and place in the freezer for 30 minutes. Run through the grinder again into a bowl.
3. In a skillet, over medium-high heat, sauté a small amount of the sausage mixture until no longer pink. Taste and adjust seasoning as desired.
4. Stuff sausage into casing as directed on pages 158–59 and twist into 6-inch (15 cm) links. Coil links and dry overnight, uncovered, on a rack over a baking sheet in the refrigerator.

Makes 2¾ lbs (1.375 kg)

Chicken Bockwurst

FOOD GRINDER ◆ FLAT BEATER ◆ SAUSAGE STUFFER

2 feet	small hog casing	60 cm
2 lbs	boneless chicken thighs, cut into 1-inch (2.5 cm) pieces (see tip, below)	1 kg
1	egg, beaten	1
1/2 cup	minced onion	125 mL
1/4 cup	sour cream	50 mL
1 tbsp	minced fresh chives	15 mL
1 tbsp	minced fresh flat-leaf parsley	15 mL
1 tsp	salt	5 mL
1/4 tsp	ground cloves	1 mL
1/4 tsp	freshly ground black pepper	1 mL
Pinch	cayenne pepper	Pinch
Pinch	ground nutmeg	Pinch

Bock means "he-goat" in German, goat possibly being the original meat in this sausage. Wurst, of course, means sausage. Today, bockwurst is generally made with veal.

1. Prepare hog casing as directed on page 158.
2. Place chicken in a shallow container in the freezer for 1 hour to facilitate grinding. Attach the food grinder, with the fine plate, to the mixer. Set to Speed 4 and run chicken through the grinder into a large bowl. Add egg, onion, sour cream, chives, parsley, salt, cloves, black pepper, cayenne pepper and nutmeg to the bowl; mix together with your hands. Cover and place in the freezer for 30 minutes. Run through the grinder again into a bowl.
3. In a skillet, over medium-high heat, sauté a small amount of the sausage mixture until no longer pink. Taste and adjust seasoning as desired.
4. Stuff sausage into casing as directed on pages 158–59 and twist into 4-inch (10 cm) links. Coil links and dry overnight, uncovered, on a rack over a baking sheet in the refrigerator.

Makes 2 lbs (1 kg)

TIPS

Don't trim away the fat or skin from the chicken thighs when you are cutting them into cubes. If purchasing bone-in thighs, you'll need about 2 3/4 lbs (1.375 kg).

These sausages are traditionally poached.

Country Turkey Sausage

FOOD GRINDER • FLAT BEATER • SAUSAGE STUFFER (OPTIONAL)

2 lbs	boneless turkey, light and dark meat (see tip, below)	1 kg
4 oz	pork fat	125 g
2 tsp	chopped fresh flat-leaf parsley	10 mL
1 ½ tsp	salt	7 mL
1 tsp	dried marjoram	5 mL
1 tsp	dried thyme	5 mL
1 tsp	freshly ground black pepper	5 mL
½ tsp	dried sage leaves	2 mL
¼ tsp	cayenne pepper	1 mL
3 feet	small hog casing (optional)	90 cm

TIPS

Don't trim away the fat or skin from the turkey when you are cutting it into cubes. If purchasing bone-in turkey, you'll need about 2¾ lbs (1.375 kg).

These sausages are traditionally poached, then browned in a skillet.

Prepare Bulk Sausage

1. Cut turkey and pork fat into 1-inch (2.5 cm) cubes. Place in a shallow container in the freezer for 30 minutes to facilitate grinding. Attach the food grinder, with the fine plate, to the mixer. Set to Speed 4 and run turkey and pork fat through the grinder into a large bowl. Add parsley, salt, marjoram, thyme, black pepper, sage and cayenne pepper; mix together with your hands. Cover and place in the freezer for 15 minutes. Run through the grinder again into a bowl.
2. In a skillet, over medium-high heat, sauté a small amount of the sausage mixture until no longer pink. Taste and adjust seasoning as desired.

To Make Links (Optional)

1. Prepare hog casing as directed on page 158.
2. Stuff sausage into casing as directed on pages 158–59 and twist into 3-inch (7.5 cm) links. Coil links and dry overnight, uncovered, on a rack over a baking sheet in the refrigerator.

Makes 2 lbs (1 kg)

Variation

If you're going to use the sausage in bulk form, try adding chopped dried apple, dried cranberries or chopped dried apricots to the sausage mixture.

Italian Turkey Sausage

FOOD GRINDER ◆ SAUSAGE STUFFER (OPTIONAL)

1 tbsp	chopped garlic	15 mL
2 tsp	salt	10 mL
1 1⁄2 tsp	whole fennel seeds	7 mL
1 tsp	crushed fennel seeds	5 mL
1⁄2 tsp	cayenne pepper	2 mL
1⁄4 tsp	freshly ground black pepper	1 mL
3 lbs	boneless turkey thighs, cut into 1-inch (2.5 cm) cubes (see tip, below)	1.5 kg

4 feet	medium hog casing (optional)	120 cm

TIP
Don't trim away the fat or skin from the turkey thighs when you are cutting them into cubes. If purchasing bone-in thighs, you'll need about 4 lbs (2 kg).

Prepare Bulk Sausage

1. In a small bowl, combine garlic, salt, fennel, cayenne pepper and black pepper. Place turkey in a shallow container and sprinkle with spice mixture. Place in the freezer for 30 minutes to facilitate grinding. Attach the food grinder, with the coarse plate, to the mixer. Set to Speed 4 and run turkey through the grinder into a large bowl.
2. In a skillet, over medium-high heat, sauté a small amount of the sausage mixture until no longer pink. Taste and adjust seasoning as desired.

To Make Links (Optional)

1. Prepare hog casing as directed on page 158.
2. Stuff sausage into casing as directed on pages 158–59 and twist into 6-inch (15 cm) links. Coil links and dry overnight, uncovered, on a rack over a baking sheet in the refrigerator.

Makes 3 1⁄2 lbs (1.75 kg)

Duck Sausage

FOOD GRINDER • FLAT BEATER • SAUSAGE STUFFER (OPTIONAL)

1 1/2 lbs	boneless duck, with leg skin, cut into 1-inch (2.5 cm) cubes	750 g
2 tbsp	unsalted butter	25 mL
1/2 cup	minced onion	125 mL
2	cloves garlic, minced	2
3/4 tsp	salt	3 mL
1/2 tsp	dried marjoram	2 mL
1/2 tsp	dried basil	2 mL
1/4 tsp	ground allspice	1 mL
1/4 tsp	freshly ground black pepper	1 mL
2 tbsp	red wine	25 mL

2 feet	small hog casing (optional)	60 cm

Duck sausage is great on pizza and in stir-fries and risottos.

TIP

When you are cutting duck into cubes, discard the breast skin, which has a lot of fat. If purchasing bone-in duck, you'll need about 3 lbs (1.5 kg).

Prepare Bulk Sausage

1. Place duck in a shallow container in the freezer for 30 minutes to facilitate grinding.
2. Meanwhile, in a skillet, melt butter over medium heat. Add onion and sauté until translucent, about 4 minutes. Add garlic, salt, marjoram, basil, allspice and pepper; sauté for 1 minute. Let cool.
3. Attach the food grinder, with the fine plate, to the mixer. Set to Speed 4 and run duck through the grinder into the mixer bowl.
4. Add onion mixture and wine to the mixer bowl. Remove the food grinder and attach the flat beater and mixer bowl to the mixer. Set to Stir and mix until well combined.
5. In a skillet, over medium-high heat, sauté a small amount of the sausage mixture until no longer pink. Taste and adjust seasoning as desired.

To Make Links (Optional)

1. Prepare hog casing as directed on page 158.
2. Stuff sausage into casing as directed on pages 158–59 and twist into 6-inch (15 cm) links. Coil links and dry overnight, uncovered, on a rack over a baking sheet in the refrigerator.

Makes 1 1/2 lbs (750 g)

Variation

Try mixing up the seasonings you use in these sausages. Other possibilities include thyme, herbes de Provence, rosemary, sage, savory, paprika, five-spice powder and quatre épices (French four-spice mixture).

Venison Sausage

FOOD GRINDER ◆ FLAT BEATER ◆ SAUSAGE STUFFER (OPTIONAL)

1¾ lbs	boneless venison shoulder	875 g
4 oz	pork fat	125 g
¼ cup	chopped fresh flat-leaf parsley	50 mL
¼ cup	white wine	50 mL
3	cloves garlic, minced	3
2 tsp	salt	10 mL
1 tsp	dried thyme	5 mL
1 tsp	dried sage leaves	5 mL
1 tsp	freshly ground black pepper	5 mL
½ tsp	ground allspice	2 mL
¼ tsp	cayenne pepper	1 mL
3 feet	medium hog casing (optional)	90 cm

Prepare Bulk Sausage

1. Cut venison and pork fat into 1-inch (2.5 cm) cubes. Place in a shallow container in the freezer for 30 minutes to facilitate grinding. Attach the food grinder, with the coarse plate, to the mixer. Set to Speed 4 and run venison and pork fat through the grinder into the mixer bowl.
2. Add parsley, wine, garlic, salt, thyme, sage, black pepper, allspice and cayenne pepper to the mixer bowl. Remove the food grinder and attach the flat beater and mixer bowl to the mixer. Set to Stir and mix until seasonings are evenly incorporated, about 1 minute.
3. In a skillet, over medium-high heat, sauté a small amount of the sausage mixture until no longer pink. Taste and adjust seasoning as desired.

To Make Links (Optional)

1. Prepare hog casing as directed on page 158.
2. Stuff sausage into casing as directed on pages 158–59 and twist into 12-inch (30 cm) links. Coil links and dry overnight, uncovered, on a rack over a baking sheet in the refrigerator.

Makes 2 lbs (1 kg)

Salmon Sausage

FOOD GRINDER ◆ FLAT BEATER ◆ SAUSAGE STUFFER (OPTIONAL)

$1\frac{1}{2}$ lbs	salmon, skinned and cut into 1-inch (2.5 cm) cubes	750 g
1 tbsp	unsalted butter	15 mL
$\frac{1}{2}$ cup	minced onion	125 mL
1	egg white	1
$\frac{1}{4}$ cup	finely diced sun-dried tomatoes	50 mL
2 tbsp	chopped capers	25 mL
1 tbsp	chopped fresh chives	15 mL
1 tbsp	chopped fresh flat-leaf parsley	15 mL
	Grated zest of 1 lemon	
1 tbsp	freshly squeezed lemon juice	15 mL
$1\frac{1}{2}$ tsp	salt	7 mL
$\frac{1}{2}$ tsp	freshly ground black pepper	2 mL
Pinch	hot pepper flakes	Pinch
2 feet	small hog casing (optional)	60 cm

TIPS

Because of the perishable nature of seafood, these sausages should be cooked and eaten the day they are made.

After they are poached, the sausages may be grilled or broiled to crisp the skins.

Prepare Bulk Sausage

1. Place salmon in a shallow container in the freezer for 30 minutes to facilitate grinding.
2. Meanwhile, in a skillet, melt butter over medium-high heat. Add onion and sauté until tender, about 4 minutes. Let cool.
3. Attach the food grinder, with the coarse plate, to the mixer. Set to Speed 4 and run salmon through the grinder into the mixer bowl.
4. Add onion, egg white, sun-dried tomato, capers, chives, parsley, lemon zest, lemon juice, salt, pepper and hot pepper flakes to the mixer bowl. Remove the food grinder and attach the flat beater and mixer bowl to the mixer. Set to Stir and mix until seasonings are evenly incorporated, about 1 minute.
5. In a skillet, over medium-high heat, sauté a small amount of the sausage mixture until fish is opaque. Taste and adjust seasoning as desired.

To Make Links (Optional)

1. Prepare hog casing as directed on page 158.
2. Stuff sausage into casing as directed on pages 158–59 and twist into 4-inch (10 cm) links. Coil links and dry for 4 hours, uncovered, on a rack over a baking sheet in the refrigerator.

To Cook

1. Cut links apart and poach in simmering water or chicken stock until sausage reaches an internal temperature of 170°F (75°C), about 7 minutes.

Makes $1\frac{1}{2}$ lbs (750 g)

Rabbit Sausage

FOOD GRINDER · FLAT BEATER · SAUSAGE STUFFER (OPTIONAL)

1¾ lbs	boneless rabbit meat	875 g
4 oz	pork fat	125 g
¼ cup	chopped fresh flat-leaf parsley	50 mL
¼ cup	white wine	50 mL
2 tsp	salt	10 mL
½ tsp	dried thyme	2 mL
½ tsp	dried summer savory	2 mL
½ tsp	minced garlic	2 mL
¼ tsp	freshly ground black pepper	1 mL
¼ tsp	celery seed	1 mL
¼ tsp	ground cardamom	1 mL
Pinch	ground allspice	Pinch
3 feet	medium hog casing (optional)	90 cm

Prepare Bulk Sausage

1. Cut rabbit and pork fat into 1-inch (2.5 cm) cubes. Place in a shallow container in the freezer for 30 minutes to facilitate grinding. Attach the food grinder, with the coarse plate, to the mixer. Set to Speed 4 and run rabbit and pork fat through the grinder into the mixer bowl.
2. Add parsley, wine, salt, thyme, savory, garlic, pepper, celery seed, cardamom and allspice to the mixer bowl. Remove the food grinder and attach the flat beater and mixer bowl to the mixer. Set to Stir and mix until seasonings are evenly incorporated, about 1 minute.
3. In a skillet, over medium-high heat, sauté a small amount of the sausage mixture until no longer pink. Taste and adjust seasoning as desired.

To Make Links (Optional)

1. Prepare hog casing as directed on page 158.
2. Stuff sausage into casing as directed on pages 158–59 and twist into 6-inch (15 cm) links. Coil links and dry overnight, uncovered, on a rack over a baking sheet in the refrigerator.

Makes 2 lbs (1 kg)

Roasted Red Pepper Vegetarian Sausage

FOOD GRINDER ◆ FLAT BEATER

- ◆ Preheat broiler
- ◆ Baking sheet

3	red bell peppers, halved and seeded	3
1/3 cup	olive oil, divided	75 mL
1/2 cup	finely chopped onion	125 mL
2	cloves garlic, minced	2
1 cup	cooked white beans	250 mL
1 tsp	freshly squeezed lemon juice	5 mL
1/2 tsp	salt	2 mL
1/2 tsp	dried basil	2 mL
1/4 tsp	freshly ground black pepper	1 mL
1/4 tsp	cayenne pepper	1 mL
1	egg yolk	1
2 1/2 cups	fresh bread crumbs, divided	625 mL
1/4 cup	chopped fresh flat-leaf parsley	50 mL
1 3/4 cups	Basil Aioli (see recipe, page 403)	425 mL

This vegetarian "sausage" goes well with grilled meats and fish.

Make ahead

Can be prepared up to 2 days ahead. Let cool, cover and refrigerate. Reheat on a baking sheet in a 400°F (200°C) oven for about 15 minutes.

1. Place red peppers skin side up on baking sheet and broil, turning occasionally, until skins blacken. Transfer to a heatproof bowl and cover with plastic wrap. When cool enough to handle, peel off the black skins and discard. Peppers should be pliable and soft. Cut into 2-inch (5 cm) pieces and set aside.
2. Meanwhile, in a large skillet, heat 2 tbsp (25 mL) of the oil over medium-high heat. Add onion and sauté for 2 minutes. Add garlic and sauté until onion is tender, about 2 minutes. Set aside.
3. In a large bowl, combine half the roasted peppers with the white beans, lemon juice, salt, basil, black pepper and cayenne pepper. Attach the food grinder, with the coarse plate, to the mixer. Set to Speed 4 and run pepper mixture through the grinder into the mixer bowl.
4. Add the remaining roasted peppers, egg yolk, 1 1/2 cups (375 mL) of the bread crumbs and parsley to the mixer bowl. Remove the food grinder and attach the flat beater and mixer bowl to the mixer. Set to Stir and mix until just combined. Form into eight 1-inch (2.5 cm) thick patties and coat with the remaining 1 cup (250 mL) bread crumbs.
5. In a large skillet, heat half of the remaining oil over medium-high heat. Add 4 of the patties and cook, flipping once, for 3 to 4 minutes per side, or until brown on both sides. Repeat with remaining patties, adding more oil as needed. Serve hot with Basil Aioli.

Makes 8 patties

Pasta

Pasta Basics

To anyone who has tasted fresh pasta, the advantage is obvious. Homemade pasta has a wonderful texture, much different from the rubbery, plastic texture of the purchased variety. And with the stand mixer and its pasta attachments, making your own pasta has never been easier. Once you've mastered the basics, you can have homemade pasta any night of the week.

Ingredients

- **Flours:** Unless otherwise specified, we've used unbleached all-purpose flour for our pasta recipes. It's the easiest flour to work with and is particularly good for the beginning pasta maker. The other flours in this chapter include semolina, which makes for a firmer texture and bite, and whole wheat flour, which gives a completely different taste and texture and is a great high-fiber alternative.
- **Eggs:** We use large eggs in our pasta recipes, but even if you use large eggs all the time, there will still be slight variations in the volume of the egg. Even a fraction of a teaspoon can affect the texture (dryness or wetness) of the dough. For that reason, we encourage you to add a little extra flour or water if necessary to make the dough smooth and elastic, but not sticky.
- **Salt:** We include salt in our recipes because it adds flavor to the pasta. Many traditional pasta recipes do not include salt, though, so feel free to leave it out.
- **Flavorings:** There are a million variations on basic pasta. We've included several in this chapter. It's fun to experiment. The unique colors and flavors of different pastas add interest to a dish. Flavorings often change the amount of moisture in a recipe, so a little extra flour might be necessary, either in the mixing or in the rolling of the dough.

Making Pasta Dough

The key to making pasta dough lies in achieving the right texture. If your dough is too dry, it won't form a ball, and you won't be able to knead it with the dough hook. If it's too wet, you will have to run it through the roller many more times than necessary to get it to be elastic. Even then, you may have difficulty separating the strands once the dough is run through the pasta cutter. That's why we suggest adding a little more flour or water to the dough as needed. Try making Basic Egg Pasta (page 192) two or three times before moving on to the flavored pastas. Once you've made pasta a few times, you'll have a better idea of how the dough is supposed to feel.

Rolling Pasta Dough

Once you've made the dough as directed in the recipe, and allowed it to rest for 20 minutes, you can proceed to rolling it out. First, cut the dough into 4 equal pieces and flatten each piece slightly. As you work with each piece of dough, keep the others wrapped in plastic wrap.

1. Attach the pasta roller to the mixer and turn the adjustment knob to setting 1. Set to Speed 4 and, working with one piece at a time, run dough through the roller. Fold dough into thirds, much as you would fold a business letter, making sure no excess flour remains inside the fold. Run dough through the roller again, open end first. Fold again and run through again, open end first. Run through the

roller once more without folding it. (This process helps make the dough more consistent and elastic.) For some of the flavored pastas, it may be necessary to repeat the folding and rolling process several more times if the dough is tearing or holes appear as you're rolling it out.

2. Turn the knob to setting 2 and run the dough through once, without folding. Repeat on setting 3. The dough will gradually become longer and thinner. Cut it in half with a pizza wheel if it becomes too long to handle easily. Continue to run dough through the roller, increasing the knob setting each time, until dough is the thickness you desire. We find that setting 5 is the optimal thickness for most pasta noodles.
3. As you finish rolling sheets of dough, lay them on a floured surface and gently rub with a little flour to help keep noodles from sticking together after cutting. The texture of the dough should look like suede or chamois. Cut sheets into 12-inch (30 cm) long pieces. If you plan to cut dough into fettuccine or linguine noodles, let it rest for 15 to 20 minutes first. This will dry the sheets out slightly and make the noodles easier to separate when cut.

Cutting Pasta Dough

Attach the fettuccine or spaghetti/linguine cutter to the mixer. Set to Speed 4 and run sheets of dough through the cutter. Lay the cut pasta on a baking sheet and sprinkle with flour, giving it a little toss to coat.

Freezing Pasta Dough

Form into loose nests on the baking sheet and place in the freezer until firm, then transfer to a plastic bag and store in the freezer for up to 6 weeks.

Cooking Fresh Pasta

Bring a large pot of water to a boil and add 2 tbsp (25 mL) salt. Add pasta, stirring for the first 30 seconds, and cook for about 2 minutes. (Add 30 seconds to the cooking time if cooking from frozen.) At this point, check for doneness. Pasta should have a firm bite, but should not be rubbery or raw-tasting. Cook for another minute, if necessary. Drain and use pasta immediately as your recipe directs.

Basic Egg Pasta

FLAT BEATER • DOUGH HOOK

$2\frac{3}{4}$ cups	unbleached all-purpose flour (approx.)	675 mL
1 tsp	salt	5 mL
4	eggs	4

TIP
Make sure to use large eggs in all pasta recipes.

1. Place flour and salt in the mixer bowl. Attach the flat beater and mixer bowl to the mixer. Set to Stir and mix briefly. Add eggs and mix until dough forms large clumps. Using your hands, form dough into a ball. If dough is shaggy and dry, and won't form a ball, add 1 tsp (5 mL) water and mix until incorporated. If it's too sticky, add 1 tbsp (15 mL) flour and mix until incorporated. If necessary, keep adding water or flour in small increments and mix until dough comes together.
2. Remove the flat beater and attach the dough hook to the mixer. Set to Speed 2 and knead for 2 minutes, until dough comes together in a firm ball. Remove dough and wrap in plastic wrap. Let rest for 20 minutes before rolling out. (For instructions on rolling and cutting pasta, see pages 190–91.)

Makes 1 lb (500 g)

Whole Wheat Pasta

FLAT BEATER • DOUGH HOOK

3 cups	whole wheat flour	750 mL
1 cup	unbleached all-purpose flour (approx.)	250 mL
1 tsp	salt	5 mL
4	eggs	4
1 tbsp	olive oil	15 mL

Whole wheat pasta is a great high-fiber alternative.

1. Place whole wheat flour, all-purpose flour and salt in the mixer bowl. Attach the flat beater and mixer bowl to the mixer. Set to Stir and mix briefly. Add eggs and olive oil; mix until dough forms large clumps. Using your hands, form dough into a ball. If dough is shaggy and dry, and won't form a ball, add 1 tsp (5 mL) water and mix until incorporated. If it's too sticky, add 1 tbsp (15 mL) flour and mix until incorporated. If necessary, keep adding water or flour in small increments and mix until dough comes together.
2. Remove the flat beater and attach the dough hook to the mixer. Set to Speed 2 and knead for 2 minutes until dough comes together in a firm ball. Remove dough and wrap in plastic wrap. Let rest for 20 minutes before rolling out. (For instructions on rolling and cutting pasta, see pages 190–91.)

Makes 1¾ lbs (875 g)

Semolina Pasta

FLAT BEATER DOUGH HOOK

2 cups	semolina (approx.)	500 g
1 tsp	salt	5 mL
3	eggs	3
1 tbsp	olive oil	15 mL

TIP
This pasta makes great fresh spaghetti. Roll out to setting 3 and use the spaghetti/linguine cutter. Use in Italian Spaghetti and Meatballs (see recipe, page 107).

1. Place semolina and salt in the mixer bowl. Attach the flat beater and mixer bowl to the mixer. Set to Stir and mix briefly. Add eggs, 3 tbsp (45 mL) water and olive oil; mix until dough forms large clumps. Using your hands, form dough into a ball. If dough is shaggy and dry, and won't form a ball, add 1 tsp (5 mL) water and mix until incorporated. If it's too sticky, add 1 tbsp (15 mL) flour and mix until incorporated. If necessary, keep adding water or flour in small increments and mix until dough comes together.
2. Remove the flat beater and attach the dough hook to the mixer. Set to Speed 2 and knead for 2 minutes, until dough comes together in a firm ball. Remove dough and wrap in plastic wrap. Let rest for 20 minutes before rolling out. (For instructions on rolling and cutting pasta, see pages 190–91.)

Makes 1 lb (500 g)

Eggless Pasta

FLAT BEATER • DOUGH HOOK

1 1/4 cups	unbleached all-purpose flour (approx.)	300 mL
1 cup	semolina	250 mL
1 tsp	salt	5 mL

1. Place all-purpose flour, semolina and salt in the mixer bowl. Attach the flat beater and mixer bowl to the mixer. Set to Stir and mix briefly. Add 3/4 cup (175 mL) water and mix until dough forms large clumps. Using your hands, form dough into a ball. If dough is shaggy and dry, and won't form a ball, add 1 tsp (5 mL) water and mix until incorporated. If it's too sticky, add 1 tbsp (15 mL) flour and mix until incorporated. If necessary, keep adding water or flour in small increments and mix until dough comes together.
2. Remove the flat beater and attach the dough hook to the mixer. Set to Speed 2 and knead for 2 minutes, until dough comes together in a firm ball. Remove dough and wrap in plastic wrap. Let rest for 20 minutes before rolling out. (For instructions on rolling and cutting pasta, see pages 190–91.)

Makes 1 lb (500 g)

Parsley Pasta

FLAT BEATER • DOUGH HOOK

$2\frac{3}{4}$ cups	unbleached all-purpose flour (approx.)	675 mL
1 tsp	salt	5 mL
4	eggs	4
$\frac{1}{3}$ cup	finely chopped fresh parsley	75 mL

TIP
Make sure to use large eggs in all pasta recipes.

1. Place flour and salt in the mixer bowl. Attach the flat beater and mixer bowl to the mixer. Set to Stir and mix briefly. Add eggs and parsley; mix until dough forms large clumps. Using your hands, form dough into a ball. If dough is shaggy and dry, and won't form a ball, add 1 tsp (5 mL) water and mix until incorporated. If it's too sticky, add 1 tbsp (15 mL) flour and mix until incorporated. If necessary, keep adding water or flour in small increments and mix until dough comes together.
2. Remove the flat beater and attach the dough hook to the mixer. Set to Speed 2 and knead for 2 minutes until dough comes together in a firm ball. Remove dough and wrap in plastic wrap. Let rest for 20 minutes before rolling out. (For instructions on rolling and cutting pasta, see pages 190–91.)

Makes 1 lb (500 g)

Rosemary Pasta

FLAT BEATER · DOUGH HOOK

1 tsp	dried rosemary	5 mL
1 tsp	olive oil	5 mL
2¾ cups	unbleached all-purpose flour (approx.)	675 mL
1 tsp	salt	5 mL
4	eggs	4

To add extra heartiness to beef stew, try pairing it with rosemary pasta.

Variations

Sage Pasta: Substitute an equal amount of dried sage leaves for the rosemary.

Thyme Pasta: Substitute an equal amount of dried thyme for the rosemary. Try pairing thyme pasta with Swedish Meatballs (see recipe, page 123).

Tarragon Pasta: Substitute 2 tsp (10 mL) dried tarragon for the rosemary.

Caper Pasta: Substitute 2 tsp (10 mL) capers (drained and rinsed if salted) for the rosemary. Caper pasta tastes great in Summer Pasta with Fresh Tomatoes and Basil (see recipe, page 108).

1. With a mortar and pestle, grind rosemary in oil. (Or, in a shallow bowl, using a fork, mash rosemary in oil.)
2. Place flour and salt in the mixer bowl. Attach the flat beater and mixer bowl to the mixer. Set to Stir and mix briefly. Add eggs and rosemary mixture; mix until dough forms large clumps. Using your hands, form dough into a ball. If dough is shaggy and dry, and won't form a ball, add 1 tsp (5 mL) water and mix until incorporated. If it's too sticky, add 1 tbsp (15 mL) flour and mix until incorporated. If necessary, keep adding water or flour in small increments and mix until dough comes together.
3. Remove the flat beater and attach the dough hook to the mixer. Set to Speed 2 and knead for 2 minutes, until dough comes together in a firm ball. Remove dough and wrap in plastic wrap. Let rest for 20 minutes before rolling out. (For instructions on rolling and cutting pasta, see pages 190–91.)

Makes 1 lb (500 g)

Saffron Pasta

FLAT BEATER • DOUGH HOOK

1/4 tsp	lightly packed saffron threads	1 mL
2 tbsp	hot water	25 mL
3	eggs	3
2 1/4 cups	unbleached all-purpose flour (approx.)	550 mL
1 tsp	salt	5 mL

1. Place saffron threads in hot water and let steep for 2 to 3 minutes, until dissolved. Add eggs and beat until well combined.
2. Place flour and salt in the mixer bowl. Attach the flat beater and mixer bowl to the mixer. Set to Stir and mix briefly. Add egg-saffron mixture and mix until dough forms large clumps. Using your hands, form dough into a ball. If dough is shaggy and dry, and won't form a ball, add 1 tsp (5 mL) water and mix until incorporated. If it's too sticky, add 1 tbsp (15 mL) flour and mix until incorporated. If necessary, keep adding water or flour in small increments and mix until dough comes together.
3. Remove the flat beater and attach the dough hook to the mixer. Set to Speed 2 and knead for 2 minutes, until dough comes together in a firm ball. Remove dough and wrap in plastic wrap. Let rest for 20 minutes before rolling out. (For instructions on rolling and cutting pasta, see pages 190–91.)

Makes 1 lb (500 g)

Cilantro and Ancho Chili Pasta

FLAT BEATER • DOUGH HOOK

$2\frac{3}{4}$ cups	unbleached all-purpose flour (approx.)	675 mL
1 tsp	salt	5 mL
2 tbsp	ancho chili powder	25 mL
4	eggs	4
$\frac{1}{3}$ cup	finely chopped fresh cilantro	75 mL

Ancho chilies are dried poblano chilies. A mild but flavorful dried chili, they can be found in powder form in many well-stocked grocery stores.

1. Place flour, salt and ancho powder in the mixer bowl. Attach the flat beater and mixer bowl to the mixer. Set to Stir and mix briefly. Add eggs and cilantro; mix until dough forms large clumps. Using your hands, form dough into a ball. If dough is shaggy and dry, and won't form a ball, add 1 tsp (5 mL) water and mix until incorporated. If it's too sticky, add 1 tbsp (15 mL) flour and mix until incorporated. If necessary, keep adding water or flour in small increments and mix until dough comes together.
2. Remove the flat beater and attach the dough hook to the mixer. Set to Speed 2 and knead for 2 minutes, until dough comes together in a firm ball. Remove dough and wrap in plastic wrap. Let rest for 20 minutes before rolling out. (For instructions on rolling and cutting pasta, see pages 190–91.)

Makes 1 lb (500 g)

TIP

Make sure to use large eggs in all pasta recipes.

Hot Chili Pasta

FLAT BEATER • DOUGH HOOK

2¾ cups	unbleached all-purpose flour (approx.)	675 mL
1 tsp	salt	5 mL
1 tsp	cayenne pepper	5 mL
4	eggs	4

TIP
Make sure to use large eggs in all pasta recipes.

1. Place flour, salt and cayenne in the mixer bowl. Attach the flat beater and mixer bowl to the mixer. Set to Stir and mix briefly. Add eggs and mix until dough forms large clumps. Using your hands, form dough into a ball. If dough is shaggy and dry, and won't form a ball, add 1 tsp (5 mL) water and mix until incorporated. If it's too sticky, add 1 tbsp (15 mL) flour and mix until incorporated. If necessary, keep adding water or flour in small increments and mix until dough comes together.
2. Remove the flat beater and attach the dough hook to the mixer. Set to Speed 2 and knead for 2 minutes, until dough comes together in a firm ball. Remove dough and wrap in plastic wrap. Let rest for 20 minutes before rolling out. (For instructions on rolling and cutting pasta, see pages 190–91.)

Makes 1 lb (500 g)

Lemon Black Pepper Pasta

FLAT BEATER ◆ DOUGH HOOK

2¾ cups	unbleached all-purpose flour (approx.)	675 mL
1 tsp	salt	5 mL
1 tsp	freshly ground black pepper	5 mL
4	eggs	4
2 tbsp	finely grated lemon zest	25 mL

Try pairing this pasta with Roasted Asparagus and Lemon Cream Sauce (see recipe, page 111).

1. Place flour, salt and pepper in the mixer bowl. Attach the flat beater and mixer bowl to the mixer. Set to Stir and mix briefly. Add eggs and lemon zest; mix until dough forms large clumps. Using your hands, form dough into a ball. If dough is shaggy and dry, and won't form a ball, add 1 tsp (5 mL) water and mix until incorporated. If it's too sticky, add 1 tbsp (15 mL) flour and mix until incorporated. If necessary, keep adding water or flour in small increments and mix until dough comes together.
2. Remove the flat beater and attach the dough hook to the mixer. Set to Speed 2 and knead for 2 minutes, until dough comes together in a firm ball. Remove dough and wrap in plastic wrap. Let rest for 20 minutes before rolling out. (For instructions on rolling and cutting pasta, see pages 190–91.)

Makes 1 lb (500 g)

Orange Pasta

FLAT BEATER • DOUGH HOOK

2¾ cups	unbleached all-purpose flour (approx.)	675 mL
¾ tsp	salt	3 mL
4	eggs	4
1 tbsp	finely grated orange zest	15 mL

The orange flavor really comes through in this pasta. It's great paired with braised chicken.

TIP
Make sure to use large eggs in all pasta recipes.

1. Place flour and salt in the mixer bowl. Attach the flat beater and mixer bowl to the mixer. Set to Stir and mix briefly. Add eggs and orange zest; mix until dough forms large clumps. Using your hands, form dough into a ball. If dough is shaggy and dry, and won't form a ball, add 1 tsp (5 mL) water and mix until incorporated. If it's too sticky, add 1 tbsp (15 mL) flour and mix until incorporated. If necessary, keep adding water or flour in small increments and mix until dough comes together.
2. Remove the flat beater and attach the dough hook to the mixer. Set to Speed 2 and knead for 2 minutes, until dough comes together in a firm ball. Remove dough and wrap in plastic wrap. Let rest for 20 minutes before rolling out. (For instructions on rolling and cutting pasta, see pages 190–91.)

Makes 1 lb (500 g)

Beet Pasta

FLAT BEATER • DOUGH HOOK

1/4 cup	drained canned beets	50 mL
1 tsp	olive oil	5 mL
2 1/4 cups	unbleached all-purpose flour (approx.)	550 mL
3/4 tsp	salt	3 mL
3	eggs	3

Though the flavor of the beets isn't dominant, beet pasta is a beautiful rosy color. To showcase the color, serve this pasta with a cream-based rather than tomato-based sauce.

1. In a small bowl, using a fork, thoroughly mash beets in oil.
2. Place flour and salt in the mixer bowl. Attach the flat beater and mixer bowl to the mixer. Set to Stir and mix briefly. Add eggs and beet mixture; mix until dough forms large clumps. Using your hands, form dough into a ball. If dough is shaggy and dry, and won't form a ball, add 1 tsp (5 mL) water and mix until incorporated. If it's too sticky, add 1 tbsp (15 mL) flour and mix until incorporated. If necessary, keep adding water or flour in small increments and mix until dough comes together.
3. Remove the flat beater and attach the dough hook to the mixer. Set to Speed 2 and knead for 2 minutes, until dough comes together in a firm ball. Remove dough and wrap in plastic wrap. Let rest for 20 minutes before rolling out. (For instructions on rolling and cutting pasta, see pages 190–91.)

Makes 1 lb (500 g)

Tomato Pasta

FLAT BEATER DOUGH HOOK

2¼ cups	unbleached all-purpose flour (approx.)	550 mL
1 tsp	salt	5 mL
3	eggs	3
3 tbsp	tomato paste	45 mL

TIP
Make sure to use large eggs in all pasta recipes.

1. Place flour and salt in the mixer bowl. Attach the flat beater and mixer bowl to the mixer. Set to Stir and mix briefly. Add eggs and tomato paste; mix until dough forms large clumps. Using your hands, form dough into a ball. If dough is shaggy and dry, and won't form a ball, add 1 tsp (5 mL) water and mix until incorporated. If it's too sticky, add 1 tbsp (15 mL) flour and mix until incorporated. If necessary, keep adding water or flour in small increments and mix until dough comes together.
2. Remove the flat beater and attach the dough hook to the mixer. Set to Speed 2 and knead for 2 minutes, until dough comes together in a firm ball. Remove dough and wrap in plastic wrap. Let rest for 20 minutes before rolling out. (For instructions on rolling and cutting pasta, see pages 190–91.)

Makes 1 lb (500 g)

Spinach Pasta

FLAT BEATER DOUGH HOOK

5 oz	frozen spinach, thawed	150 g
2 1⁄4 cups	unbleached all-purpose flour (approx.)	550 mL
1 tsp	salt	5 mL
3	eggs	3

This vibrant green pasta makes lovely ravioli or lasagna.

TIP

In place of frozen spinach, cook 8 oz (250 g) fresh until tender. Let cool and squeeze dry as directed.

1. Squeeze out as much water as possible from spinach and chop finely.
2. Place flour and salt in the mixer bowl. Attach the flat beater and mixer bowl to the mixer. Set to Stir and mix briefly. Add spinach and eggs; mix until dough forms large clumps. Using your hands, form dough into a ball. If dough is shaggy and dry, and won't form a ball, add 1 tsp (5 mL) water and mix until incorporated. If it's too sticky, add 1 tbsp (15 mL) flour and mix until incorporated. If necessary, keep adding water or flour in small increments and mix until dough comes together.
3. Remove the flat beater and attach the dough hook to the mixer. Set to Speed 2 and knead for 2 minutes, until dough comes together in a firm ball. Remove dough and wrap in plastic wrap. Let rest for 20 minutes before rolling out. (For instructions on rolling and cutting pasta, see pages 190–91.)

Makes 1 1⁄4 lbs (625 g)

Olivada Pasta

FLAT BEATER · DOUGH HOOK

2¼ cups	unbleached all-purpose flour (approx.)	550 mL
½ tsp	salt	2 mL
3	eggs	3
3 tbsp	olive paste	45 mL

TIP
Make sure to use large eggs in all pasta recipes.

1. Place flour and salt in the mixer bowl. Attach the flat beater and mixer bowl to the mixer. Set to Stir and mix briefly. Add eggs and olive paste; mix until dough forms large clumps. Using your hands, form dough into a ball. If dough is shaggy and dry, and won't form a ball, add 1 tsp (5 mL) water and mix until incorporated. If it's too sticky, add 1 tbsp (15 mL) of flour and mix until incorporated. If necessary, keep adding water or flour in small increments and mix until dough comes together.
2. Remove the flat beater and attach the dough hook to the mixer. Set to Speed 2 and knead for 2 minutes, until dough comes together in a firm ball. Remove dough and wrap in plastic wrap. Let rest for 20 minutes before rolling out. (For instructions on rolling and cutting pasta, see pages 190–91.)

Makes 1 lb (500 g)

Breads

Bread and Baking Basics

Baking can be a tricky business. Here are a few tips to help you along the way.

Ingredients

- **Flour:** For the best results, use the flour specified in the recipe.
- **Yeast:** We use active dry yeast. As long as it is used before its best-before date, it's the most reliable type of yeast. If you have a large jar of yeast, 2¼ tsp (11 mL) can be used in place of one (¼ oz/7 g) package.
- **Liquids:** The liquid used in a bread recipe shouldn't be too hot. Yeast can be killed at temperatures above 115°F (45°C). We use liquid at about 100°F (38°C), which should feel just warm. For water, warm water from the tap is fine. Warm milk in the microwave, stirring afterward to make sure there are no hot spots. Test with your finger; it should be lukewarm (or, for more precision, use an instant-read thermometer).

Equipment

- **Scoops:** An assortment of ice cream–style scoops can save you time and make your end product look more professional as each cookie, muffin or biscuit will be the same size. We recommend a small scoop for cookies and a large ice cream scoop for muffins and biscuits.
- **Dough knife:** Dough knives cut dough beautifully and scrape and clean up when you are done. A dough knife is a good investment: you will use it more than you think.
- **Rubber spatulas:** Having an assortment of spatulas is a great help. A large spatula works best for folding egg whites and whipped cream into soufflés. Use medium and small spatulas to scrape down the mixer bowl when mixing, or to scrape out that last bit of an ingredient from a measuring cup or spoon.
- **Towels:** Used to cover bread as it rises. Any clean, dry kitchen towel will do.
- **Kitchen scale:** Although not a necessary tool, a kitchen scale is helpful when portioning dough into rolls of equal size. It's also handy when you have a 1-lb (500 g) bag of chocolate and need to measure 4 oz (125 g) for a recipe.
- **Baking stones or unglazed clay oven tiles:** Rustic breads are usually baked directly on hot tiles. When the wet dough hits the hot tile, steam rises, making the loaf crusty. The clay stones or tiles are placed on a rack in the oven before the oven is preheated. If you can't find the tiles, try using a pizza stone.
- **Baking sheets:** These 18- by 12- by 1-inch (45 by 30 by 2.5 cm) pans are more durable than most cookie sheets. They won't warp in the oven and have many uses. It's good to have two or three.
- **Parchment paper:** A brilliant invention, parchment paper is a great timesaver. When you use it to line baking sheets, you lose none of your baked goods to sticking, cracking and breaking — and you often don't even have to wash the pan. We use it to line cake pans to ensure that the cake releases, and even when roasting vegetables or meats to save time on cleanup. Parchment paper can be found in most grocery stores and comes unbleached (brown) or bleached, on rolls or in sheets.
- **Spray bottle:** Professional bread ovens have steam injection systems that intermittently spray steam into the hot oven, creating crusty rustic loaves. When you're making ciabatta and French bread at home, use a

spray bottle to spray water into the oven two or three times during baking. This helps create the nice crust that is typical of these breads. Use fresh water each time.
- **Instant-read thermometer:** With an instant-read thermometer, you won't have to guess when breads and meats are done. Every kitchen should have one or two. To measure the internal temperature of bread, stick the thermometer into the center. Bread is done when it reaches an internal temperature of 200°F (100°C).
- **Wire cooling racks:** Baked goods cool best when elevated. When left to cool on the counter, condensation builds up between the baked good and the pan, creating a soggy bottom.

Techniques

- **Measure flour by the scoop-and-fill method:** Before you measure, fluff flour with a large spoon; otherwise, it may be tightly packed and could alter your measurements. To fill a 1-cup (250 mL) measure, use a 1/4-cup (50 mL) measure to scoop flour into the cup. When full, clear the excess by scraping a flat knife across the top.
- **Find the best rising spot:** Any draft-free spot is good. Some bakers use their microwave ovens. We like to let our bread rise on a counter close to a warm range. Too much heat is bad, as is too much cold. A spot between 70°F and 80°F (20°C and 25°C) is optimal.

Farmhouse White Bread

FLAT BEATER · DOUGH HOOK

◆ Two 9- by 5-inch (2 L) loaf pans, greased

1½ cups	homogenized (whole) milk	375 mL
¼ cup	unsalted butter, cut into pieces	50 mL
1	package (¼ oz/7 g) active dry yeast	1
½ cup	warm water (see tip, below)	125 mL
2 tbsp	granulated sugar	25 mL
1 tbsp	salt	15 mL
5 to 6 cups	unbleached all-purpose flour (approx.), divided	1.25 to 1.5 L
1½ tsp	unsalted butter, softened	7 mL
1	egg, beaten with 1 tbsp (15 mL) water	1

TIP

The water should be around 100°F (38°C). Yeast can be killed at temperatures above 115°F (45°C). Water at 100°F (38°C) will feel just warm.

1. In a small saucepan, heat milk and the ¼ cup (50 mL) butter over medium heat until butter is melted. Let cool to around 100°F (38°C).
2. In the mixer bowl, stir together yeast, water and sugar. Let stand until yeast begins to foam, about 5 minutes. Add warm milk mixture and salt. Attach the flat beater and mixer bowl to the mixer. Set to Speed 2 and mix until well combined. Add 4 cups (1 L) of the flour, ½ cup (125 mL) at a time, and mix until a dough forms.
3. Remove the flat beater and attach the dough hook. Set to Speed 2 and knead, adding flour ½ cup (125 mL) at a time, until dough forms a smooth and elastic ball that cleans the bowl. Continue to knead for 2 minutes, adding flour 1 tbsp (15 mL) at a time as necessary to keep dough from clinging to the bowl. (You may not need all of the flour. Save the remainder for dusting.) Using your hands, form dough into a ball. Place back in the mixer bowl, rub with softened butter and cover loosely with plastic wrap. Let rise in a warm, draft-free place for 1 to 2 hours, or until doubled in bulk.
4. Uncover dough and punch down several times to work out air bubbles. Form back into a ball. Cover with plastic wrap and let rise until doubled in bulk, about 1 hour.

5. Turn dough out onto a lightly floured work surface and cut in half. As you work with one piece of dough, keep the other covered. Working with one piece at a time, pat dough into a 10- by 8-inch (25 by 20 cm) rectangle. Starting with a long side, roll dough up jelly-roll style, then fold under the ends. Pinch the seams closed and place in prepared loaf pan, seam side down. Repeat with remaining dough. Cover loosely with plastic wrap and let rise for 45 to 60 minutes, or until the top of the dough is nearly level with the top of the loaf pan. Meanwhile, place oven rack in the middle position and preheat oven to 375°F (190°C).
6. Using a pastry brush, coat tops of loaves with egg wash. Bake for 25 to 30 minutes, or until loaves are golden and reach an internal temperature of 200°F (100°C). Remove from pans and let cool completely on wire racks before slicing.

Makes 2 loaves

Make ahead

Prepare dough through Step 3 in the evening and let rise overnight in the refrigerator. Let stand at room temperature for 1 hour before shaping.

Wrap baked bread in plastic wrap and then foil and store in the freezer for up to 2 weeks.

Variations

Herb Bread: Add 1 tsp (5 mL) each dried oregano, basil and thyme to the milk and butter in Step 1.

Cheese Bread: Before rolling dough up jelly-roll style in Step 5, sprinkle each half with 3/4 cup (175 mL) shredded Asiago, Cheddar, Swiss or mozzarella cheese, or any shredded cheese of your choice.

Cinnamon Bread: Before rolling dough up jelly-roll style in Step 5, sprinkle each half with a mixture of 1/3 cup (75 mL) granulated sugar and 2 tsp (10 mL) ground cinnamon.

Pumpernickel Bread

FLAT BEATER DOUGH HOOK

◆ 9- by 5-inch (2 L) loaf pan, greased

1	package (1/4 oz/7 g) active dry yeast	1
1 1/4 cups	warm water (see tip, opposite)	300 mL
1 tbsp	granulated sugar	15 mL
2 cups	rye flour	500 mL
1 cup	unbleached all-purpose flour (approx.)	250 mL
1 cup	whole wheat flour	250 mL
1/2 cup	cornmeal	125 mL
3 tbsp	fancy molasses	45 mL
3 tbsp	unsalted butter, softened, divided	45 mL
1 tbsp	salt	15 mL

Make ahead

Prepare dough through Step 4 in the evening and let rise overnight in the refrigerator.

Wrap baked bread in plastic wrap and then foil and store in the freezer for up to 2 weeks.

1. In the mixer bowl, stir together yeast, water and sugar. Let stand until yeast begins to foam, about 5 minutes.
2. Meanwhile, in a medium bowl, combine rye flour, all-purpose flour, whole wheat flour, and cornmeal. Set aside.
3. Add molasses, 2 tbsp (25 mL) of the butter and salt to the mixer bowl. Attach the flat beater and mixer bowl to the mixer. Set to Speed 2 and mix until combined. Add 3 cups (750 mL) of the flour mixture and mix until a dough forms.
4. Remove the flat beater and attach the dough hook. Set to Speed 2 and knead, adding flour mixture 1/2 cup (125 mL) at a time, until a slightly stiff but workable dough forms (see tip, opposite) (You may not need all of the flour mixture. Save the remainder for dusting.) It may be a bit sticky, heavy, and difficult to blend. As you knead, adding more flour as necessary, the dough should become smooth and fairly elastic. It may take 4 to 6 minutes of kneading or longer until the dough is only slightly sticky. Using your hands, form dough into a ball. Place back in the mixer bowl, rub with the remaining 1 tbsp (15 mL) butter and cover loosely with plastic wrap. Let rise in a warm, draft-free place for 2 to 2 1/2 hours, or until doubled in bulk.

5. Uncover dough and punch down several times to work out air bubbles. Pat dough into a 10- by 8-inch (25 by 20 cm) rectangle. Starting with a long side, roll dough up jelly-roll style, then fold under the ends. Pinch the seams closed and place in prepared loaf pan, seam side down. Cover loosely with plastic wrap and let rise for 2 to 3 hours, or until the top of the dough is nearly level with the top of the loaf pan. Meanwhile, place oven rack in the middle position and preheat oven to 375°F (190°C).
6. Bake for 35 to 45 minutes, or until loaf sounds hollow when tapped on the top and reaches an internal temperature of 200°F (100°C). Remove from pan and let cool completely on a wire rack before slicing.

Makes 1 loaf

TIPS

The water should be around 100°F (38°C). Yeast can be killed at temperatures above 115°F (45°C). Water at 100°F (38°C) will feel just warm.

The dough may be a bit sticky, heavy and difficult to blend. As the mixer kneads, the dough should become smooth and fairly elastic. It may take 4 to 6 minutes of kneading or longer before the dough is only slightly sticky.

Multigrain Bread

FLAT BEATER ◆ DOUGH HOOK

◆ Two 9- by 5-inch (2 L) loaf pans, greased

1/4 cup	wheat berries	50 mL
1	package (1/4 oz/7 g) active dry yeast	1
1/4 cup	warm water (see tip, opposite)	50 mL
3 cups	unbleached all-purpose flour (approx.)	750 mL
1/2 cup	old-fashioned rolled oats	125 mL
1/2 cup	walnut halves, toasted (see tip, opposite) and finely chopped	125 mL
1 cup	whole wheat flour	250 mL
1/2 cup	natural wheat bran	125 mL
1/3 cup	turbinado sugar	75 mL
1/4 cup	flax seeds	50 mL
1/4 cup	pumpkin seeds	50 mL
1/4 cup	sesame seeds	50 mL
2 tsp	salt	10 mL
1	egg	1
1 1/2 cups	cool water	375 mL
1/4 cup	unsalted butter, melted	50 mL

Multigrain bread is delicious toasted for breakfast. It is also a healthful alternative to white bread for sandwiches or French toast.

1. In a small saucepan, over medium-high heat, cook wheat berries in 3/4 cup (175 mL) water until water boils. Reduce heat to low and simmer until wheat berries are tender, about 40 minutes. Drain and set aside.
2. In the mixer bowl, stir together yeast and warm water. Let stand until yeast begins to foam, about 5 minutes. Add wheat berries, all-purpose flour, rolled oats, walnuts, whole wheat flour, bran, sugar, flax, pumpkin and sesame seeds, salt, egg, cool water and butter. Attach the flat beater and mixer bowl to the mixer. Set to Stir and mix until a dough forms.
3. Remove the flat beater and attach the dough hook. Set to Speed 2 and knead until dough clings to the dough hook and just cleans the sides of the bowl, about 5 minutes. If dough is too sticky and wet, add all-purpose flour 1 tbsp (15 mL) at a time. Remove the mixer bowl and cover loosely with plastic wrap. Let rise in a warm, draft-free place until doubled in bulk, about 1 hour.

4. Uncover dough and punch down several times to work out air bubbles. Turn dough out onto a floured work surface and cut in half. As you work with one piece of dough, keep the other covered. Working with one piece at a time, pat dough into a 15- by 9-inch (38 by 23 cm) rectangle. Starting with a long side, roll dough up jelly-roll style and place in prepared loaf pan, seam side down. Repeat with remaining dough. Cover with towels and let rise for 45 minutes to 1 hour, or until the top of the dough is nearly level with the top of the loaf pan. Meanwhile, place oven rack in the middle position and preheat oven to 375°F (190°C).
5. Using a sharp knife, make 3 parallel slashes down the middle of the loaves. Bake for about 30 minutes, or until loaves sound hollow when tapped on the top and reach an internal temperature of 200°F (100°C). Remove from pans and let cool completely on wire racks before slicing.

Makes 2 loaves

Make ahead

Prepare dough through Step 3 in the evening and let rise overnight in the refrigerator. Let stand at room temperature for 1 hour before shaping.

Wrap baked bread in plastic wrap and then foil and store in the freezer for up to 2 weeks.

TIPS

The water should be around 100°F (38°C). Yeast can be killed at temperatures above 115°F (45°C). Water at 100°F (38°C) will feel just warm.

You can use the grain mill attachment to process your own fresh flours.

To toast nuts, spread them on a baking sheet and toast in a 350°F (180°C) oven for 7 to 8 minutes, or until lightly browned.

To brown the bottoms and sides of the loaves, remove from the pans and return to the oven on a baking sheet for the last 5 minutes.

French Baguettes

FLAT BEATER · DOUGH HOOK

- 2 rimless baking sheets, lined with parchment paper
- Clay oven tiles

1	package (1⁄4 oz/7 g) active dry yeast	1
1⁄3 cup	warm water (see tip, opposite)	75 mL
4 1⁄2 cups	all-purpose unbleached flour (approx.)	1.05 L
1 1⁄2 cups	cool water	375 mL
1 tbsp	salt	15 mL
	Vegetable cooking spray	

1. In a small bowl, stir together yeast, warm water and a pinch of flour. Let stand until yeast begins to foam, about 5 minutes. Stir in cool water.

2. Place flour and salt in the mixer bowl. Attach the flat beater and mixer bowl to the mixer. Set to Stir and mix in yeast mixture, stopping mixer from time to time to push loose flour on the sides of the bowl into the wet dough mass in the center, until a dough forms.

3. Remove the flat beater and attach the dough hook. Set to Speed 2 and knead until dough is smooth and elastic, about 8 minutes. Remove the dough hook and scrape off loose dough. Remove the mixer bowl and cover loosely with plastic wrap. Let dough rise in a warm, draft-free place for 2 hours, until doubled in bulk.

4. Uncover dough and punch down several times to work out air bubbles. Cover bowl with plastic wrap and place in the refrigerator to rise overnight. Five hours before you plan to bake the bread, remove dough from the refrigerator and let it warm up on the counter for about 2 hours.

5. Turn dough out onto a floured work surface. Pat into a 12- by 14-inch (30 by 35 cm) rectangle and cut lengthwise into 4 pieces. As you work with each piece of dough, keep the rest covered. Working with one piece at a time, starting with a long side, roll dough up jelly-roll style. Arrange 2 loaves, seam side down, on each baking sheet, 5 inches (12 cm) apart. Pull up the parchment paper to form a hill between the loaves (this will keep the loaves from sticking together as they rise). Spray with cooking spray and cover loosely with towels. Let rise until dough is 1 1⁄2 times its size, about 1 1⁄2 hours. Meanwhile, place oven racks in the lower middle and upper middle positions, line with clay oven tiles and preheat oven to 450°F (230°C).

6. Spray loaves and the inside of the oven with water and place baking sheets on the hot tiles. Remove baking sheets much as a magician would pull a tablecloth from a set table, leaving the parchment paper and loaves on the tiles. Maintain space between the loaves so they don't stick together as they puff in the oven. Spray loaves again in 2 minutes and again 2 minutes after that. Bake for about 22 to 25 minutes, or until loaves are firm and crusty and reach an internal temperature of 200°F (100°C). Let cool on wire racks for at least 1 hour before slicing.

Makes 4 baguettes

Make ahead

Wrap bread in plastic wrap and then foil and store in the freezer for up to 2 weeks. Crisp in a 350°F (180°C) oven before serving, and it will be almost as good as the day you made it.

TIPS

The water should be around 100°F (38°C). Yeast can be killed at temperatures above 115°F (45°C). Water at 100°F (38°C) will feel just warm.

If you don't have enough tiles, bake loaves 2 at a time in the middle of the oven. The extra 20 or so minutes of rise won't hurt the second batch.

Brioche

FLAT BEATER ◆ DOUGH HOOK

◆ Two 8- by 4-inch (1.5 L) loaf pans, greased

2	packages (each 1/4 oz/7 g) active dry yeast	2
1/3 cup	warm water (see tip, opposite)	75 mL
2 tsp	granulated sugar	10 mL
4 cups	unbleached all-purpose flour	1 L
6	eggs, at room temperature, beaten	6
1 tbsp	granulated sugar	15 mL
2 tsp	salt	10 mL
1 1/2 cups	unsalted butter, softened and cut into 25 pieces	375 mL
	Vegetable cooking spray	
1	egg, beaten	1

Leftover brioche makes the best bread pudding and French toast.

1. In a small bowl, stir together yeast, water and the 2 tsp (10 mL) sugar. Let stand until yeast begins to foam, about 5 minutes.
2. Place flour in the mixer bowl. Make a well in the center and add eggs, the 1 tbsp (15 mL) sugar, salt and yeast mixture. Attach the flat beater and mixer bowl to the mixer. Set to Stir and mix until a dough forms.
3. Remove the flat beater and attach the dough hook. Set to Speed 2 and knead until dough is stretchy, about 4 minutes. Add butter, one piece at a time, incorporating one piece before adding the next. Increase to Speed 4 if the dough isn't accepting the butter readily. When all of the butter has been absorbed, the dough will look fluffy. Remove the mixer bowl and cover with plastic wrap. Let dough rise in a warm, draft-free place until doubled in bulk, about 2 hours.
4. Uncover dough and punch down several times to work out air bubbles. Cover with plastic wrap and let rise for 1 hour, then chill in the refrigerator for 2 hours.

5. Turn cold dough out onto a floured work surface and cut in half. As you work with one piece of dough, keep the other covered. Working with one piece at a time, pat dough into an 8- by 4-inch (20 by 10 cm) rectangle. Loosely form into a loaf and place in prepared loaf pan. Repeat with remaining dough. Spray the top of the loaves with cooking spray and cover loosely with plastic wrap. Let rise for 1½ to 2 hours, or until the top of the dough is nearly level with the top of the loaf pan. Meanwhile, place oven rack in the middle position and preheat oven to 375°F (190°C).
6. Using a pastry brush, coat tops of loaves with egg. Bake for about 40 minutes, or until browned and loaves reach an internal temperature of 190°F (88°C). Remove from pans and let cool on wire racks for at least 1 hour before slicing.

Makes 2 loaves

Make ahead

Can be prepared through Step 4 up to 1 day ahead. Cover bowl with a plate and a weight and keep in the refrigerator overnight. (The plate and weight will keep the dough from escaping the bowl.) Let stand at room temperature for 1 hour before shaping.

TIP

The water should be around 100°F (38°C). Yeast can be killed at temperatures above 115°F (45°C). Water at 100°F (38°C) will feel just warm.

Focaccia with Caramelized Onions

FLAT BEATER   DOUGH HOOK

- 13- by 9-inch (3 L) baking pan, generously greased
- Baking stone (optional)

Dough		
1	package (1/4 oz/7 g) active dry yeast	1
1 1/3 cup	warm water (see tip, below)	325 mL
1 tsp	granulated sugar	5 mL
3 1/4 cups	unbleached all-purpose flour (approx.)	800 mL
3 tbsp	extra-virgin olive oil	45 mL
1 1/2 tsp	salt	7 mL
Topping		
2 tbsp	extra-virgin olive oil, divided	25 mL
2	large onions, sliced into 1/4-inch (0.5 cm) slices	2
	Coarse sea salt	

Make ahead

Prepare dough through Step 2 in the evening and let rise overnight in the refrigerator. Let stand at room temperature for 1 hour before shaping.

Wrap baked bread in plastic wrap and then foil and store in the freezer for up to 2 weeks.

TIP

The water should be around 100°F (38°C). Yeast can be killed at temperatures above 115°F (45°C). Water at 100°F (38°C) will feel just warm.

1. *Prepare the dough:* In the mixer bowl, stir together yeast, water and sugar. Let stand until yeast begins to foam, about 5 minutes. Add flour, oil and salt. Attach the flat beater and mixer bowl to the mixer. Set to Speed 2 and mix until a dough forms.
2. Remove the flat beater and attach the dough hook. Set to Speed 4 and knead until dough is soft, smooth and slightly sticky, about 3 to 4 minutes. If dough is sticking to the bottom of the bowl, add flour 1 tbsp (15 mL) at a time. Using your hands, form dough into a ball. Place back in the mixer bowl, brush with olive oil and cover with a towel. Let rise in a warm, draft-free place for 1 to 1 1/2 hours, or until doubled in bulk.
3. Press dough evenly into prepared baking pan and cover with a towel. Let rise until again doubled in bulk, about 1 hour.
4. *Meanwhile, prepare the topping:* In a large skillet, heat 1 tbsp (15 mL) of the olive oil over medium heat. Add onions and cook, stirring frequently, for 15 to 20 minutes, or until golden brown. Meanwhile, place oven rack in the middle position, add a baking stone if you have one and preheat oven to 425°F (220°C).
5. Using your fingertips, make shallow indentations all over dough. Brush with the remaining 1 tbsp (15 mL) oil, letting it pool in the indentations. Arrange caramelized onions on top and gently press into dough. Sprinkle lightly with sea salt. Place pan on baking stone, if using, and bake for 20 to 25 minutes, or until focaccia is golden and reaches an internal temperature of 200°F (100°C). Using a large spatula, slip focaccia off pan and onto a rack to cool. Cut into large squares and serve warm or at room temperature.

Serves 8 to 10

Rosemary Focaccia with Tomatoes and Fresh Mozzarella

FLAT BEATER DOUGH HOOK

- 13- by 9-inch (3 L) baking pan, generously greased
- Baking stone (optional)

Dough		
1	package (1/4 oz/7 g) active dry yeast	1
1 1/3 cup	warm water (see tip, page 220)	325 mL
1 tsp	granulated sugar	5 mL
3 1/4 cups	unbleached all-purpose flour (approx.)	800 mL
1 tbsp	finely chopped fresh rosemary	15 mL
1 1/2 tsp	salt	7 mL
3 tbsp	extra-virgin olive oil	45 mL
Topping		
2 tbsp	extra-virgin olive oil	25 mL
2	cloves garlic, thinly sliced	2
2	sprigs fresh rosemary	2
1	large tomato, thinly sliced	1
6 oz	mozzarella cheese, sliced into 1/4 inch (0.5 cm) slices	175 g
	Coarse sea salt	

Make ahead

Prepare dough through Step 2 in the evening and let rise overnight in the refrigerator. Let stand at room temperature for 1 hour before shaping.

Wrap baked bread in plastic wrap and then foil and store in the freezer for up to 2 weeks.

1. *Prepare the dough:* In the mixer bowl, stir together yeast, water and sugar. Let stand until yeast begins to foam, about 5 minutes. Add flour, rosemary, salt and oil. Attach the flat beater and mixer bowl to the mixer. Set to Speed 2 and mix until a dough forms.
2. Remove the flat beater and attach the dough hook. Set to Speed 4 and knead until dough is soft, smooth and slightly sticky, about 3 to 4 minutes. If dough is sticking to the bottom of the bowl, add flour 1 tbsp (15 mL) at a time. Using your hands, form dough into a ball. Place back in the mixer bowl, brush with olive oil and cover with a towel. Let rise in a warm, draft-free place for 1 to 1 1/2 hours, or until doubled in bulk.
3. Press dough evenly into prepared baking pan and cover with a towel. Let rise until again doubled in bulk, about 1 hour. Meanwhile, place oven rack in the middle position, add a baking stone if you have one and preheat oven to 425°F (220°C).
4. *Prepare the topping:* In a small saucepan, heat oil over low heat. Add garlic and rosemary; cook, stirring, until garlic is tender but not browned, about 5 minutes.
5. Using your fingertips, make shallow indentations all over dough. Brush with garlic-rosemary oil, letting it pool in the indentations. Arrange tomato and mozzarella slices on top and sprinkle lightly with sea salt. Place pan on baking stone, if using, and bake for 20 to 25 minutes, or until focaccia is golden and reaches an internal temperature of 200°F (100°C). Using a large spatula, slip focaccia off pan and onto a rack to cool. Cut into large squares and serve warm or at room temperature.

Serves 8 to 10

Ciabatta

FLAT BEATER • DOUGH HOOK

- Rimless baking sheet
- Clay oven tiles

2 tsp	active dry yeast	10 mL
1/2 cup	warm water (see tip, opposite)	125 mL
6 cups	unbleached all-purpose flour (approx.)	1.5 L
1 tbsp	salt	15 mL
2 1/2 cups	cool water	625 mL

Ciabatta dough is the stickiest dough ever, but don't let that scare you. Just use lots of flour when handling it. The results are definitely worth it.

1. In the mixer bowl, stir together yeast and water. Let stand until yeast begins to foam, about 5 minutes. Add flour, salt and cold water. Attach the flat beater and mixer bowl to the mixer. Set to Stir and mix until a dough forms.
2. Remove the flat beater and attach the dough hook. Set to Speed 2 and knead until dough is stretchy, about 8 minutes. Remove the mixer bowl and cover with plastic wrap. Let dough rise in a warm, draft-free place until tripled in bulk, about 4 hours.
3. Turn dough out onto a generously floured work surface. Using a pastry knife or a metal dough knife, fold dough into thirds, much as you would fold a business letter. Flour the top and pat dough down. Cover with a towel and let stand for about 20 minutes. Flip dough, fold it again and let stand for 20 minutes. (This process tightens the dough so the loaves will have a nice shape.) Dip a metal pastry scraper into cool water and cut dough crosswise into 4 loaves.
4. Cut 4 sheets of parchment paper into pieces 3 inches (7.5 cm) larger on all sides than the loaves. Liberally flour dough, place on parchment paper and cover with towels. Let rise until doubled in bulk, about 2 hours. Meanwhile, place oven rack in the middle position, line with clay oven tiles and preheat oven to 450°F (230°C).

5. Carefully slide 2 of the loaves, with parchment paper, onto baking sheet. Place baking sheet on the hot tiles and remove it much as a magician would pull a tablecloth from a set table, leaving the parchment paper and loaves on the tiles. Make sure the loaves do not touch and have enough room to expand. Spray loaves and the inside of the oven with water. Shut the door quickly. Spray again 3 times, at 2-minute intervals. Bake for 25 to 30 minutes, or until loaves reach an internal temperature of 200°F (100°C). Let cool completely on wire racks. Repeat with the remaining loaves.

Makes 4 loaves

Make ahead

Wrap bread in plastic wrap and then foil and store in the freezer for up to 6 weeks. Reheat frozen loaf, unwrapped, in a 350°F (180°C) oven for about 15 minutes to bring back the crusty exterior. Let cool on the counter for about 10 minutes before slicing.

TIP

The water should be around 100°F (38°C). Yeast can be killed at temperatures above 115°F (45°C). Water at 100°F (38°C) will feel just warm.

Monkey Bread

FLAT BEATER ◆ DOUGH HOOK

◆ 10-inch (3 L) Bundt pan, sprayed with vegetable spray

Dough		
1	envelope (¼ oz/7 g) active dry yeast	1
¼ cup	warm water (see tip, page 220)	50 mL
⅓ cup	granulated sugar	75 mL
1 tsp	salt	5 mL
1	egg	1
1 cup	warm homogenized (whole) milk (see tip, page 233)	250 mL
¼ cup	unsalted butter, softened, divided	50 mL
4 cups	unbleached all-purpose flour, divided	1 L
Coating		
6 tbsp	unsalted butter, melted	90 mL
½ cup	lightly packed light brown sugar	125 mL
2 tsp	ground cinnamon	10 mL
Icing		
2 cups	confectioner's (icing) sugar, sifted	500 mL
¼ cup	homogenized (whole) milk	50 mL

Make ahead

Prepare dough through Step 2 in the evening and let rise overnight in the refrigerator. Let stand at room temperature for 1 hour before shaping.

Wrap baked bread in plastic wrap and then foil and store in the freezer for up to 2 weeks.

1. *Prepare the dough:* In the mixer bowl, stir together yeast, water and a pinch of the sugar. Let stand until yeast begins to foam, about 5 minutes. Add sugar, salt, egg, milk and 3 tbsp (45 mL) of the butter. Attach the flat beater and mixer bowl to the mixer. Set to Stir and mix until combined. Mix in 2 cups (500 mL) of the flour, in 4 additions, until a dough forms.

2. Remove the flat beater and attach the dough hook. Set to Speed 2 and mix in the remaining flour, in 4 additions. Continue kneading until dough is stretchy, about 1 minute. Using your hands, form dough into a ball. Place back in the mixer bowl, rub with the remaining 1 tbsp (15 mL) butter and cover with plastic wrap. Let rise in a warm, draft-free place until doubled in bulk, about 1 hour.

4. *Prepare the coating:* Place butter in a small bowl. In another bowl, combine brown sugar and cinnamon.

5. Cut dough into ½-inch (1 cm) pieces and roll into balls. Coat balls in melted butter, then roll in sugar-cinnamon mixture. Place in prepared pan, with balls touching, in layers as necessary. Cover with plastic wrap and let rise until doubled in bulk, about 1 hour. Meanwhile, place oven rack in the middle position and preheat oven to 350°F (180°C).

6. Bake for 30 to 35 minutes, or until top is golden. Let cool in pan on a wire rack for 15 minutes. Invert onto a serving plate, and let cool for 20 minutes. To serve, pull bread apart.

7. *Prepare the icing:* In a small bowl, stir together confectioner's sugar and milk until smooth. Drizzle over loaf.

Serves 6 to 8

Cinnamon Rolls (page 248)

Blue Cheese and Walnut Mini Muffins (page 268)

Linzertorte Cookies with Raspberry Filling (page 288)
and Grandma Re's Rugalach (page 291)

Cranberry Maple Squares (page 318)

Irish Soda Bread

FLAT BEATER

- Preheat oven to 375°F (190°C)
- Baking sheet, lined with parchment paper

4 cups	unbleached all-purpose flour	1 L
1 1/2 tsp	baking soda	7 mL
1 1/2 tsp	salt	7 mL
3 tbsp	granulated sugar	45 mL
3 tbsp	unsalted butter, softened	45 mL
1 cup	dried currants	250 mL
1 3/4 cups	buttermilk	425 mL
2 tbsp	unsalted butter, melted	25 mL

Make ahead

Store tightly wrapped in foil in the freezer for up to 2 weeks.

1. Sift flour, baking soda and salt into the mixer bowl. Attach the flat beater and mixer bowl to the mixer. Set to Stir and mix in sugar and softened butter until mixture resembles coarse crumbs. Add currants and buttermilk; mix until dough is evenly moistened but still lumpy.
2. Remove the flat beater and attach the dough hook. Set to Speed 2 and knead until a soft, slightly less sticky dough forms, about 1 minute.
3. Divide dough in half and form each half into a ball. Pat each ball into a domed 6-inch (15 cm) round and place on prepared baking sheet, at least 4 inches (10 cm) apart. Using a sharp knife, cut a 1/2-inch (1 cm) deep X into the top of each loaf. Brush loaves with melted butter.
4. Bake in middle of preheated oven for 35 to 40 minutes, or until loaves are golden brown, sound hollow when tapped on the bottom and reach an internal temperature of 200°F (100°C). Let cool completely on wire racks.

Makes two 6-inch (15 cm) loaves

Cardamom Bread

FLAT BEATER   DOUGH HOOK

◆ Baking sheet, lined with parchment paper

1 1/2 cups	homogenized (whole) milk	375 mL
1/2 cup	fancy molasses	125 mL
1/4 cup	unsalted butter, cut into pieces	50 mL
2 tbsp	liquid honey	25 mL
1 1/2 tbsp	active dry yeast	22 mL
3 1/4 cups	unbleached all-purpose flour	800 mL
2 cups	rye flour	500 mL
2 tsp	ground cardamom	10 mL
1 tsp	salt	5 mL
1 tsp	ground aniseed	5 mL
	Grated zest of 1 orange	
2 tbsp	unsalted butter, melted	25 mL

Slightly sweet and deeply colored from the molasses, cardamom bread makes a tasty sandwich bread or accompaniment to soups and stews.

1. In a small saucepan, combine milk, molasses, 1/4 cup (50 mL) butter and honey; heat over medium heat until butter is melted. Let cool to around 100°F (38°C) and add yeast. Let stand until yeast begins to foam, about 5 minutes.
2. In the mixer bowl, whisk together all-purpose flour, rye flour, cardamom, salt, aniseed and zest. Attach the flat beater and mixer bowl to the mixer. Set to Stir and mix in wet ingredients, stopping the mixer occasionally to push dry ingredients into the wet center, until a rough dough forms.
3. Remove the flat beater and attach the dough hook. Set to Speed 2 and knead until dough is smooth and elastic, about 10 minutes. Remove the mixer bowl and cover loosely with plastic wrap. Let dough rise in a warm, draft-free place until doubled in bulk, about 3 hours.
4. Uncover dough and punch down several times to work out air bubbles. Turn dough out onto a lightly floured work surface and cut in half. As you work with one piece of dough, keep the other covered. Working with one piece at a time, pat dough into a 10- by 8-inch (25 by 20 cm) rectangle. Starting with a long side, roll dough up jelly-roll style. Shape into a football and place on prepared baking sheet, seam side down. Repeat with remaining dough, making sure loaves do not touch. Cover with towels and let rise for 40 to 60 minutes, or until doubled in bulk. Meanwhile, place oven rack in the middle position and preheat oven to 375°F (190°C).

5. Using a sharp knife, make 3 slashes in the top of each loaf. Brush with melted butter. Bake for 15 minutes, then reduce temperature to 350°F (180°C). Bake until loaves reach an internal temperature of 200°F (100°C), about 20 minutes. Remove from pans and let cool completely on wire racks before slicing.

Makes 2 loaves

Make ahead

Store bread tightly wrapped in plastic wrap at room temperature for up to 6 days.

TIP

Cardamom is a member of the ginger family. It has a lemony flavor and is used mainly in Indian and Middle Eastern cuisines. You will also find it in many Scandinavian breads and pastries. It can be found in the pod, whole or ground. We like to buy our spices whole, if possible, and grind them ourselves for a more vibrant flavor.

Olive Oil Bread with Rosemary and Walnuts

FLAT BEATER DOUGH HOOK

- 2 rimless baking sheets, lined with parchment paper
- Clay oven tiles
- Water sprayer

3 1/2 cups	unbleached all-purpose flour (approx.)	875 mL
1 1/2 cups	whole wheat flour	375 mL
1	package (1/4 oz/7 g) active dry yeast	1
1 1/2 cups	warm water (see tip, opposite)	375 mL
1 tsp	granulated sugar	5 mL
1/2 cup	extra-virgin olive oil	125 mL
2 tbsp	finely chopped fresh rosemary	25 mL
1 tbsp	salt	15 mL
1 1/2 cups	chopped walnuts, toasted (see tip, page 215)	375 mL
1 tbsp	butter, softened	15 mL

1. In a medium bowl, combine all-purpose flour and whole wheat flour.
2. In the mixer bowl, stir together yeast, water and sugar. Let stand until yeast begins to foam, about 5 minutes. Add oil, rosemary and salt. Attach the flat beater and mixer bowl to the mixer. Set to Speed 2 and mix well. Add 3 cups (750 mL) of the flour mixture and mix just until a dough forms.
3. Remove the flat beater and attach the dough hook. Set to Speed 2 and knead, adding flour 1/4 cup (50 mL) at a time until dough clings to the dough hook and just cleans the sides of the bowl. Add walnuts and knead for 2 minutes, adding more flour if necessary to keep the dough from clinging to the bowl. (You may not need all of the flour. Save the remainder for dusting when shaping your loaves.) Form dough into a ball. Return dough to the mixer bowl, rub with butter and cover the bowl with greased plastic wrap. Let dough rise in a warm, draft-free place until doubled in bulk, 1 to 2 hours.
4. Uncover dough and punch down several times to work out air bubbles. Form into a ball, turn over in the bowl, cover bowl and let rise for 1 hour.

5. Uncover dough and turn out onto a lightly floured surface. Divide dough in half and form each half into a smooth 5-inch (12.5 cm) round. Place rounds on prepared baking sheets. Cover with plastic wrap and let rise until nearly doubled in bulk, 45 to 60 minutes. Meanwhile, place oven rack in the lower third of oven, line with clay oven tiles and preheat oven to 400°F (200°C).
6. Spray loaves and the inside of the oven with water and place baking sheets on the hot tiles. Remove baking sheets much as a magician would pull a tablecloth from a set table, leaving the parchment paper and loaves on the tiles. Make sure the loaves do not touch and have enough room to expand. Spray loaves again in 2 minutes and again 2 minutes after that. Bake for 25 to 30 minutes, or until loaves are golden and crusty and reach an internal temperature of 200°F (100°C). Let cool completely on wire racks before slicing.

Makes 2 loaves

TIPS

The water should be around 100°F (38°C). Yeast can be killed at temperatures above 115°F (45°C). Water at 100°F (38°C) will feel just warm.

When adding the walnuts to the dough, you may find that they accumulate at the bottom of the mixer bowl rather than mixing into the dough. If this happens, stop the mixer, lift the dough out and knead the nuts in by hand to begin the process, then return dough to the mixer to finish kneading.

Sun-Dried Tomato Bread with Pine Nuts

FLAT BEATER DOUGH HOOK

◆ 9- by 5-inch (2 L) loaf pan, greased

3/4 cup	chopped drained oil-packed sun-dried tomatoes	175 mL
1 tbsp	oil from sun-dried tomatoes or olive oil	15 mL
1	clove garlic, minced	1
1/4 cup	minced onion	50 mL
2 tbsp	fresh rosemary	25 mL
1/3 cup	pine nuts	75 mL
1	package (1/4 oz/7 g) active dry yeast	1
1/3 cup	warm water (see tip, opposite)	75 mL
3 1/2 cups	unbleached all-purpose flour (approx.)	875 mL
2 tsp	salt	10 mL
1 cup	cool water	250 mL
2 tsp	oil from sun-dried tomatoes	10 mL
1/2 cup	shredded Asiago cheese	125 mL

1. In a medium skillet, heat the 1 tbsp (15 mL) oil over medium heat. Add garlic and onion; sauté until onion is translucent, about 3 minutes. Add rosemary and sauté for 1 minute. Let cool.
2. Meanwhile, in a microwave-safe bowl, microwave pine nuts on High for 30 seconds. Stir with a fork and microwave for another 30 seconds; repeat if necessary until toasted. Let cool.
3. In the mixer bowl, stir together yeast and warm water. Let stand until yeast begins to foam, about 5 minutes. Add onion mixture, flour, sun-dried tomatoes, salt, cool water and the 2 tsp (10 mL) oil. Attach the flat beater and the mixer bowl to the mixer. Set to Stir and mix until a dough forms.
4. Remove the flat beater and attach the dough hook. Set to Speed 2 and knead until dough is smooth and elastic, about 5 minutes. Knead in pine nuts. If dough is sticky, add flour 1 tbsp (15 mL) at a time. Remove the mixer bowl and cover with plastic wrap. Let dough rise in a warm, draft-free place until doubled in bulk, about 1 hour.
5. Uncover dough and punch down several times to work out air bubbles. Turn out onto a lightly floured work surface. Pat dough into a 15- by 9-inch (38 by 23 cm) rectangle. Sprinkle with cheese. Starting with a long side, roll dough up jelly-roll style and place in prepared loaf pan, seam side down. Cover with a towel and let rise until the top of the dough is just above the top of the loaf pan, about 45 minutes. Meanwhile, place oven rack in the middle position and preheat oven to 400°F (200°C).

6. Using a sharp knife, make a crisscross slash in the top of the loaf. Bake for 15 minutes. Reduce temperature to 375°F (190°C) and bake until loaf is golden brown and reaches an internal temperature of 200°F (100°C), about 25 minutes. Remove from pan and let cool on a wire rack for 5 minutes. Serve warm or cool.

Makes 1 loaf

Variation

Make individual rolls by shaping dough in ⅓-cup (75 mL) portions into balls and sprinkling with cheese. Arrange rolls on a baking sheet lined with parchment paper, at least 2 inches (5 cm) apart. Cover with a towel and let rise until slightly puffed, about 30 minutes. Bake at 400°F (200°C) for about 15 to 20 minutes, or until rolls are light brown and reach an internal temperature of 200°F (100°C).

Make ahead

Prepare dough through Step 4 in the evening and let rise overnight in the refrigerator. Let stand at room temperature for 1 hour before shaping.

Wrap baked bread in plastic wrap and then foil and store in the freezer for up to 2 weeks.

TIP

The water should be around 100°F (38°C). Yeast can be killed at temperatures above 115°F (45°C). Water at 100°F (38°C) will feel just warm.

Walnut Bread

FLAT BEATER · DOUGH HOOK

- Baking sheet, greased

1/2 cup	unsalted butter	125 mL
3/4 cup	finely chopped onion	175 mL
5 cups	unbleached all-purpose flour	1.25 L
1 cup	whole wheat flour	250 mL
1	envelope (1/4 oz/7 g) active dry yeast	1
2 cups	warm homogenized (whole) milk (see tip, opposite)	500 mL
2 tbsp	granulated sugar	25 mL
2 1/2 tsp	salt	12 mL
2 tsp	unsalted butter, softened	10 mL
3/4 cup	coarsely chopped toasted walnuts (see tip, opposite)	175 mL

Make ahead

Prepare dough through Step 4 in the evening and let rise overnight in the refrigerator.

Wrap baked bread in plastic wrap and then foil and store in the freezer for up to 2 weeks.

1. In a large heavy skillet, melt the 1/2 cup (125 mL) butter over medium heat. Add onion and sauté until tender, about 5 minutes. Let cool.
2. In a medium bowl, combine all-purpose and whole wheat flours. Set aside.
3. In the mixer bowl, stir together yeast, milk and sugar. Let stand until yeast begins to foam, about 5 minutes. Add onion mixture, 3 cups (750 mL) of the flour mixture and salt. Attach the flat beater and the mixer bowl to the mixer. Set to Speed 2 and mix until a dough forms.
4. Remove the flat beater and attach the dough hook. Set to Speed 2 and knead, adding flour mixture 1/2 cup (125 mL) at a time until dough clings to the dough hook and just cleans the sides of the bowl. (You may not need all of the flour mixture. Save the remainder for dusting.) Continue to knead for 4 minutes. Using your hands, form dough into a ball. Place back in the mixer bowl, coat with softened butter and cover with a towel. Let rise in a warm, draft-free place for 1 to 2 hours, or until doubled in bulk.
5. Uncover dough and punch down several times to work out air bubbles. Sprinkle with walnuts. Return the bowl to the mixer, with the dough hook still attached. Set to Speed 4 and knead just long enough to incorporate the nuts.

6. Turn dough out onto a floured work surface and cut in half. Shape each half into a 6-inch (15 cm) round loaf. Place on prepared baking sheet, 4 inches (10 cm) apart. Flatten slightly and cover with a towel. Let rise until almost doubled in bulk, about 45 minutes. Meanwhile, place oven rack in the middle position and preheat oven to 400°F (200°C).
7. Bake until loaves are golden brown, sound hollow when tapped on the bottom and reach an internal temperature of 200°F (100°C), about 25 minutes. Let cool on wire racks before slicing.

Makes 2 loaves

TIPS

The milk should be around 100°F (38°C). Yeast can be killed at temperatures above 115°F (45°C). Milk at 100°F (38°C) will feel just warm.

To toast nuts, spread them on a baking sheet and toast in a 350°F (180°C) oven for 7 to 8 minutes, or until lightly browned.

Basic Pizza Dough

FLAT BEATER ◆ DOUGH HOOK

- ◆ Pizza stone or clay oven tiles
- ◆ Pizza peel or rimless baking sheet

1	package (1/4 oz/7 g) active dry yeast	1
1 1/3 cups	warm water (see tip, opposite)	325 mL
1 tbsp	granulated sugar	15 mL
1 tbsp	extra-virgin olive oil	15 mL
3 1/3 cups	unbleached all-purpose flour	825 mL
1 tbsp	salt	15 mL
	Cornmeal	

Make ahead

The dough can be made 1 day ahead and kept in a bowl, tightly covered with plastic wrap, in the refrigerator. It can also be frozen for up to 4 weeks. Thaw overnight in the refrigerator. In either case, let warm to room temperature before shaping.

1. In a bowl, stir together yeast, water and sugar. Let stand until yeast begins to foam, 3 to 4 minutes. Stir in oil.
2. Place flour and salt in the mixer bowl. Attach the flat beater and mixer bowl to the mixer. Set to Speed 2 and mix until salt is blended evenly into the flour. Quickly pour in yeast mixture and mix until a dough forms.
3. Remove the flat beater and attach the dough hook. Set to Speed 2 and knead until dough is smooth and elastic and cleans the sides of the bowl, about 3 minutes. Remove the mixer bowl and cover with plastic wrap or a towel. Let dough rise in a warm, draft-free place until doubled in bulk, about 45 minutes.
4. Place pizza stone or tiles on oven rack and preheat oven to 450°F (230°C).
5. Uncover dough and punch down several times to work out air bubbles. Turn out onto a floured work surface and cut in half. As you work with the first piece of dough, keep the other covered. Roll one piece of dough into a 12-inch (30 cm) round. Transfer to peel or baking sheet sprinkled with cornmeal. Open the oven door and place the front edge of the peel at the back edge of the stone. Tilt the peel slightly and pull it back toward you, transferring the dough to the stone. Bake for about 2 minutes, or until the dough has firmed up. To retrieve the dough, slide the peel under it, scooping it up. Repeat with the second piece of dough.

6. Top the first pizza shell with desired toppings (see "Pizza possibilities," below) and return to the oven in the same manner. Bake for 12 to 15 minutes, or until cheese is golden and bottom is crispy. Transfer to a cutting board and let cool for about 3 minutes before slicing. Repeat with second pizza shell.

Makes two 12-inch (30 cm) pizza shells

Pizza possibilities

You can top pizza with almost anything, but here are a few tips: We like to use a combination of grated mozzarella, fontina, and Parmesan cheeses. For pizza sauce, you can use a basic tomato sauce, but we also like to use pesto. If you add fresh tomatoes, make sure to slice them thinly so they cook properly. Here are some topping combinations we especially enjoy:

- Red bell pepper, kalamata olives and feta cheese
- Pesto, thinly sliced tomatoes and fontina cheese
- Marinara Sauce (page 409), pepperoni, sausage and mozzarella cheese
- Garlic, marinated artichokes and Asiago cheese
- Sautéed wild mushrooms, onions and goat cheese
- Garlic oil and a mixture of Asiago, mozzarella and Parmesan cheeses
- Pesto, red bell pepper, kalamata olives, cilantro, red onion and Monterey Jack cheese

TIPS

The water should be around 100°F (38°C). Yeast can be killed at temperatures above 115°F (45°C). Water at 100°F (38°C) will feel just warm.

The reason we partially bake the pizza before topping it is because once the dough is on the peel, it begins to attract moisture. In the time it takes to top a pizza, the dough might stick to the peel, making a mess when you try to get it onto the hot stones. By quickly laying the dough on the peel and immediately getting it into the oven, you guarantee that it won't stick and make a mess of your oven, floor and stone.

Baking pizza on a hot pizza stone or tiles gives the best result, and if you plan to make pizza once in a while the stone and peel are well worth the investment. However, if you don't own either of those tools, you can still make a good pizza. Prepare the pizza on a rimless baking sheet, place it in the oven and cook for 5 minutes, or until the dough has stiffened a bit. Then slide the pizza onto the oven rack and continue cooking until the bottom is crispy and the top is golden and bubbly.

Parmesan Bread Sticks

FLAT BEATER DOUGH HOOK

- 2 baking sheets, lined with parchment paper

1 cup	homogenized (whole) milk	250 mL
1/4 cup	unsalted butter, cut into pieces	50 mL
1	envelope (1/4 oz/7 g) active dry yeast	1
1/4 cup	warm water (see tip, opposite)	50 mL
1 tbsp	granulated sugar	15 mL
1	egg	1
4 cups	sifted unbleached all-purpose flour (approx.), divided	1 L
2 tsp	salt	10 mL
1/2 cup	unsalted butter, melted, divided	125 mL
1 1/2 cups	freshly grated Parmesan cheese	375 mL

1. In a small saucepan, heat milk and the 1/4 cup (50 mL) butter over medium heat until butter is melted. Let cool to around 100°F (38°C).
2. In the mixer bowl, stir together yeast, water and sugar. Let stand until yeast begins to foam, about 5 minutes. Add milk mixture and egg. Attach the flat beater and mixer bowl to the mixer. Set to Speed 2 and mix until combined. Add 1 1/2 cups (375 mL) of the flour and salt; mix until a wet, sticky dough forms (this is called a sponge). Remove the mixer bowl and cover loosely with plastic wrap. Let rise in a warm, draft-free place until doubled in bulk, about 1 hour.
3. Remove the flat beater and attach the dough hook and mixer bowl to the mixer. Set to Speed 2 and add the remaining flour, 1/2 cup (125 mL) at a time, until dough clings to the dough hook and just cleans the sides of the bowl. (You may not need all of the flour. Save the remainder for dusting.) Continue kneading for 4 minutes, until dough is smooth and elastic. Using your hands, form dough into a ball. Place back in the mixer bowl, brush lightly with melted butter and cover loosely with plastic wrap. Let rise for 1 to 2 hours, or until doubled in bulk. Meanwhile, place oven racks in the lower middle and upper middle positions and preheat oven to 375°F (190°C).

4. Place remaining melted butter and Parmesan cheese in separate shallow dishes. Uncover dough and punch down several times to work out air bubbles. Divide dough into 16 pieces, cover loosely with plastic wrap and let rest for 5 minutes. As you work with each piece of dough, keep the rest covered. Working with one piece at a time, roll dough between the palms of your hands. Make it as long as you like, but not longer than the baking sheets. Dip in melted butter, letting excess drip off, then lightly coat with Parmesan. Place on prepared baking sheet. Repeat with remaining dough.
5. Bake until golden brown, about 15 minutes. Remove bread sticks to a wire rack and let cool. Serve warm or at room temperature.

Makes 16 bread sticks

Make ahead

Store bread sticks in a large heavy-duty plastic bag at room temperature for up to 2 days. Or freeze in a doubled plastic bag for up to 2 weeks. To reheat, wrap in foil and heat in a 350°F (180°C) oven until warm, about 15 minutes.

TIP

The water should be around 100°F (38°C). Yeast can be killed at temperatures above 115°F (45°C). Water at 100°F (38°C) will feel just warm.

Sandwich Buns

FLAT BEATER   DOUGH HOOK

- 2 large baking sheets, lined with parchment paper and sprinkled with cornmeal

1 cup	homogenized (whole) milk	250 mL
1⁄3 cup	unsalted butter, cut into pieces	75 mL
1	package (1⁄4 oz/7 g) active dry yeast	1
3⁄4 cup	warm water (see tip, opposite)	175 mL
2 tbsp	granulated sugar	25 mL
2 1⁄2 tsp	salt	12 mL
2	eggs, at room temperature	2
5 1⁄2 to 6 cups	unbleached all-purpose flour (approx.), divided	1.375 to 1.5 L
1 tbsp	unsalted butter, softened	15 mL
1	egg white, beaten with 1 tsp (5 mL) water (optional)	1
	Sesame or poppy seeds (optional)	

1. In a small saucepan, heat milk and the 1⁄3 cup (75 mL) butter over medium heat until butter is melted. Let cool to around 100°F (38°C).
2. In the mixer bowl, stir together yeast, water and a pinch of sugar. Let stand until yeast begins to foam, about 5 minutes. Add milk mixture, sugar, salt and eggs. Attach the flat beater and mixer bowl to the mixer. Set to Speed 2 and mix until combined. Add 4 cups (1 L) of the flour and mix until a dough forms.
3. Remove the flat beater and attach the dough hook. Set to Speed 2 and knead, adding flour 1⁄2 cup (125 mL) at a time, until dough forms a smooth and elastic ball that cleans the bowl. Continue to knead for 2 minutes, adding flour 1 tbsp (15 mL) at a time as necessary to keep dough from clinging to the bowl. (You may not need all of the flour. Save the remainder for dusting.) Using your hands, form dough into a ball. Place back in the mixer bowl, rub with softened butter and cover loosely with plastic wrap. Let rise in a warm, draft-free place for 1 to 2 hours, or until doubled in bulk.
4. Uncover dough and punch down several times to work out air bubbles. Turn over in the bowl. Cover with plastic wrap and let rise until doubled in bulk, about 1 hour.

5. Uncover dough and punch down again. Turn dough out onto a lightly floured work surface and cut into 12 equal pieces. As you work with each piece of dough, keep the rest covered. Working with one piece at a time, shape dough into a smooth ball. Flatten slightly with the palm of your hand and place on prepared baking sheet. If desired, brush tops with egg wash and sprinkle with sesame seeds. Repeat with remaining dough, placing at least 4 inches (10 cm) apart on sheets. Cover with towels and let rise for 30 minutes, until slightly risen. Flatten gently again. Meanwhile, place oven racks in the lower middle and upper middle positions and preheat oven to 375°F (190°C).
6. Bake for 25 to 30 minutes, switching baking sheets halfway through, until buns are golden and reach an internal temperature of 200°F (100°C). Remove to wire racks and let cool completely.

Makes 12 buns

Make ahead

Store buns in a large heavy-duty plastic bag at room temperature for up to 2 days. Or freeze in a doubled plastic bag for up to 2 weeks. To thaw, let stand on the counter in bags until soft.

TIP

The water should be around 100°F (38°C). Yeast can be killed at temperatures above 115°F (45°C). Water at 100°F (38°C) will feel just warm.

Croissants

FLAT BEATER ◆ DOUGH HOOK

- Baking sheet, lined with parchment paper

1	package ($\frac{1}{4}$ oz/7 g) active dry yeast	1
$1\frac{1}{2}$ cups	milk, warmed to about 110°F (43°C) (see tip, opposite)	375 mL
2 tbsp	granulated sugar	25 mL
$3\frac{1}{2}$ cups	unbleached all-purpose flour	875 mL
$2\frac{1}{2}$ tsp	salt	12 mL
$2\frac{1}{2}$	sticks cold, unsalted butter (10 oz/300 g)	$2\frac{1}{2}$
1	egg, beaten with 2 tbsp (25 mL) water	1

Thanks to Julia Child and Simone Beck's Mastering the Art of French Cooking *for inspiring this recipe.*

1. In a bowl, stir together yeast, warm milk and sugar. Let stand until yeast begins to foam, 3 to 4 minutes. Stir briefly to dissolve the sugar.
2. Place flour and salt in the mixer bowl. Attach the flat beater and mixer bowl to the mixer. Set to Stir and mix until combined. Add milk mixture, increase to Speed 2 and mix until a dough forms.
3. Remove the flat beater and attach the dough hook. Set to Speed 2 and knead until dough is smooth and elastic, about 4 minutes. Remove the mixer bowl and cover with plastic wrap. Let dough rise in a warm, draft-free place until tripled in bulk, $2\frac{1}{2}$ to 3 hours.
4. Deflate the dough by loosening up the sides with a rubber spatula. Cover and refrigerate for 30 minutes. (This will make the dough easier to handle.)
5. Turn dough out onto a floured work surface. Using a floured rolling pin, roll out into a 20- by 14-inch (50 by 35 cm) rectangle.
6. On another floured work surface, lay out the butter with the two full sticks side by side and the half stick across the top end to form what looks like two columns with a top. Generously flour the butter and, with a rolling pin, pound the butter into one large flat piece that measures roughly 14 by 12 inches (35 by 30 cm). Transfer the butter to the dough, covering two-thirds of the dough and leaving a 1-inch (2.5 cm) border around the edges. (If the butter breaks into pieces, just piece it back together on the dough.)
7. Starting at the section of dough that isn't covered in butter, fold dough up and over half of the butter-covered dough. Fold the other end of the dough up and over the previous fold. You now have 3 layers of dough, covering 2 layers of butter. (This is called turn 1.)

8. Turn the dough so that an open end is facing you and roll out into an 18- by 10-inch (45 by 25 cm) rectangle. Brush any flour from the top of the dough with a dry pastry brush and fold into thirds as before. Wrap tightly in plastic wrap and refrigerate for 1 hour.
9. Roll out chilled dough into an 18- by 10-inch (45 by 25 cm) rectangle. Fold into thirds, then roll out again and fold again, making 4 total turns. Rewrap the dough and refrigerate for 1 hour or store in a sealable plastic bag overnight to be baked the next day.
10. About 2 hours before you need the croissants, roll out dough on a lightly floured work surface into a 24- by 8-inch (60 by 20 cm) rectangle. Cut in half crosswise and refrigerate one half while you shape the other. Roll into a 24- by 8-inch (60 by 20 cm) rectangle and cut into 6 squares. Refrigerate 5 of the squares while shaping the first one. Cut the square on the diagonal to make 2 triangles and roll out each triangle from the wide end to the tip until it is about 7 inches (18 cm) long. Make a 1-inch (2.5 cm) cut in the middle of the wide end and roll from the wide end to the tip, forming a roll. Bend the ends down to form a crescent and arrange 3 inches (7.5 cm) apart on prepared baking sheet. Repeat with the remaining squares. (It is important to keep the dough cold. If it starts to look oily or becomes difficult to work with, return it to the refrigerator to firm up.) Cover croissants with a towel and let rise for 1 hour. Meanwhile, preheat oven to 450°F (230°C).
11. Brush croissants with egg wash and bake for 12 to 15 minutes, or until puffed and browned. Serve hot or at room temperature.

Makes 24 croissants

TIP

Warm milk in a microwave-safe measuring cup or bowl in the microwave on High for 30 seconds.

Make ahead

Since they are so full of butterfat, these rolls freeze well for up to 2 weeks. To reheat, place thawed rolls on a baking sheet and warm in a 400°F (200°C) oven for 5 minutes.

Popovers

WIRE WHIP

- Preheat oven to 450°F (230°C)
- 12-cup muffin tin, generously greased

4	eggs	4
2 cups	unbleached all-purpose flour	500 mL
1 tsp	salt	5 mL
2 cups	homogenized (whole) milk	500 mL
1 tbsp	unsalted butter, melted	15 mL

TIP
Do not open the oven while popovers are cooking. The heat loss will deflate them, and they won't be nicely puffed.

1. Break eggs into the mixer bowl. Attach the whip and mixer bowl to the mixer. Set to Speed 2 and beat well. Add flour, salt, milk and butter; beat, scraping down bowl as necessary, until just combined.
2. Fill muffin cups three-quarters full. Bake in middle of preheated oven for 15 minutes, then reduce temperature to 350°F (180°C) and bake for 20 minutes, until well browned and crusty. Remove to a wire rack, puncture sides with a sharp knife to let steam escape and serve immediately.

Makes 12 large popovers

Variation

Herbed Popovers: Add 2 cloves garlic, finely minced, and 2 tbsp (25 mL) finely minced fresh rosemary with the flour.

Onion Rolls

FLAT BEATER · DOUGH HOOK

- 2 baking sheets, lined with parchment paper

1	package (1/4 oz/7 g) active dry yeast	1
1 1/3 cups	warm homogenized (whole) milk (see tip, below)	325 mL
4 cups	unbleached all-purpose flour (approx.)	1 L
1/4 cup	granulated sugar	50 mL
1 1/2 tsp	salt	7 mL
1	egg, lightly beaten	1
2 tbsp	olive oil	25 mL
2 tsp	olive oil	10 mL
1/2 cup	diced onion	125 mL
1	egg, beaten with 1 tsp (5 mL) water	1

Make ahead

Prepare dough through Step 2 in the evening and let rise overnight in the refrigerator. Let stand at room temperature for 1 hour before shaping

Store rolls in a large heavy-duty plastic bag at room temperature for up to 2 days. Or freeze in a doubled plastic bag for up to 2 weeks.

TIPS

The milk should be around 100°F (38°C). Yeast can be killed at temperatures above 115°F (45°C). Milk at 100°F (38°C) will feel just warm.

To make sandwich buns, divide dough into 10 large rolls instead of 18 smaller ones. Because of their larger size, they will take a few more minutes to bake. These buns are delicious wrapped around a hamburger.

1. In the mixer bowl, stir together yeast and milk. Let stand until yeast starts to foam, about 5 minutes. Add flour, sugar and salt. Attach the flat beater and mixer bowl to the mixer. Set to Stir and mix until combined. Add egg and the 2 tbsp (25 mL) olive oil; mix until a dough forms, about 1 minute.
2. Remove the flat beater and attach the dough hook. Set to Speed 2 and knead until dough forms a smooth and elastic ball that cleans the bowl, about 10 minutes. If dough is sticky, add flour 1 tbsp (15 mL) at a time as necessary to tighten it up. Remove the mixer bowl and cover loosely with plastic wrap. Let dough rise in a warm, draft-free place until doubled in bulk, about 2 hours.
3. Meanwhile, in a small skillet, heat the 2 tsp (5 mL) olive oil. Add onion and sauté until tender and beginning to turn golden brown, about 12 minutes. Let cool to room temperature.
4. Uncover dough and punch down several times to work out air bubbles. Add cooled onions. Return the bowl to the mixer, with the dough hook still attached. Set to Speed 4 and knead just long enough to incorporate the onions.
5. Divide dough into 18 equal pieces and roll into tightly formed balls. Arrange on prepared baking sheets, about 2 inches (5 cm) apart. Cover with a towel and let rise until nearly doubled in bulk, about 1 hour. Meanwhile, place oven racks in the lower middle and upper middle positions and preheat oven to 400°F (200°C).

5. Brush rolls with egg wash and bake until they are nicely browned and reach an internal temperature of 200°F (100°C), about 15 minutes. For the best texture, let cool on wire racks for at least 15 minutes before serving.

Makes 18 rolls

Kalamata Olive Rolls

FLAT BEATER DOUGH HOOK

- Large baking sheet, lined with parchment paper

1	package (1/4 oz/7 g) active dry yeast	1
1 1/2 cups	warm water (see tip, below)	375 mL
4 cups	unbleached all-purpose flour (approx.)	1 L
2 tsp	salt	10 mL
1/2 tsp	cracked black pepper (optional)	2 mL
1/3 cup	olive oil, divided	75 mL
1/2 cup	chopped pitted kalamata olives	125 mL
	Coarse sea salt	

Make ahead

Prepare dough through Step 2 in the evening and let rise overnight in the refrigerator. Let stand at room temperature for 1 hour before serving.

Store rolls in a large heavy-duty plastic bag at room temperature for up to 2 days. Or freeze in a doubled plastic bag for up to 2 weeks.

TIP

The water should be around 100°F (38°C). Yeast can be killed at temperatures above 115°F (45°C). Water at 100°F (38°C) will feel just warm.

1. In the mixer bowl, stir together yeast and water. Let stand until yeast starts to foam, about 5 minutes. Add flour, salt, cracked black pepper (if using) and 1/4 cup (50 mL) of the olive oil. Attach the flat beater and mixer bowl to the mixer. Set to Stir and mix, stopping the mixer occasionally to scrape down bowl, until a dough forms.
2. Remove the flat beater and attach the dough hook. Set to Speed 2 and knead until dough is smooth and elastic, about 7 minutes. If dough is not cleaning the bowl, add flour 1 tbsp (15 mL) at a time as necessary. Remove the mixer bowl and cover loosely with plastic wrap. Let dough rise in a warm, draft-free place until doubled in bulk, about 2 hours.
3. Uncover dough and punch down several times to work out air bubbles. Turn dough out onto a lightly floured surface and knead in olives by hand. Divide dough into 12 equal pieces and roll into tightly formed balls. Arrange on prepared baking sheet, about 2 inches (5 cm) apart. Cover with a towel and let rise until doubled in bulk, about 1 1/2 hours. Meanwhile, place oven rack in the middle position and preheat oven to 400°F (200°C).
4. Brush rolls with the remaining olive oil and sprinkle with sea salt. Bake until rolls are golden brown and reach an internal temperature of 200°F (100°C), about 20 minutes. Let cool on a wire rack. Serve warm or cool.

Makes 12 rolls

Cloverleaf Rolls

FLAT BEATER • DOUGH HOOK

- 2 baking sheets, lined with parchment paper

1	package (1/4 oz/7 g) active dry yeast	1
1 1/3 cups	warm homogenized (whole) milk (see tip, below)	325 mL
4 cups	unbleached all-purpose flour (approx.)	1 L
1/4 cup	granulated sugar	50 mL
1 1/2 tsp	salt	7 mL
1	egg, lightly beaten	1
2 tbsp	unsalted butter, melted	25 mL
1	egg, beaten with 1 tsp (5 mL) water	1

Make ahead

Prepare dough through Step 2 in the evening and let rise overnight in the refrigerator. Let stand at room temperature for 1 hour before shaping.

Store rolls in a large heavy-duty plastic bag at room temperature for up to 2 days. Or freeze in a doubled plastic bag for up to 2 weeks.

TIP

The milk should be around 100°F (38°C). Yeast can be killed at temperatures above 115°F (45°C). Milk at 100°F (38°C) will feel just warm.

1. In the mixer bowl, stir together yeast and milk. Let stand until yeast starts to foam, about 5 minutes. Add flour, sugar and salt. Attach the flat beater and mixer bowl to the mixer. Set to Stir and mix until combined. Add egg and butter; mix until a dough forms.
2. Remove the flat beater and attach the dough hook. Set to Speed 2 and knead until dough forms a smooth and elastic ball that cleans the bowl, about 10 minutes. If dough is sticky, add flour 1 tbsp (15 mL) at a time as necessary. Remove the mixer bowl and cover loosely with plastic wrap. Let dough rise in a warm, draft-free place until doubled in bulk, about 2 hours.
3. Uncover dough and punch down several times to work out air bubbles. Turn dough out onto a lightly floured surface. Divide into 18 equal pieces and roll into tightly formed balls. Arrange on prepared baking sheets, about 2 inches (5 cm) apart. Cover with a towel and let rise until nearly doubled in bulk, about 1 hour. Meanwhile, place oven racks in the lower middle and upper middle positions and preheat oven to 400°F (200°C).
4. Using kitchen shears, make two right-angle cuts on each roll to create a cloverleaf shape. Brush with egg wash and bake until rolls are nicely browned and reach an internal temperature of 200°F (100°C), about 15 minutes. For the best texture, let cool on wire racks for at least 15 minutes before serving.

Makes 18 rolls

Grandma Gray's Nut Rolls

FLAT BEATER   DOUGH HOOK

- 2 baking sheets, lined with parchment paper

Dough		
2	packages (each 1/4 oz/7 g) active dry yeast	2
2 cups	cooled scalded homogenized (whole) milk, divided (see tip, opposite)	500 mL
1 cup	granulated sugar	250 mL
1 tsp	salt	5 mL
1 cup	unsalted butter, softened	250 mL
2	eggs, beaten	2
7 cups	unbleached all-purpose flour (approx.), divided	1.75 L
Filling		
2	eggs, beaten	2
2 lbs	walnut halves, finely ground (about 5 cups/1.25 L)	1 kg
2 cups	granulated sugar	500 mL
1 1/3 cups	homogenized (whole) milk	325 mL
1 cup	unsalted butter, melted	250 mL
1/4 tsp	salt	1 mL
1	egg, beaten	1

Grandma Gray made these rich, buttery walnut rolls every holiday, much to the delight of family and friends. They're the perfect gift during the holidays.

1. *Prepare the dough:* In a small bowl, stir together yeast and 1 cup (250 mL) of the milk. Let stand until yeast begins to foam, about 5 minutes.
2. Place sugar, salt and butter in the mixer bowl. Attach the flat beater and mixer bowl to the mixer. Set to Speed 4 and mix until light and fluffy, about 2 minutes. Add eggs and beat for 1 minute. Set to Stir and add yeast mixture and 3 cups (750 mL) of the flour. Increase to Speed 2 and beat until well mixed, about 1 minute. Beat in the remaining flour alternately with the remaining milk, making 3 additions of dry and 2 of wet.
3. Remove the flat beater and attach the dough hook. Set to Speed 2 and knead until dough is smooth and elastic, about 10 minutes. Remove the mixer bowl and cover loosely with plastic wrap. Let rise in a warm, draft-free place until doubled in bulk, about 2 hours.
4. *Meanwhile, prepare the filling:* In a large saucepan, over medium heat, cook eggs, walnuts, sugar, milk, butter and salt, stirring constantly, for 10 to 15 minutes, or until thickened. Be careful that the bottom doesn't scorch. Let cool.

5. Uncover dough and punch down several times to work out air bubbles. Turn out onto a lightly floured work surface and divide into 5 equal parts. As you work with each piece of dough, keep the rest covered. Working with one piece at a time, roll out dough into a 12-inch (30 cm) square. It will be thin. Spread with one-fifth of the filling, leaving a 1-inch (2.5 cm) border. Starting from the far edge, roll up dough tightly jelly-roll style. Pinch ends together and place seam side down on prepared baking sheet. Repeat with remaining dough, leaving 4 to 5 inches (10 to 13 cm) between rolls. Cover with towels and let rise for 30 minutes. Meanwhile, place oven racks in the lower middle and upper middle positions and preheat oven to 350°F (180°C).
6. Brush rolls with egg wash and bake for 45 to 50 minutes, or until rolls are golden brown and reach an internal temperature of 200°F (100°C). Let cool completely on a wire rack before slicing.

Makes five 14-inch (35 cm) rolls

Make ahead

Prepare dough through Step 3 in the evening and let rise overnight in the refrigerator. Let stand at room temperature for 1 hour before serving.

Store rolls in a large heavy-duty plastic bag at room temperature for up to 2 days. Or freeze in a doubled plastic bag for up to 2 weeks.

TIPS

To scald milk, place in a heavy saucepan and bring to a simmer over medium heat. Remove from heat and let cool.

After cooling, the milk should be around 100°F (38°C). Yeast can be killed at temperatures above 115°F (45°C). Milk at 100°F (38°C) will feel just warm.

Cinnamon Rolls

FLAT BEATER ◆ DOUGH HOOK

◆ 13- by 9-inch (3 L) baking pan, lined with parchment paper

Dough		
3 cups	unbleached all-purpose flour	750 mL
1/4 cup	granulated sugar	50 mL
1 tsp	salt	5 mL
1 tbsp	active dry yeast	15 mL
1/4 cup	warm homogenized (whole) milk (see tip, page 245)	50 mL
3	eggs	3
3/4 cup	unsalted butter, cut into 12 pieces	175 mL
Cinnamon Butter		
1 cup	lightly packed light brown sugar	250 mL
1/4 cup	unbleached all-purpose flour	50 mL
2 1/4 tsp	ground cinnamon	11 mL
Pinch	salt	Pinch
1/2 cup	unsalted butter, softened	125 mL
3/4 cup	pecan halves, toasted (see tip, opposite) and coarsely ground	175 mL
Glaze		
1 1/2 cup	confectioner's (icing) sugar, sifted	375 mL
3 tbsp	whipping (35%) cream	15 mL

1. *Prepare the dough:* In a medium bowl, combine flour, sugar and salt. Set aside.
2. In the mixer bowl, stir together yeast and milk. Let stand until yeast begins to foam, about 5 minutes. Add eggs. Attach the flat beater and mixer bowl to the mixer. Set to Stir and mix until combined. Increase to Speed 2 and mix in flour mixture, 1/2 cup (125 mL) at a time, until incorporated.
3. Remove the flat beater and attach the dough hook. Set to Speed 2 and add butter, one piece at a time, incorporating each piece before adding the next. Continue kneading until dough is smooth and elastic, about 3 minutes. Place in a separate large bowl and cover with a towel. Let rise in a warm, draft-free place until doubled in bulk, about 1 1/2 hours.
4. *Meanwhile, prepare the cinnamon butter:* Place brown sugar, flour, cinnamon, salt and butter in clean mixer bowl. Remove the dough hook and attach the flat beater and mixer bowl to the mixer. Set to Speed 2 and mix until smooth.
5. Uncover dough and punch down several times to work out air bubbles. Turn dough out onto a lightly floured board and roll out into an 18- by 11-inch (45 by 28 cm) rectangle. Spread evenly with cinnamon butter, leaving a 1-inch (2.5 cm) border, and sprinkle with ground pecans. Starting with a long side, roll dough up jelly-roll style and pinch ends together. Cut into 12 equal pieces and place cut side up in prepared pan. Cover with plastic wrap and let rise for 45 to 60 minutes, or until doubled. Meanwhile, place oven rack in the middle position and preheat oven to 350°F (180°C).

6. Bake until rolls are golden brown and reach an internal temperature of 200°F (100°C), about 35 minutes. Let cool in pan on a wire rack for 5 minutes. Remove from pan and let cool on a wire rack.
7. *Meanwhile, prepare the glaze:* In a small bowl, whisk together confectioner's sugar and whipping cream. Add water as needed until a glaze consistency is reached.
8. Place a baking sheet under the wire rack. Drizzle glaze over warm rolls and serve warm or at room temperature.

Makes 12 rolls

Make ahead

Prepare dough through Step 4 in the evening and let rise overnight in the refrigerator. Let stand at room temperature for 1 hour before shaping.

Store rolls in a large heavy-duty plastic bag at room temperature for up to 2 days. Or freeze in a doubled plastic bag for up to 2 weeks.

TIP

To toast pecan halves, spread out on a baking sheet and bake at 350°F (180°C) for about 8 minutes, giving pan a toss halfway through. Let cool.

Blueberry Cream Cheese Danish

FLAT BEATER ◆ DOUGH HOOK

◆ 2 baking sheets, lined with parchment paper

2	packages (each 1/4 oz/7 g) active dry yeast	2
1/4 cup	warm water (see tip, page 244)	50 mL
3/4 cup	granulated sugar, divided	175 mL
2/3 cup	milk, warmed to about 110°F (43°C) (see tip, opposite)	150 mL
3	egg yolks	3
1 tsp	vanilla	5 mL
1 tsp	salt	5 mL
3 1/2 cups	unbleached all-purpose flour (approx.), divided	875 mL
3	sticks unsalted butter (12 oz/375 g), chilled	3
Filling		
8 oz	cream cheese, softened	250 g
1/4 cup	granulated sugar	50 mL
1	egg yolk	1
2 tbsp	unbleached all-purpose flour	25 mL
	Grated zest of 1 lemon	
1 tbsp	freshly squeezed lemon juice	15 mL
1 tsp	vanilla	5 mL
1/4 tsp	salt	1 mL
1 cup	blueberries or raspberries	250 mL
1	egg, beaten with 1 tbsp (15 mL) water	1
Glaze		
1 cup	confectioner's (icing) sugar	250 mL
2 tbsp	freshly squeezed lemon juice	25 mL

1. In the mixer bowl, stir together yeast, water and 2 tbsp (25 mL) of the sugar. Let stand until yeast begins to foam, about 5 minutes. Add the remaining sugar, milk, egg yolks, vanilla, salt and 2 1/2 cups (625 mL) of the flour. Attach the flat beater and mixer bowl to the mixer. Set to Speed 2 and mix until a dough forms.
2. Remove the flat beater and attach the dough hook. Add the remaining flour, set to Speed 2 and knead for 2 or 3 minutes, or until dough cleans the sides of the bowl and is no longer sticky. Remove the mixer bowl, cover with plastic wrap and refrigerate for 30 minutes.
3. On a generously floured work surface, roll out dough into a 12-inch (30 cm) square. On another generously floured work surface, lay the sticks of butter side by side. Sprinkle the tops with more flour and pound with a rolling pin into a 6-inch (15 cm) square. Center the butter diagonally on the dough and fold in the corners of the dough so that they meet in the center, like an envelope, enclosing the butter completely.
4. Using a rolling pin, flatten the dough with gentle, uniform pressure until it measures 18 by 8 inches (45 by 20 cm). Brush any excess flour from the dough with a dry pastry brush. Fold the top quarter of the dough down to the center. Fold the bottom quarter up to the center, leaving a 1/2-inch (1 cm) space between the two ends. Fold the top half over the bottom half, like closing a book. With a short side facing you, roll out into an 18- by 8-inch (45 by 20 cm) rectangle. Fold again in the same manner. (You have just completed 2 turns.) Wrap dough in plastic wrap and refrigerate for 1 hour.

5. Roll out and fold dough again, making 2 more turns. Wrap in plastic wrap and refrigerate for at least 2 hours or overnight (if refrigerating overnight, place wrapped dough in a large sealable bag to prevent it from escaping the wrapping and drying out).
6. *Prepare the filling:* Place cream cheese and sugar in clean mixer bowl. Attach the flat beater and mixer bowl to the mixer. Set to Speed 4 and beat until combined. Reduce to Speed 2 and add egg yolk, flour, lemon zest, lemon juice, vanilla and salt. Increase to Speed 4 and beat until well blended, about 30 seconds. Remove the mixer bowl, cover with plastic wrap and refrigerate for at least 1 hour or for up to 24 hours.
7. Cut dough in half and return one half to the refrigerator. On a lightly floured work surface, roll the other half out into a 16- by 8-inch (40 by 20 cm) rectangle. Cut into eight 4-inch (10 cm) squares. Pull two opposite corners to stretch them (so that they will cover the filling). Lay out the squares 3 inches (7.5 cm) apart on prepared baking sheets and dollop a heaping tablespoon (15 mL) of filling in the center of each sheet. Top with a few blueberries. Brush the elongated flaps with egg wash (so that they will stick). Fold flaps over the berries so that the filling and berries are enclosed, leaving remaining two corners flat. Brush top of dough with egg wash. Let rise for 30 to 45 minutes, or until slightly risen and puffy. Meanwhile, preheat oven to 375°F (190°C).
8. Bake for 25 to 30 minutes, or until golden. Let cool on baking sheets on a wire rack. Repeat with the remaining dough and filling.
9. *Prepare the glaze:* In a small bowl, combine confectioner's sugar and lemon juice. Drizzle over Danish while still warm. Serve warm or at room temperature.

Makes 16 Danish

TIP

Warm milk in a microwave-safe measuring cup or bowl in the microwave on High for 30 seconds.

Sticky Buns

FLAT BEATER DOUGH HOOK

- 13- by 9-inch (3 L) baking pan, greased
- Baking sheet

3 cups	unbleached all-purpose flour	750 mL
1/3 cup	granulated sugar, divided	75 mL
1 tsp	salt	5 mL
1 tbsp	active dry yeast	15 mL
1/3 cup	milk, warmed to about 110°F (43°C) (see tip, below)	75 mL
3	eggs	3
1/2 cup	unsalted butter, softened	125 mL
2 tsp	ground cinnamon	10 mL
Topping		
3/4 cup	packed brown sugar	175 mL
1/3 cup	unsalted butter, softened	75 mL
2 tbsp	dark corn syrup	25 mL
2 tbsp	water	25 mL
2 1/2 cups	pecans, toasted (see tip, page 249) and chopped	625 mL
Glaze		
1 cup	confectioner's (icing) sugar	250 mL
3 tbsp	whipping (35%) cream	45 mL

1. In a medium bowl, combine flour, 1/4 cup (50 mL) of the granulated sugar and salt. Set aside.
2. In a small bowl, stir together yeast and milk. Let stand until yeast begins to foam, 3 to 4 minutes.
3. Place eggs in the mixer bowl and add the yeast mixture. Attach the flat beater and mixer bowl to the mixer. Set to Stir and mix to combine. Add dry ingredients, increase to Speed 2 and mix until a rough dough forms.
4. Remove the flat beater and attach the dough hook. Set to Speed 2 and mix in butter, 1 tbsp (15 mL) at a time, until completely incorporated, scraping the sides of the bowl as necessary.
5. On a lightly floured work surface, knead dough by hand for 2 to 3 minutes, or until smooth and satiny. Place dough in a bowl, cover with a towel, and let rise until doubled in bulk, about 1 1/2 hours.
6. On a lightly floured work surface, roll out dough into an 18- by 11-inch (45 by 28 cm) rectangle. Combine cinnamon and the remaining granulated sugar and sprinkle evenly over the dough. Starting from one long end, roll up into a log. Pinch the ends of the log to seal it and cut into 12 even pieces.
7. *Prepare the topping:* In a small bowl, combine brown sugar, butter, corn syrup and water. Spread evenly in prepared pan. Sprinkle with nuts. Arrange buns cut side up in the pan. Cover with plastic wrap and let rise until doubled in bulk, 45 to 60 minutes. Meanwhile, preheat oven to 350°F (180°C).
8. Remove the plastic wrap and bake for 35 to 40 minutes, or until a tester inserted in the center comes out clean. Let cool for 30 minutes before turning buns out onto baking sheet.
9. *Prepare the glaze:* In a small bowl, combine confectioner's sugar and cream, adding water if needed for the desired consistency. Drizzle over the top of the buns. Separate buns and serve warm.

Makes 12 buns

TIP

Warm milk in a microwave-safe measuring cup or bowl in the microwave on High for 30 seconds.

Buttermilk Biscuits

FLAT BEATER

- Preheat oven to 425°F (220°C)
- Baking sheet, lined with parchment paper

3 cups	unbleached all-purpose flour	750 mL
4 tsp	baking powder	20 mL
1 tbsp	granulated sugar	15 mL
1 1/2 tsp	salt	7 mL
1 tsp	baking soda	5 mL
3/4 cup	chilled unsalted butter, cut into 1/4-inch (0.5 cm) pieces	175 mL
1 cup	buttermilk	250 mL
1/3 cup	whipping (35%) cream	75 mL

1. Place flour, baking powder, sugar, salt and baking soda in the mixer bowl. Attach the flat beater and mixer bowl to the mixer. Set to Stir and mix until combined. Increase to Speed 2 and mix in butter, one piece at a time, until mixture resembles coarse meal. Decrease to Stir and mix in buttermilk and whipping cream just until evenly moistened.
2. Using a large ice cream scoop or spoon, scoop dough onto prepared baking sheet, spacing 2 inches (5 cm) apart. Bake in middle of preheated oven for 15 to 18 minutes, or until golden brown on top. Let cool slightly on a wire rack and serve warm.

Makes 16 biscuits

Make ahead

Store tightly wrapped in foil in the freezer for up to 2 weeks. Warm in a 350°F (180°C) oven for 10 minutes.

Buckwheat Biscuits

FLAT BEATER

- Preheat oven to 425°F (220°C)
- 9-inch (23 cm) round cake pan, greased

2½ cups	unbleached all-purpose flour (approx.), divided	625 mL
½ cup	buckwheat flour	125 mL
3 tbsp	granulated sugar	45 mL
2 tsp	baking powder	10 mL
1 tsp	salt	5 mL
1 tsp	baking soda	5 mL
¼ cup	unsalted butter, cut into ¼-inch (0.5 cm) pieces	50 mL
1 cup	buttermilk	250 mL
2 tbsp	unsalted butter, melted	25 mL

Make ahead

Store tightly wrapped in foil in the freezer for up to 2 weeks. Warm in a 350°F (180°C) oven for 10 minutes.

1. Place 1½ cups (375 mL) of the all-purpose flour, buckwheat flour, sugar, baking powder, salt and baking soda in the mixer bowl. Attach the flat beater and mixer bowl to the mixer. Set to Stir and mix until combined. Mix in the ¼ cup (50 mL) butter, one piece at a time, until mixture resembles coarse meal, about 1 minute. Mix in buttermilk until a loose dough forms, about 5 seconds. Let stand for 5 minutes to allow dough to firm up.
2. Place the remaining 1 cup (250 mL) flour in a shallow bowl. Using an ice cream scoop, scoop up a biscuit-sized piece of dough and drop it into the flour. Sprinkle a little flour on top of the dough, pick it up and shape it into a round 1 inch (2.5 cm) high and 2 inches (5 cm) wide. Place in prepared pan. Repeat with remaining dough. Arrange snugly in the pan and brush with melted butter.
3. Bake in middle of preheated oven for 12 to 15 minutes, or until biscuits are lightly browned and have risen to double their size. Let cool on a wire rack.

Makes 12 biscuits

Cheddar Cheese Biscuits

FLAT BEATER

- Preheat oven to 400°F (200°C)
- Baking sheet, lined with parchment paper

2 cups	unbleached all-purpose flour	500 mL
2½ tsp	baking powder	12 mL
2 tsp	granulated sugar	10 mL
½ tsp	baking soda	2 mL
½ tsp	salt	2 mL
⅓ cup	chilled unsalted butter, cut into ¼-inch (0.5 cm) pieces	75 mL
1 cup	shredded extra-sharp Cheddar cheese	250 mL
1 cup	cold buttermilk (approx.)	250 mL

1. Place flour, baking powder, sugar, baking soda and salt in the mixer bowl. Attach the flat beater and mixer bowl to the mixer. Set to Stir and mix until combined. Set to Speed 2 and mix in butter, one piece at a time, until mixture resembles coarse meal. Add cheese and mix just until combined. With the mixer running, slowly add enough buttermilk to bind dough.
2. Turn out onto a floured work surface and pat out dough to ½-inch (1 cm) thickness. Using a 2-inch (5 cm) cookie cutter, cut out biscuits. Gather scraps, pat out to ½-inch (1 cm) thickness and cut additional biscuits. Place on prepared baking sheet, spacing 2 inches (5 cm) apart.
3. Bake in middle of preheated oven for 15 to 18 minutes, or until firm and golden brown. Let cool slightly on a wire rack. Serve warm.

Makes about 12 biscuits

Make ahead

Store tightly wrapped in foil in the freezer for up to 2 weeks. Warm in a 350°F (180°C) oven for 10 minutes.

Lemon-Thyme Biscuits

FLAT BEATER

- Preheat oven to 400°F (200°C)
- Large baking sheet, lined with parchment paper

2 cups	unbleached all-purpose flour	500 mL
3 tbsp	granulated sugar	45 mL
2 tsp	baking powder	10 mL
1 tsp	baking soda	5 mL
1 tsp	dried thyme (or 1 tbsp/ 15 mL chopped fresh)	5 mL
1/2 tsp	salt	2 mL
	Grated zest of 2 lemons	
2/3 cup	unsalted butter, cut into 1/4-inch (0.5 cm) pieces	150 mL
3/4 cup	buttermilk	175 mL

TIP
Substitute other herbs, such as rosemary, chives or basil, for the thyme.

1. Place flour, sugar, baking powder, baking soda, thyme, salt and lemon zest in the mixer bowl. Attach the flat beater and mixer bowl to the mixer. Set to Stir and mix until combined. Set to Speed 2 and mix in butter, one piece at a time, until mixture resembles coarse meal. Decrease to Stir and mix in buttermilk until a dough forms.
2. Using a large ice cream scoop or spoon, scoop biscuits onto prepared baking sheet, spacing 2 inches (5 cm) apart. Bake in middle of preheated oven for 13 to 15 minutes, or until firm and golden brown. Let cool on a wire rack. Serve warm or at room temperature.

Makes 8 biscuits

Make ahead

Store tightly wrapped in foil in the freezer for up to 2 weeks. Warm in a 350°F (180°C) oven for 10 minutes.

Toasted Oatmeal Scones with Maple Glaze

ROTOR SLICER/SHREDDER
FLAT BEATER

- Preheat oven to 425°F (220°C)
- Baking sheet
- Rimmed baking sheet, lined with parchment paper

3/4 cup	unsalted butter	175 mL
1 1/3 cups	old-fashioned rolled oats	325 mL
1 2/3 cups	unbleached all-purpose flour	400 mL
1/3 cup	packed light brown sugar	75 mL
2 tsp	baking powder	10 mL
3/4 tsp	baking soda	4 mL
3/4 tsp	salt	4 mL
2/3 cup	well-shaken buttermilk	150 mL
1	egg, lightly beaten	1
2 tbsp	whipping (35%) cream	25 mL
2 tbsp	granulated sugar	25 mL
Glaze		
1 1/2 cups	confectioner's (icing) sugar	375 mL
3 tbsp	pure maple syrup	45 mL
1 tbsp	milk	15 mL

In this recipe, we use a couple of unusual techniques to ensure a flaky and flavorful scone. We toast the oatmeal, which gives the scones a deep, nutty flavor, and we freeze and grate the butter before briefly mixing it into the dough. When the dough bakes, the butter melts, leaving flaky little pockets inside the scones. Tea, anyone?

1. Place butter in the freezer for 20 minutes.
2. Spread oats evenly on baking sheet and bake in preheated oven, stirring halfway through, for 5 minutes, or until oats are just beginning to brown. Let cool.
3. Place cooled oats, flour, brown sugar, baking powder, baking soda and salt in the mixer bowl. Attach the slicer/shredder, with the coarse shredder, to the mixer (or use a box grater). Set to Speed 4 and shred the frozen butter into the mixer bowl. Using a wooden spoon, stir briefly to combine. Place bowl in freezer for 20 minutes.
4. Attach the flat beater and the mixer bowl to the mixer. Add buttermilk and egg. Set to Speed 2 and mix until just combined.
5. On a floured work surface, knead dough gently until it comes together in a ball. Pat into a 9-inch (23 cm) square, about 1/2 inch (1 cm) thick. Cut into nine 3-inch (7.5 cm) squares. Cut each square diagonally to form 2 triangles. Place 2 inches (5 cm) apart on prepared baking sheet.
6. Brush tops of scones with cream and sprinkle with granulated sugar. Bake until golden brown, about 16 minutes. Let cool on baking sheet on a wire rack.
7. *Meanwhile, prepare the glaze:* In a medium bowl, whisk together confectioner's sugar, maple syrup and milk. Drizzle over cooled scones.

Makes 18 scones

Lower-Fat Oatmeal Scones with Currants and Walnuts

FLAT BEATER

- Preheat oven to 400°F (200°C)
- Baking sheet, lined with parchment paper

1¾ cups	unbleached all-purpose flour	425 mL
½ cup	old-fashioned rolled oats	125 mL
⅓ cup	lightly packed light brown sugar	75 mL
2 tsp	baking powder	10 mL
1 tsp	baking soda	5 mL
½ tsp	salt	2 mL
¼ cup	unsalted butter, cut into pieces	50 mL
½ cup	dried currants	125 mL
½ cup	walnut halves, chopped	125 mL
	Grated zest of 1 lemon	
1 cup	buttermilk	250 mL
2 tbsp	buttermilk	25 mL
3 tbsp	turbinado or coarse sugar	45 mL

1. Place flour, oats, brown sugar, baking powder, baking soda and salt in the mixer bowl. Attach the flat beater and mixer bowl to the mixer. Set to Stir and mix until combined. Set to Speed 2 and mix in butter, one piece at a time, until mixture resembles coarse meal. Add currants, walnuts and lemon zest; mix until combined. Quickly add the 1 cup (250 mL) buttermilk and mix just until incorporated. Let stand for 5 minutes. (The oatmeal will absorb much of the buttermilk, and the dough will become drier and easier to work with.)
2. Turn mixture out onto a lightly floured surface. Sprinkle with flour and pat into a 10-inch (25 cm) disk. Cut into 8 wedges and arrange 2 inches (5 cm) apart on prepared baking sheet. Brush with the 2 tbsp (25 mL) buttermilk and sprinkle with turbinado sugar.
3. Bake in middle of preheated oven for 15 to 20 minutes, or until firm and light golden. Let cool on a wire rack. Serve warm or at room temperature.

Makes 8 scones

Make ahead

Store tightly wrapped in foil in the freezer for up to 2 weeks. Warm in a 350°F (180°C) oven for 10 minutes.

Sour Cherry Scones with Orange Glaze

FLAT BEATER

- ◆ Preheat oven to 400°F (200°C)
- ◆ Baking sheet, lined with parchment paper

2 1/4 cups	unbleached all-purpose flour	550 mL
1/3 cup	granulated sugar	75 mL
2 tsp	baking powder	10 mL
1 tsp	baking soda	5 mL
1/4 tsp	salt	1 mL
	Grated zest of 1 orange	
2/3 cup	unsalted butter, cut into 1/4-inch (0.5 cm) pieces	150 mL
1/2 cup	buttermilk	125 mL
1 1/2 cups	pitted sour cherries (see tip, below)	375 mL
2 tbsp	buttermilk	25 mL
Glaze		
3/4 cup	confectioner's (icing) sugar, sifted	175 mL
1 tbsp	orange juice	15 mL

TIP

You can use fresh, frozen or canned sour cherries. If using canned, drain and dry them before adding to the mixer bowl.

1. Place flour, sugar, baking powder, baking soda, salt and orange zest in the mixer bowl. Attach the flat beater and mixer bowl to the mixer. Set to Stir and mix until combined. Increase to Speed 2 and mix in butter, one piece at a time, until mixture resembles coarse meal. Decrease to Stir and mix in the 2/3 cup (150 mL) buttermilk and cherries until just combined, about 6 seconds.
2. Turn mixture out onto a lightly floured surface and divide into 2 mounds. Working with one mound at a time, sprinkle top with a little flour and pat into a 5-inch (12 cm) disk. Cut each into 8 wedges and arrange 2 inches (5 cm) apart on prepared baking sheet. Brush with the 2 tbsp (25 mL) buttermilk.
3. Bake in middle of preheated oven for 20 to 25 minutes, or until firm and golden brown. Let cool on a wire rack.
4. *Meanwhile, prepare the glaze:* In a small bowl, whisk together confectioner's sugar and orange juice until smooth.
5. Drizzle glaze over warm scones and serve warm or at room temperature.

Makes 16 scones

Make ahead

Store tightly wrapped in foil in the freezer for up to 2 weeks. Warm in a 350°F (180°C) oven for 10 minutes.

Coconut Scones with Dried Pineapple and Macadamia Nuts

FLAT BEATER

- Preheat oven to 400°F (200°C)
- Baking sheet, lined with parchment paper

2 cups	unbleached all-purpose flour	500 mL
1 cup	sweetened flaked coconut	250 mL
1⁄3 cup	granulated sugar	75 mL
1 tbsp	baking powder	15 mL
1⁄2 tsp	salt	2 mL
	Grated zest of 1 orange	
1⁄2 cup	cold unsalted butter, cut into small pieces	125 mL
1	egg, beaten	1
1⁄2 cup	chopped dried pineapple	125 mL
1⁄2 cup	chopped macadamia nuts	125 mL
1⁄3 cup	half-and-half (10%) cream	75 mL
1⁄2 tsp	coconut extract	2 mL
2 tbsp	half-and-half (10%) cream	25 mL
2 tbsp	turbinado or raw sugar	25 mL

1. Place flour, coconut, granulated sugar, baking powder, salt, orange zest and butter in the mixer bowl. Attach the flat beater and mixer bowl to the mixer. Set to Speed 2 and mix until crumbly, about 2 minutes. Stop the mixer and add egg, pineapple, nuts, the 1⁄3 cup (75 mL) cream and coconut extract. Set to Speed 2 and mix just until a dough forms.
2. Turn dough out onto a lightly floured work surface and press into an 8-inch (20 cm) disk. Cut into 8 wedges. Place 2 inches (5 cm) apart on prepared baking sheet.
3. Brush tops of scones with the 2 tbsp (25 mL) cream and sprinkle with turbinado sugar. Bake in preheated oven for about 20 minutes, or until lightly browned and firm. Let cool on baking sheet on a wire rack. Serve warm or at room temperature.

Makes 8 scones

Lemon Blueberry Muffins

FLAT BEATER

- Preheat oven to 375°F (190°C), with rack in lower middle position
- 12-cup muffin tin, lightly greased

2 cups	unbleached all-purpose flour	500 mL
1 tbsp	baking powder	15 mL
1/2 tsp	salt	2 mL
3/4 cup	granulated sugar	175 mL
	Finely grated zest of 1 lemon	
1/2 cup	unsalted butter, softened	125 mL
2	eggs, at room temperature	2
1/2 cup	homogenized (whole) milk	125 mL
1 cup	fresh or frozen blueberries	250 mL
1 tbsp	unbleached all-purpose flour	15 mL
Glaze		
3/4 cup	confectioner's (icing) sugar, sifted	175 mL
1 1/2 tbsp	freshly squeezed lemon juice	22 mL

1. In a medium bowl, combine the 2 cups (500 mL) flour, baking powder and salt. Set aside.
2. Place sugar, lemon zest and butter in the mixer bowl. Attach the flat beater and mixer bowl to the mixer. Set to Speed 4 and beat until light and fluffy, about 2 minutes. Stop mixer to scrape down bowl. Set to Speed 4 and add eggs, one at a time, beating well after each addition. Stop mixer to scrape down bowl. Set to Speed 2 and beat in flour mixture alternately with milk, making 3 additions of dry and 2 of wet. Remove the mixer bowl and scrape it down.
3. In a small bowl, quickly toss blueberries with the 1 tbsp (15 mL) flour. Using a large spatula, carefully fold blueberries into batter.
4. Divide batter evenly among muffin cups. Bake in middle of preheated oven for 20 to 25 minutes, or until golden brown. Let cool in tin on a wire rack for about 5 minutes. Remove muffins to rack.
5. *Meanwhile, prepare the glaze:* In a small bowl, whisk together confectioner's sugar and lemon juice until smooth. Brush on warm muffins.

Makes 12 muffins

Make ahead

Store tightly wrapped in foil in the freezer for up to 2 weeks.

Raisin Bran Muffins

FLAT BEATER

- Preheat oven to 400°F (200°C), with rack in lower middle position
- 12-cup muffin tin, greased and floured

1 cup	raisins	250 mL
1/2 cup	hot water	125 mL
1 1/2 cups	whole wheat flour	375 mL
1 cup	unbleached all-purpose flour	250 mL
1 cup	natural wheat bran	250 mL
1/2 cup	lightly packed light brown sugar	125 mL
1 tsp	baking powder	5 mL
1 tsp	salt	5 mL
1/2 tsp	baking soda	2 mL
2	eggs, beaten	2
1 1/2 cups	small-curd cottage cheese	375 mL
1/2 cup	vegetable oil	125 mL
1/2 cup	homogenized (whole) milk	125 mL

1. Plump raisins in hot water for 10 minutes; drain.
2. Place raisins, whole wheat flour, all-purpose flour, bran, brown sugar, baking powder, salt and baking soda in the mixer bowl. Attach the flat beater and mixer bowl to the mixer. Set to Stir and mix until combined.
3. In a medium bowl, combine eggs, cottage cheese and oil. Add to the mixer bowl and mix until dry ingredients are moistened.
4. Divide batter evenly among muffin cups. Bake in middle of preheated oven until a toothpick inserted in center comes out clean, about 20 minutes. Remove muffins from tins and let cool slightly on a wire rack. Serve warm.

Makes 12 muffins

Make ahead

Store tightly wrapped in foil in the freezer for up to 2 weeks.

Double Chocolate Muffins

FLAT BEATER

- Preheat oven to 375°F (190°C), with rack in lower middle position
- 12-cup muffin tin, lightly greased

1¾ cups	unbleached all-purpose flour	425 mL
¼ cup	unsweetened cocoa powder	50 mL
1 tsp	baking soda	5 mL
½ tsp	salt	2 mL
¾ cup	granulated sugar	175 mL
½ cup	unsalted butter, softened	125 mL
2	eggs	2
1 tsp	vanilla	5 mL
⅔ cup	sour cream	150 mL
½ cup	milk	125 mL
¾ cup	semisweet chocolate chips	175 mL

1. In a medium bowl, combine flour, cocoa, baking soda and salt. Set aside.
2. Place sugar and butter in the mixer bowl. Attach the flat beater and mixer bowl to the mixer. Set to Speed 4 and beat until light and fluffy, about 2 minutes. Stop mixer to scrape down bowl. Set to Speed 4 and add eggs, one at a time, beating well after each addition, then add vanilla. Stop mixer to scrape down bowl.
3. In a small bowl, combine sour cream and milk. Set mixer to Speed 2 and mix in flour mixture alternately with sour cream mixture, making 3 additions of dry and 2 of wet. Stop mixer to scrape down bowl. Set to Stir and mix in chocolate chips.
4. Using a large ice cream scoop, divide batter evenly among prepared muffin cups. Bake in preheated oven for about 20 minutes, or until a tester comes out with just a few moist crumbs attached. Let cool in tin on a wire rack for 5 minutes. Remove muffins from tin and let cool completely on rack.

Makes 12 muffins

Banana Chocolate Chunk Muffins

FLAT BEATER

- Preheat oven to 375°F (190°C), with rack in lower middle position
- 12-cup muffin tin, lightly greased

2 1/4 cups	unbleached all-purpose flour	550 mL
2 tsp	baking powder	10 mL
1 tsp	salt	5 mL
1/2 tsp	baking soda	2 mL
1 cup	granulated sugar	250 mL
1/2 cup	unsalted butter, softened	125 mL
2	eggs	2
1 cup	mashed bananas (about 2)	250 mL
1 cup	lower-fat plain yogurt	250 mL
1 cup	semisweet chocolate chunks or chips	250 mL

1. In a medium bowl, combine flour, baking powder, salt and baking soda. Set aside.
2. Place sugar and butter in the mixer bowl. Attach the flat beater and mixer bowl to the mixer. Set to Speed 4 and beat until light and fluffy, about 2 minutes. Stop mixer to scrape down bowl. Set to Speed 4 and add eggs, one at a time, beating well after each addition. Add bananas and beat well. Stop mixer to scrape down bowl. Set to Speed 2 and beat in flour mixture alternately with yogurt, making 3 additions of dry and 2 of wet. Stop mixer to scrape down bowl. Set to Stir and mix in chocolate chunks.
3. Divide batter evenly among muffin cups. Bake in middle of preheated oven for 25 to 30 minutes, or until golden brown. Let cool in tin on a wire rack for 5 minutes. Serve warm or let cool completely.

Makes 12 muffins

Make ahead

Store tightly wrapped in foil in the freezer for up to 2 weeks.

Orange Date Muffins

FLAT BEATER

- Preheat oven to 400°F (200°C), with rack in lower middle position
- 12-cup muffin tin, greased and floured

2 cups	unbleached all-purpose flour	500 mL
1 1/2 tsp	baking powder	7 mL
1 tsp	baking soda	5 mL
3/4 tsp	salt	3 mL
3/4 cup	granulated sugar	175 mL
1/2 cup	unsalted butter, softened	125 mL
1	egg	1
1/4 cup	sour cream	50 mL
2 tbsp	grated orange zest	25 mL
1/4 cup	freshly squeezed orange juice	50 mL
1/2 tsp	orange extract	2 mL
1 cup	coarsely chopped pitted dates	250 mL
1/2 cup	walnut halves, toasted (see tip, page 215) and chopped	125 mL

1. In a medium bowl, combine flour, baking powder, baking soda and salt.
2. Place sugar and butter in the mixer bowl. Attach the flat beater and mixer bowl to the mixer. Set to Speed 4 and beat until light and fluffy, about 2 minutes. Stop mixer to scrape down bowl. Decrease to Stir and add egg, sour cream, orange zest, orange juice and orange extract; mix until combined. Add flour mixture and mix until just combined. Set to Stir and mix in dates and walnuts, if using.
3. Divide batter evenly among muffin cups. Bake in middle of preheated oven until golden brown, about 20 minutes. Remove muffins from tins and let cool on a wire rack. Serve warm or let cool completely.

Makes 12 muffins

Make ahead

Store tightly wrapped in foil in the freezer for up to 2 weeks.

TIPS

These muffins are also great baked in three 12-cup mini-muffin tins for 15 minutes.

One large orange yields about 2 tbsp (25 mL) zest and 1/4 cup (50 mL) juice.

Pumpkin Walnut Muffins

FLAT BEATER

- Preheat oven to 350°F (180°C), with rack in lower middle position
- 12-cup muffin tin, lightly greased

2¼ cups	unbleached all-purpose flour	550 mL
1½ tsp	ground cinnamon	7 mL
1 tsp	baking soda	5 mL
¾ tsp	salt	3 mL
½ tsp	ground ginger	2 mL
Pinch	ground cloves	Pinch
1 cup	granulated sugar	250 mL
½ cup	unsalted butter, softened	125 mL
2	eggs	2
1 cup	canned pumpkin purée (not pie filling)	250 mL
½ cup	buttermilk	125 mL
1 cup	walnut halves, coarsely chopped	250 mL

1. In a medium bowl, combine flour, cinnamon, baking soda, salt, ginger and cloves. Set aside.
2. Place sugar and butter in the mixer bowl. Attach the flat beater and mixer bowl to the mixer. Set to Speed 4 and beat until light and fluffy, about 2 minutes. Stop mixer to scrape down bowl. Set to Speed 4 and add eggs, one at a time, beating well after each addition. Add pumpkin and beat well. Stop mixer to scrape down bowl. Set to Speed 2 and beat in flour mixture alternately with buttermilk, making 3 additions of dry and 2 of wet. Stop mixer to scrape down bowl. Set to Stir and mix in walnuts.
3. Divide batter evenly among muffin cups. Bake in middle of preheated oven for 20 to 25 minutes, or until golden brown. Let cool in tin on a wire rack for 5 minutes. Remove muffins to rack to cool completely. Serve at room temperature.

Makes 12 muffins

Make ahead

Store tightly wrapped in foil in the freezer for up to 2 weeks.

Sunrise Zucchini Muffins

FLAT BEATER

- Preheat oven to 400°F (200°C), with rack in lower middle position
- 12-cup muffin tin, greased and floured

2 cups	unbleached all-purpose flour	500 mL
1 cup	shredded zucchini	250 mL
1/2 cup	whole wheat flour	125 mL
1/2 cup	raisins	125 mL
1/2 cup	granulated sugar	125 mL
1 tbsp	baking powder	15 mL
1 tbsp	grated orange zest	15 mL
1 tsp	baking soda	5 mL
3/4 tsp	salt	3 mL
1/2 tsp	ground cinnamon	2 mL
1/4 tsp	ground nutmeg	1 mL
2	eggs, beaten	2
1/2 cup	homogenized (whole) milk	125 mL
1/3 cup	vegetable oil	75 mL
1/4 cup	freshly squeezed orange juice	50 mL

1. Place all-purpose flour, zucchini, whole wheat flour, raisins, sugar, baking powder, orange zest, baking soda, salt, cinnamon and nutmeg in the mixer bowl. Attach the flat beater and mixer bowl to the mixer. Set to Stir and mix until combined.
2. In a small bowl, combine eggs, milk, oil and orange juice. Add to the mixer bowl and mix until just combined.
3. Divide batter evenly among muffin cups. Bake in middle of preheated oven for 10 minutes, then reduce temperature to 375°F (190°C) and bake until golden, about 10 minutes. Remove muffins from tins and let cool on a wire rack. Serve warm or let cool completely.

Makes 12 muffins

Make ahead

Store tightly wrapped in foil in the freezer for up to 2 weeks.

Blue Cheese and Walnut Mini Muffins

FLAT BEATER

- Preheat oven to 400°F (200°C)
- 36 mini-muffin cups, lightly greased

1 cup + 2 tbsp	unbleached all-purpose flour	275 mL
1/3 cup	cornmeal	75 mL
2 tsp	baking powder	10 mL
1/2 tsp	salt	2 mL
1/4 tsp	freshly ground black pepper	1 mL
4 oz	crumbled blue cheese (about 1 cup/250 mL)	125 g
2 tbsp	unsalted butter, softened	25 mL
2	eggs	2
1/2 cup	homogenized (whole) milk	125 mL
1 cup	walnut halves, toasted (see tip, page 215) and finely chopped	250 mL

1. In a medium bowl, combine flour, cornmeal, baking powder, salt and pepper. Set aside.
2. Place cheese and butter in the mixer bowl. Attach the flat beater and mixer bowl to the mixer. Set to Speed 2 and beat until combined. Add eggs and beat for 2 minutes, stopping once to scrape down bowl. Decrease speed to Stir and mix in flour mixture alternately with milk, making 3 additions of dry and 2 of wet. Add walnuts and mix until just combined.
3. Spoon into prepared muffin cups and bake in middle of preheated oven until a tester inserted in the center of a muffin comes out clean, about 10 minutes. Remove muffins from tins and let cool on a wire rack. Serve warm or at room temperature.

Makes 36 mini muffins

Make ahead

Store tightly wrapped in foil in the freezer for up to 2 weeks.

Banana Walnut Bread

FLAT BEATER

- Preheat oven to 350°F (180°C)
- 9- by 5-inch (2 L) loaf pan, greased

1/2 cup	homogenized (whole) milk	125 mL
2 tsp	freshly squeezed lemon juice	10 mL
2 cups	sifted unbleached all-purpose flour	500 mL
1 tsp	baking powder	5 mL
1/2 tsp	salt	2 mL
1/2 tsp	baking soda	2 mL
1 cup	granulated sugar	250 mL
1/2 cup	unsalted butter, softened	125 mL
2	eggs	2
2	very ripe bananas, mashed (about 1 cup/250 mL)	2
1 cup	walnut halves, toasted (see tip, page 215) and chopped	250 mL

1. In a small bowl, combine milk and lemon juice. Let stand until milk curdles, about 1 minute. Set aside.
2. In a medium bowl, whisk together flour, baking powder, salt and baking soda. Set aside.
3. Place sugar and butter in the mixer bowl. Attach the flat beater and mixer bowl to the mixer. Set to Speed 2 and beat until light and fluffy, about 2 minutes. Add eggs, one at a time, and beat until combined. Add bananas and beat until combined. (Mixture will look curdled.) Beat in flour mixture alternately with milk mixture, making 3 additions of dry and 2 of wet. Stop mixer to scrape down bowl. Add walnuts, set to Stir and mix just until incorporated.
4. Pour batter into prepared pan and bake in middle of preheated oven for 45 to 60 minutes, or until a tester inserted in the center comes out clean. Let cool in pan on a wire rack for 10 minutes, then invert bread onto rack to cool completely.

Makes 1 loaf

Make ahead

Store tightly wrapped in foil in the freezer for up to 2 months.

Cranberry Pecan Bread

FLAT BEATER

- Preheat oven to 350°F (180°C)
- 9- by 5-inch (2 L) loaf pan, greased and floured

1 cup	dried cranberries	250 mL
1/2 cup	orange juice	125 mL
2 cups	unbleached all-purpose flour	500 mL
1 1/2 tsp	baking soda	7 mL
1/2 tsp	salt	2 mL
3/4 cup	granulated sugar	175 mL
2	eggs	2
3/4 cup	sour cream	175 mL
1/3 cup	vegetable oil	75 mL
1 tsp	vanilla	5 mL
3/4 cup	pecan halves, toasted (see tip, page 249) and chopped	75 mL

Cranberry pecan bread is delicious spread with cream cheese and made into finger sandwiches for a tea tray. For a more uptown presentation, try sweetening a little goat cheese with honey as a spread.

1. In a small saucepan, over medium heat, bring cranberries and orange juice to a simmer. Let cool.
2. In a medium bowl, whisk together flour, baking soda and salt.
3. Place sugar, eggs, sour cream, oil and vanilla in the mixer bowl. Attach flat beater and mixer bowl to the mixer. Set to Stir and mix until incorporated. Add flour mixture and mix for 1 minute. Add cranberry mixture and pecans; mix just until incorporated.
4. Pour batter into prepared pan and bake in middle of preheated oven for 55 to 60 minutes, or until a tester inserted in the center comes out clean. Let cool in pan on a wire rack for 10 minutes, then invert bread onto rack to cool completely.

Makes 1 loaf

Make ahead

Store tightly wrapped in foil in the freezer for up to 2 months.

Chocolate Chip Macadamia Bread

FLAT BEATER

- Preheat oven to 375°F (190°C)
- 9- by 5-inch (2 L) loaf pan, greased

2 cups	unbleached all-purpose flour	500 mL
1 1/2 tsp	baking powder	7 mL
1/2 tsp	salt	2 mL
1 cup	granulated sugar	250 mL
1/2 cup	unsalted butter	125 mL
2	eggs	2
1 tsp	vanilla	5 mL
1/2 cup	homogenized (whole) milk	125 mL
1 cup	semisweet chocolate chips	250 mL
1/2 cup	coarsely chopped macadamia nuts	125 mL

1. In a medium bowl, combine flour, baking powder and salt.
2. Place sugar and butter in the mixer bowl. Attach the flat beater and mixer bowl to the mixer. Set to Speed 4 and beat until light and fluffy, about 2 minutes. Stop mixer to scrape down bowl. Set to Speed 4 and beat in eggs, one at a time, and vanilla. Stop mixer to scrape down bowl. Beat in flour mixture alternately with milk, making 3 additions of dry and 2 of wet. Stop mixer to scrape down bowl. Add chocolate chips and macadamia nuts; set to Stir and mix just until incorporated.
3. Spread batter evenly in prepared pan and bake in the lower third of preheated oven for 35 to 45 minutes, or until a tester inserted in the center comes out clean. Let cool in pan on a wire rack for 10 minutes, then invert bread onto rack to cool completely.

Makes 1 loaf

Make ahead

Store tightly wrapped in foil in the freezer for up to 2 months.

Chai Fruit Bread

FLAT BEATER

- Preheat oven to 350°F (180°C)
- 9- by 5-inch (2 L) loaf pan, greased and floured

2½ cups	unbleached all-purpose flour	625 mL
2½ tsp	ground cinnamon	12 mL
2 tsp	baking powder	10 mL
1 tsp	salt	5 mL
½ tsp	baking soda	2 mL
½ cup	boiling water	125 mL
1 cup	dried currants	250 mL
1 cup	chopped stemmed dried figs	250 mL
¼ cup	spiced chai powder	50 mL
1 cup	firmly packed light brown sugar	250 mL
	Grated zest of 1 orange	
1	egg, lightly beaten	1
⅔ cup	buttermilk	150 mL
½ cup	vegetable oil	125 mL
1 tsp	orange extract	5 mL

1. In a medium bowl, whisk together flour, cinnamon, baking powder, salt and baking soda.
2. Pour boiling water into the mixer bowl and add currants, figs and chai powder. Cover with plastic wrap and let stand for 10 minutes, until fruit is softened. Add brown sugar, orange zest, egg, buttermilk, oil and orange extract. Attach the flat beater and mixer bowl to the mixer. Set to Stir and mix for 1 minute, then add flour mixture in 3 additions. Set to Speed 2 and mix for 1 minute, stopping occasionally to scrape down bowl.
3. Pour batter into prepared loaf pan and bake in middle of preheated oven for 55 to 60 minutes, or until a tester inserted in the center comes out clean. Let cool in pan on a wire rack for 10 minutes, then invert bread onto rack to cool completely.

Makes 1 loaf

Make ahead

Store tightly wrapped in foil in the freezer for up to 2 months.

TIP

Spiced chai powder is an instant mix that can be found in specialty grocery stores.

Apple Streusel Coffee Cake

FLAT BEATER

- Preheat oven to 350°F (180°C)
- 10-inch (3 L) Bundt pan, greased and floured

2 cups	unbleached all-purpose flour	500 mL
1 tsp	baking powder	5 mL
1 tsp	baking soda	5 mL
1 tsp	salt	5 mL
1 cup	granulated sugar	250 mL
1/2 cup	unsalted butter, softened	125 mL
2	eggs	2
1 cup	sour cream	250 mL
2 tsp	vanilla	10 mL
1 cup	pecan halves, chopped	250 mL
3/4 cup	firmly packed light brown sugar	175 mL
2 tsp	ground cinnamon	10 mL
2	Granny Smith apples, peeled and each sliced into 12 slices	2

1. In a medium bowl, whisk together flour, baking powder, baking soda and salt.
2. Place granulated sugar and butter in the mixer bowl. Attach the flat beater and mixer bowl to the mixer. Set to Speed 4 and beat until light and fluffy, about 2 minutes. Stop mixer to scrape down bowl. Decrease to Stir and add eggs, sour cream and vanilla; mix until combined. Add flour mixture and mix until smooth.
3. In another bowl, combine pecans, brown sugar and cinnamon.
4. Sprinkle one-third of the pecan mixture into the bottom of prepared pan. Top with half of the batter, half of the apples and another third of the pecan mixture. Repeat layers.
5. Bake in middle of preheated oven for 50 to 60 minutes, or until a tester inserted in the center comes out clean. Let cool in pan on a wire rack for 30 minutes. Invert cake onto rack. Serve warm or room temperature.

Serves 12

Make ahead

Store tightly wrapped in foil in the freezer for up to 1 month.

Raspberry Cream Cheese Coffee Cake

FLAT BEATER

- Preheat oven to 350°F (180°C)
- 10-inch (4 L) tube pan with a removable bottom, greased and floured

3 cups	unbleached all-purpose flour	750 mL
2 tsp	baking powder	10 mL
1 tsp	baking soda	5 mL
1 tsp	salt	5 mL
8 oz	cream cheese, softened	250 mL
2 1/4 cups	granulated sugar, divided	550 mL
1 tbsp	freshly squeezed lemon juice	15 mL
1 tsp	vanilla	5 mL
Pinch	salt	Pinch
1 cup	unsalted butter, softened	250 mL
3	eggs	3
1 1/2 tsp	vanilla	7 mL
1 1/4 cups	sour cream	300 mL
1/2 cup	seedless raspberry jam	125 mL
1 1/2 cups	confectioner's (icing) sugar	375 mL
3 tbsp	homogenized (whole) milk	45 mL
1/4 tsp	almond extract	1 mL

1. In a large bowl, combine flour, baking powder, baking soda and salt. Set aside.
2. Place cream cheese, 1/4 cup (50 mL) of the granulated sugar, lemon juice, vanilla and salt in the mixer bowl. Attach the flat beater and mixer bowl to the mixer. Set to Speed 4 and beat until smooth, about 2 minutes. Transfer to another bowl and set aside.
3. Place butter and the remaining granulated sugar in clean mixer bowl. Attach the mixer bowl to the mixer. Set to Speed 4 and beat until light and fluffy, about 2 minutes. Stop mixer to scrape down bowl. Set to Speed 4 and add eggs, one at a time, beating well after each addition, then add vanilla. Stop mixer to scrape down bowl. Set to Speed 2 and mix in flour mixture alternately with sour cream, making 3 additions of dry and 2 of wet.
4. Measure out 1 cup (250 mL) of the cake batter and combine thoroughly with the cream cheese mixture.
5. Pour remaining batter into prepared pan. Drop cream cheese mixture by spoonfuls on top. Spoon raspberry jam on top of cream cheese. Using a knife, gently swirl cream cheese and jam together, creating a marbled effect.

6. Bake in preheated oven for 60 to 75 minutes, or until a tester comes out with just a few moist crumbs attached. Let cool in pan on a wire rack for 10 minutes. Remove the tube section from the pan and run a thin knife under the cake to release the bottom. Using two long spatulas, transfer cake to rack to cool completely. Once cool, transfer to a serving plate.
7. In a medium bowl, whisk together confectioner's sugar, milk and almond extract until smooth. Drizzle over cooled cake.

Serves 12

Variation

Try using apricot, strawberry or fig jam instead of raspberry.

TIP

Room temperature eggs and butter will result in a lighter and less dense cake.

Cinnamon Swirl Coffee Cake with Orange and Chocolate

FLAT BEATER

- Preheat oven to 350°F (180°C)
- 9-inch (23 cm) springform pan, greased and lined with parchment paper, parchment greased and floured

1 cup	chopped pecans	250 mL
1 cup	packed brown sugar	250 mL
1 cup	semisweet chocolate chips	250 mL
1 cup	unsalted butter, softened, divided	250 mL
1 tbsp	ground cinnamon	15 mL
1 tbsp	unsweetened cocoa powder	15 mL
3 cups	cake flour	750 mL
1 ½ tsp	baking powder	7 mL
1 ½ tsp	baking soda	7 mL
½ tsp	salt	2 mL
1 ⅓ cups	granulated sugar	325 mL
3	eggs	3
2 cups	sour cream	500 mL
1 tbsp	vanilla	15 mL
	Grated zest and juice of 1 orange	
¼ cup	confectioner's (icing) sugar	50 mL

1. In a large bowl, combine pecans, brown sugar, chocolate chips, ¼ cup (50 mL) of the butter, cinnamon and cocoa powder. Using your fingertips, rub the ingredients together. Set aside.
2. In another bowl, sift together flour, baking powder, baking soda and salt. Set aside.
3. Place granulated sugar and the remaining butter in the mixer bowl. Attach the flat beater and mixer bowl to the mixer. Set to Speed 4 and beat until light and fluffy. Stop mixer to scrape down bowl. Set to Speed 4 and beat in eggs, one at a time. Beat in sour cream, vanilla, orange zest and orange juice. Stop mixer to scrape down bowl. Set to Speed 2 and mix in flour mixture, ¼ cup (50 mL) at a time, just until mixed.
4. Spoon half the batter into prepared pan and sprinkle with half the nut mixture. Swirl a knife through the topping and down into the batter to mix it lightly. Spoon in the remaining batter and sprinkle with the remaining topping.
5. Bake in preheated oven for 75 minutes, or until a tester inserted in the center comes out clean. Let cool in pan on a wire rack for 30 minutes. Run a knife around the sides to loosen the cake and remove the sides. Invert onto a large plate and peel away the parchment. Invert onto a serving platter and dust with confectioner's sugar. Serve warm or at room temperature.

Serves 12

Cookies, Bars and Squares

Soft Sugar Cookies

FLAT BEATER

- Preheat oven to 350°F (180°C)
- Baking sheets, lined with parchment paper

3 cups	unbleached all-purpose flour	750 mL
1 1/2 tsp	ground nutmeg	7 mL
1 tsp	baking powder	5 mL
1/2 tsp	baking soda	2 mL
1/4 tsp	salt	1 mL
3/4 cup	unsalted butter, softened	175 mL
3 cups	confectioner's (icing) sugar, sifted, divided	750 mL
2	eggs	2
2 tsp	vanilla	10 mL
1/4 cup	buttermilk	50 mL

1. In a medium bowl, whisk together flour, nutmeg, baking powder, baking soda and salt.
2. Place butter in the mixer bowl. Attach the flat beater and mixer bowl to the mixer. Set to Speed 4 and beat until soft and creamy. Reduce speed to Stir and mix in 2 1/2 cups (625 mL) of the confectioner's sugar, in 3 additions. Mix in eggs, one at a time, and vanilla. Mix in flour mixture alternately with buttermilk, making 3 additions of each. Remove the mixer bowl and scrape down with a spatula to incorporate any unmixed ingredients.
3. Drop by rounded tablespoonfuls (15 mL), 2 inches (5 cm) apart, onto prepared baking sheets. Bake in middle of preheated oven for 12 to 15 minutes, or until golden around the edges but still soft in the middle. Transfer to wire racks and let cool. Sift the remaining 1/2 cup (125 mL) confectioner's sugar over cooled cookies.

Makes about 4 dozen cookies

Variation

Substitute 2 tsp (10 mL) of orange or lemon extract for the vanilla.

Make ahead

Store in an airtight container in the freezer for up to 4 weeks.

TIP

Use a small ice cream scoop or a tablespoon to scoop dough onto the baking sheets.

Holiday Sugar Cookies

FLAT BEATER

- Baking sheets, lined with parchment paper
- Assorted 2- to 3-inch (5 to 7.5 cm) cookie cutters

3 cups	unbleached all-purpose flour	750 mL
1 tsp	baking powder	5 mL
1/2 tsp	salt	2 mL
1 cup	granulated sugar	250 mL
1 cup	unsalted butter, softened	250 mL
1	egg	1
1/2 tsp	almond extract	2 mL

TIPS

Rolling out cookie dough between pieces of parchment paper eliminates the need for additional flour. This will help keep your cookies tender and allow you to reroll dough scraps more than once.

If you are baking more than one sheet of cookies at a time, switch rack positions halfway through.

1. In a medium bowl, whisk together flour, baking powder and salt.
2. Place sugar and butter in the mixer bowl. Attach the flat beater and mixer bowl to the mixer. Set to Speed 4 and beat until light and fluffy. Beat in egg and almond extract. Reduce speed to Stir and mix in flour mixture, in 3 additions. Divide dough in half and flatten each half into a disk.
3. Working with one disk at a time, roll out dough between two pieces of parchment paper to 1/4-inch (0.5 cm) thickness (dough will be very soft). Using assorted cookie cutters, cut out cookies. Place 1 inch (2.5 cm) apart on prepared baking sheets. Repeat with remaining dough. Refrigerate cookies on baking sheets for at least 15 minutes before baking. Preheat oven to 350°F (180°C).
4. Bake in middle of preheated oven until light golden at edges, about 12 minutes. Transfer to wire racks and let cool completely.

Makes about 3 dozen cookies

Make ahead

Can be prepared through Step 2 up to 1 day ahead. Wrap disks in plastic wrap and refrigerate. Soften dough slightly at room temperature before rolling out.

Store baked cookies in an airtight container at room temperature for up to 1 week or in the freezer for up to 4 weeks.

Full Moon Cookies

FLAT BEATER

- Baking sheets, lined with parchment paper
- 5-inch (12 cm) round cookie cutter
- 2- to 3-inch (5 to 7.5 cm) Halloween cookie cutters

Basic Dough		
2½ cups	unbleached all-purpose flour	625 mL
1 tsp	baking powder	5 mL
½ tsp	salt	2 mL
¾ cup	granulated sugar	175 mL
½ cup	unsalted butter, softened	125 mL
2	eggs	2
½ tsp	almond extract	2 mL
Chocolate Dough		
2¼ cups	unbleached all-purpose flour	550 mL
¼ cup	unsweetened cocoa powder	50 mL
1 tsp	baking powder	5 mL
½ tsp	salt	2 mL
¾ cup	granulated sugar	175 mL
½ cup	unsalted butter, softened	125 mL
2	eggs	2
½ tsp	almond extract	2 mL
	Black and orange candies	

Meredith makes these fun cookies every Halloween for neighborhood kids. To personalize them, write the children's names on them with black frosting.

1. *Prepare the basic dough:* In a medium bowl, whisk together flour, baking powder and salt.
2. Place sugar and butter in the mixer bowl. Attach the flat beater and mixer bowl to the mixer. Set to Speed 4 and beat until light and fluffy. Beat in eggs, one at a time, and almond extract. Reduce speed to Stir and mix in flour mixture, in 3 additions. Flatten dough into a disk, wrap in plastic wrap and refrigerate for 3 to 4 hours, until firm. Clean the mixer bowl and flat beater.
3. *Prepare the chocolate dough:* In a medium bowl, whisk together flour, cocoa, baking powder and salt.
4. Place sugar and butter in the mixer bowl. Attach the flat beater and mixer bowl to the mixer. Set to Speed 4 and beat until light and fluffy. Beat in eggs and almond extract. Reduce speed to Stir and mix in flour mixture, in 3 additions. Flatten dough into a disk, wrap in plastic wrap and refrigerate for 3 to 4 hours, until firm.
5. On a lightly floured work surface, roll out basic dough to ⅛-inch (0.25 cm) thickness. Cut out 5-inch (13 cm) rounds (these will represent the full moon) and place 1 inch (2.5 cm) apart on prepared baking sheets. Reroll scraps and repeat. Place in refrigerator while you're rolling out chocolate dough. Preheat oven to 350°F (180°C).

6. Roll out chocolate dough to 1⁄8-inch (0.25 cm) thickness. Cut out Halloween shapes (owls, cats, bats, witches). Reroll scraps. Decorate with candies and place on dough rounds, slightly off-center, as if the shape is being seen in front of a full moon.
7. Bake in middle of preheated oven for 12 to 14 minutes, or until edges are lightly colored. Transfer to a wire rack and let cool completely.

Makes 12 big cookies

Make ahead

Store in an airtight container in the freezer for up to 4 weeks.

TIPS

Use your imagination when decorating the cookies; we use the candies to make eyes or brooms.

This recipe will make extra chocolate dough. You can either halve the ingredients for the chocolate dough or make extra chocolate cookies.

Snickerdoodles

FLAT BEATER

- Baking sheets, lined with parchment paper

3 cups	unbleached all-purpose flour	750 mL
2 tsp	baking powder	10 mL
1 tsp	baking soda	5 mL
1/2 tsp	ground cinnamon	2 mL
1/4 tsp	salt	1 mL
1 3/4 cups	granulated sugar	425 mL
1 cup	unsalted butter, softened	250 mL
2	eggs	2
2 tsp	vanilla	10 mL
Topping		
1/2 cup	granulated sugar	125 mL
1 tsp	ground cinnamon	5 mL

1. In a medium bowl, whisk together flour, baking powder, baking soda, cinnamon and salt.
2. Place sugar and butter in the mixer bowl. Attach the flat beater and mixer bowl to the mixer. Set to Speed 4 and beat until light and fluffy. Beat in eggs, one at a time, and vanilla. Reduce speed to Stir and mix in flour mixture, in 3 additions. Cover and refrigerate for 1 hour, until firm. Preheat oven to 375°F (190°C).
3. *Prepare the topping:* In a small bowl, whisk together sugar and cinnamon.
4. Form balls of dough about the size of a walnut. Roll in cinnamon sugar to coat. Place 2 1/2 inches (6 cm) apart on prepared baking sheets. Bake in middle of preheated oven for 10 to 12 minutes, or until puffed and slightly cracked. Let cool on sheets for 5 minutes, then transfer to wire racks to cool completely.

Makes 4 dozen cookies

Make ahead

Store in an airtight container in the freezer for up to 4 weeks.

Crispy Oatmeal Cookies

FLAT BEATER

- Preheat oven to 350°F (180°C)
- Baking sheets, lined with parchment paper

1 1/4 cups	unbleached all-purpose flour	300 mL
1 tsp	salt	5 mL
1 tsp	baking soda	5 mL
1 tsp	ground cinnamon	5 mL
1 1/2 cups	unsalted butter, softened	375 mL
1 cup	lightly packed light brown sugar	250 mL
1/2 cup	granulated sugar	125 mL
1	egg	1
1 tsp	vanilla	5 mL
3 cups	old-fashioned rolled oats	750 mL
2 cups	walnut halves, chopped	500 mL
1 cup	dried cranberries	250 mL

1. In a small bowl, whisk together flour, salt, baking soda and cinnamon.
2. Place butter in the mixer bowl. Attach the flat beater and mixer bowl to the mixer. Set to Speed 4 and beat until soft and creamy. Beat in brown sugar and granulated sugar until light and fluffy. Beat in egg and vanilla. Reduce speed to Stir and mix in flour mixture, in 3 additions. Mix in oats, walnuts and cranberries until evenly incorporated.
3. Drop by rounded teaspoonfuls (5 mL), 2 inches (5 cm) apart, onto prepared baking sheets. Bake in middle of preheated oven for 8 to 10 minutes, or until lightly browned. Let cool on sheets for 5 minutes, then transfer to wire racks to cool completely.

Makes 6 dozen cookies

Variations

Substitute pecans or slivered almonds for the walnuts.

Add 1 cup (250 mL) chocolate chips, raisins or other dried fruit, such as currants or chopped apricots.

Make ahead

Store in an airtight container in the freezer for up to 4 weeks.

The Ultimate Chocolate Chip Cookie

FLAT BEATER

- Preheat oven to 350°F (180°C)
- Baking sheets, lined with parchment paper

2½ cups	unbleached all-purpose flour	625 mL
1 tsp	baking soda	5 mL
1 tsp	salt	5 mL
1 cup	unsalted butter, softened	250 mL
¾ cup	lightly packed light brown sugar	175 mL
½ cup	granulated sugar	125 mL
2	eggs	2
2 tsp	vanilla	10 mL
2 cups	semisweet chocolate chips (about 12 oz/375 g)	500 mL
1 cup	walnut halves, toasted (see tip, below) and coarsely chopped	250 mL

TIPS

To toast nuts, spread them on a baking sheet and toast in a 350°F (180°C) oven for 7 to 8 minutes, or until lightly browned.

If you prefer your cookies crunchy rather than chewy, bake for an additional 3 minutes, until light brown.

1. In a medium bowl, whisk together flour, baking soda, and salt.
2. Place butter, brown sugar and granulated sugar in the mixer bowl. Attach the flat beater and mixer bowl to the mixer. Set to Speed 4 and beat until light and fluffy. Beat in eggs, one at a time, and vanilla. Reduce speed to Stir and mix in flour mixture, in 3 additions. Mix in chocolate chips and walnuts, if using, until evenly incorporated.
3. Drop by rounded tablespoonfuls (15 mL), about 2 inches (5 cm) apart, onto prepared baking sheets. Bake in middle of preheated oven until brown around the edges yet soft in the center, about 12 minutes. Let cool on sheets for 1 minute, then transfer to wire racks to cool completely.

Makes 4 dozen cookies

Make ahead

Store in an airtight container in the freezer for up to 4 weeks.

Oatmeal Chocolate Chip Cookies

FLAT BEATER

- Preheat oven to 350°F (180°C)
- Baking sheets, lined with parchment paper

2 cups	unbleached all-purpose flour	500 mL
1 tsp	baking soda	5 mL
1 tsp	salt	5 mL
1/2 tsp	ground cinnamon	2 mL
1/4 tsp	ground nutmeg	1 mL
1 cup	unsalted butter, softened	250 mL
1 cup	firmly packed light brown sugar	250 mL
1/2 cup	granulated sugar	125 mL
2	eggs	2
1 tsp	vanilla	5 mL
2 cups	semisweet chocolate chips (about 12 oz/375 g)	500 mL
1 1/2 cups	old-fashioned rolled oats	375 mL

1. In a medium bowl, whisk together flour, baking soda, salt, cinnamon and nutmeg.
2. Place butter in the mixer bowl. Attach the flat beater and mixer bowl to the mixer. Set to Speed 4 and beat until soft and creamy. Increase to Speed 6 and beat in brown sugar and granulated sugar until light and fluffy. Beat in eggs, one at a time, and vanilla. Reduce speed to Stir and mix in flour mixture, in 3 additions. Mix in chocolate chips and oats until evenly incorporated.
3. Drop by rounded tablespoonfuls (15 mL), 2 inches (5 cm) apart, onto prepared baking sheets. Bake in middle of preheated oven for 10 to 12 minutes, or until golden and slightly firm to the touch. Let cool on sheets for 5 minutes, then transfer to wire racks to cool completely.

Makes 4 dozen cookies

Variation

Substitute walnuts or pecans for a portion of the chocolate chips. Use 1 cup (250 mL) nut halves, chopped, and 1 1/2 cups (375 mL) chocolate chips. Or use peanut butter chocolate chips, white chocolate chips, etc.

Make ahead

Store in an airtight container in the freezer for up to 4 weeks.

Peanut Butter Cookies

FLAT BEATER

- Preheat oven to 350°F (180°C)
- Baking sheets, lined with parchment paper

2½ cups	unbleached all-purpose flour	625 mL
¾ tsp	salt	3 mL
½ tsp	baking soda	2 mL
½ tsp	baking powder	2 mL
1 cup	unsalted butter, softened	250 mL
1 cup	lightly packed light brown sugar	250 mL
1 cup	granulated sugar	250 mL
1 cup	peanut butter (crunchy or creamy)	250 mL
2	eggs	2
2 tsp	vanilla	10 mL

1. In a medium bowl, whisk together flour, salt, baking soda and baking powder.
2. Place butter in the mixer bowl. Attach the flat beater and mixer bowl to the mixer. Set to Speed 4 and beat until soft and creamy. Beat in brown sugar and granulated sugar until light and fluffy. Beat in peanut butter until fully incorporated. Beat in eggs, one at a time, and vanilla. Reduce speed to Stir and mix in flour mixture, in 3 additions.
3. Scoop out 2 tbsp (25 mL) of dough for each cookie, roll into balls and place 2 inches (5 cm) apart on prepared baking sheets. Press each ball with the tines of a fork dipped in cold water to make a crisscross design. Bake in middle of preheated oven for 10 to 12 minutes, or until puffed and slightly brown along edges (they will not look fully baked). Let cool on sheets until set, about 4 minutes, then transfer to wire racks to cool completely.

Makes 4 dozen cookies

Make ahead

Store in an airtight container in the refrigerator for up to 1 week or in the freezer for up to 4 weeks.

Lemon Drop Cookies

FLAT BEATER

- Preheat oven to 375°F (190°C)
- Baking sheets, lined with parchment paper

3 cups	sifted unbleached all-purpose flour	750 mL
2 tsp	baking powder	10 mL
1 tsp	salt	5 mL
1 1/2 cups	granulated sugar	375 mL
3/4 cup	unsalted butter, softened	175 mL
3 tbsp	grated lemon zest	45 mL
1/4 cup	freshly squeezed lemon juice	50 mL
3	eggs	3
Glaze		
2 cups	confectioner's (icing) sugar, sifted	500 mL
1/4 cup	freshly squeezed lemon juice	50 mL

1. In a medium bowl, whisk together flour, baking powder and salt.
2. Place sugar and butter in the mixer bowl. Attach the flat beater and mixer bowl to the mixer. Set to Speed 4 and beat until light and fluffy. Beat in lemon zest and juice. Beat in eggs, one at a time. Reduce speed to Stir and mix in flour mixture, in 3 additions.
3. Drop by tablespoonfuls (15 mL), 2 inches (5 cm) apart, onto prepared baking sheets. Bake in middle of preheated oven for 8 to 10 minutes, or until just firm to the touch. Let cool on sheets for 1 minute, then transfer to wire racks to cool completely.
4. *Prepare the glaze:* In a medium bowl, whisk together confectioner's sugar and lemon juice until smooth.
5. Using a pastry brush, brush glaze on each cookie. Place on racks and let stand for 10 to 15 minutes, or until glaze is set.

Makes 5 dozen cookies

Make ahead

Store in an airtight container in the freezer for up to 4 weeks.

Linzertorte Cookies with Raspberry Filling

FLAT BEATER

- Baking sheets, lined with parchment paper
- 2½-inch (6 cm) round cookie cutter
- 1½-inch (4 cm) round cookie cutter

2 cups	unbleached all-purpose flour	500 mL
½ tsp	ground cinnamon	2 mL
¼ tsp	ground cloves	1 mL
Pinch	salt	Pinch
1 cup	confectioner's (icing) sugar, sifted	250 mL
1 cup	unsalted butter, softened	250 mL
1	egg	1
1 cup	unblanched almonds, finely ground	250 mL
½ cup	seedless raspberry jam (see tip, below)	125 mL
	Additional confectioner's (icing) sugar	

Make ahead

Store in an airtight container in the freezer for up to 4 weeks.

TIP

If you can only find raspberry jam with seeds, strain it through a fine-mesh sieve to remove the seeds.

1. In a small bowl, whisk together flour, cinnamon, cloves and salt.
2. Place confectioner's sugar and butter in the mixer bowl. Attach the flat beater and mixer bowl to the mixer. Set to Speed 4 and beat until light and fluffy. Beat in egg. Reduce speed to Stir and mix in flour mixture, in 3 additions. Mix in almonds. Divide dough in half and flatten each half into a disk. Wrap in plastic wrap and refrigerate for 1 hour, until firm.
3. Working with one disk at a time, on a lightly floured work surface, roll out dough to ⅛-inch (0.25 cm) thickness. Cut out rounds with the larger cutter, then cut the centers out of half of the rounds to make rings. Re-roll the scraps and cut out more rounds and rings. Using a metal spatula, transfer rounds and rings to separate prepared baking sheets, grouping rings together and rounds together for even baking, and placing them at least 2 inches (5 cm) apart. Refrigerate for 1 hour, until cold. Meanwhile, preheat oven to 350°F (180°C).
4. Bake in middle of preheated oven for 10 to 15 minutes, or until lightly browned. Transfer to wire racks and let cool completely. Spread rounds with raspberry jam and top each with a ring. Sift confectioner's sugar over cookies.

Makes 2 dozen cookies

Easy Chocolate-Hazelnut Turnovers (page 342)

Plum Upside-Down Cake (page 356)

Orange Shortcakes (page 357)

Homemade Wasabi Mayonnaise (page 401)
and Tomatillo Salsa (page 407)

Russian Wedding Cakes

FLAT BEATER

- Baking sheets, lined with parchment paper

1 cup	unsalted butter, softened	250 mL
2 cups	confectioner's (icing) sugar, sifted, divided	500 mL
2 tsp	vanilla	10 mL
2 cups	unbleached all-purpose flour	500 mL
1/2 tsp	salt	2 mL
1 cup	walnut halves, toasted (see tip, page 284) and coarsely ground	250 mL

These buttery sugar-covered cookies are known by many names, including Russian Tea Cakes, Mexican Wedding Cakes and Snowballs.

Make ahead

Store in an airtight container at room temperature for up to 2 days or in the freezer for up to 4 weeks.

1. Place butter in the mixer bowl. Attach the flat beater and mixer bowl to the mixer. Set to Speed 4 and beat until soft and creamy. Beat in 1/2 cup (125 mL) of the confectioner's sugar and vanilla until light and fluffy. Reduce speed to Stir and mix in flour, in 3 additions, and salt. Mix in walnuts. Form dough into a ball, wrap in plastic wrap and refrigerate until cold, about 30 minutes. Preheat oven to 350°F (180°C).
2. Sift the remaining 1 1/2 cups (375 mL) confectioner's sugar into a pie plate or shallow dish. Set aside.
3. Roll dough into 1-inch (2.5 cm) balls and place 1/2 inch (1 cm) apart on prepared baking sheets. Bake in middle of preheated oven for 12 to 15 minutes, or until golden brown on bottom and pale golden on top. Let cool on sheets for 5 minutes. Gently toss in confectioner's sugar to coat. Transfer to wire racks and let cool completely. Sift the sugar left in the pie plate over cookies.

Makes about 4 dozen cookies

Aunt Jane's Walnut Refrigerator Cookies

FLAT BEATER

- Baking sheets, lined with parchment paper

3½ cups	unbleached all-purpose flour	875 mL
1 tsp	baking soda	5 mL
1 tsp	cream of tartar	5 mL
¾ tsp	salt	3 mL
2 cups	lightly packed light brown sugar	500 mL
1 cup	unsalted butter, softened	250 mL
2	eggs	2
2 tsp	vanilla	10 mL
1 cup	walnut halves, coarsely chopped	250 mL

Meredith's Aunt Jane made these wonderful walnut cookies every time an abundance of black walnuts was available. Black walnuts lend an unusual fragrant quality to these cookies, but they are equally wonderful made with regular walnuts or pecans.

1. In a medium bowl, whisk together flour, baking soda, cream of tartar and salt.
2. Place brown sugar and butter in the mixer bowl. Attach the flat beater and mixer bowl to the mixer. Set to Speed 4 and beat until light and fluffy. Beat in eggs, one at a time, and vanilla. Reduce speed to Stir and mix in flour mixture, in 3 additions. Mix in walnuts until evenly incorporated.
3. Divide dough in half and place each half on a large piece of parchment paper or waxed paper. Form two logs, approximately 2 inches (5 cm) in diameter, roll up in paper and twist ends to close. Refrigerate until firm, for at least 2 hours or overnight. Preheat oven to 375°F (190°C).
4. Working with one log at a time, slice dough into ¼-inch (0.5 cm) thick slices and place 1½ inches (4 cm) apart on baking sheets. Bake in middle of preheated oven for 12 to 15 minutes, or until golden brown around the edges. Transfer to wire racks and let cool completely.

Makes 5 dozen cookies

Make ahead

Store dough logs in an airtight container in the refrigerator for up to 3 days or in the freezer for up to 1 month. Thaw frozen dough overnight in the refrigerator before baking.

Store baked cookies in an airtight container in the freezer for up to 4 weeks.

Grandma Re's Rugalach

FLAT BEATER

- Baking sheets, lined with parchment paper

Cookie Dough		
1 lb	cream cheese, softened	500 g
2 cups	unsalted butter, softened	500 mL
4¾ cups	unbleached all-purpose flour	1.175 L
¼ tsp	salt	1 mL
Nut Filling		
¾ cup	homogenized (whole) milk	175 mL
¼ cup	unsalted butter, cut into pieces	50 mL
1 cup	granulated sugar	250 mL
4 cups	walnut or pecan halves, ground (1½ lbs/750 g)	1 L
½ tsp	vanilla	2 mL
	Confectioner's (icing) sugar	

Although Carla's Grandma Re didn't have a passion for baking, she could always be counted on to make these rich, nut-filled cookies at Christmastime.

Make ahead

Store dough in an airtight container in the refrigerator for up to 24 hours. Soften for 30 minutes at room temperature before rolling out.

Store baked cookies in an airtight container in the freezer for up to 4 weeks.

TIP

The nut filling can also be used to fill pastries and breads.

1. *Prepare the dough:* Place cream cheese and butter in the mixer bowl. Attach the flat beater and mixer bowl to the mixer. Set to Speed 4 and beat until smooth. Reduce speed to Stir and mix in flour, in 3 additions, and salt. Divide dough into 8 disks, wrap in plastic wrap and refrigerate for 1 hour, until firm.
2. *Meanwhile, prepare the filling:* In a medium saucepan, bring milk, butter and sugar to a boil over medium heat. Add walnuts and cook, stirring constantly, until thick, about 5 minutes. Remove from heat and add vanilla. Let cool. Preheat oven to 325°F (160°C).
3. Using a fine-mesh sieve, sprinkle confectioner's sugar over a work surface. As you work with each piece of dough, keep the rest refrigerated. Working with one disk at a time, lay dough on work surface and sprinkle with confectioner's sugar. Roll into a 10-inch (25 cm) round and spread thinly with ⅓ cup (75 mL) filling. Using a pastry wheel or a sharp knife, cut dough into 8 wedges. Beginning at the large end of each wedge, roll towards the small pointed end. Repeat with remaining dough.
4. Place cookies 2 inches (5 cm) apart on prepared baking sheets. Bake in middle of preheated oven for 15 to 20 minutes, or until golden brown. Transfer to wire racks and let cool completely.

Makes 6 dozen cookies

Variation

Try other fillings, such as canned apricot filling, almond filling or poppy seed filling.

Chocolate Crackle Cookies

WIRE WHIP

- Preheat oven to 350°F (180°C)
- Baking sheets, lined with parchment paper

3	egg whites	3
1 tsp	vanilla	5 mL
1 1/2 cups	confectioner's (icing) sugar, sifted	375 mL
1/3 cup	unsweetened cocoa powder, sifted	125 mL
Pinch	salt	Pinch
1 cup	walnut halves, chopped	250 mL
2 tbsp	unbleached all-purpose flour	25 mL

1. Place egg whites and vanilla in the mixer bowl. Attach the whip and mixer bowl to the mixer. Set to Speed 8 and beat until whites form soft peaks. Reduce speed to Stir and mix in confectioner's sugar, cocoa and salt until incorporated. Stop mixer and add walnuts and flour. Set to Stir and mix until well combined.
2. Drop by rounded tablespoonfuls (15 mL), 3 inches (7.5 cm) apart, onto prepared baking sheets. Bake in middle of preheated oven until firm around the edges but still soft in the middle, about 10 minutes. Transfer to wire racks and let cool.

Makes 2 dozen cookies

Make ahead

Store in an airtight container at room temperature for up to 5 days. Do not freeze.

Spiced Pumpkin and Walnut Cookies

FLAT BEATER ◆ WIRE WHIP

- ◆ Preheat oven to 350°F (180°C)
- ◆ Baking sheets, lined with parchment paper

2 cups	unbleached all-purpose flour	500 mL
1 tsp	ground cinnamon	5 mL
1 tsp	baking powder	5 mL
1/2 tsp	baking soda	2 mL
1/2 tsp	salt	2 mL
1/4 tsp	ground ginger	1 mL
Pinch	ground cloves	Pinch
1 cup	granulated sugar	250 mL
1 cup	unsalted butter, softened	250 mL
1	egg	1
1 cup	canned pumpkin purée (not pie filling)	250 mL
1 tsp	vanilla	5 mL
1 cup	walnut halves, toasted (see tip, page 284) and coarsely chopped	250 mL
Icing		
2 cups	confectioner's (icing) sugar, sifted	500 mL
1/4 cup	unsalted butter, softened	50 mL
3 tbsp	whipping (35%) cream	45 mL
3 tbsp	pure maple syrup	45 mL
1/2 tsp	maple extract	2 mL

1. In a medium bowl, whisk together flour, cinnamon, baking powder, baking soda, salt, ginger and cloves.
2. Place sugar and butter in the mixer bowl. Attach the flat beater and mixer bowl to the mixer. Set to Speed 4 and beat until light and fluffy. Beat in egg, pumpkin and vanilla. Reduce speed to Stir and mix in flour mixture, in 3 additions. Mix in walnuts until evenly incorporated.
3. Drop by rounded teaspoonfuls (5 mL), 2 inches (5 cm) apart, onto prepared baking sheets. Bake in middle of preheated oven until golden, about 15 minutes. Transfer to wire racks and let cool.
4. *Meanwhile, prepare the icing:* Place confectioner's sugar and butter in clean mixer bowl. Remove the flat beater and attach the whip and mixer bowl to the mixer. Set to Speed 4 and beat until light and fluffy. Beat in whipping cream, maple syrup and maple extract until smooth.
5. Spread a dollop of icing on each cookie. Let stand for 15 to 20 minutes, or until icing is set.

Makes 4 dozen cookies

Make ahead

Store in an airtight container at room temperature for up to 5 days or in the freezer for up to 4 weeks.

Hermit Cookies

FLAT BEATER

- Preheat oven to 350°F (180°C)
- Baking sheets, lined with parchment paper

1 1/2 cups	unbleached all-purpose flour	375 mL
1 tsp	ground cinnamon	5 mL
1/2 tsp	baking soda	2 mL
1/2 tsp	salt	2 mL
1/2 tsp	ground nutmeg	2 mL
1/2 tsp	ground ginger	2 mL
1/4 tsp	ground cloves	1 mL
1/2 cup	vegetable shortening	125 mL
1/2 cup	unsalted butter, softened	125 mL
1 cup	lightly packed light brown sugar	250 mL
1	egg	1
1 tsp	vanilla	5 mL
1 cup	raisins	250 mL
1 cup	walnut halves, toasted (see tip, page 284) and chopped	250 mL
	Confectioner's (icing) sugar	

1. In a small bowl, whisk together flour, cinnamon, baking soda, salt, nutmeg, ginger and cloves.
2. Place shortening and butter in the mixer bowl. Attach the flat beater and mixer bowl to the mixer. Set to Speed 4 and beat until soft and creamy. Beat in brown sugar until light and fluffy. Beat in egg and vanilla. Reduce speed to Stir and mix in flour mixture, in 3 additions. Mix in raisins and walnuts until evenly incorporated.
3. Drop by rounded teaspoonfuls (5 mL), 2 inches (5 cm) apart, onto prepared baking sheets. Bake in middle of preheated oven until golden around the edges and almost set in the middle, about 10 minutes. Transfer to wire racks and let cool. Sift confectioner's sugar over cooled cookies.

Makes 3 dozen cookies

Make ahead

Store in an airtight container at room temperature for up to 5 days or in the freezer for up to 4 weeks.

Molasses Cookies

FLAT BEATER

- Preheat oven to 350°F (180°C)
- Baking sheets, lined with parchment paper

3 1/2 cups	unbleached all-purpose flour	875 mL
1 tbsp	ground ginger	15 mL
2 tsp	ground cinnamon	10 mL
2 tsp	baking soda	10 mL
3/4 tsp	salt	3 mL
1/2 tsp	freshly ground white pepper	2 mL
1/2 tsp	ground allspice	2 mL
1 1/2 cups	granulated sugar, divided	375 mL
1 cup	firmly packed light brown sugar	250 mL
2 cups	unsalted butter, softened	500 mL
1	egg	1
1/2 cup	fancy molasses	125 mL

The white pepper in these cookies gives them lots of interesting spice.

1. In a large bowl, whisk together flour, ginger, cinnamon, baking soda, salt, pepper and allspice.
2. Place 1 cup (250 mL) of the granulated sugar, brown sugar and butter in the mixer bowl. Attach the flat beater and mixer bowl to the mixer. Set to Speed 4 and beat until light and fluffy. Beat in egg and molasses. Reduce speed to Stir and mix in flour mixture, 1/2 cup (125 mL) at a time.
3. Scoop out 1 tbsp (15 mL) of dough for each cookie and roll into balls. Drop balls into the remaining 1/2 cup (125 mL) sugar and roll to coat. Place 2 inches (5 cm) apart on prepared sheets. Bake in middle of preheated oven until set around the edges but still soft in the middle, about 8 minutes. Let cool on sheets for 5 minutes, then transfer to wire racks to cool completely.

Makes 4 dozen cookies

Make ahead

Store in an airtight container at room temperature for up to 5 days or in the freezer for up to 4 weeks.

Gingerbread Cookies

FLAT BEATER

- Baking sheets, lined with parchment paper
- Assorted 3- to 4-inch (7.5 to 10 cm) cookie cutters

5 cups	unbleached all-purpose flour	1.25 L
1 tbsp	ground ginger	15 mL
1½ tsp	baking soda	7 mL
1 tsp	ground cinnamon	5 mL
1 tsp	ground cloves	5 mL
½ tsp	salt	2 mL
1 cup	granulated sugar	250 mL
1 cup	vegetable shortening	250 mL
1	egg	1
1 cup	fancy molasses	250 mL
2 tbsp	cider vinegar	25 mL
Butter Frosting		
6 tbsp	unsalted butter, softened	90 mL
4½ cups	confectioner's (icing) sugar, sifted	1.125 mL
¼ cup	whipping (35 %) cream (approx.)	50 mL
1 tsp	vanilla	5 mL

Make ahead

Store frosting, covered, in the refrigerator for up to 3 days. Give it a good stir before using to lighten it and break up any dried edges.

Store cookies in an airtight container in the refrigerator for up to 3 days or in the freezer for up to 4 weeks. Allow frosting to dry before stacking cookies for storage. Bring to room temperature before serving.

1. In a large bowl, whisk together flour, ginger, baking soda, cinnamon, cloves and salt.
2. Place sugar and shortening in the mixer bowl. Attach the flat beater and mixer bowl to the mixer. Set to Speed 4 and beat until light and fluffy. Beat in egg. Beat in molasses and vinegar. Reduce speed to Stir and mix in flour mixture, in 3 additions. Divide dough into 3 disks, wrap in plastic wrap and refrigerate for at least 3 hours, until firm, or overnight. Clean the mixer bowl and flat beater. Preheat oven to 375°F (190°C).
3. *Prepare the frosting:* Place butter in the mixer bowl. Attach the flat beater and mixer bowl to the mixer. Set to Speed 4 and beat until smooth and creamy. Reduce speed to Stir and mix in confectioner's sugar in 2 additions, adding whipping cream as necessary to make a smooth frosting. Mix in vanilla. Set aside.
4. As you work with each piece of dough, keep the rest in the refrigerator. Working with one disk at a time, on a lightly floured work surface, roll out dough to ⅛-inch (0.25 cm) thickness. Cut out with cookie cutters and place 2 inches (5 cm) apart on prepared baking sheets. Bake in middle of preheated oven until puffy and soft, about 5 minutes. Transfer to wire racks and let cool completely. Frost as desired with butter frosting.

Makes about 4 dozen cookies

TIP

Try tinting the frosting with food coloring.

Soft Gingersnap Cookies

FLAT BEATER

- Preheat oven to 325°F (160°C)
- Baking sheets, lined with parchment paper

2 cups	unbleached all-purpose flour	500 mL
1 tbsp	ground ginger	15 mL
1 tsp	ground cinnamon	5 mL
1 tsp	baking soda	5 mL
1⁄4 tsp	salt	1 mL
Pinch	ground allspice	Pinch
1 cup	unsalted butter, softened	250 mL
1 cup	firmly packed dark brown sugar	250 mL
1	egg	1
1 tsp	vanilla	5 mL
1⁄2 cup	granulated sugar	125 mL
1⁄4 cup	slivered crystallized ginger (optional)	50 mL

1. In a medium bowl, whisk together flour, ginger, cinnamon, baking soda, salt and allspice.
2. Place butter in the mixer bowl. Attach the flat beater and mixer bowl to the mixer. Set to Speed 4 and beat until soft and creamy. Beat in brown sugar until light and fluffy. Beat in egg and vanilla until incorporated. Reduce speed to Stir and mix in flour mixture, in 3 additions.
3. Scoop out 1 tbsp (15 mL) of dough for each cookie and roll into balls. Drop balls into granulated sugar and roll to coat. Place 2 inches (5 cm) apart on prepared baking sheets. If desired, gently push a small piece of crystallized ginger into the center of each cookie. Bake in middle of preheated oven until set around the edges but still soft in the middle, about 8 minutes. Let cool on sheets on wire racks for 5 minutes, then transfer to racks to cool completely.

Makes 3 dozen cookies

Make ahead

Store in an airtight container at room temperature for up to 5 days or in the freezer for up to 4 weeks.

Almond Macaroons

FLAT BEATER

- Preheat oven to 350°F (180°C)
- Baking sheets, lined with parchment paper

8 oz	almond paste	250 g
1 cup	granulated sugar	250 mL
Pinch	salt	Pinch
2	egg whites, at room temperature	2
1/2 tsp	almond extract	2 mL
1/4 cup	slivered blanched almonds	50 mL

Make ahead

Store in an airtight container at room temperature for up to 1 week or in the freezer for up to 4 weeks.

1. Crumble almond paste with your hands. Place almond paste, sugar and salt in the mixer bowl. Attach the flat beater and mixer bowl to the mixer. Set to Stir and mix until crumbly, about 5 minutes.
2. In a small bowl, whisk together egg whites and almond extract. Set mixer to Speed 2 and beat in egg white mixture, in 3 additions, until smooth.
3. Drop by rounded tablespoonfuls (15 mL), 2 inches (5 cm) apart, onto prepared baking sheets. Push a few slivered almonds into the center of each cookie. Bake in middle of preheated oven until golden and firm on the edges but still soft in the middle, about 10 minutes. Let cool completely on sheets on wire racks.

Makes 2 dozen cookies

Black-and-White Coconut Macaroons

WIRE WHIP

- Preheat oven to 325°F (160°C)
- Baking sheets, lined with parchment paper

4	egg whites, at room temperature	4
1⅔ cups	confectioner's (icing) sugar, sifted	400 mL
1 tsp	vanilla	5 mL
2⅓ cups	sweetened flaked coconut	575 mL
⅓ cup	unbleached all-purpose flour	75 mL
2 oz	bittersweet chocolate, chopped	60 g

Make ahead

Store in an airtight container at room temperature for up to 1 week or in the freezer for up to 4 weeks.

1. Place egg whites in the mixer. Attach the whip and mixer bowl to the mixer. Set to Speed 4 and beat until foamy. Increase to Speed 8 and beat until soft peaks form. Reduce to Speed 4 and beat in confectioner's sugar, in 4 additions, and vanilla until stiff, glossy peaks form. Remove the mixer bowl.
2. In a medium bowl, combine coconut and flour. Using a large rubber spatula, fold into the egg whites.
3. Drop by rounded tablespoonfuls (15 mL), 2 inches (5 cm) apart, onto prepared baking sheets. Bake in middle of preheated oven until light golden and slightly firm to the touch, about 20 minutes. Transfer to wire racks and let cool completely.
4. Meanwhile, in a heatproof bowl set over a small saucepan of hot, not boiling water, heat chocolate, stirring, until half melted. Remove from heat and stir until no lumps remain. (Or, in a microwave-safe bowl, microwave chocolate on Medium (50%) until half melted, about 45 seconds. Stir until no lumps remain.)
5. Line a baking sheet with a clean sheet of parchment paper. Dip the bottom ¼ inch (0.5 cm) of the cookies in chocolate and place on baking sheet. Refrigerate until chocolate is set.

Makes 2 dozen cookies

Almond Meringue Cookies

WIRE WHIP

- Preheat oven to 300°F (150°C)
- Baking sheets, lined with parchment paper
- Pastry bag with ½-inch (1 cm) plain tip (optional)

1 cup	granulated sugar, divided	250 mL
¾ cup	blanched almonds, toasted (see tip, page 284) and finely ground	175 mL
1 tbsp	cornstarch	15 mL
4	egg whites, at room temperature	4
Pinch	salt	Pinch
½ tsp	vanilla	2 mL
¼ tsp	almond extract	1 mL

TIP
If you don't have a pastry bag, you can use a small plastic baggie with a hole cut in the corner.

1. In a small bowl, whisk together ½ cup (125 mL) of the sugar, almonds and cornstarch.
2. Place egg whites and salt in the mixer bowl. Attach the whip and mixer bowl to the mixer. Set to Speed 4 and beat until foamy. Increase to Speed 8 and beat until soft peaks form. Beat in the remaining sugar, 1 tbsp (15 mL) at a time, until stiff, glossy peaks form. Add vanilla and almond extract and beat for 1 minute. Remove the mixer bowl.
3. Using a large rubber spatula, gently fold sugar mixture into the egg whites, in 3 additions.
4. Spoon into pastry bag and pipe 3-inch (7.5 cm) long fingers, 1 inch (2.5 cm) apart, onto prepared baking sheets. (Or drop by tablespoonfuls/15 mL, 1 inch/2.5 cm apart, onto prepared baking sheets.) Bake in middle of preheated oven until firm to the touch, about 25 minutes. Let cool on sheets on wire racks.

Makes 3 dozen cookies

Make ahead

Store in an airtight container at room temperature for up to 1 week or in the freezer for up to 4 weeks.

Chocolate Meringue Cookies

WIRE WHIP

- Preheat oven to 275°F (140°C)
- Baking sheets, lined with parchment paper
- Pastry bag with ½-inch (1 cm) star tip (optional)

4	egg whites, at room temperature	4
Pinch	salt	Pinch
¼ tsp	cider vinegar	1 mL
1 cup	granulated sugar	250 mL
2 tsp	unsweetened cocoa powder	10 mL
2 tsp	orange-flavored liqueur	10 mL
	Additional unsweetened cocoa powder	

1. Place egg whites and salt in the mixer bowl. Attach the whip and mixer bowl to the mixer. Set to Speed 4 and beat until foamy. Increase to Speed 8 and beat in vinegar until soft peaks form. Beat in sugar, 1 tbsp (15 mL) at a time, until stiff, glossy peaks form. Reduce speed to Stir and mix in cocoa and liqueur.
2. Spoon into pastry bag and pipe 1-inch (2.5 cm) rosettes, 2 inches (5 cm) apart, onto prepared baking sheets. (Or drop by tablespoonfuls/15 mL, 2 inches/5 cm apart, onto prepared baking sheets). Using a small sifter or wire-mesh strainer, sprinkle with cocoa. Bake in middle of preheated oven until firm to the touch, about 30 minutes. Turn the oven off. Let meringues cool completely on sheets in the oven. Peel from the paper when cool to the touch.

Makes 2 dozen cookies

TIP

If you don't have a pastry bag, you can use a small plastic baggie with a hole cut in the corner.

Make ahead

Store in an airtight container at room temperature for up to 1 week or in the freezer for up to 4 weeks.

Meringue Surprise Cookies

WIRE WHIP

- Preheat oven to 300°F (150°C)
- Baking sheets, lined with parchment paper

4	egg whites	4
1/4 tsp	salt	1 mL
1 cup	granulated sugar	250 mL
1 cup	candy-coated chocolate pieces	250 mL

The candy coating from the chocolate pieces bleeds inside the cookies and makes them multi-colored and festive.

TIP
It's important to store these cookies in an airtight container, especially when you are making them on a humid or rainy day. Moisture in the air tends to soften meringue, changing its texture from crispy to chewy.

1. Place egg whites and salt in the mixer bowl. Attach the whip and mixer bowl to the mixer. Set to Speed 4 and beat until foamy. Increase to Speed 8 and beat until soft peaks form. Beat in sugar, 1 tbsp (15 mL) at a time, until stiff, glossy peaks form. Remove the mixer bowl and, using a large rubber spatula, carefully fold in chocolate candies.
2. Drop by rounded tablespoonfuls (15 mL), 2 inches (5 cm) apart, onto prepared baking sheets. Bake in middle of preheated oven until set, about 30 minutes. Turn the oven off. Let meringues cool on sheets in the oven for at least 2 hours or overnight, until crisp and dry.

Makes 3 dozen cookies

Make ahead

Store in an airtight container at room temperature for up to 1 week. Do not freeze.

Ladyfingers

WIRE WHIP

- Preheat oven to 300°F (150°C)
- Baking sheets, lined with parchment paper and sprinkled with confectioner's sugar
- Pastry bag with ½-inch (1 cm) plain tip

3	egg whites	3
Pinch	salt	Pinch
1 tbsp	granulated sugar	15 mL
3	egg yolks	3
½ cup	granulated sugar	125 mL
1 tsp	vanilla	5 mL
½ cup	unbleached all-purpose flour, sifted	125 mL
	Confectioner's (icing) sugar, sifted	

Ladyfingers can be used in tiramisu, trifles, charlottes and many other desserts that incorporate sponge layers. Homemade ladyfingers are far superior to store-bought.

TIPS

Adequately beat the yolk mixture and do not overbeat the egg whites to ensure fluffy, instead of crisp, ladyfingers.

If you don't have a pastry bag, you can use a small plastic baggie with a hole cut in the corner.

1. Place egg whites and salt in the mixer bowl. Attach the whip and mixer bowl to the mixer. Set to Speed 4 and beat until foamy. Increase to Speed 8 and beat until soft peaks form. Beat in the 1 tbsp (15 mL) sugar until stiff, glossy peaks form. Transfer to a large bowl and reattach the mixer bowl and whip to the mixer.
2. Place yolks in the mixer bowl and beat on Speed 8 until thick and lemon-colored. Beat in sugar in a steady stream. Beat in vanilla. Continue beating for at least 4 minutes, or until mixture is thick and pale and forms a ribbon when the whip is lifted from the batter. Remove the mixer bowl.
3. Using a large rubber spatula, gently fold whites and flour into the yolk mixture, making 4 additions of each, until batter is light and fluffy. Be careful not to overmix or you will deflate the batter.
4. Spoon into pastry bag and pipe 4-inch (10 cm) fingers, 1 inch (2.5 cm) apart, onto prepared baking sheets. Sprinkle with confectioner's sugar. Bake in middle of preheated oven for 15 to 20 minutes, or until tops spring back when lightly touched. Let cool on sheets on wire racks.

Makes 2 dozen ladyfingers

Make ahead

Store in an airtight container at room temperature for up to 2 days or in the freezer for up to 2 weeks.

Shortbread

FLAT BEATER

- Preheat oven to 350°F (180°C)
- Baking sheets, lined with parchment paper

2 cups	unbleached all-purpose flour	500 mL
1/4 tsp	baking powder	1 mL
1/4 tsp	salt	1 mL
1 cup	unsalted butter, softened	250 mL
1/2 cup	confectioner's (icing) sugar, sifted	125 mL
2 tbsp	turbinado or granulated sugar	25 mL

Make ahead

Store between sheets of waxed paper in an airtight container at room temperature for up to 1 week or in the freezer for up to 4 weeks.

1. In a small bowl, whisk together flour, baking powder and salt.
2. Place butter in the mixer bowl. Attach the flat beater and mixer bowl to the mixer. Set to Speed 4 and beat until soft and creamy. Stop mixer and add confectioner's sugar. Set to Stir and mix for 30 seconds so the sugar doesn't fly all over, then increase to Speed 6 and beat until light and fluffy. Reduce speed to Stir and mix in flour mixture, in 3 additions.
3. Divide dough in half and place each half on a prepared baking sheet. Pat each into an 8-inch (20 cm) round, 1/4 inch (0.5 cm) thick. Using a ruler or sharp spatula, mark 8 wedges in the top of each round. Press the tines of a fork around the edges and poke holes in the center. Sprinkle with turbinado sugar.
4. Bake in middle of preheated oven until golden around the edges and set in the middle, about 15 minutes. Cut into wedges while still warm. Let cool on sheets on wire racks.

Makes 16 wedges

Chocolate Orange Shortbreads

FLAT BEATER

- Baking sheets, lined with parchment paper
- 2-inch (5 cm) round cookie cutter
- Pastry bag with 1⁄8-inch (0.25 cm) plain tip

1 1⁄4 cups	unbleached all-purpose flour	300 mL
1⁄4 cup	cornstarch	50 mL
1⁄4 cup	unsweetened cocoa powder (preferably Dutch-process)	50 mL
1⁄2 tsp	salt	2 mL
1 cup	unsalted butter, softened	250 mL
1 tbsp	finely grated orange zest	15 mL
1 cup	confectioner's (icing) sugar, sifted	250 mL
1 tsp	vanilla	5 mL
3 oz	bittersweet or semisweet chocolate, chopped	90 g

Make ahead

Store in a single layer between sheets of waxed paper in airtight containers at room temperature for up to 2 days or in the freezer for up to 4 weeks.

TIP

If you don't have a pastry bag, you can use a small plastic baggie with a hole cut in the corner.

1. In a medium bowl, whisk together flour, cornstarch, cocoa and salt.
2. Place butter in the mixer bowl. Attach the flat beater and mixer bowl to the mixer. Set to Speed 4 and beat until soft and creamy. Beat in orange zest. Reduce to Speed 2 and beat in confectioner's sugar and vanilla. Reduce to Stir and mix in flour mixture, in 3 additions. Form dough into a disk, wrap in plastic wrap and refrigerate for 30 minutes. Position oven racks in the top and bottom third and preheat oven to 350°F (180°C).
3. On a lightly floured work surface, working with once piece of dough at a time, roll out dough to 1⁄4-inch (0.5 cm) thickness. Cut into 2-inch (3 cm) rounds and place 1 1⁄2 inches (4 cm) apart on prepared baking sheets. Re-roll scraps and repeat with remaining dough. Bake in middle of preheated oven for 5 minutes, then rotate sheets. Bake for about 5 minutes longer, or until shortbread looks dry and feels firm to touch. Let cool on sheets for 1 minute, then remove to wire racks to cool completely.
4. Meanwhile, in a heatproof bowl set over a small saucepan of hot, not boiling water, heat chocolate, stirring, until half melted. Remove from heat and stir until no lumps remain. (Or, in a microwave-safe bowl, microwave chocolate on Medium (50%) until half melted, about 45 seconds. Stir until no lumps remain.) Spoon into pastry bag and pipe decoratively over cookies. Let stand until chocolate sets, about 1 hour.

Makes 2 dozen cookies

Hazelnut and Cranberry Biscotti

FLAT BEATER

- Preheat oven to 350°F (180°C)
- Large baking sheet, lined with parchment paper

2¾ cups	unbleached all-purpose flour	675 mL
1½ cups	granulated sugar	375 mL
½ cup	unsalted butter, cut into small pieces	125 mL
1½ tsp	baking powder	7 mL
¾ tsp	salt	3 mL
2	eggs	2
¼ cup	brandy	50 mL
½ tsp	almond extract	2 mL
1⅔ cups	hazelnuts, toasted, husked (see tip, below) and coarsely chopped	400 mL
1 cup	dried cranberries (about 6 oz/175 g)	250 mL

TIP

To husk hazelnuts, spread nuts out on a baking sheet and bake in a 350°F (180°C) oven for about 10 minutes. Dump nuts into a clean, dry kitchen towel. Fold the towel over to cover the nuts and let cool for about 5 minutes. Rub vigorously to remove the husks from the nuts.

1. Place flour, sugar, butter, baking powder and salt in the mixer bowl. Attach the flat beater and mixer bowl to the mixer. Set to Speed 2 and beat until mixture resembles coarse crumbs.
2. In a small bowl, whisk together eggs, brandy and almond extract. Add to the mixer bowl along with hazelnuts and cranberries. Set to Speed 2 and beat until a moist dough forms. Divide dough into thirds and place 3 inches (7.5 cm) apart on prepared baking sheet. Shape into three 12- by 2-inch (30 by 5 cm) logs.
3. Bake in middle of preheated oven until set but still soft, about 30 minutes. Let cool completely on sheet on a wire rack. Reduce oven temperature to 300°F (150°C).
4. Place logs on a cutting board and cut crosswise into ¾-inch (2 cm) thick slices. Return to baking sheet, cut side up, and bake for 10 minutes. Turn over and bake for another 15 minutes.

Makes 40 biscotti

Make ahead

Store in an airtight container at room temperature for up to 2 weeks or in the freezer for up to 4 weeks.

Almond Biscotti with Cinnamon

FLAT BEATER

- Preheat oven to 350°F (180°C)
- Large baking sheet, lined with parchment paper

2¾ cups	unbleached all-purpose flour	675 mL
1½ cups	granulated sugar	375 mL
½ cup	unsalted butter, cut into small pieces	125 mL
2½ tsp	baking powder	12 mL
1¼ tsp	ground cinnamon	6 mL
1 tsp	salt	5 mL
1⅔ cups	almonds, toasted (see tip, page 284) and coarsely chopped	400 mL
2	eggs	2
¼ cup + 1 tbsp	milk	65 mL
1 tsp	vanilla	5 mL

1. Place flour, sugar, butter, baking powder, cinnamon and salt in the mixer bowl. Attach the flat beater and mixer bowl to the mixer. Set to Speed 2 and beat until mixture resembles coarse crumbs.
2. In a small bowl, whisk together eggs, milk and vanilla. Add to the mixer bowl along with almonds. Set to Speed 2 and beat until a moist dough forms. Divide dough into thirds and place 3 inches (7.5 cm) apart on prepared baking sheet. Shape into three 12- by 2-inch (30 by 5 cm) logs.
3. Bake in middle of preheated oven until set but still soft, about 30 minutes. Let cool completely on sheet on a wire rack. Reduce oven temperature to 300°F (150°C).
4. Place logs on a cutting board and cut crosswise into ¾-inch (2 cm) thick slices. Return to baking sheet, cut side up, and bake for 10 minutes. Turn over and bake for another 15 minutes.

Makes 40 biscotti

Make ahead

Store in an airtight container at room temperature for up to 2 weeks or in the freezer for up to 4 weeks.

Orange, Apricot and White Chocolate Biscotti

FLAT BEATER

- Preheat oven to 350°F (180°C)
- Large baking sheet, lined with parchment paper

2¾ cups	unbleached all-purpose flour	675 mL
1½ cups	granulated sugar	375 mL
½ cup	unsalted butter, cut into small pieces	125 mL
1½ tsp	baking powder	7 mL
¾ tsp	salt	3 mL
	Finely grated zest of 1 orange	
2	eggs	2
¼ cup	orange-flavored liqueur	50 mL
½ tsp	almond extract	2 mL
1⅔ cups	almonds, toasted (see tip, page 284) and coarsely chopped	400 mL
1 cup	dried apricots, coarsely chopped	250 mL
5 oz	white chocolate, chopped	150 g

1. Place flour, sugar, butter, baking powder, salt and orange zest in the mixer bowl. Attach the flat beater and mixer bowl to the mixer. Set to Speed 2 and beat until mixture resembles coarse crumbs.
2. In a small bowl, whisk together eggs, orange liqueur and almond extract. Add to the mixer bowl along with almonds, apricots and white chocolate. Set to Speed 2 and beat until a moist dough forms. Divide dough into thirds and place 3 inches (7.5 cm) apart on prepared baking sheet. Shape into three 12- by 2-inch (30 by 5 cm) logs.
3. Bake in middle of preheated oven until set but still soft, about 30 minutes. Let cool completely on sheet on a wire rack. Reduce oven temperature to 300°F (150°C).
4. Place logs on a cutting board and cut crosswise into ¾-inch (2 cm) thick slices. Return to baking sheet, cut side up, and bake for 10 minutes. Turn over and bake for another 15 minutes.

Makes 40 biscotti

Make ahead

Store in an airtight container at room temperature for up to 2 weeks or in the freezer for up to 4 weeks.

Chocolate Cherry Biscotti

FLAT BEATER

- Preheat oven to 350°F (180°C)
- Large baking sheet, lined with parchment paper

2¾ cups	unbleached all-purpose flour	675 mL
1¼ cups	granulated sugar	300 mL
½ cup	unsalted butter, cut into small pieces	125 mL
2 tbsp	unsweetened cocoa powder	25 mL
1½ tsp	baking powder	7 mL
¾ tsp	salt	3 mL
3	eggs, lightly beaten	3
1¾ cups	chopped bittersweet chocolate (about 10 oz/300 g)	425 mL
1 cup	dried cherries	250 mL
1 tbsp	grated orange zest	15 mL

1. Place flour, sugar, butter, cocoa, baking powder and salt in the mixer bowl. Attach the flat beater and mixer bowl to the mixer. Set to Speed 2 and beat until mixture resembles coarse crumbs. Beat in eggs, chocolate, cherries and orange zest until a moist dough forms. Divide dough into thirds and place 3 inches (7.5 cm) apart on prepared baking sheet. Shape into three 12- by 2-inch (30 by 5 cm) logs.
2. Bake in middle of preheated oven until set but still soft, about 30 minutes. Let cool completely on sheet on a wire rack. Reduce oven temperature to 300°F (150°C).
3. Place logs on a cutting board and cut crosswise into ¾-inch (2 cm) thick slices. Return to baking sheet, cut side up, and bake for 10 minutes. Turn over and bake for another 15 minutes.

Makes 40 biscotti

Make ahead

Store in an airtight container at room temperature for up to 2 weeks or in the freezer for up to 4 weeks.

Decadent Bittersweet Brownies

FLAT BEATER

- Preheat oven to 350°F (180°C)
- 8-inch (2 L) square metal baking pan, greased and floured

1 cup + 2 tbsp	granulated sugar	275 mL
1/2 cup	unsalted butter, softened	125 mL
3	eggs	3
1 tsp	vanilla	5 mL
5 oz	bittersweet chocolate, melted (see tip, below)	150 g
3 oz	unsweetened chocolate, melted	90 g
1 cup	unbleached all-purpose flour	250 mL
1/2 tsp	salt	2 mL
3/4 cup	walnut halves, coarsely chopped (optional)	175 mL

TIP
To melt chocolate, first break it into small pieces. In a heatproof bowl set over a small saucepan of gently simmering water, heat chocolate, stirring, until half melted. Remove from heat and stir until no lumps remain. (Or, in a microwave-safe bowl, microwave chocolate on Medium (50%) until half melted, about 45 seconds. Stir until no lumps remain.)

1. Place sugar and butter in the mixer bowl. Attach the flat beater and mixer bowl to the mixer. Set to Speed 4 and beat until light and fluffy. Beat in eggs, one at a time, and vanilla. Beat in chocolate until smooth. Reduce speed to Stir and mix in flour and salt until just combined. Mix in walnuts, if using, until evenly incorporated.
2. Spread batter in prepared pan and smooth top. Bake in middle of preheated oven for 35 to 40 minutes, or until a tester inserted in the center comes out with moist, sticky crumbs attached. Let cool in pan on a wire rack. Cut into squares.

Makes 16 brownies

Make ahead

Store in an airtight container at room temperature for up to 5 days or in the freezer for up to 4 weeks.

Cream Cheese Brownies

FLAT BEATER

- Preheat oven to 350°F (180°C)
- 8- or 9-inch (2 or 2.5 L) square metal baking pan, greased and floured

Chocolate Batter		
1 cup + 2 tbsp	granulated sugar	275 mL
½ cup	unsalted butter, softened	125 mL
3	eggs	3
1 tsp	vanilla	5 mL
3 oz	unsweetened chocolate, melted (see tip, page 310)	90 g
1 cup	unbleached all-purpose flour	250 mL
½ tsp	salt	2 mL
Cream Cheese Layer		
1	egg	1
8 oz	cream cheese, softened	250 g
⅓ cup	granulated sugar	75 mL
½ tsp	vanilla	2 mL
Pinch	salt	Pinch
½ cup	chocolate chips	125 mL

1. *Prepare the chocolate batter:* Place sugar and butter in the mixer bowl. Attach the flat beater and mixer bowl to the mixer. Set to Speed 4 and beat until light and fluffy. Beat in eggs, one at a time, and vanilla. Beat in chocolate until smooth. Reduce speed to Stir and mix in flour, in 3 additions, and salt until just combined. Transfer to a large bowl and clean the mixer bowl and flat beater.
2. *Prepare the cream cheese layer:* Place egg, cream cheese, sugar, vanilla and salt in the mixer bowl. Attach the flat beater and mixer bowl to the mixer. Set to Speed 4 and beat until well combined.
3. Spread two-thirds of the batter in prepared pan and smooth top. Using a rubber spatula, spread cream cheese layer over batter. Drop the remaining batter in spoonfuls over cream cheese layer. Using the tip of a knife, gently swirl through batter to form a marble design. Sprinkle with chocolate chips. Bake in middle of preheated oven for 30 to 35 minutes for 9-inch (2.5 L) pan or 45 to 50 minutes for 8-inch (2 L) pan, or until a tester inserted in the center comes out with moist, sticky crumbs attached. Let cool in pan on a wire rack. Cut into squares.

Makes 16 brownies

Make ahead

Store in an airtight container at room temperature for up to 5 days or in the freezer for up to 4 weeks.

Grasshopper Brownies

FLAT BEATER ◆ WIRE WHIP

- ◆ Preheat oven to 350°F (180°C)
- ◆ 8-inch (2 L) square metal baking pan, greased and floured

1 cup + 2 tbsp	granulated sugar	275 mL
½ cup	unsalted butter, softened	125 mL
3	eggs	3
½ tsp	vanilla	2 mL
5 oz	semisweet chocolate, melted (see tip, page 310)	150 g
3 oz	unsweetened chocolate, melted	90 g
½ tsp	peppermint extract	2 mL
1 cup	unbleached all-purpose flour	250 mL
½ tsp	salt	2 mL
Mint Topping		
1 cup	confectioner's (icing) sugar, sifted	250 mL
2 tbsp	unsalted butter, softened	25 mL
1 tbsp	milk	15 mL
¼ tsp	peppermint extract	1 mL
2	drops green food coloring	2
Chocolate Topping		
6 oz	semisweet chocolate, chopped	175 g
2 tbsp	unsalted butter	25 mL

1. Place sugar and butter in the mixer bowl. Attach the flat beater and mixer bowl to the mixer. Set to Speed 4 and beat until light and fluffy. Beat in eggs, one at a time, and vanilla. Beat in chocolate and peppermint extract until smooth. Reduce speed to Stir and mix in flour, in 3 additions, and salt until just combined.
2. Spread batter in prepared pan and smooth top. Bake in middle of preheated oven for 35 to 40 minutes, or until a tester inserted in the center comes out with moist, sticky crumbs attached. Let cool slightly in pan on a wire rack.
3. *Meanwhile, prepare the mint topping:* Place confectioner's sugar, butter, milk, peppermint extract and food coloring in clean mixer bowl. Attach the whip and mixer bowl to the mixer. Set to Speed 4 and beat until creamy. Spread over warm brownies. Cover and refrigerate until set, about 1 hour.
4. *Prepare the chocolate topping:* In a small saucepan, over low heat, heat chocolate and butter, stirring constantly, until smooth. Let cool slightly. Spread evenly over mint topping. Cover and refrigerate until set, about 1 hour. Cut into squares.

Makes 16 brownies

Make ahead

Store in an airtight container in the refrigerator for up to 3 days or in the freezer for up to 4 weeks.

Blondies

FLAT BEATER

- Preheat oven to 350°F (180°C)
- 13- by 9-inch (3 L) metal baking pan, lightly greased

2¼ cups	unbleached all-purpose flour	550 mL
2¼ tsp	baking powder	11 mL
1 tsp	salt	5 mL
1 cup	firmly packed light brown sugar	250 mL
½ cup	granulated sugar	125 mL
⅔ cup	unsalted butter, softened	150 mL
3	eggs	3
2 tsp	vanilla	10 mL
2 cups	semisweet chocolate chips (about 12 oz/375 g)	500 mL
1 cup	pecan halves, coarsely chopped	250 mL

1. In a medium bowl, whisk together flour, baking powder, and salt.
2. Place brown sugar, granulated sugar and butter in the mixer bowl. Attach the flat beater and mixer bowl to the mixer. Set to Speed 4 and beat until light and fluffy. Beat in eggs, one at a time, and vanilla. Reduce speed to Stir and mix in flour mixture, in 3 additions. Mix in chocolate chips and pecans until evenly incorporated.
3. Spread batter in prepared pan and smooth top. Bake in middle of preheated oven for 25 to 30 minutes, or until golden brown and a tester inserted in the center comes out clean. Let cool in pan on a wire rack. Cut into bars.

Makes 18 bars

Make ahead

Store in an airtight container at room temperature for up to 3 days or in the freezer for up to 4 weeks.

Walnut Apricot Bars

FLAT BEATER

- Preheat oven to 325°F (160°C)
- 13- by 9-inch (3 L) metal baking pan, greased

2 cups	unsalted butter, softened	500 mL
2 cups	granulated sugar	500 mL
2	eggs	2
4 cups	unbleached all-purpose flour	1 L
2 cups	walnut halves, lightly toasted (see tip, page 284) and chopped	500 mL
1 ½ cups	apricot preserves	375 mL

Make ahead

Store in an airtight container at room temperature for up to 5 days or in the freezer for up to 4 weeks.

1. Place butter in the mixer bowl. Attach the flat beater and mixer bowl to the mixer. Set to Speed 4 and beat until soft and creamy. Beat in sugar until light and fluffy. Beat in eggs, one at a time. Reduce speed to Stir and mix in flour, in 3 additions. Mix in walnuts until evenly incorporated.
2. With lightly floured fingers, press half of the dough into prepared pan. Spread apricot preserves over dough, leaving a 1-inch (2.5 cm) border. Flatten walnut-size pieces of the remaining dough between the palms of your hands. Lay on top of preserves, leaving open spots where preserves peek through. (The dough will spread a little as it cooks.)
3. Bake in middle of preheated oven until set and golden brown, about 1 hour. Let cool in pan on a wire rack. Cut into bars.

Makes 24 bars

Variations

Use pecans or slivered almonds instead of walnuts.

Substitute raspberry, strawberry or plum preserves for the apricot.

Linzertorte Bars

FLAT BEATER

- 8-inch (2 L) square metal baking pan, lined with parchment paper

1 ½ cups	unbleached all-purpose flour	375 mL
¾ tsp	baking powder	4 mL
½ tsp	ground cinnamon	2 mL
¼ tsp	salt	1 mL
Pinch	ground allspice	Pinch
½ cup	firmly packed light brown sugar	125 mL
¼ cup	granulated sugar	50 mL
½ cup	unsalted butter, softened	125 mL
1	egg	1
½ cup	almonds, toasted (see tip, page 284) and finely ground	125 mL
1 tsp	grated lemon zest	5 mL
¾ cup	seedless raspberry jam (see tip, below)	175 mL
2 tsp	freshly squeezed lemon juice	10 mL
	Confectioner's (icing) sugar	

TIP

If you can only find raspberry jam with seeds, strain it through a fine-mesh sieve to remove the seeds.

1. In a small bowl, whisk together flour, baking powder, cinnamon, salt and allspice.
2. Place brown sugar, granulated sugar and butter in the mixer bowl. Attach the flat beater and mixer bowl to the mixer. Set to Speed 4 and beat until light and fluffy. Beat in egg, almonds and lemon zest. Reduce speed to Stir and mix in flour mixture, in 3 additions.
3. With lightly floured fingers, press two-thirds of the dough into prepared pan. Roll out the remaining dough between two sheets of waxed paper to ⅛-inch (0.25 cm) thickness. Slide onto a baking sheet and refrigerate the rolled-out portion until firm, about 15 minutes. Preheat oven to 375°F (190°C).
4. In a small bowl, combine jam and lemon juice. Spread evenly over dough in pan, leaving a ½-inch (1 cm) border. Peel off top sheet of paper from rolled dough and cut dough diagonally into ½-inch (1 cm) thick strips. Arrange strips in a lattice pattern over jam, pressing at edges to adhere.
5. Bake in middle of preheated oven until golden brown and firm to the touch, about 30 minutes. Let cool in pan on a wire rack. Sift confectioner's sugar over top and cut into bars.

Makes 24 bars

Make ahead

Store in an airtight container at room temperature for up to 3 days or in the freezer for up to 4 weeks.

Coconut Macadamia Bars

FLAT BEATER   WIRE WHIP

- Preheat oven to 350°F (180°C)
- 13- by 9-inch (3 L) metal baking pan, greased

Shortbread		
2 cups	unbleached all-purpose flour	500 mL
1 cup	unsalted butter, softened	250 mL
2/3 cup	confectioner's (icing) sugar, sifted	150 mL
1/2 tsp	salt	2 mL
Topping		
1 cup	firmly packed light brown sugar	250 mL
1/2 cup	unsalted butter, melted	125 mL
1/4 cup	whipping (35%) cream	50 mL
1 tbsp	freshly squeezed lemon juice	15 mL
1/4 tsp	salt	1 mL
2 2/3 cups	sweetened flaked coconut	650 mL
1 1/3 cups	macadamia nuts (large pieces halved)	325 mL

TIP
If you cannot find macadamia nuts, hazelnuts, walnuts or pecans also work well.

1. *Prepare the shortbread:* Place flour, butter, confectioner's sugar and salt in the mixer bowl. Attach the flat beater and mixer bowl to the mixer. Set to Speed 4 and beat until a dough forms. Press evenly into prepared pan and bake in preheated oven for 20 to 25 minutes, or until pale golden. Reduce oven temperature to 325°F (160°C).
2. *Meanwhile, prepare the topping:* Place brown sugar, butter, whipping cream, lemon juice and salt in clean mixer bowl. Remove the flat beater and attach the whip and mixer bowl to the mixer. Set to Speed 4 and beat until well combined. Remove the mixer bowl. Using a rubber spatula, stir in coconut and nuts until evenly incorporated.
3. Spread topping over warm shortbread. Bake in middle of preheated oven for 35 to 45 minutes, or until top is golden and center is bubbling. Let cool completely in pan on a wire rack. Cut into bars.

Makes about 40 bars

Make ahead

Store in an airtight container in the refrigerator for up to 4 days or in the freezer for up to 3 weeks. Serve cold or at room temperature.

Deluxe Lemon Squares

FLAT BEATER   WIRE WHIP

- Preheat oven to 350°F (180°C)
- 13- by 9-inch (3 L) metal baking pan, greased

Crust		
1 1/2 cups	unbleached all-purpose flour	375 mL
1/2 cup	confectioner's (icing) sugar, sifted	125 mL
3/4 cup	unsalted butter, cut into small pieces	175 mL
1/2 tsp	grated lemon zest	2 mL
Pinch	salt	Pinch
Topping		
6	eggs	6
3 cups	granulated sugar	750 mL
1 cup	freshly squeezed lemon juice	250 mL
1/2 cup	unbleached all-purpose flour	125 mL
1/4 tsp	baking powder	1 mL
Pinch	salt	Pinch
	Confectioner's (icing) sugar	

1. *Prepare the crust:* Place flour, confectioner's sugar, butter, lemon zest and salt in the mixer bowl. Attach the flat beater and mixer bowl to the mixer. Set to Speed 2 and beat until mixture resembles coarse crumbs. Press evenly into prepared pan and bake in preheated oven until golden, about 20 minutes. Let cool in pan on a wire rack.
2. *Prepare the filling:* Place eggs and sugar in clean mixer bowl. Attach the whip and mixer bowl to the mixer. Set to Speed 4 and beat until smooth. Beat in lemon juice. Reduce speed to Stir and mix in flour, baking powder and salt.
3. Pour filling over baked crust. Bake in middle of preheated oven for 25 to 30 minutes, or until filling is set. Let cool in pan on a wire rack for 30 minutes. Sift confectioner's sugar over top and cut into squares.

Makes 48 squares

Make ahead

Store in an airtight container in the refrigerator for up to 4 days or in the freezer for up to 4 weeks.

Cranberry Maple Squares

FLAT BEATER ◆ WIRE WHIP

- Preheat oven to 350°F (180°C)
- 13- by 9-inch (3 L) metal baking pan, greased and lined with greased parchment paper

2 cups	unbleached all-purpose flour	500 mL
1⁄4 cup	granulated sugar	50 mL
2⁄3 cup	cold unsalted butter, cut into small pieces	150 mL
1 tsp	baking powder	5 mL
1⁄4 tsp	salt	1 mL
2	eggs	2
Filling		
3⁄4 cup	lightly packed light brown sugar	175 mL
1⁄2 cup	unsalted butter, softened	125 mL
1⁄4 cup	pure maple syrup	50 mL
4	eggs	4
1 1⁄4 cups	pecan halves, chopped	300 mL
1 1⁄2 cups	dried cranberries	375 mL
Pinch	salt	Pinch

1. Place flour, sugar, butter, baking powder and salt in the mixer bowl. Attach the flat beater and mixer bowl to the mixer. Set to Speed 2 and beat until mixture resembles coarse crumbs. Beat in eggs, one at a time, until dough forms a ball.
2. On a floured work surface, roll out dough into a 13- by 9-inch (33 by 23 cm) rectangle. Carefully fold twice so it is easier to transfer to the prepared pan. Unfold into the pan, pressing evenly into the bottom and 1 inch (2.5 cm) up the sides. Refrigerate while you prepare the filling.
3. *Prepare the filling:* Place brown sugar and butter in clean mixer bowl. Remove the flat beater and attach the whip and mixer bowl to the mixer. Set to Speed 4 and beat until light and fluffy. Beat in maple syrup. Beat in eggs, one at a time, until smooth. Remove the mixer bowl. Using a rubber spatula, stir in pecans, cranberries and salt until evenly incorporated.
4. Pour filling into dough and spread evenly in the pan. Bake in lower third of preheated oven for 35 to 40 minutes, or until pastry is golden and filling is set. Let cool completely in pan on a wire rack. Cut into squares.

Makes 24 squares

Make ahead

Store in an airtight container at room temperature for up to 3 days or in the freezer for up to 4 weeks.

Desserts

continued on next page

Flaky Pastry

FLAT BEATER

1 1⁄2 cups	unbleached all-purpose flour	375 mL
1⁄4 tsp	salt	1 mL
2⁄3 cup	cold unsalted butter, cut into 1⁄4-inch (0.5 cm) pieces	150 mL
1⁄3 cup	ice water	75 mL

TIP

For tender, flaky pastry, make sure not to overmix the dough. As soon as it comes together, stop the mixer.

1. Place flour, salt and butter in the mixer bowl. Attach the flat beater and mixer bowl to the mixer. Set to Speed 2 and mix for 30 seconds. Increase to Speed 4 and mix until only small lumps of butter remain. Quickly add ice water and mix until dough comes together. Form dough into a disk, wrap in plastic wrap and refrigerate for about 30 minutes, or until chilled, to make it easier to roll out.

To Roll Pastry

Place dough on a lightly floured work surface and lightly dust the top with flour. Roll out gently but firmly, picking dough up after each roll and rotating it from 12 o'clock to 3 o'clock. (This keeps the dough from sticking and helps it stay round.) Add more flour to the work surface as necessary. When you have rolled dough to desired thickness (usually about 1⁄8-inch/0.25 cm thick), fold it in half and then in half again to prevent it from tearing while in transit from the work surface to the pie plate. Trim edge to 1 inch (2.5 cm) beyond pie plate, fold under and flute or crimp edges. Use as directed in the recipe.

To Freeze Rolled Dough

Wrap between sheets of parchment paper, place on a baking sheet and freeze for up to 6 weeks. To thaw, let stand at room temperature for about 30 minutes. It is ready to use when it becomes pliable and fits easily into the pie plate.

Makes one 10-inch (25 cm) shell

Tender Pastry

FLAT BEATER

1 1/2 cups	unbleached all-purpose flour	375 mL
1/4 tsp	salt	1 mL
6 tbsp	cold unsalted butter	90 mL
3 tbsp	cold vegetable shortening	45 mL
1/3 cup	ice water	75 mL

Butter's role in pastry is to give lots of wonderful flavor and create flaky layers. Shortening helps to make pastry more tender and crumbly. In this recipe, we've combined the best of both worlds.

TIP

For tender, flaky pastry, make sure not to overmix the dough. As soon as it comes together, stop the mixer.

1. Place flour, salt, butter and shortening in the mixer bowl. Attach the flat beater and mixer bowl to the mixer. Set to Speed 2 and mix for 30 seconds. Increase to Speed 4 and mix until only small lumps of butter remain. Quickly add ice water and mix until dough comes together. Form dough into a disk, wrap in plastic wrap and refrigerate for about 30 minutes, or until chilled, to make it easier to roll out.
2. See page 321 for instructions on rolling pastry and freezing rolled dough.

Makes one 9-inch (23 cm) shell

Puff Pastry

FLAT BEATER

1 ½ cups	unbleached all-purpose flour	375 mL
½ cup	cake flour	125 mL
½ tsp	salt	2 mL
1 cup	unsalted butter, cut into 10 pieces	250 mL
½ cup	ice water (approx.)	125 mL

Make ahead

Store pastry cylinder, tightly wrapped in plastic wrap, in the refrigerator for up to 2 days. Or roll out, wrap between sheets of parchment paper, place on a baking sheet and freeze for up to 2 months.

TIP

Puff pastry is more buttery and flaky than regular pastry. It can be used in place of regular pastry for a richer crust.

1. Place all-purpose flour, cake flour, salt and butter in the mixer bowl. Cover with plastic wrap and freeze for 1 hour. Attach the flat beater and mixer bowl to the mixer. Set to Stir and mix for about 1 minute, until butter is the size of peas. Add ice water in a steady stream and mix until dough comes together in 2 or 3 clumps. Do not overmix.
2. Turn dough out onto a lightly floured work surface and pat into an 8- by 4-inch (20 by 10 cm) rectangle. Using a metal spatula for support, fold dough into thirds, much as you would fold a business letter. (This is called a turn.) Turn the open end toward you. Using a rolling pin, roll out to an 8- by 4-inch (20 by 10 cm) rectangle. Fold into thirds again, wrap in plastic wrap and refrigerate for 30 minutes.
3. Place pastry on floured work surface and roll out to an 8- by 4-inch (20 by 10 cm) rectangle. Fold into thirds and turn the open end toward you. Roll out to a 12- by 4-inch (30 by 10 cm) rectangle. Starting with a short side, roll up jelly-roll style to form a tight cylinder. Wrap in plastic and refrigerate for 30 minutes. Roll out as directed in the recipe.

Makes one 25- by 10-inch (63 by 25 cm) rectangle (about 1 ¼ lbs/625 g)

Sour Cream Pastry

FLAT BEATER

2¼ cups	unbleached all-purpose flour	550 mL
½ tsp	salt	2 mL
¾ cup	cold unsalted butter, cut into ¼-inch (0.5 cm) pieces	175 mL
½ cup	sour cream	125 mL

1. Place flour, salt and butter in the mixer bowl. Attach the flat beater and mixer bowl to the mixer. Set to Speed 2 and beat until mixture resembles coarse meal. Stop mixer and add sour cream. Set to Speed 2 and beat until dough begins to come together. Add 1 tbsp (15 mL) water if dough looks shaggy and dry. Cut dough in half and form each half into a disk. Wrap in plastic wrap and refrigerate for at least 1 hour, until firm, or for up to 24 hours. See page 321 for instructions on rolling out pastry and freezing dough.

Makes enough pastry for two 9-inch (23 cm) pie crusts

Cream Cheese Pastry

FLAT BEATER

2½ cups	unbleached all-purpose flour	625 mL
½ tsp	salt	2 mL
½ cup	cold unsalted butter, cut into ¼-inch (0.5 cm) pieces	125 mL
¼ cup	cold vegetable shortening	50 mL
1	egg, beaten	1
8 oz	cream cheese, softened and cut into 8 pieces	250 g

1. Place flour, salt and butter in the mixer bowl. Attach the flat beater and mixer bowl to the mixer. Set to Stir and mix until butter is in pea-size chunks and the mixture resembles cornmeal. Set to Speed 2 and beat in shortening for 1 minute, then beat in egg and cream cheese until dough comes together. Cut dough in half and form each half into a disk. Wrap in plastic wrap and refrigerate for 30 minutes, or until chilled. See page 321 for instructions on rolling out pastry and freezing dough.

Makes enough pastry for two 9-inch (23 cm) pie crusts

Brown Butter Pie Crust

FLAT BEATER

◆ 9-inch (23 cm) pie plate

1/2 cup	unsalted butter	125 mL
1 1/4 cups	unbleached all-purpose flour	300 mL
2 tbsp	granulated sugar	25 mL
1/4 tsp	salt	1 mL
1 tbsp	white vinegar	15 mL

TIP
Browning the butter gives this crust a unique nutty flavor and texture, different from any other type of pastry crust. Be careful when browning the butter: it can go from browned to burnt quickly, so watch it closely.

1. In a small saucepan, melt butter over medium-low heat, stirring occasionally, for 5 to 7 minutes, or until butter browns. Pour into the mixer bowl and add flour, sugar, salt and vinegar. Attach the flat beater and mixer bowl to the mixer. Set to Speed 2 and mix until combined. Press into the bottom and sides of pie plate.

Makes one 9-inch (23 cm) pie crust

Make ahead

Store covered with plastic wrap in the refrigerator for up to 2 days.

Mile-High Meringue

WIRE WHIP

1 tbsp	cornstarch	15 mL
1⁄3 cup	water	75 mL
6	egg whites	6
1⁄2 tsp	cream of tartar	2 mL
Pinch	salt	Pinch
3⁄4 cup	granulated sugar	175 mL
1⁄2 tsp	vanilla	2 mL

This is the type of meringue topping you see piled high on pies in your neighborhood diner. It's soft and tender, with a subtle vanilla flavor. We use a mixture of cornstarch and water to help stabilize the egg whites and give the meringue a nice smooth texture after it's baked.

1. In a small saucepan, whisk together cornstarch and water. Cook over medium heat, whisking constantly, until thick but not stiff. Do not overcook.
2. Place egg whites, cream of tartar and salt in the mixer bowl. Attach the whip and mixer bowl to the mixer. Set to Speed 6 and beat until soft peaks form. Gradually beat in sugar. Add vanilla and beat in cornstarch mixture, 1 tbsp (15 mL) at a time, until stiff peaks form, 1 to 2 minutes. Use to top pie as directed in recipes.

Makes enough for one 9-inch (23 cm) pie

Peach Crumb Pie

FLAT BEATER

◆ Preheat oven to 375°F (190°C)

1	Brown Butter Pie Crust (see recipe, page 325)	1
Topping		
1 cup	unbleached all-purpose flour	250 mL
1 cup	granulated sugar	250 mL
1/2 tsp	salt	2 mL
1/2 cup	cold unsalted butter, cut into 1/4-inch (0.5 cm) pieces	125 mL
1/2 cup	sliced almonds	125 mL
Filling		
7	peaches, peeled (see tip, below)	7
3 tbsp	granulated sugar	45 mL
1 tbsp	unbleached all-purpose flour	15 mL
1/2 tsp	ground cinnamon	2 mL
1/4 tsp	salt	1 mL
	Vanilla ice cream	

TIP

To peel peaches, bring a large pot of water to a boil. Using a paring knife, score peach bottoms lightly with an X. Gently drop peaches in boiling water for 30 seconds to 1 minute. Using a slotted spoon, remove peaches and place in ice water for 1 minute. The skins should slip off easily. If they don't, place peaches back in boiling water for 30 seconds.

1. Chill pie crust for 30 minutes. Line with a piece of parchment paper with a 4-inch (10 cm) overhang, fill with pie weights (rice or dried beans) and bake in lower third of preheated oven for 20 minutes. Remove parchment paper and weights and bake for 10 to 15 minutes, or until brown and crisp. Let cool on a wire rack.
2. *Prepare the topping:* Place flour, sugar, salt and butter in the mixer bowl. Attach the flat beater and mixer bowl to the mixer. Set to Speed 2 and mix until large clumps form that crumble when pinched. Be careful not to overmix. Remove the mixer bowl and, with a wooden spoon, lightly toss in almonds.
3. *Prepare the filling:* Cut peaches in half, each half into 4 wedges, and each wedge in half crosswise. Toss with sugar, flour, cinnamon and salt.
4. Spoon filling into cooled pie crust and cover evenly with topping. Bake in middle of oven until top is golden brown and peaches are bubbling, about 50 minutes. Let cool on a wire rack. Serve warm or at room temperature with ice cream.

Serves 8

Make ahead

Store loosely covered with plastic wrap at room temperature for up to 1 day.

Apple Streusel Pie

FLAT BEATER ROTOR
SLICER/SHREDDER

- Preheat oven to 350°F (180°C)
- 10-inch (25 cm) deep-dish pie plate

Streusel Topping		
1 cup	unbleached all-purpose flour	250 mL
1/3 cup	lightly packed light brown sugar	75 mL
1/3 cup	granulated sugar	75 mL
1/4 tsp	salt	1 mL
1/2 cup	unsalted butter, cut into 8 pieces	125 mL
3/4 cup	walnut halves, coarsely chopped	175 mL
Filling		
2 lbs	Granny Smith apples, peeled and quartered (about 4)	1 kg
1 lb	Golden Delicious apples, peeled and quartered (about 2)	500 g
3/4 cup	granulated sugar	175 mL
3 tbsp	unbleached all-purpose flour	45 mL
1/2 tsp	ground cinnamon	2 mL
1/4 tsp	salt	1 mL
1 tbsp	freshly squeezed lemon juice	15 mL

1/2	recipe Sour Cream Pastry (page 324)	1/2
1	egg	1
1 cup	whipping (35%) cream	250 mL
	French Vanilla Ice Cream (see recipe, page 391) or Sweetened Whipped Cream (see recipe, page 416)	

1. *Prepare the streusel topping:* Place flour, brown sugar, granulated sugar, salt and butter in the mixer bowl. Attach the flat beater and mixer bowl to the mixer. Set to Speed 2 and mix until coarse crumbs form. Mix in walnuts until evenly incorporated. Remove the mixer bowl and set aside.
2. *Prepare the filling:* Remove the flat beater and attach the slicer/shredder, with the thick slicer, to the mixer. Set to Speed 4 and slice apples into a large bowl. Sprinkle with sugar, flour, cinnamon, salt and lemon juice and toss to coat.
3. Roll out pastry and fit into pie plate. Trim and flute or crimp edge. Pour apples into pie shell.
4. In a small bowl, using a fork, mix together egg and whipping cream. Pour over apples.
5. Bake in lower third of preheated oven for 40 minutes. Remove from oven and sprinkle with streusel topping. Bake until top is golden brown and apples are tender, about 20 minutes. Remove and let cool on rack. Serve warm or at room temperature with ice cream or whipped cream.

Serves 10 to 12

Make ahead

Store loosely covered with plastic wrap in the refrigerator for up to 1 day.

Mile-High Lemon Meringue Pie

- Preheat oven to 375°F (190°C), with rack in lower middle position
- 9-inch (23 cm) pie plate

1	recipe Flaky Pastry (page 321) or Tender Pastry (page 322)	1
1	recipe Mile-High Meringue (page 326)	1
Filling		
1 1/3 cups	granulated sugar	325 mL
1/3 cup	cornstarch	75 mL
1/4 tsp	salt	1 mL
1 1/2 cups	water	375 mL
4	egg yolks	4
3 tbsp	unsalted butter	45 mL
1 tbsp	finely grated lemon zest	15 mL
1/2 cup	freshly squeezed lemon juice	125 mL

1. Roll out pastry and fit into pie plate. Trim and flute or crimp edge. Chill for 30 minutes. Line with a piece of parchment paper with a 4-inch (10 cm) overhang, fill with pie weights (rice or dried beans) and bake in preheated oven for 20 minutes. Remove parchment paper and weights and bake for 10 to 15 minutes, or until brown and crisp. Let cool on a wire rack. Reduce oven temperature to 325°F (160°C).
2. *Prepare the filling:* In a heavy saucepan, whisk together sugar, cornstarch and salt. Whisk in water and cook over medium heat, stirring constantly, until thickened, about 2 minutes.
3. In a medium bowl, beat egg yolks. Gradually whisk in about 1/2 cup (125 mL) of the hot sugar mixture. Pour egg mixture into the saucepan, whisking constantly. Cook, stirring constantly, until thick and bubbly, about 3 minutes. Remove from heat and whisk in butter, lemon zest and lemon juice. Pour into pie shell and top with meringue while filling is still hot. Make sure meringue completely covers filling and goes right to the edge of the crust.
4. Bake for 20 to 30 minutes, or until meringue is golden. Let cool completely on a wire rack before slicing.

Serves 8

Banana Cream Pie

WIRE WHIP

- Preheat oven to 375°F (190°C)
- 9-inch (23 cm) tart pan with removable bottom
- Pastry bag fitted with a ½-inch (1 cm) star tip (optional)

½	recipe Cream Cheese Pastry (page 324)	½
2 cups	half-and-half (10%) cream	500 mL
6	egg yolks	6
1 cup	granulated sugar	250 mL
¼ cup	unbleached all-purpose flour	50 mL
Pinch	salt	Pinch
1 tsp	vanilla	5 mL
1	recipe Italian Meringue (page 415)	1
3	bananas, sliced into ¼-inch (0.5 cm) slices	3

Make ahead

Store loosely covered with plastic wrap in the refrigerator for up to 1 day.

1. On a lightly floured work surface, roll pastry out to a 12-inch (30 cm) circle, about ¼ inch (0.5 cm) thick. Carefully place inside tart pan and press into every corner of the pan so it fits tightly. Roll the rolling pin over the edge of the pan to shave off any excess dough. Chill for 30 minutes. Line with a piece of parchment paper with a 4-inch (10 cm) overhang, fill with pie weights (rice or dried beans) and bake in lower third of preheated oven for 20 minutes. Remove parchment paper and weights and bake for 10 to 15 minutes, or until brown and crisp. Let cool on a wire rack.
2. In a medium saucepan, bring cream to a simmer over medium heat. Remove from heat.
3. In a medium bowl, whisk together egg yolks, sugar, flour and salt until light. Whisk in hot cream, in 3 additions, until thoroughly combined. Transfer to the saucepan and cook over medium heat, stirring constantly, until mixture begins to bubble. Cook for 1 minute longer, then remove from heat and stir in vanilla. Transfer to a bowl and refrigerate for at least 2 hours, until chilled. Preheat the broiler.
4. Lay banana slices in the cooled tart shell, completely covering the bottom. Spread evenly with cooled pastry cream. Spread with meringue. (Or, using a pastry bag with a star tip, pipe rosettes of meringue to completely cover pastry cream layer.) Place pie under broiler until meringue is golden, about 1 minute. (Or brown with a kitchen torch.) Cover and refrigerate for at least 3 hours, or until ready to serve.

Serves 8

Coconut Cream Pie

WIRE WHIP

- Preheat oven to 375°F (190°C), with rack in lower middle position
- 9-inch (23 cm) pie plate

1	recipe Flaky Pastry (page 321)	1
1 1/2 cups	half-and-half (10%) cream	375 mL
3/4 cup	granulated sugar, divided	175 mL
3 tbsp	unbleached all-purpose flour	45 mL
2	eggs, beaten	2
1	egg yolk	1
1 1/2 cups	sweetened flaked coconut, divided	375 mL
2 tbsp	unsalted butter	25 mL
1 tsp	vanilla	5 mL
1/2 tsp	coconut extract, divided	2 mL
1 1/4 cups	whipping (35%) cream, chilled	300 mL

Make ahead

Store loosely covered with plastic wrap in the refrigerator for up to 6 hours.

1. Roll out pastry and fit into pie plate. Trim and flute or crimp edge. Chill for 30 minutes. Line with a piece of parchment paper with a 4-inch (10 cm) overhang, fill with pie weights (rice or dried beans) and bake in preheated oven for 20 minutes. Remove parchment paper and weights and bake for 10 to 15 minutes, or until brown and crisp. Let cool on a wire rack.
2. In a saucepan, heat cream over medium-high heat until steaming. Remove from heat and set aside.
3. In a large saucepan, combine 1/2 cup (125 mL) of the sugar and the flour. Beat in eggs, egg yolk and 1/2 cup (125 mL) of the coconut. Add 1 cup (250 mL) of the hot cream, 1/4 cup (50 mL) at a time, whisking until combined. Pour in the remaining cream in a steady stream. Cook over medium heat, stirring, until custard boils and thickens, about 4 minutes. Boil for 1 minute more, then transfer to a large bowl. Stir in butter, vanilla and half the coconut extract. Place plastic wrap directly on the surface of the custard and refrigerate for at least 2 hours, until chilled, or for up to 24 hours.
4. In a skillet, over medium heat, toast the remaining coconut, without stirring, until starting to color, about 3 minutes. Stir the coconut constantly, until evenly browned, about 4 minutes. Transfer to a plate and let cool.
5. Place whipping cream, remaining sugar and remaining coconut extract in the mixer bowl. Attach the whip and mixer bowl to the mixer. Set to Speed 6 and beat until stiff peaks form. Set aside.
6. Spread chilled custard over the bottom of the baked shell and top with the whipped cream. Sprinkle with toasted coconut.

Serves 8

Butterscotch Pie

- Preheat oven to 375°F (190°C)
- 9-inch (23 cm) pie plate

1	recipe Flaky Pastry (page 321)	1
2 cups	homogenized (whole) milk	500 mL
½ cup	unsalted butter	125 mL
1 cup	lightly packed light brown sugar	250 mL
1 cup	whipping (35%) cream	250 mL
3	egg yolks	3
¼ cup	cornstarch	50 mL
¼ tsp	salt	1 mL
1½ tsp	vanilla	7 mL
1	recipe Italian Meringue (page 415)	1

Make ahead

Store loosely covered with plastic wrap in the refrigerator for up to 1 day.

1. Roll out pastry and fit into pie plate. Trim and flute or crimp edge. Chill for 30 minutes. Line with a piece of parchment paper with a 4-inch (10 cm) overhang, fill with pie weights (rice or dried beans) and bake in lower third of preheated oven for 20 minutes. Remove parchment paper and weights and bake for 10 to 15 minutes, or until brown and crisp. Let cool on a wire rack.
2. In a large saucepan, bring milk to a simmer over medium heat. Remove from heat and set aside.
3. Meanwhile, in a heavy saucepan, melt butter over medium heat. Stir in brown sugar. Increase heat to medium-high and cook, stirring occasionally, until bubbling all over. Carefully add whipping cream (mixture will bubble and steam), stirring constantly. Reduce heat to medium-low and cook, stirring, until sugar is dissolved, about 1 minute. Whisk into hot milk.
4. Place egg yolks in a medium bowl and gradually whisk in about ½ cup (125 mL) of the hot milk mixture in a thin, steady stream. Whisk in cornstarch and salt until dissolved. Whisk back into the saucepan. Cook over medium-high heat, whisking constantly, until thick and gently boiling. (The whisk will leave trail marks on the bottom of the pan and a few large bubbles will boil up to the top.) Cook, whisking, for 2 minutes longer, then remove from heat and whisk in vanilla. Pour into cooled pie crust and refrigerate, uncovered, for at least 2 hours or overnight. Preheat the broiler.
5. Spread meringue on top of chilled pie and place under broiler until lightly browned, about 1 minute. (Or brown with a kitchen torch.) Cover and refrigerate for at least 3 hours, or until ready to serve.

Serves 8

Texas Pecan Pie

WIRE WHIP

- Preheat oven to 350°F (180°C)
- 9-inch (23 cm) round cake pan with 1½-inch (4 cm) sides

1	recipe Flaky Pastry (page 321)	1
3	eggs	3
1 cup	packed light brown sugar	250 mL
1 cup	light corn syrup	250 mL
3 tbsp	unsalted butter, melted	45 mL
2 tsp	vanilla	10 mL
¼ tsp	salt	1 mL
1 cup	finely chopped pecans	250 mL
1 cup	pecan halves	250 mL

1. On a floured work surface, roll out pastry into a 13-inch (33 cm) round. Fit into cake pan and trim to align with pan edges. Freeze for 15 minutes.
2. Place eggs, brown sugar, corn syrup, butter, vanilla and salt in the mixer bowl. Attach the whip and mixer bowl to the mixer. Set to Speed 4 and mix for 1 minute. Mix in chopped pecans until just combined. Pour into crust. Arrange pecan halves decoratively on top.
3. Bake in preheated oven for 75 minutes, or until set. Let cool on a wire rack.

Serves 8 to 10

Pumpkin Pie

FLAT BEATER

- Preheat oven to 350°F (180°C), with rack in lower middle position
- 9-inch (23 cm) pie plate

1	recipe Flaky Pastry (page 321)	1
3	eggs, beaten	3
1	can (14 oz/398 mL) pumpkin purée (not pie filling)	1
1/2 cup	whipping (35%) cream	125 mL
1/2 cup	lightly packed brown sugar	125 mL
1 tsp	ground cinnamon	5 mL
1/2 tsp	ground ginger	2 mL
1/2 tsp	salt	2 mL
Pinch	ground cloves	Pinch
	Sweetened Whipped Cream (see recipe, page 416	

1. Roll out pastry and fit into pie plate. Trim and flute or crimp edge. Place in the refrigerator until ready to fill.
2. Place eggs, pumpkin purée, cream, brown sugar, cinnamon, ginger, salt and cloves in the mixer bowl. Attach the flat beater and mixer bowl to the mixer. Set to Speed 4 and beat until blended. Pour into chilled crust.
3. Bake in preheated oven for 50 minutes, or until custard is set and crust is browned. Let cool on a wire rack. When no longer hot, refrigerate to further set the custard. Serve cold, with sweetened whipped cream.

Serves 8

Chocolate Cream Pie

WIRE WHIP

- Preheat oven to 375°F (190°C), with rack in lower middle position
- 9-inch (23 cm) pie plate

1	recipe Flaky Pastry (page 321) or Tender Pastry (page 322)	1
Filling		
3 cups	milk	750 mL
4 oz	bittersweet chocolate, chopped	125 g
3 oz	unsweetened chocolate, chopped	90 g
1 cup	granulated sugar	250 mL
1/2 cup	cornstarch	125 mL
1/4 tsp	salt	1 mL
3	egg yolks	3
2 tbsp	unsalted butter, cut into small pieces, softened	25 mL
1 tsp	vanilla	5 mL
Topping		
1 1/2 cups	whipping (35%) cream, chilled	375 mL
2 1/2 tbsp	granulated sugar (or to taste)	32 mL
	Grated bittersweet chocolate	

TIP

To prevent lumps from forming in your custard, make sure you whisk the sugar and cornstarch together thoroughly before pouring in the hot milk mixture.

1. Roll out pastry and fit into pie plate. Trim and flute or crimp edge. Chill for 30 minutes. Line with a piece of parchment paper with a 4-inch (10 cm) overhang, fill with pie weights (rice or dried beans) and bake in preheated oven for 20 minutes. Remove parchment paper and weights and bake for 10 to 15 minutes, or until brown and crisp. Let cool on a wire rack.
2. *Prepare the filling:* In a large saucepan, bring milk to a simmer over medium heat. Whisk in bittersweet and unsweetened chocolate until smooth. Immediately remove from heat.
3. In a heavy saucepan, whisk together sugar and cornstarch. Gradually add the hot milk mixture, whisking constantly. Cook over medium heat, stirring constantly, until thickened, about 2 minutes.
4. In a medium bowl, beat egg yolks. Whisk in about 1/2 cup (125 mL) of the hot milk mixture. Pour egg mixture into the saucepan, whisking constantly. Cook, stirring constantly, until thick and bubbly, about 3 minutes. Remove from heat and whisk in butter and vanilla. Pour into pie shell and refrigerate, uncovered, for at least 2 hours, until chilled, or overnight.
5. *Prepare the topping:* Place cream and sugar in the mixer bowl. Attach the whip and mixer bowl to the mixer. Set to Speed 6 and beat until stiff peaks form. Spread over the custard. Sprinkle with grated chocolate. Refrigerate until ready to serve.

Serves 8

Black Bottom Pie

WIRE WHIP

- Preheat oven to 375°F (190°C)
- 9-inch (23 cm) pie plate

1	recipe Flaky Pastry (page 321)	1
1½ tsp	powdered gelatin	7 mL
¼ cup	cold water	50 mL
4	egg yolks	4
¾ cup	granulated sugar, divided	175 mL
2 tbsp	cornstarch	25 mL
2 cups	milk	500 mL
2 oz	bittersweet chocolate, melted (see tip, opposite)	60 g
2 tsp	vanilla	10 mL
4	egg whites, at room temperature	4
¼ tsp	salt	1 mL
¼ tsp	cream of tartar	1 mL
1 tbsp	dark rum (optional)	15 mL
1½ cups	whipping (35%) cream	375 mL
3 tbsp	confectioner's (icing) sugar, sifted	45 mL
¼ cup	chocolate shavings	50 mL

This recipe contains raw egg whites. If the food safety of raw eggs is a concern for you, use pasteurized eggs. Many grocery stores now carry pasteurized eggs in their shells.

1. Roll out pastry and fit into pie plate. Trim and flute or crimp edge. Chill for 30 minutes. Line with a piece of parchment paper with a 4-inch (10 cm) overhang, fill with pie weights (rice or dried beans) and bake in lower third of preheated oven for 20 minutes. Remove parchment paper and weights and bake for 10 to 15 minutes, or until brown and crisp. Let cool on a wire rack.
2. In a small bowl, sprinkle gelatin over water and let soften for 5 minutes.
3. In a medium bowl, whisk together egg yolks, ¼ cup (50 mL) of the sugar and cornstarch. Set aside.
4. In a medium saucepan, bring milk and ¼ cup (50 mL) of the sugar just to a simmer over medium heat. Gradually whisk milk mixture into the yolk mixture until combined. Whisk back into saucepan and cook, stirring constantly, until mixture has boiled and thickened, about 3 minutes. Remove from heat.
5. Measure 1 cup (250 mL) of the custard into a small bowl and add chocolate and vanilla. Place bowl in an ice bath and let cool completely. When cool, spread evenly in pie crust. Refrigerate until set, about 5 minutes. Meanwhile, whisk gelatin into the remaining custard, stirring until gelatin is dissolved. Place bowl in an ice bath and let cool until just beginning to set.

6. Place egg whites, salt and cream of tartar in the mixer bowl. Attach the whip and mixer bowl to the mixer. Set to Speed 4 and beat until foamy. Increase to Speed 8 and beat until soft peaks form. Beat in the remaining 1⁄4 cup (50 mL) sugar, in 2 additions, until stiff, glossy peaks form.
7. Stir one-quarter of the meringue and rum, if using, into the custard to lighten. Gently fold in the remaining meringue. Spread over chocolate layer in pie plate. Cover with plastic wrap and refrigerate until set, for at least 3 hours or overnight. Clean the mixer bowl and whip.
8. Place whipping cream and confectioner's sugar in the mixer bowl. Attach the whip and mixer bowl to the mixer. Set to Speed 8 and beat until firm. Spread over custard and sprinkle with chocolate shavings. Cover and refrigerate for 3 to 8 hours, or until ready to serve.

Serves 8

Make ahead

Store loosely covered with plastic wrap in the refrigerator for up to 1 day.

TIPS

To melt chocolate, first break it into small pieces. In a heatproof bowl set over a small saucepan of gently simmering water, heat chocolate, stirring, until half melted. Remove from heat and stir until no lumps remain. (Or, in a microwave-safe bowl, microwave chocolate on Medium (50 %) until half melted, about 45 seconds. Stir until no lumps remain.)

To shave chocolate, run a vegetable peeler along the edge of a block of chocolate.

Chocolate Truffle Tart

- Preheat oven to 350°F (180°C)
- 10-inch (25 cm) tart pan with removable bottom

1	recipe Flaky Pastry (page 321)	1
1 cup	whipping (35%) cream	250 mL
1/2 cup	milk	125 mL
10 oz	bittersweet chocolate, chopped	300 g
2 tbsp	granulated sugar	25 mL
1/4 tsp	salt	1 mL
	Finely grated zest of 1 orange	
2	eggs	2
2 cups	Sweetened Whipped Cream (see recipe, page 416)	500 mL

Make ahead

Store tart wrapped in plastic wrap in the refrigerator for up to 1 day. Bring back to room temperature before serving to allow the chocolate to soften.

1. On a lightly floured work surface, roll pastry out to a 12-inch (30 cm) circle, about 1/4 inch (0.5 cm) thick. Carefully place inside tart pan and press into every corner of the pan so it fits tightly. Roll the rolling pin over the edge of the pan to shave off any excess dough. Chill for 30 minutes. Line with a piece of parchment paper with a 4-inch (10 cm) overhang, fill with pie weights (rice or dried beans) and bake in lower third of preheated oven for 20 minutes. Remove parchment paper and weights and let cool on a wire rack.
2. In a heavy medium saucepan, bring whipping cream and milk to a simmer over medium heat. Remove from heat, add chocolate and stir until melted and smooth. Stir in sugar, salt and orange zest until well incorporated.
3. In a small bowl, whisk eggs until blended. Stir into the chocolate mixture until completely blended.
4. Pour into cooled tart shell and bake in middle of oven for 15 to 20 minutes, or until filling is set and surface is glossy. Do not overbake. Let cool completely on a wire rack. Cut into slices and garnish each with a dollop of whipped cream.

Serves 10 to 12

Rustic Pear Frangipane Tart

FLAT BEATER

- Preheat oven to 375°F (190°C)
- Large baking sheet, lined with parchment paper

1	recipe Flaky Pastry recipe (page 321)	1
1/2 cup	unsalted butter, softened	125 mL
1/3 cup	granulated sugar, divided	75 mL
1	egg	1
1 cup	ground blanched almonds	250 mL
1 tsp	vanilla	5 mL
1/4 tsp	salt	1 mL
1/4 tsp	almond extract	1 mL
4	ripe but firm pears, peeled and thinly sliced	4
1/2 cup	apricot jam	125 mL
	French Vanilla Ice Cream (see recipe, page 391) or Sweetened Whipped Cream (see recipe, page 416)	

Frangipane is an almond-flavored pastry cream that pairs beautifully with fruit.

1. On a lightly floured work surface, roll pastry out to a 12-inch (30 cm) circle. Place on prepared baking sheet and refrigerate while you prepare the rest of the ingredients.

2. Place butter and 1/4 cup (50 mL) of the sugar in the mixer bowl. Attach the flat beater and mixer bowl to the mixer. Set to Speed 4 and beat until light and fluffy. Beat in egg, almonds, vanilla, salt and almond extract.

3. Spread frangipane mixture on pastry, leaving a 1 1/2-inch (4 cm) border. Place pear slices on top, in concentric circles. Gently fold up the edges of the pastry over the filling. Sprinkle with the remaining sugar. Bake in lower third of preheated oven for 25 to 35 minutes, or until pears are tender and crust is golden.

4. In a small saucepan, heat apricot jam over low heat until melted. Brush the top of the tart with jam and let cool on a wire rack. Cut into wedges and serve with ice cream or whipped cream.

Serves 6 to 8

Make ahead

Store loosely covered with plastic wrap in the refrigerator for up to 1 day.

Lattice-Topped Nectarine Tart

FLAT BEATER

- Preheat oven to 400°F (200°C), with rack in lower middle position
- 9-inch (23 cm) pie plate
- Baking sheet

6	nectarines, cut into 1-inch (2.5 cm) slices	6
1/3 cup	granulated sugar	75 mL
2 tbsp	unbleached all-purpose flour	25 mL
Pinch	ground nutmeg	Pinch
Pinch	salt	Pinch
	Grated zest of 1 lemon	
2 tbsp	freshly squeezed lemon juice	25 mL
2	recipes Flaky Pastry (page 321)	2
3 tbsp	unsalted butter, cubed	45 mL
1	egg, beaten	1
2 tbsp	granulated sugar	25 mL
	Vanilla ice cream	

1. In a large bowl, combine nectarines, the 1/3 cup (75 mL) sugar, flour, nutmeg, salt, lemon zest and lemon juice. Taste and adjust flavoring with sugar or lemon juice, if necessary.
2. Roll out one disk of pastry to a 14-inch (35 cm) circle. Fold pastry in half, then into quarters, and place in pie plate. Open pastry out, spread fruit mixture evenly over the bottom and dot with butter. Trim edges of pastry so that there is a 1-inch (2.5 cm) overhang. Refrigerate while you roll out the top.
3. Roll out the second disk of pastry to a 14-inch (35 cm) circle. Using a pizza cutter or pastry wheel, cut strips of pastry about 3/4 inch (2 cm) wide and long enough to fit across the pie. Arrange strips in a lattice pattern over the top of the pie. Trim the pastry and roll up the overhang to enclose the ends of the lattice. Crimp the pastry around the rim. Brush with beaten egg and sprinkle with the 2 tbsp (25 mL) sugar.
4. Place on baking sheet and bake in preheated oven, turning halfway through, for 45 to 60 minutes, or until golden on top and crisp on the bottom. Let cool on a wire rack. Serve warm with vanilla ice cream.

Serves 8

Individual Plum Tartlets with Frangipane

- Preheat oven to 425°F (220°C), with rack in lower middle position
- Baking sheet, lined with parchment paper

Filling		
1 1/2 lbs	plums (about 6 small or 3 large), cut into 1-inch (2.5 cm) slices	750 g
1/3 cup	granulated sugar (approx.)	75 mL
2 tbsp	unbleached all-purpose flour	25 mL
1 tbsp	freshly squeezed lemon juice	15 mL
Pinch	salt	Pinch
Pinch	ground nutmeg	Pinch
Frangipane		
3/4 cup	blanched almonds	175 mL
1/4 cup	granulated sugar	50 mL
1	egg	1
3 tbsp	unsalted butter, softened	45 mL
2 tsp	unbleached all-purpose flour	10 mL
1/2 tsp	almond extract	2 mL
Pinch	salt	Pinch

1	recipe Flaky Pastry (page 321)	1
1	egg, beaten with 1 tbsp (15 mL) water	1
	Additional granulated sugar	
	Vanilla ice cream	

Make ahead

The tartlets can be made up to 6 hours ahead and kept at room temperature. Reheat in a 350°F (180°C) oven for about 10 minutes.

1. *Prepare the filling:* In a large bowl, combine plums, sugar, flour, lemon juice, salt and nutmeg. Taste and adjust flavoring with sugar, if necessary.
2. *Prepare the frangipane:* In a food processor, process almonds and sugar until finely ground. Add egg, butter, flour, almond extract and salt; pulse until well combined and thick.
3. Roll out pastry into a 15- by 10-inch (38 by 25 cm) rectangle. Cut into 6 squares and arrange on prepared baking sheet. Place a large spoonful of frangipane in the center of each pastry square. Divide the filling among the squares. (Be careful not to overfill them; you will need to pull the pastry up and over the tops. You may have some filling and frangipane left over.) Bring the two opposite corners of the pastry up and over the filling. Pinch the open corners to form a cup, so that the filling doesn't escape. Brush with egg wash and sprinkle with sugar.
4. Bake in preheated oven for 25 minutes, or until golden and crisp on the bottom. Let cool slightly on baking sheet on a wire rack. Serve warm with a scoop of ice cream.

Makes 6 tartlets

Variations

Combine 1 cup (250 mL) sour cream, 3 tbsp (45 mL) packed brown sugar and 1 tsp (5 mL) vanilla. Top the tartlets with sweetened sour cream instead of serving with ice cream.

If plums don't look good, try making these tartlets with nectarines.

Easy Chocolate-Hazelnut Turnovers

- Preheat oven to 400°F (200°C)
- 2 large baking sheets, lined with parchment paper

8 oz	bittersweet chocolate, finely chopped	250 g
3/4 cup	hazelnuts, toasted, husked (see tip, page 306), and finely chopped	175 mL
1	recipe Puff Pastry (page 323)	1
1	egg, beaten with 2 tbsp (25 mL) water	1
	Turbinado or granulated sugar	

Make ahead

Store in an airtight container in the refrigerator for up to 1 day. Warm in a 350°F (180°C) oven for 10 minutes.

1. In a heatproof bowl set over a saucepan of hot, not boiling water, melt chocolate, stirring frequently until smooth. Remove from heat and stir in hazelnuts. Let stand over hot water while you prepare the pastry.
2. On a lightly floured work surface, roll pastry out to a 25- by 10-inch (63 cm by 25 cm) rectangle. Trim edges so they are straight and cut into ten 5-inch (13 cm) squares. Divide chocolate mixture among the squares, placing the filling in the center of each square. Working with one square at a time, brush edges lightly with egg wash, then fold over the corners to form a triangle. Press down on the edges gently with the tines of a fork to seal. Make two small slits on the top of each turnover with a sharp knife. Place at least 2 inches (5 cm) apart on prepared baking sheets. Brush tops lightly with egg wash and sprinkle with sugar.
3. Bake in upper and lower thirds of preheated oven for 15 to 20 minutes, rotating and switching pans halfway through, or until golden brown. Serve warm or at room temperature.

Makes 10 turnovers

Floating Islands

WIRE WHIP

4 cups	milk	1 L
8	egg whites, at room temperature	8
1 cup	granulated sugar, divided	250 mL
8	egg yolks	8
1 tsp	vanilla	5 mL
	Chocolate Sauce (see recipe, page 375)	
½ cup	sliced almonds, toasted (see tip, below)	125 mL

TIP
To toast sliced almonds, spread them on a baking sheet and toast in a 350°F (180°C) oven for 3 to 4 minutes, or until lightly browned.

1. In a large saucepan, bring milk to a simmer over medium heat.
2. Place egg whites in the mixer bowl. Attach the whip and mixer bowl to the mixer. Set to Speed 4 and beat until foamy. Increase to Speed 8 and beat until soft peaks form. Beat in ½ cup (125 mL) of the sugar, in 4 additions, and continue beating until stiff, glossy peaks form. Working in batches of 2 or 3 islands at a time, using a large spoon, scoop about one-sixth of the egg white mixture and carefully place on surface of simmering milk, leaving enough room in pan for islands to float. Cook for about 3 minutes or until bottom is set. Carefully flip over and cook for about 3 minutes longer or until set Remove with a slotted spoon and place on a serving plate. Repeat with the remaining egg whites. Set aside.
3. Place egg yolks and the remaining ½ cup (125 mL) sugar in clean mixer bowl. Attach the whip and mixer bowl to the mixer. Set to Speed 6 and beat until thick and pale yellow. Reduce speed to Stir and slowly ladle in about 1 cup (250 mL) of the warm milk. Return to saucepan. Cook over low heat, stirring constantly without letting it come to a boil, until mixture thickens enough to coat the back of a spoon. Immediately strain into a bowl and add vanilla. Ladle around poached meringues. Drizzle with chocolate sauce and sprinkle with almonds.

Serves 6

Chocolate Napoleon with Berries and Raspberry Coulis

FRUIT/VEGETABLE STRAINER

- Preheat oven to 400°F (200°C)
- Baking sheet, lined with parchment paper

2 cups	milk	500 mL
1/2 cup	granulated sugar	125 mL
1/4 cup	unbleached all-purpose flour	50 mL
Pinch	salt	Pinch
6	egg yolks	6
6 oz	semisweet or bittersweet chocolate, finely chopped	175 g
1 tsp	vanilla	5 mL
1	recipe Puff Pastry (page 323)	1
3 tbsp	confectioner's (icing) sugar, sifted	45 mL
1	package (10 oz/300 g) frozen raspberries in syrup, thawed	1
2 tsp	freshly squeezed lemon juice	10 mL
2 cups	fresh raspberries	500 mL
	Additional fresh raspberries and confectioner's (icing) sugar	

It's fun to put the coulis in a small squeeze bottle with a fine tip so that you can decorate plates with lines, squiggles or pools. The bottle gives you more control and allows you to use your imagination.

1. In a heavy saucepan, heat milk over medium heat until almost simmering. Remove from heat.
2. In a medium bowl, combine sugar, flour and salt; whisk in egg yolks. (The mixture will be tight at first but will loosen as the sugar melts.) Gradually whisk in heated milk in a thin, steady stream until smooth. Return to the saucepan and cook over medium heat, whisking constantly, until mixture comes to a boil and thickens to pudding consistency. Boil for 1 minute more, whisking. Remove from heat. Stir in chocolate and vanilla until chocolate has melted. Transfer to a heatproof bowl and cover with plastic wrap directly on the surface. Refrigerate until cold, at least 3 hours.
3. On a floured work surface, roll pastry out to a 12- by 8-inch (30 cm by 20 cm) rectangle. Cut into 12 rectangles, about 4 by 2 inches (10 cm by 5 cm). Place 2 inches (5 cm) apart on prepared baking sheet, and prick each rectangle 4 to 5 times with a fork. Sprinkle with confectioner's sugar and bake in middle of preheated oven until golden and crispy, about 10 minutes. Let cool completely on sheet on a wire rack.
4. Attach the fruit/vegetable strainer to the mixer. Set to Speed 4 and run thawed raspberries through the strainer into a large bowl, with another bowl to catch the solids. Discard solids. Strain through a fine-mesh sieve and discard any seeds. Season with lemon juice. Transfer to a squeeze bottle, if using.

5. Place one piece of pastry on a serving plate and top with one-eighth of chocolate pastry cream and one-eighth of fresh raspberries. Repeat layers with remaining cream and berries and top with a piece of pastry. Garnish with a splash of raspberry coulis and fresh berries and dust with confectioner's sugar. Serve immediately or chill in the refrigerator for up to 30 minutes.

Serves 4

Make ahead

The raspberry coulis can be prepared up to 3 days ahead. Store in the refrigerator.

Variations

Instead of the chocolate pastry cream, spread pastry with Lemon Curd (see recipe, page 412) or Orange Curd (see recipe, page 413). Layer with fresh blueberries, blackberries or strawberries instead of raspberries.

The chocolate sauce on page 375 makes a great addition to this dessert. Before you assemble the napoleons, create fun patterns and designs on each serving plate with chocolate sauce and raspberry coulis.

Sugar-and-Spice Cake

FLAT BEATER

- Preheat oven to 350°F (180°C)
- 10-inch (3 L) Bundt pan, generously greased and floured

2 cups	unbleached all-purpose flour	500 mL
1 1/2 tsp	ground cinnamon	7 mL
1 1/2 tsp	ground allspice	7 mL
1 1/2 tsp	ground nutmeg	7 mL
1 tsp	baking soda	5 mL
1 tsp	baking powder	5 mL
1/2 tsp	salt	2 mL
1 1/2 cups	granulated sugar	375 mL
1 cup	unsalted butter, softened	250 mL
4	eggs	4
1 tsp	vanilla	5 mL
1 cup	sour cream	250 mL
	Confectioner's (icing) sugar, sifted	

1. In a medium bowl, whisk together flour, cinnamon, allspice, nutmeg, baking soda, baking powder and salt.
2. Place sugar and butter in the mixer bowl. Attach the flat beater and mixer bowl to the mixer. Set to Speed 4 and beat until light and fluffy, about 2 minutes. Beat in eggs, one at a time, and vanilla. Reduce speed to Stir and mix in flour mixture alternately with sour cream, making 3 additions of flour and 2 of sour cream.
3. Spoon batter into prepared pan and smooth top. Bake in middle of preheated oven for 40 to 50 minutes, or until a tester inserted in the center comes out clean. Let cool in pan on a wire rack for 10 minutes, then invert onto rack to cool completely. Transfer to a serving plate and sprinkle with confectioner's sugar.

Serves 10 to 12

Make ahead

Store cake wrapped in plastic wrap at room temperature for up to 1 day.

Ginger Molasses Cake with Apple Glaze

FLAT BEATER • WIRE WHIP

- Preheat oven to 350°F (180°C)
- 9-inch (23 cm) round metal cake pan, greased

2 cups	unbleached all-purpose flour	500 mL
2 tsp	ground ginger	10 mL
1 ½ tsp	baking soda	7 mL
1 tsp	ground cinnamon	5 mL
½ tsp	salt	2 mL
¼ tsp	ground allspice	1 mL
¼ tsp	ground nutmeg	1 mL
Pinch	freshly ground white pepper	Pinch
½ cup	firmly packed light brown sugar	125 mL
½ cup	unsalted butter, softened	125 mL
2	egg yolks	2
½ cup	sour cream	125 mL
½ cup	fancy molasses	125 mL
1 tsp	rum extract	5 mL
2	egg whites	2
¼ cup	granulated sugar	50 mL
½ cup	apple jelly	125 mL
	Confectioner's (icing) sugar, sifted	

TIP
Try placing a paper doily on top of the cake before dusting with confectioner's sugar. Carefully lift off after dusting. It will leave an impressive design.

1. In a small bowl, whisk together flour, ginger, baking soda, cinnamon, salt, allspice, nutmeg and white pepper.
2. Place brown sugar and butter in the mixer bowl. Attach the flat beater and mixer bowl to the mixer. Set to Speed 4 and beat until light and fluffy. Beat in egg yolks, one at a time. Beat in sour cream, molasses and rum extract until smooth. Reduce speed to Stir and mix in flour mixture, in 3 additions, until just combined. Transfer to a large bowl. Clean the mixer bowl.
3. Place egg whites in mixer bowl. Remove the flat beater and attach the whip and mixer bowl to the mixer. Set to Speed 4 and beat until foamy. Increase to Speed 8 and beat until soft peaks form. Beat in granulated sugar until stiff, glossy peaks form.
4. Using a large rubber spatula, gently fold egg whites into the batter, in 3 additions. Do not completely incorporate the whites in the first 2 additions; let some streaks of white remain. With the third addition, fold until no streaks remain.
5. Gently spoon batter into prepared pan and smooth top. Bake in middle of preheated oven for 30 to 35 minutes, or until top of cake springs back when touched. Let cool in pan on a wire rack for 5 minutes, then invert onto rack to cool for 10 minutes.
6. In a small saucepan, heat jelly over medium heat until it liquefies. Brush over warm cake and let cool completely. Dust with confectioner's sugar.

Serves 8

Make ahead

Store cake wrapped in plastic wrap at room temperature for up to 1 day.

Orange Chocolate Chip Bundt Cake

FLAT BEATER

- Preheat oven to 350°F (180°C)
- 10-inch (3 L) Bundt pan, generously greased and floured

Cake		
2½ cups	unbleached all-purpose flour	625 mL
1½ tsp	salt	7 mL
1 tsp	baking powder	5 mL
2 cups	granulated sugar	500 mL
½ cup	unsalted butter, softened	125 mL
¾ cup	vegetable oil	175 mL
5	eggs	5
1 tbsp	vanilla	15 mL
	Grated zest of one orange	
½ cup	freshly squeezed orange juice	125 mL
2 cups	semisweet chocolate chips (about 12 oz/375 g)	500 mL
Glaze		
1⅓ cup	confectioner's (icing) sugar, sifted	325 mL
½ cup	frozen orange juice concentrate, thawed	125 mL
1 tbsp	unsalted butter, melted	15 mL

1. *Prepare the cake:* In a medium bowl, whisk together flour, baking powder and salt.
2. Place sugar and butter in the mixer bowl. Attach the flat beater and mixer bowl to the mixer. Set to Speed 4 and beat until light and fluffy. Slowly beat in oil. Beat in eggs, one at a time, and vanilla. Reduce speed to Stir and mix in flour mixture alternately with orange juice, making 3 additions of dry and 2 of wet. Mix in chocolate chips and orange zest until evenly incorporated.
3. Spoon batter into prepared pan and smooth top. Bake in middle of preheated oven for 45 to 50 minutes, or until a tester inserted in the center comes out clean. Let cool in pan on a wire rack for 30 minutes, then invert onto rack to cool completely.
4. *Prepare the glaze:* In a small bowl, whisk together confectioner's sugar, orange juice concentrate and butter until smooth.
5. Transfer cake to a serving plate and drizzle with glaze. Let stand for at least 20 minutes before slicing and serving.

Serves 10 to 12

Make ahead

Store cake wrapped in plastic wrap at room temperature for up to 2 days.

Yellow Cake with Chocolate Fudge Frosting

FLAT BEATER WIRE WHIP

- Preheat oven to 350°F (180°C)
- Two 9-inch (23 cm) round metal cake pans, greased and lined with greased and floured parchment paper

Cake		
2½ cups	cake flour	625 mL
1 tbsp	baking powder	15 mL
½ tsp	salt	2 mL
1⅓ cups	granulated sugar	325 mL
¾ cup	unsalted butter, softened	175 mL
6	egg yolks	6
1 tsp	vanilla	5 mL
1 cup	milk	250 mL
Chocolate Fudge Frosting		
½ cup	unsalted butter, softened	125 mL
4 cups	confectioner's (icing) sugar, sifted	1 L
6 tbsp	whipping (35%) cream	90 mL
2 oz	unsweetened chocolate, melted and cooled (see tip, page 337)	60 g
1 tsp	vanilla	5 mL
Pinch	salt	Pinch

TIP

An offset spatula makes frosting so much easier because of the angle of the blade. Once you use one, you will never use a butter knife to frost a cake again.

1. *Prepare the cake:* In a medium bowl, whisk together flour, baking powder and salt.
2. Place sugar and butter in the mixer bowl. Attach the flat beater and mixer bowl to the mixer. Set to Speed 4 and beat until light and fluffy. Beat in egg yolks, one at a time, and vanilla. Reduce speed to Stir and mix in flour mixture alternately with milk, making 3 additions of dry and 2 of wet.
3. Divide batter between prepared pans and smooth tops. Bake in middle of preheated oven for 20 to 25 minutes, or until a tester inserted in the center comes out clean and top of cake springs back when touched. Let cool in pans on wire racks for 10 minutes, then invert onto racks, peel off paper and let cool completely before frosting, at least 1 hour.
3. *Prepare the frosting:* Place butter in clean mixer bowl. Attach the whip and mixer bowl to the mixer. Set to Speed 4 and beat until soft and creamy. Reduce to Speed 2 and beat in confectioner's sugar alternately with cream, making 3 additions of sugar and 2 of cream. Beat in chocolate, vanilla and salt until smooth.
4. *To assemble:* Place one cake layer, flat side up, on a cake stand or platter and, using an offset spatula, spread about 1 cup (250 mL) of the frosting over the top. Add the remaining cake layer, flat side up, and spread the remaining frosting over the top and sides of the cake.

Serves 10 to 12

Make ahead

Store cake wrapped in plastic wrap at room temperature for up to 2 days.

Sour Cream Chocolate Cake

FLAT BEATER ◆ WIRE WHIP

- Preheat oven to 350°F (180°C)
- Two 9-inch (23 cm) round metal cake pans, greased and lined with greased and floured parchment paper

Cake		
2 cups	unbleached all-purpose flour	500 mL
2 cups	granulated sugar	500 mL
1 1/4 tsp	baking powder	6 mL
1 tsp	salt	5 mL
1/2 tsp	baking soda	2 mL
2	eggs, at room temperature	2
4 oz	unsweetened chocolate, melted (see tip, page 337)	125 g
1 cup	sour cream, at room temperature	250 mL
3/4 cup	milk	175 mL
1/4 cup	unsalted butter, softened	50 mL
2 tsp	vanilla	10 mL
Frosting		
4 oz	unsweetened chocolate, chopped	125 g
1/2 cup	unsalted butter	125 mL
4 cups	confectioner's (icing) sugar, sifted	1 L
1/2 cup	sour cream	125 mL
1/4 cup	whipping (35%) cream	50 mL
2 tsp	vanilla	10 mL
1/4 tsp	salt	1 mL

1. *Prepare the cake:* Place flour, sugar, baking powder, salt, baking soda, eggs, chocolate, sour cream, milk, butter and vanilla in the mixer bowl. Attach the flat beater and mixer bowl to the mixer. Set to Stir and mix for 30 seconds. Increase to Speed 4 and beat for 2 minutes, stopping twice to scrape down sides.
2. Divide batter between prepared pans and smooth tops. Bake in middle of preheated oven for 25 to 30 minutes, or until a tester inserted in the center comes out clean and edges of cake begin to pull away from sides of pans. Let cool in pans on wire racks for 5 minutes, then invert onto racks, peel off paper and let cool completely.
3. *Prepare the frosting:* In a heatproof bowl set over a small saucepan of hot, not boiling water, melt chocolate and butter, stirring frequently until smooth. Let cool completely.
4. Place chocolate mixture, confectioner's sugar, sour cream, cream, vanilla and salt in clean mixer bowl. Attach the whip and mixer bowl to the mixer. Set to Stir and mix for 30 seconds. Increase to Speed 4 and beat, stopping once to scrape down bowl, until frosting is smooth, creamy and a spreadable consistency.
5. *To assemble:* Place one cake layer, flat side up, on a cake stand or platter and, using an offset spatula, spread about 1 cup (250 mL) of the frosting over the top. Add the remaining cake layer, flat side up, and spread the remaining frosting over the top and sides of the cake.

Serves 8 to 10

Make ahead

Store cake wrapped in plastic wrap at room temperature for up to 2 days.

German Chocolate Cake with Coconut Pecan Frosting

FLAT BEATER

- Preheat oven to 350°F (180°C)
- Two 9-inch (23 cm) round metal cake pans, greased and lined with greased and floured parchment paper

Cake		
2 cups	unbleached all-purpose flour	500 mL
½ cup	unsweetened cocoa powder, sifted	125 mL
1 tsp	baking soda	5 mL
½ tsp	baking powder	2 mL
¼ tsp	salt	1 mL
1 ½ cups	granulated sugar	375 mL
½ cup	unsalted butter, softened	125 mL
½ cup	vegetable shortening	125 mL
4	eggs	4
1 tsp	vanilla	5 mL
1 cup	buttermilk	250 mL
Coconut Pecan Frosting		
1 cup	firmly packed light brown sugar	250 mL
1 cup	firmly packed sweetened flaked coconut	250 mL
⅔ cup	whipping (35%) cream	150 mL
½ cup	pecan halves, chopped	125 mL
¼ cup	unsalted butter	50 mL

1. *Prepare the cake:* In a medium bowl, whisk together flour, cocoa, baking soda, baking powder and salt.
2. Place sugar, butter and shortening in the mixer bowl. Attach the flat beater and mixer bowl to the mixer. Set to Speed 4 and beat until light and fluffy. Beat in eggs, one at a time, and vanilla until smooth. Reduce speed to Stir and mix in flour mixture alternately with buttermilk, making 3 additions of each.
3. Divide batter between prepared pans and smooth tops. Bake in middle of preheated oven until firm to the touch, about 35 minutes. Let cool in pans for 5 minutes, then invert onto racks, peel off paper and let cool completely.
4. *Prepare the frosting:* In a medium saucepan, bring brown sugar, coconut, whipping cream, pecans and butter to a boil over medium heat. Cook, stirring, until slightly thickened, about 2 minutes. Remove from heat.
5. *To assemble:* Place one cake layer, flat side up, on a cake stand or platter and, using an offset spatula, spread about 1 cup (250 mL) of the frosting over the top. Add the remaining cake layer, flat side up, and spread the remaining frosting over the top of the cake. Serve warm or cooled to room temperature.

Serves 10

Make ahead

Store cake wrapped in plastic wrap at room temperature for up to 2 days.

Mexican Chocolate Soufflé Cake

WIRE WHIP

- Preheat oven to 325°F (160°C)
- 9-inch (23 cm) springform pan, greased

Cake		
10 oz	bittersweet chocolate, chopped	300 g
3⁄4 cup	unsalted butter, cut into 12 pieces	175 mL
3⁄4 cup	granulated sugar, divided	175 mL
1⁄2 tsp	ground cinnamon	2 mL
1 1⁄2 tsp	vanilla	7 mL
6	egg yolks	6
1⁄4 cup	unbleached all-purpose flour	50 mL
6	egg whites, at room temperature	6
1⁄4 tsp	salt	1 mL
Cinnamon Whipped Cream		
1 cup	cold whipping (35%) cream	250 mL
3 tbsp	confectioner's (icing) sugar, sifted	45 mL
1⁄2 tsp	ground cinnamon	2 mL

1. *Prepare the cake:* Place chocolate and butter in the mixer bowl. Set bowl over a saucepan of simmering water, making sure the bottom of the bowl doesn't touch the water. Melt chocolate, stirring frequently. Let cool completely.
2. Attach the whip and mixer bowl to the mixer. Set to Speed 4 and beat in 6 tbsp (90 mL) of the sugar, cinnamon and vanilla. Beat in egg yolks, one at a time. Reduce speed to Stir and mix in flour. Transfer to a large bowl and clean the mixer bowl and whip.
3. Place egg whites and salt in the mixer bowl. Attach the whip and mixer bowl to the mixer. Set to Speed 4 and beat until foamy. Increase to Speed 8 and beat until soft peaks form. Beat in the remaining sugar, in 3 additions, until stiff, glossy peaks form.
4. Using a large rubber spatula, gently fold egg whites into the batter, in 4 additions. Do not completely incorporate the egg whites in the first 3 additions; let some streaks of white remain. With the fourth addition, fold until no streaks remain. Clean the mixer bowl and whip.
5. Spoon batter into prepared pan and smooth top. Bake in middle of preheated oven for 35 to 40 minutes, or until a tester inserted in the center comes out with moist crumbs attached. Let cake cool in pan on a wire rack for 10 minutes. Remove sides of pan and let cool completely. (Cake will fall during cooling, creating cracks in the top of the crust.)

6. *Meanwhile, prepare the cinnamon whipped cream:* Place whipped cream, sugar and cinnamon in the mixer bowl. Attach the whip and mixer bowl to the mixer. Set to Speed 2 and gradually increase to Speed 8, beating just until soft peaks form. Serve immediately or refrigerate for up to 1 hour.
7. Cut cake into wedges and serve with cinnamon whipped cream.

Serves 10 to 12

Make ahead

Store cake wrapped in plastic wrap at room temperature for up to 1 day.

TIPS

Eggs separate more easily when cold, but beat up to a higher volume if they are brought to room temperature first. For this recipe, let eggs sit at room temperature for 30 minutes before using.

It's very difficult to remove this cake from the bottom of the springform pan. For the sake of stability, we usually just leave it on when we transfer the cake to a serving platter.

Chocolate Amaretto Cake

FLAT BEATER · WIRE WHIP

- Preheat oven to 350°F (180°C)
- Two 8-inch (20 cm) round metal cake pans, greased and lined with greased and floured parchment paper

Cake		
3/4 cup	cake flour, sifted	175 mL
1/4 cup	almond flour or finely ground blanched almonds	50 mL
1/4 tsp	salt	1 mL
1/2 cup	milk	125 mL
1/2 cup	unsalted butter	125 mL
7 oz	bittersweet or semisweet chocolate, chopped	225 g
5	egg yolks	5
1/2 cup	granulated sugar, divided	125 mL
2 tbsp	amaretto liqueur	25 mL
1/2 tsp	vanilla	2 mL
5	egg whites, at room temperature	5

Amaretto Ganache		
1/2 cup	whipping (35%) cream	125 mL
8 oz	bittersweet or semisweet chocolate, broken into pieces if in bar form	250 g
3 tbsp	amaretto liqueur	45 mL

1. *Prepare the cake:* In a small bowl, whisk together cake flour, almond flour and salt. Set aside.
2. In a medium saucepan, heat milk and butter over medium heat until butter is melted and milk is steaming. Remove from heat and add chocolate. Let melt for a few moments, then stir until smooth. Set aside.
3. Place egg yolks and 1/4 cup (50 mL) of the sugar in the mixer bowl. Attach the flat beater and mixer bowl to the mixer. Set to Speed 6 and beat until light-colored and thick, about 5 minutes. Beat in chocolate mixture, amaretto and vanilla until combined. Transfer to a large bowl and clean the mixer bowl.
4. Place egg whites in the mixer bowl. Attach the whip and mixer bowl to the mixer. Set to Speed 4 and beat until foamy. Increase to Speed 8 and beat until soft peaks form. Beat in the remaining 1/4 cup (50 mL) sugar until stiff, glossy peaks form. Remove from the mixer.
5. Using a large rubber spatula, alternately fold flour mixture and egg whites into the yolk mixture, making 3 additions of each.
6. Divide batter between prepared pans and smooth tops. Bake in middle of preheated oven for 30 to 35 minutes or until cake rises and then falls and pulls away from the sides of the pan. Let cool in pans on wire racks for 5 minutes, then invert onto racks, peel off paper and let cool completely.
7. *Prepare the ganache:* In a medium saucepan, heat whipping cream over medium heat until steaming. Remove from heat and add chocolate. Let melt for a few moments, then stir until silky and smooth. Stir in amaretto. Let cool slightly: it will thicken somewhat and give better coverage.

8. *To assemble:* Place one cake layer, flat side up, on a cake stand or platter and top with about one-third of the ganache. Smooth with a rubber spatula or offset palette knife, letting excess ganache drip down the sides. Add the remaining cake layer, flat side up, and top with half of the remaining ganache, smoothing and letting excess drip down the sides. Refrigerate cake for 30 minutes (keep remaining ganache at room temperature). Top with the remaining ganache, smoothing and letting excess drip down the sides. Refrigerate for 3 hours. Bring to room temperature before serving.

Serves 8 to 10

Make ahead

Store cake wrapped in plastic wrap at room temperature for up to 2 days.

Variation

After smoothing the ganache over the first cake layer, add a layer of fresh raspberries, top with another layer of ganache, then top with the second cake layer. Proceed with the recipe as directed and garnish with raspberry coulis (see page 344, Step 4).

TIP

The smooth, shiny surface of this cake lends itself to many different garnishes. For a beautiful finish, look for candied flowers in cake decorating shops.

Plum Upside-Down Cake

FLAT BEATER

- Preheat oven to 350°F (180°C)
- 9-inch (23 cm) round metal cake pan

1 cup	unbleached all-purpose flour	250 mL
1/2 tsp	baking powder	2 mL
1/2 tsp	baking soda	2 mL
1/4 tsp	salt	1 mL
3/4 cup	granulated sugar, divided	175 mL
6 tbsp	unsalted butter, softened	90 mL
1	egg	1
	Grated zest of 1 lemon	
1/3 cup	buttermilk	75 mL
1 tsp	vanilla	5 mL
2 tbsp	unsalted butter	25 mL
3	plums, each cut into 12 slices	3
2 tsp	freshly squeezed lemon juice	10 mL
	Sweetened Whipped Cream (see recipe, page 416) or ice cream	

Make ahead

Store cake wrapped in plastic wrap at room temperature for up to 1 day.

1. In a small bowl, whisk together flour, baking powder, baking soda and salt.
2. Place 1/2 cup (125 mL) of the sugar and the 6 tbsp (90 mL) butter in the mixer bowl. Attach the flat beater and mixer bowl to the mixer. Set to Speed 4 and beat until light and fluffy. Beat in egg and lemon zest. Reduce speed to Stir and mix in flour mixture alternately with buttermilk, making 3 additions of dry and 2 of wet. Mix in vanilla.
3. In cake pan, melt the 2 tbsp (25 mL) butter over medium heat. Add the remaining 1/4 cup (50 mL) sugar and cook, stirring, until foamy, about 2 minutes. Carefully remove from heat and place plum slices in a decorative pattern on top of sugar mixture, working from the center out, overlapping slightly. Sprinkle with lemon juice. Return pan to medium heat and cook, undisturbed, until juices bubble up around the plums, about 4 minutes. Carefully remove from heat and add batter evenly to the pan, covering the fruit. Try not to disturb the placement of the fruit slices.
4. Bake in middle of preheated oven until a tester inserted in the center comes out clean, about 25 minutes. Let cool in pan on a wire rack for 10 minutes, then invert onto a serving plate. Serve warm or at room temperature with whipped cream or ice cream.

Serves 8

Orange Shortcakes

FLAT BEATER

- Preheat oven to 350°F (180°C)
- Baking sheet, lined with parchment paper
- 3-inch (7.5 cm) round cookie cutter

1 1⁄2 cup	unbleached all-purpose flour	375 mL
1⁄4 cup	granulated sugar	50 mL
2 1⁄2 tsp	baking powder	12 mL
1⁄2 tsp	salt	2 mL
6 tbsp	cold unsalted butter, cut into 1⁄4-inch (0.5 cm) pieces	90 mL
	Grated zest of 1 orange	
1⁄2 cup	whipping (35%) cream	125 mL
2 tbsp	unsalted butter, melted	25 mL
2 tbsp	coarse sugar (optional)	25 mL
	Seasonal fruit, chopped and lightly sweetened	
	Lightly whipped cream	

1. Place flour, granulated sugar, baking powder and salt in the mixer bowl. Attach the flat beater and mixer bowl to the mixer. Set to Stir and mix until combined. Increase to Speed 4 and beat in cold butter and orange zest until butter is the size of peas. Reduce speed to Stir and mix in whipping cream until a dough forms.
2. Turn dough out onto a floured work surface and roll out to 1⁄2-inch (1 cm) thickness. Cut out six 3-inch (7.5 cm) rounds and place 2 inches (5 cm) apart on prepared baking sheet. Reroll scraps. Brush with melted butter and sprinkle with coarse sugar, if using. Bake in middle of preheated oven until golden, about 20 minutes. Transfer to a wire rack and let cool completely.
3. Slice shortcakes in half horizontally. Place seasonal fruit and whipped cream on bottom half and cover with top half.

Serves 6

Make ahead

Store shortcakes, unfilled, wrapped in plastic wrap at room temperature for up to 1 day.

Coconut Cake with Meringue Frosting

FLAT BEATER • WIRE WHIP

- Preheat oven to 350°F (180°C)
- Two 8-inch (20 cm) round metal cake pans, greased and lined with greased and floured parchment paper

Cake		
2 cups	cake flour, sifted	500 mL
1 1/2 tsp	baking powder	7 mL
1/4 tsp	baking soda	1 mL
1/4 tsp	salt	1 mL
1 cup	granulated sugar	250 mL
1/2 cup	unsalted butter, softened	125 mL
5	egg yolks	5
1 tsp	coconut extract	5 mL
1/2 tsp	vanilla	2 mL
3/4 cup	canned unsweetened coconut milk	175 mL
1 cup	toasted sweetened shredded coconut (see tip, opposite)	250 mL
6	egg whites, at room temperature	6
Meringue Frosting		
1 cup	granulated sugar	250 mL
4	egg whites	4
1/2 cup	seedless raspberry jam	125 mL
2 cups	toasted sweetened shredded coconut	500 mL

1. *Prepare the cake:* In a medium bowl, whisk together flour, baking powder, baking soda and salt.
2. Place sugar and butter in the mixer bowl. Attach the flat beater and mixer bowl to the mixer. Set to Speed 4 and beat until light and fluffy. Beat in egg yolks, one at a time. Beat in coconut extract and vanilla. Reduce speed to Stir and mix in flour mixture alternately with coconut milk, making 3 additions of dry and 2 of wet. Mix in coconut. Transfer to a medium bowl. Clean the mixer bowl.
3. Place egg whites in the mixer bowl. Remove the flat beater and attach the whip and mixer bowl to the mixer. Set to Speed 4 and beat until foamy. Increase to Speed 8 and beat until soft peaks form. Remove the bowl from the mixer.
4. Using a large rubber spatula, gently fold egg whites into the batter, in 3 additions. Do not completely incorporate the egg whites in the first 2 additions; let some streaks of white remain. With the third addition, fold until no streaks remain. Clean the mixer bowl and whip.
5. Divide batter between prepared pans and smooth tops. Bake in middle of preheated oven until tops spring back when lightly pressed, about 25 minutes. Cool in pans on wire racks for 5 minutes, then invert onto racks, peel off paper, and let cool completely.

6. *Prepare the frosting:* In a medium saucepan, bring sugar and 1⁄4 cup (50 mL) water to a boil over medium-high heat, swirling the pan occasionally to encourage even melting. Boil to the soft-ball stage (see tip, at right), about 4 minutes. Remove from heat.
7. Meanwhile, place egg whites in the mixer bowl. Attach the whip and mixer bowl to the mixer. Set to Speed 4 and beat until foamy. Increase to Speed 8 and beat until soft peaks form. With the motor running, gradually pour in hot syrup in a steady stream until incorporated. Continue to beat until bowl is cool to the touch, about 5 minutes.
8. *To assemble:* Place one cake layer, flat side up, on a cake stand or platter and, using an offset spatula, spread raspberry jam over the top. Add the remaining cake layer, flat side up, and spread frosting over the top and sides of the cake. Cover top and sides with coconut.

Serves 10 to 12

TIPS

To toast coconut, spread on a baking sheet and bake in a 350°F (180°C) oven for 5 minutes. Stir the coconut and bake until the coconut is golden and toasted, another 2 or 3 minutes. Remove from the oven and cool.

Syrup at the soft-ball stage measures between 234°F and 240°F (112°C and 115°C) on a candy thermometer. If you don't have a candy thermometer, drop 1⁄4 tsp (1 mL) of the syrup into very cold water. If it forms a soft ball that flattens of its own accord when removed, it is ready. If it doesn't, cook for another minute and try again.

Carrot Cake with Cream Cheese Frosting

ROTOR SLICER/SHREDDER
FLAT BEATER

- Preheat oven to 350°F (180°C)
- Two 9-inch (23 cm) round metal cake pans, greased and lined with greased and floured parchment paper

Cake		
5	medium carrots	5
2 cups	unbleached all-purpose flour	500 mL
2 tsp	baking soda	10 mL
2 tsp	ground cinnamon	10 mL
1 tsp	salt	5 mL
1/2 tsp	baking powder	2 mL
Pinch	ground allspice	Pinch
4	eggs	4
1 cup	granulated sugar	250 mL
1/2 cup	lightly packed light brown sugar	125 mL
1/2 cup	vegetable oil	125 mL
1 tsp	grated lemon zest	5 mL
Cream Cheese Frosting		
8 oz	cream cheese, softened	250 g
2/3 cup	unsalted butter, softened	150 mL
2 tsp	vanilla	10 mL
5 cups	confectioner's (icing) sugar, sifted	1.125 L
1 tsp	milk, if necessary (approx.)	5 mL
1 cup	walnut halves, toasted (see tip, opposite) and chopped	250 mL

1. *Prepare the cake:* Attach the slice/shredder, with the coarse shredder, to the mixer. Set to Speed 4 and shred carrots into a medium bowl. (Or shred by hand with a box grater.) Measure out 3 cups (750 mL) of grated carrots and set aside.
2. In a medium bowl, whisk together flour, baking soda, cinnamon, salt, baking powder and allspice.
3. Place eggs, sugar, brown sugar, oil and lemon zest in the mixer bowl. Attach the flat beater and mixer bowl to the mixer. Set to Speed 4 and beat until combined. Set to Stir and mix in flour mixture, in 3 additions. Increase to Speed 4 and beat in carrots until evenly incorporated.
4. Divide batter between prepared pans and smooth tops. Bake in middle of preheated oven for 25 to 30 minutes, or until tops feel firm to the touch and a tester inserted in the centers comes out clean. Let cool in pans on wire racks for 10 minutes, then invert onto racks, peel off paper and let cool completely.
5. *Prepare the frosting:* Clean the mixer bowl and flat beater. Place cream cheese, butter and vanilla in the mixer bowl. Attach the flat beater and mixer bowl to the mixer. Set to Speed 4 and beat until smooth and creamy. Reduce speed to Stir and mix in confectioner's sugar, in 3 additions. Increase to Speed 4 and beat until frosting is a spreadable consistency. Thin, if necessary, with milk.

6. *To assemble:* Place one cake layer, flat side up, on a cake stand or platter and, using an offset spatula, spread 1/2 cup (125 mL) of the frosting over the top. Add the remaining cake layer, flat side up, and spread the remaining frosting over the top and sides of the cake. Press toasted walnuts into the sides.

Serves 10 to 12

Make ahead

Store unfrosted cake wrapped in plastic wrap at room temperature for up to 3 days.

TIPS

A medium lemon will yield about 2 to 3 tsp (10 to 15 mL) zest.

To toast nuts, spread them on a baking sheet and toast in a 350°F (180°C) oven for 7 to 8 minutes, or until lightly browned.

Switch the pans' positions in the oven and rotate them 180 degrees about halfway through to ensure even baking.

Angel Food Cake

WIRE WHIP

- Preheat oven to 375°F (190°C)
- 10-inch (4 L) tube pan, ungreased

1 cup	sifted cake flour	250 mL
1 1/4 cups	granulated sugar, divided	300 mL
1 1/2 cups	egg whites (10 to 11), at room temperature	375 mL
1 tbsp	warm water	15 mL
2 tsp	vanilla	10 mL
1 tsp	cream of tartar	5 mL
1/2 tsp	salt	2 mL

1. In a small bowl, whisk together flour and 1/4 cup (50 mL) of the sugar.
2. Place egg whites and water in mixer bowl. Attach the whip and mixer bowl to the mixer. Set to Speed 4 and beat until foamy. Increase to Speed 8 and beat in vanilla, cream of tartar and salt until soft peaks form. Beat in the remaining 1 cup (250 mL) sugar, in 3 additions, until stiff, glossy peaks form. Reduce speed to Stir and mix in flour mixture, in 3 additions, mixing just until the flour is incorporated.
3. Spoon batter into pan and smooth top. Bake in lower third of preheated oven until golden and a tester inserted in the center comes out clean, about 40 minutes. Immediately invert pan and, using the hole in the tube, hang upside down on an inverted funnel or the neck of a bottle. Let cool completely. Turn pan right side up. Run a long, thin knife around tube and outer edges of pan. Remove outer rim and run knife under bottom of cake. Invert to release cake, then invert again onto a serving plate.

Serves 8

Variations

Cocoa Angel Food Cake: Decrease the amount of cake flour to 3/4 cup (175 mL) and sift 1/3 cup (75 mL) unsweetened cocoa powder with the flour and sugar.

Orange Angel Food Cake: Add the grated zest of 1 orange to the mixer bowl when you add the flour mixture. Top with orange glaze: Sift 2 cups (500 mL) confectioner's (icing) sugar into a small saucepan and stir in 3 tbsp (45 mL) orange juice, 1 tbsp (15 mL) orange-flavored liqueur and a pinch of salt to make a smooth paste. Heat over medium-high heat until just warm to the touch. Drizzle over cake.

Make ahead

Store cake wrapped in plastic wrap at room temperature for up to 2 days.

Sponge Cake

WIRE WHIP

- Preheat oven to 350°F (180°C)
- 18- by 12-inch (45 by 30 cm) rimmed baking sheet, lined with parchment paper

1 1/2 cups	cake flour	375 mL
2 tsp	baking powder	10 mL
1/4 tsp	salt	1 mL
7	egg yolks	7
1 1/4 cups	granulated sugar	300 mL
1/4 cup	boiling water	50 mL
1 1/2 tsp	vanilla	7 mL
7	egg whites, at room temperature	7

This is delicious in trifles, tiramisu and jelly rolls. Cut into finger-length shapes, it can be used instead of ladyfingers in many recipes.

Make ahead

Store wrapped in plastic wrap in the freezer for up to 2 months.

1. In a medium bowl, whisk together flour, baking powder and salt.
2. Place egg yolks and sugar in the mixer bowl. Attach the whip and mixer bowl to the mixer. Set to Speed 6 and beat until thick and pale yellow. Slowly beat in boiling water and vanilla until thick. Remove the mixer bowl and, using a large rubber spatula, fold in flour mixture, in 3 additions. Transfer to a large bowl and clean the mixer bowl and whip.
3. Place egg whites in the mixer bowl. Attach the whip and mixer bowl to the mixer. Set to Speed 4 and beat until foamy. Increase to Speed 8 and beat until soft peaks form. Using a large rubber spatula, gently fold egg whites into the batter, making 3 additions. Do not completely incorporate the whites in the first 2 additions; let some streaks of white remain. With the third addition, fold until no streaks remain.
4. Spread batter evenly on prepared baking sheet. Bake in middle of preheated oven until golden and center springs back when lightly pressed, about 15 minutes. Let cool completely on baking sheet on a wire rack, then invert onto a cutting board and peel off paper.

Makes one 18- by 12-inch (45 by 30 cm) sheet cake

Maple Pound Cake with Maple Glaze

FLAT BEATER

- Preheat oven to 350°F (180°C)
- 10-inch (3 L) Bundt pan, greased and floured

Cake		
2 cups	unbleached all-purpose flour	500 mL
1 tsp	baking powder	5 mL
½ tsp	salt	2 mL
1¾ cups	granulated sugar	425 mL
8 oz	cream cheese (not lower-fat), softened	250 g
1 cup	unsalted butter, softened	250 mL
4	eggs	4
2 tsp	maple extract	10 mL
Glaze		
¼ cup	hot water	50 mL
¼ cup	pure maple syrup	50 mL

1. *Prepare the cake:* In a medium bowl, whisk together flour, baking powder and salt.
2. Place sugar, cream cheese and butter in the mixer bowl. Attach the flat beater and mixer bowl to the mixer. Set to Speed 4 and beat until soft and creamy. Beat in eggs, one at a time, and maple extract. Reduce speed to Stir and mix in flour mixture, in 3 additions.
3. Spoon batter into prepared pan and smooth top. Bake in middle of preheated oven for about 1 hour, or until a tester inserted in the center comes out clean. Let cool in pan on a wire rack for 5 minutes, then invert onto rack.
4. *Prepare the glaze:* In a small bowl, combine water and maple syrup.
5. Place a plate or tray under the rack to catch glaze as it drips down the cake. Using a pastry brush, brush warm cake with glaze until it has absorbed as much glaze as possible. Let cool completely on rack before transferring to a serving plate.

Serves 10 to 12

Make ahead

Store cake wrapped in plastic wrap at room temperature for up to 2 days.

Cream Cheese Pound Cake with Lemon Glaze

FLAT BEATER

- Preheat oven to 350°F (180°C)
- 9- by 5-inch (2 L) loaf pan, greased and floured

Cake		
2 cups	unbleached all-purpose flour	500 mL
1 tsp	baking powder	5 mL
1⁄4 tsp	salt	1 mL
1 1⁄2 cups	granulated sugar	375 mL
6 oz	cream cheese, softened	175 g
1 cup	unsalted butter, softened	250 mL
4	eggs	4
2 tsp	grated lemon zest	10 mL
2 tsp	vanilla	10 mL
Glaze		
1 cup	confectioner's (icing) sugar, sifted	250 mL
	Juice of 1 lemon	

1. *Prepare the cake:* In a medium bowl, whisk together flour, baking powder and salt.
2. Place sugar, cream cheese and butter in the mixer bowl. Attach the flat beater and mixer bowl to the mixer. Set to Speed 4 and beat until soft and creamy. Beat in eggs, one at a time. Beat in lemon zest and vanilla. Reduce speed to Stir and mix in flour mixture, in 3 additions.
3. Spoon batter into prepared pan and smooth top. Bake in middle of preheated oven for 1 to 1 1⁄4 hours, or until a tester inserted in the center comes out clean. Let cool in pan on a wire rack for 5 minutes, then invert onto rack to cool completely.
4. *Prepare the glaze:* In a small bowl, stir together confectioner's sugar and lemon juice, adding water as necessary to make a drizzling consistency.
5. Drizzle glaze over cooled cake.

Serves 10 to 12

Make ahead

This cake is better when prepared a day or two in advance. Let glaze dry, then wrap in plastic wrap and store at room temperature for up to 2 days.

Dark Chocolate Pound Cake with White Chocolate Glaze

FLAT BEATER

- Preheat oven to 350°F (180°C)
- 10-inch (3 L) Bundt pan, greased and floured

2¼ cups	cake flour	550 mL
¾ cup	unsweetened cocoa powder (preferably Dutch-process)	175 mL
½ tsp	salt	2 mL
½ tsp	baking soda	2 mL
1½ cups	unsalted butter, softened	375 mL
1 cup	granulated sugar	250 mL
1 cup	packed dark brown sugar	250 mL
1 cup	sour cream	250 mL
5	eggs	5
4 oz	bittersweet chocolate, melted (see tip, page 337)	125 g
2 tsp	vanilla	10 mL
Glaze		
3 tbsp	whipping (35%) cream	45 mL
4 oz	white chocolate, chopped	125 g
1 cup	raspberries (optional)	250 mL

1. In a large bowl, sift together flour, cocoa, salt and baking soda. Set aside.
2. Place butter, granulated sugar and brown sugar in the mixer bowl. Attach the flat beater and mixer bowl to the mixer. Set to Speed 4 and beat until light and fluffy, about 2 minutes. Stop mixer to scrape down bowl. Add sour cream, set to Speed 4 and beat until incorporated. Beat in eggs, one at a time. Stop mixer to scrape down bowl. Add melted chocolate and vanilla, set to Speed 2 and mix until combined. Mix in flour mixture, ¼ cup (50 mL) at a time, until combined.
3. Pour batter into prepared pan and bake in preheated oven for 60 to 75 minutes, or until a tester inserted into the center comes out clean. Let cool in pan on a wire rack for 30 minutes before turning out onto a cake plate.
4. *Prepare the glaze:* In a small saucepan, heat cream over medium heat until steaming. Remove from heat and stir in white chocolate until melted. Drizzle over top and sides of cake.
5. Serve warm or at room temperature, garnished with raspberries, if desired.

Serves 10

Ginger Pound Cake

FLAT BEATER

- Preheat oven to 350°F (180°C)
- 9- by 5-inch (2 L) metal loaf pan, greased and floured

2 cups	granulated sugar, divided	500 mL
1/2 cup	water	125 mL
1	5-inch (12.5 cm) knob gingerroot, peeled and very thinly sliced, divided	1
1/2 cup	milk	125 mL
2 cups	unbleached all-purpose flour	500 mL
1/2 tsp	baking powder	2 mL
1/4 tsp	salt	1 mL
1 cup	unsalted butter, softened	250 mL
3	eggs	3
	Grated zest of 1 lemon	
1 tsp	vanilla	5 mL
1/2 cup	confectioner's (icing) sugar	125 mL

TIP

The easiest way to peel gingerroot is by scraping the skin from the root using the tip of a spoon. That way, you don't lose as much of the flavorful root along with the skin.

1. In a medium saucepan, bring 1/2 cup (125 mL) of the granulated sugar, water and half the ginger to a simmer over medium heat. Reduce heat and simmer gently for 20 minutes, or until the ginger is tender and translucent. Remove ginger with a slotted spoon and toss with 2 tbsp (25 mL) granulated sugar. Lay out on a rack to dry for 2 to 4 hours. Reserve the syrup.
2. In a small saucepan, bring the remaining ginger and milk to a simmer over medium heat. Cover, remove from heat and let stand for 30 to 60 minutes so that the ginger flavors the milk. Remove ginger with a slotted spoon and discard.
3. In a medium bowl, combine flour, baking powder and salt. Set aside.
4. Place the remaining sugar and butter in the mixer bowl. Attach the flat beater and mixer bowl to the mixer. Set to Speed 4 and beat until light and fluffy. Beat in eggs, one at a time, then lemon zest and vanilla. Stop mixer to scrape down bowl. Set to Speed 2 and mix in flour mixture alternately with milk, making 4 additions of dry and 3 of wet.
5. Pour batter into prepared pan and bake in preheated oven for about 75 minutes, or until a tester inserted in the center comes out with just a few moist crumbs attached. Let cool in pan on a wire rack for 30 minutes, then turn out onto rack to cool completely.
6. In a small bowl, combine confectioner's sugar and as much of the ginger syrup as needed to make a pourable glaze. Drizzle cake with glaze and, while wet, decorate top with candied ginger. Let dry for 30 minutes, until firm, before serving.

Serves 10

Pumpkin Cheesecake

FLAT BEATER

- Preheat oven to 350°F (180°C)
- 9-inch (23 cm) springform pan
- Large roasting pan

Crust		
2¼ cups	ground gingersnap cookies	550 mL
1½ cups	pecan halves, toasted (see tip, page 361) and ground	375 mL
¼ cup	lightly packed light brown sugar	50 mL
½ cup	unsalted butter, melted	125 mL
Filling		
1½ lbs	cream cheese, softened	750 g
1½ cups	granulated sugar	375 mL
1	can (14 oz/398 g) pumpkin purée (not pie filling) (about 1¾ cups/425 mL)	1
½ cup	whipping (35%) cream	125 mL
1 tsp	ground cinnamon	5 mL
½ tsp	salt	2 mL
½ tsp	ground ginger	2 mL
¼ tsp	ground cloves	1 mL
¼ tsp	ground allspice	1 mL
1 tsp	vanilla	5 mL
1 tbsp	freshly squeezed lemon juice	15 mL
4	eggs	4
	Boiling water	

Make ahead

Store wrapped in plastic wrap in the refrigerator for up to 1 day.

1. *Prepare the crust:* In a medium bowl, combine gingersnaps, pecans and brown sugar. Add melted butter and stir to combine. Press into bottom and 2 inches (5 cm) up sides of springform pan.
2. *Prepare the filling:* Place cream cheese and sugar in the mixer bowl. Attach the flat beater and mixer bowl to the mixer. Set to Speed 4 and beat until light and fluffy, stopping mixer once to scrape down bowl. Beat in pumpkin, whipping cream, cinnamon, salt, ginger, cloves, allspice, vanilla and lemon juice until well combined. Beat in eggs, one at a time.
3. Line outside of springform pan, up to the top edge, with a double layer of foil. Set inside roasting pan and pour filling into crust (it will almost fill pan). Set roasting pan in middle of preheated oven and pour in enough boiling water to reach halfway up the sides of the springform pan. Bake until cheesecake puffs around the edges and center moves only slightly when pan is shaken, about 1½ hours. Run a small, sharp knife around edges of pan to loosen cheesecake. Transfer roasting pan to a wire rack and let cool for 45 minutes. Remove springform pan from water, place on rack and let cool to room temperature, about 2 hours. Cover tightly with plastic wrap and refrigerate overnight.

Serves 10

TIP

To help keep the top from cracking, it's important to loosen the cake from the pan immediately after removing it from the oven. This allows the cake to contract without sticking to the sides, which would pull on the top and create cracks.

Gingerbread with Warm Apples

FLAT BEATER

- Preheat oven to 350°F (180°C)
- 9-inch (2.5 L) square metal baking pan, greased

2 cups	unbleached all-purpose flour	500 mL
2 tsp	ground ginger	10 mL
1 tsp	ground cinnamon	5 mL
1 tsp	baking soda	5 mL
1/2 tsp	salt	2 mL
1/4 tsp	ground nutmeg	1 mL
1/4 tsp	ground allspice	1 mL
1/4 tsp	freshly ground white pepper	1 mL
1/2 cup	firmly packed light brown sugar	125 mL
1/2 cup	unsalted butter, softened	125 mL
2	eggs	2
1/2 cup	sour cream	125 mL
1/2 cup	fancy molasses	125 mL
1/4 cup	dark rum or apple cider	50 mL
4	Crispin (Mutsu) or Gala apples, peeled and cut into eighths (about 2 lbs/1 kg)	4
2 tbsp	granulated sugar	25 mL
2 tbsp	freshly squeezed lemon juice	25 mL
	Sweetened Whipped Cream (see recipe, page 416)	

1. In a medium bowl, whisk together flour, ginger, cinnamon, baking soda, salt, nutmeg, allspice and white pepper.
2. Place brown sugar and butter in the mixer bowl. Attach the flat beater and mixer bowl to the mixer. Set to Speed 4 and beat until light and fluffy. Beat in eggs, one at a time, sour cream, molasses and rum. Reduce speed to Stir and mix in flour mixture, in 2 additions.
3. Spoon batter into prepared pan and smooth top. Bake in middle of preheated oven until a tester inserted in the center comes out clean, about 30 minutes. Let cool in pan on a wire rack for 10 minutes, then invert onto rack to cool completely.
4. In a medium saucepan, over medium heat, cook apples, sugar and lemon juice, stirring often, until apples are soft, about 10 minutes.
5. Cut cake into squares and serve with warm apples and whipped cream.

Serves 8

Make ahead

Store cake wrapped in plastic wrap at room temperature for up to 1 day.

Lemon Blueberry Trifle

FRUIT/VEGETABLE STRAINER
WIRE WHIP

- Trifle bowl or 10-cup (2.5 L) bowl

1	package (16 oz/454 g) frozen blueberries, thawed and drained	1
1/2 cup	granulated sugar	125 mL
2 tbsp	lemon juice	25 mL
1 cup	cold whipping (35%) cream	250 mL
2 1/2 cups	Lemon Curd (see recipe, page 412), cooled	625 mL
1/2	Sponge Cake (see recipe, page 363), cut into small pieces	1/2
1 cup	fresh blueberries (optional)	250 mL

1. In a small saucepan, heat blueberries, sugar and 3 tbsp (45 mL) water over medium heat until blueberries begin to soften, about 5 minutes.
2. Attach the fruit/vegetable strainer to the mixer. Set to Speed 4 and run half the berry mixture through the strainer into a medium bowl, with another bowl to catch the solids. Discard solids. Add whole-berry mixture to the strained sauce. Add lemon juice and refrigerate for up to 24 hours, until ready to assemble trifle.
3. Place whipping cream in the mixer bowl. Attach the whip and mixer bowl to the mixer. Set to Speed 8 and beat until firm. Fold into lemon curd.
4. Pour 1/2 cup (125 mL) of the blueberry sauce into the trifle bowl. Top with a 1/2-inch (1 cm) thick layer of lemon curd, followed by a layer of cake pieces. Repeat layers at least twice more and top with a final layer of lemon curd. Cover and refrigerate for at least 8 hours or for up to 24 hours to let flavors and textures develop. Serve cold, garnished with fresh blueberries, if using.

Serves 12

South Seas Trifle

WIRE WHIP · FRUIT/VEGETABLE STRAINER

◆ Trifle bowl or 2 ½ quart (2.5 L) bowl

Sabayon		
8	egg yolks	8
½ cup	granulated sugar	125 mL
½ cup	freshly squeezed orange juice	125 mL
¼ cup	orange-flavored liqueur or orange juice	50 mL
1 cup	cold whipping (35%) cream	250 mL
Mango Sauce		
4	mangoes, peeled and diced	4
½ cup	granulated sugar	125 mL
2 tbsp	dark rum or orange juice	25 mL
2 tbsp	freshly squeezed lemon juice	25 mL
½	Sponge Cake (see recipe, page 363)	½
1 cup	seedless blackberry or raspberry jam	250 mL

1. *Prepare the sabayon:* Place egg yolks, sugar, orange juice and orange liqueur in the mixer bowl. Attach the whip and mixer bowl to the mixer. Set to Speed 4 and beat until smooth. Set mixer bowl over a saucepan of simmering water, making sure the bottom of the bowl doesn't touch the water, and whisk briskly until the sabayon has tripled in volume, about 5 minutes. Reattach the mixer bowl to the mixer, with the whip still attached. Set to Speed 4 and beat until bowl is cool to the touch. Transfer to a large bowl and clean the mixer bowl and whip.
2. Place whipping cream in the mixer bowl. Attach the whip and mixer bowl to the mixer. Set to Speed 8 and beat until firm. Fold into cooled sabayon.
3. *Prepare the mango sauce:* In a large saucepan, over medium heat, cook mangoes, sugar and rum, stirring occasionally, until mango is tender, about 20 minutes.
4. Attach the fruit/vegetable strainer to the mixer. Set to Speed 4 and run mango mixture through the strainer into a large bowl, with another bowl to catch the solids. Discard solids. Add lemon juice to the mango purée and refrigerate for up to 24 hours, until ready to assemble trifle.
5. Slice sponge cake in half horizontally. Spread blackberry jam over cut side of bottom half of the cake and top with the other half to make a big jelly sandwich. Cut into 4- by 2-inch (10 cm by 5 cm) fingers.
6. Pour ½ cup (125 mL) of the mango sauce into the trifle bowl. Top with 1 cup (250 mL) of sabayon, then a layer of cake fingers, with the long cut side up. Repeat layers twice more and top with a final layer of sabayon. Arrange the remaining cake fingers, jelly side out, around the perimeter of the bowl. (This will look pretty if you are using a glass trifle bowl.) Cover and refrigerate for at least 8 hours or for up to 24 hours to let flavors and textures develop. Serve cold.

Serves 12

Summer Trifle

WIRE WHIP FRUIT/VEGETABLE STRAINER

◆ Trifle bowl or 10-cup (2.5 L) bowl

Vanilla Cream		
4	egg yolks	4
1/2 cup	granulated sugar	125 mL
Pinch	salt	Pinch
12 oz	cream cheese, softened and cut into 8 pieces	375 g
1 tsp	vanilla	5 mL
4	egg whites, at room temperature	4
1 lb	frozen peaches or frozen mixed fruit, thawed, drained and chopped	500 g
Raspberry Sauce		
3	packages (each 12 oz/375 g) frozen raspberries in syrup, thawed	3
1/4 cup	eau de vie framboise (raspberry liqueur) (optional)	50 mL
1/2	Sponge Cake (see recipe, page 363), cut into small pieces	1/2
1 cup	fresh raspberries (optional)	250 mL

This recipe contains raw eggs. If the food safety of raw eggs is a concern for you, use pasteurized eggs. Many grocery stores now carry pasteurized eggs in their shells.

1. *Prepare the vanilla cream:* Place egg yolks, sugar and salt in the mixer bowl. Attach the whip and mixer bowl to the mixer. Set to Speed 8 and beat until thick, about 3 minutes. Reduce to Speed 2 and beat in cream cheese and vanilla. Increase to Speed 8 and beat until smooth. Transfer to a large bowl. Clean the mixer bowl and whip.
2. Place egg whites in the mixer bowl. Attach the whip and mixer bowl to the mixer. Set to Speed 4 and beat until foamy. Increase to Speed 8 and beat until soft peaks form. Fold into cream cheese mixture, then fold in peaches.
3. *Prepare the raspberry sauce:* Attach the fruit/vegetable strainer to the mixer. Set to Speed 4 and run raspberries and their syrup through strainer into a large bowl, with another bowl to catch the solids. Discard solids. Push through a fine-mesh strainer and discard seeds. Add framboise, if using. You should have about 1 cup (250 mL) raspberry sauce.
4. Pour 3 tbsp (45 mL) of the raspberry sauce into the trifle bowl. Top with a thin layer of vanilla cream, then a layer of cake pieces. Repeat layers at least twice more and top with a final layer of cream. Cover and refrigerate for at least 8 hours or for up to 24 hours to let flavors and textures develop. Serve cold, garnished with fresh raspberries, if using.

Serves 12

Tiramisu

WIRE WHIP

◆ 13- by 9-inch (3 L) glass baking dish

7	egg yolks	7
1/2 cup	granulated sugar	125 mL
1/3 cup	sweet Marsala	75 mL
8 oz	mascarpone, softened	250 g
1 cup	cold whipping (35%) cream	250 mL
1 1/4 cup	brewed espresso, at room temperature	300 mL
1/4 cup	rum	50 mL
1 tsp	vanilla	5 mL
48	Ladyfingers (see recipe, page 303)	48
2 oz	semisweet or bittersweet chocolate, grated	60 g

1. Place egg yolks and sugar in the mixer bowl. Attach the whip and mixer bowl to the mixer. Set to Speed 6 and beat until thick and pale yellow.
2. Set mixer bowl over a saucepan of simmering water, making sure the bottom of the bowl doesn't touch the water. Add Marsala and cook, whisking constantly, until thick and doubled in volume. Remove from heat and gently stir in mascarpone until completely blended. Transfer to another bowl and let cool completely. Clean the mixer bowl and whip and refrigerate until chilled.
3. Place whipping cream in chilled mixer bowl. Attach the whip and mixer bowl to the mixer. Set to Speed 8 and beat until soft peaks form. Fold into mascarpone mixture until blended.
4. In a shallow bowl, combine espresso, rum and vanilla. Quickly dip 24 of the ladyfingers in the coffee mixture and arrange in a single layer in baking dish. (Do not soak the cookies or they will become too moist and fall apart.) Using a rubber spatula, spread half of the mascarpone cream evenly on ladyfingers. Repeat with a second layer of dipped ladyfingers and the remaining mascarpone cream. Sprinkle with chocolate. Refrigerate for at least 2 hours or for up to 24 hours.

Serves 8 to 10

Vanilla Soufflé with Chocolate Sauce

WIRE WHIP

- Preheat oven to 425°F (220°C)
- 8-inch (20 cm) soufflé dish

3 tbsp	granulated sugar	45 mL
1 1⁄4 cups	milk	300 mL
1	vanilla bean, split lengthwise	1
1⁄2 cup	granulated sugar	125 mL
1⁄4 cup	unbleached all-purpose flour	50 mL
6	egg yolks	6
3 tbsp	unsalted butter, softened	45 mL
6	egg whites, at room temperature	6
Pinch	salt	Pinch
2 tbsp	granulated sugar	25 mL
1 tbsp	confectioner's (icing) sugar, sifted	15 mL
1 cup	Chocolate Sauce (see recipe, opposite)	250 mL

Make ahead

The soufflé base can be prepared through Step 2 up to 7 hours ahead. Cover tightly with plastic wrap and refrigerate.

1. Make a collar for soufflé dish (see tip, opposite). Fit collar around dish. Sprinkle the 3 tbsp (45 mL) of sugar into the dish and roll it around to coat the sides and bottom evenly. Knock out the excess. Set prepared dish aside.
2. In a medium saucepan, bring milk and vanilla bean to a simmer over medium heat. Remove vanilla bean and scrape out seeds. Add seeds back to the milk. (Save the pods for another use.) Place the 1⁄2 cup (125 mL) sugar and flour in another saucepan. Using a whisk, gradually beat the hot milk into the sugar mixture until blended. Bring to a boil over medium-high heat, whisking constantly. Boil, whisking constantly, until thick, about 30 seconds. Remove from heat and beat with a wooden spoon to cool slightly. Transfer to a large bowl. This is your soufflé base.
3. Whisk egg yolks into the warm soufflé base, one at a time. Beat in half of the 3 tbsp (45 mL) butter and dot top with the remaining butter to keep a skin from forming.
4. Place egg whites and salt in the mixer bowl. Attach the whip and mixer bowl to the mixer. Set to Speed 4 and beat until foamy. Increase to Speed 8 and beat until soft peaks form. Gradually beat in the 2 tbsp (25 mL) sugar until stiff, glossy peaks form.

5. Using a large rubber spatula, gently fold egg whites into the soufflé base, in 4 additions. Do not completely incorporate the egg whites in the first 3 additions; let some streaks of white remain. With the fourth addition, fold until no streaks remain. Be careful not to overmix.
6. Gently spoon into prepared dish. Place in middle of preheated oven and immediately reduce temperature to 375°F (190°C). Bake for about 20 minutes, or until soufflé begins to rise and brown. Sprinkle top with confectioner's (icing) sugar. Bake for 20 to 25 minutes longer, or until soufflé is firm on the outside edges and slightly creamy in the middle. Carefully remove the collar and serve immediately with chocolate sauce.

Serves 4

TIPS

To make a collar for soufflé dish: Measure out a strip of foil that will fit all the way around the soufflé dish. Fold into thirds lengthwise. Using 1 tbsp (15 mL) softened butter, grease the dish and the top 2½ inches (6 cm) of foil on the side that does not have folded edges. Wrap the foil around the outside of the dish, creating a collar with buttered foil extending 2 inches (5 cm) higher than the top of the dish. Secure with a straight pin or paper clip.

Used vanilla pods can be rinsed and dried and stored in a sugar canister for 2 weeks to make vanilla sugar, which can be used in baking, coffee, tea or whatever you desire.

Chocolate Sauce

6 oz	bittersweet chocolate	175 g
¼ cup	whipping (35%) cream	50 mL

Make ahead

Store chocolate sauce in an airtight container in the refrigerator for up to 1 week. Warm in the microwave for 30 seconds, stir and heat for another 20 seconds. Repeat until smooth and warm.

1. In a heatproof bowl set over a saucepan of hot, not boiling water, melt chocolate, stirring frequently until smooth. Stir in whipping cream and thin with water as necessary. (Be careful not to overheat the chocolate or it will become grainy.) Serve warm or at room temperature.

Makes 1 cup (250 mL)

Classic Chocolate Soufflé

WIRE WHIP

- Preheat oven to 425°F (220°C)
- 8-inch (20 cm) soufflé dish

8 oz	bittersweet chocolate, chopped	250 g
1/4 cup	strong brewed coffee	50 mL
3 tbsp	granulated sugar	45 mL
1 1/4 cups	milk	300 mL
1/3 cup	granulated sugar	75 mL
1/4 cup	unbleached all-purpose flour	50 mL
1 tbsp	vanilla	15 mL
6	egg yolks	6
3 tbsp	unsalted butter, softened	45 mL
6	egg whites, at room temperature	6
Pinch	salt	Pinch
2 tbsp	granulated sugar	25 mL

Make ahead

The soufflé base can be prepared through Step 3 up to 7 hours ahead. Cover tightly with plastic wrap and refrigerate.

1. In a heatproof bowl set over a saucepan of hot, not boiling water, melt chocolate in coffee, stirring often, until smooth. Set aside.
2. Make a collar for soufflé dish (see tip, page 375). Sprinkle the 3 tbsp (45 mL) of sugar into the dish and roll it around to coat the sides and bottom evenly. Knock out the excess. Set prepared dish aside.
3. In a medium saucepan, bring milk to a simmer over medium heat. Place the 1/3 cup (75 mL) sugar and flour in another saucepan. Using a whisk, gradually beat the hot milk into the sugar mixture until blended. Bring to a boil over medium-high heat, whisking. Boil, whisking constantly, until thick, about 30 seconds. Remove from heat and stir in melted chocolate and vanilla. Transfer to a large bowl.
4. Whisk egg yolks into the warm soufflé base, one at a time. Beat in half of the 3 tbsp (45 mL) butter and dot top with the remaining butter.
5. Place egg whites and salt in the mixer bowl. Attach the whip and mixer bowl to the mixer. Set to Speed 4 and beat until foamy. Increase to Speed 8 and beat until soft peaks form. Gradually beat in the 2 tbsp (25 mL) sugar until stiff, glossy peaks form.
6. Using a large rubber spatula, gently fold egg whites into the soufflé base, in 4 additions. Do not completely incorporate the egg whites in the first 3 additions; let some streaks of white remain. With the fourth addition, fold until no streaks remain. Be careful not to overmix.
7. Gently spoon into prepared dish. Place in middle of preheated oven and immediately reduce temperature to 375°F (190°C). Bake for 40 to 45 minutes, or until soufflé is firm on the outside edges and slightly creamy in the middle. Carefully remove the collar and serve immediately.

Serves 4

Cappuccino Soufflé

WIRE WHIP

- Preheat oven to 400°F (200°C)
- 8-inch (20 cm) soufflé dish

3 tbsp	granulated sugar	45 mL
1 cup	milk	250 mL
1/3 cup	granulated sugar	75 mL
2 tbsp	instant espresso powder	25 mL
3 tbsp	unsalted butter	45 mL
1/4 cup	unbleached all-purpose flour	50 mL
1/4 tsp	ground cinnamon	1 mL
4	egg yolks, at room temperature	4
1 tbsp	vanilla	15 mL
5	egg whites, at room temperature	5
Pinch	salt	Pinch
2 tbsp	granulated sugar	25 mL
	Sifted confectioners (icing) sugar	

Make ahead

The soufflé base can be prepared through Step 3 up to 7 hours ahead. Cover tightly with plastic wrap and refrigerate.

1. Make a collar for soufflé dish (see tip, page 375). Sprinkle the 3 tbsp (45 mL) of sugar into the dish and roll it around to coat the sides and bottom evenly. Knock out the excess. Set prepared dish aside.
2. In a medium saucepan, bring milk, the 1/3 cup (75 mL) sugar and espresso powder to a simmer over medium heat, stirring to melt sugar. Remove from heat.
3. In another saucepan, melt the 3 tbsp (45 mL) butter over medium heat. Add flour and cinnamon; cook, stirring, until foamy. Using a whisk, gradually beat the hot milk into the flour mixture until blended. Bring to a boil over medium-high heat, whisking. Boil, whisking constantly, until thick, about 1 minute. Let cool for a few minutes. Transfer to a large bowl.
4. Whisk egg yolks into the warm soufflé base, one at a time. Whisk in vanilla.
5. Place egg whites and salt in the mixer bowl. Attach the whip and mixer bowl to the mixer. Set to Speed 4 and beat until foamy. Increase to Speed 8 and beat until soft peaks form. Gradually beat in the 2 tbsp (25 mL) sugar until stiff, glossy peaks form.
6. Using a large rubber spatula, gently fold egg whites into the soufflé base, in 4 additions. Do not completely incorporate the egg whites in the first 3 additions; let some streaks of white remain. With the fourth addition, fold until no streaks remain. Be careful not to overmix.
7. Gently spoon into prepared dish. Place in middle of preheated oven and immediately reduce temperature to 375°F (190°C). Bake for 40 to 45 minutes, or until soufflé is firm on the outside edges and slightly creamy in the middle. Carefully remove the collar and dust top with confectioner's sugar. Serve immediately.

Serves 6

Citrus Soufflé with Lemon Sauce

WIRE WHIP

◆ 8-inch (20 cm) soufflé dish

1	envelope (1/4 oz/7 g) unflavored gelatin	1
1/4 cup	cold water	50 mL
7	egg yolks	7
1 2/3 cups	granulated sugar, divided	400 mL
	Grated zest of 2 lemons	
3/4 cup	freshly squeezed lemon juice	175 mL
Pinch	salt	Pinch
7	egg whites, at room temperature	7
1 1/2 cups	cold whipping (35%) cream	375 mL

This recipe contains raw egg whites. If the food safety of raw eggs is a concern for you, use pasteurized eggs. Many grocery stores now carry pasteurized eggs in their shells.

1. Measure out a strip of foil that will fit all the way around the soufflé dish and fold it so that it rises 2 inches (5 cm) above the rim. Brush the inside of the collar with vegetable oil and tie to the dish with string.
2. In a small microwave-safe bowl, sprinkle gelatin over cold water and let soften for 5 minutes. Microwave on High for 10 seconds. Stir, then heat for 5 seconds. The gelatin should be melted. If it isn't, heat for 5 seconds more. Stir again.
3. In a heavy saucepan, whisk together egg yolks, 1 1/2 cups (375 mL) of the sugar, lemon zest, lemon juice and salt; cook over medium heat, stirring constantly, until mixture begins to thicken. (Do not let boil or the eggs will scramble.) Transfer to a large bowl and beat with a wooden spoon for 2 minutes to cool slightly. Remove 1/3 cup (75 mL) to use as lemon sauce; cover and refrigerate. Stir gelatin into hot lemon mixture.
4. Place egg whites in the mixer bowl. Attach the whip and mixer bowl to the mixer. Set to Speed 4 and beat until foamy. Increase to Speed 8 and beat until soft peaks form. Gradually beat in the remaining sugar until stiff, glossy peaks form. Transfer to another bowl and clean the mixer bowl and whip.
5. Place whipping cream in the mixer bowl. Attach the whip and mixer bowl to the mixer. Set to Speed 8 and beat until firm.
6. Place bowl of lemon mixture in an ice bath. Using a large rubber spatula, gently fold in egg whites, in 3 additions, then whipped cream.
7. Gently spoon into prepared dish and smooth top. Refrigerate for 3 hours, until set, or for up to 24 hours. Carefully remove the collar. Spoon into 8 serving dishes and dollop with reserved lemon sauce.

Serves 8

Frozen Raspberry Soufflé

FRUIT/VEGETABLE STRAINER
WIRE WHIP

◆ 8-inch (20 cm) soufflé dish

2	packages (each 12 oz/375 g) frozen unsweetened raspberries (about 3 cups/750 mL)	2
2 tbsp	raspberry brandy (optional)	25 mL
1 tbsp	freshly squeezed lemon juice	15 mL
2/3 cup	granulated sugar	150 mL
1 tsp	corn syrup	5 mL
4	egg whites, at room temperature	4
Pinch	salt	Pinch
1 cup	cold whipping (35%) cream	250 mL
1/4 cup	granulated sugar	50 mL
1/4 cup	fresh raspberries (optional)	50 mL

TIP
Syrup at the soft-ball stage measures between 234°F and 240°F (112°C and 115°C) on a candy thermometer. If you don't have a candy thermometer, drop 1/4 tsp (1 mL) of the syrup into very cold water. If it forms a soft ball that flattens of its own accord when removed, it is ready. If it doesn't, cook for another minute and try again.

1. Measure out a strip of foil that will fit all the way around the soufflé dish and fold it so that it rises 2 inches (5 cm) above the rim. Brush the inside of the collar with vegetable oil and tie to the dish with string.
2. Attach the fruit/vegetable strainer to the mixer. Set to Speed 4 and run raspberries through the strainer into a large bowl, with another bowl to catch the solids. Discard solids. Strain through a fine-mesh sieve and discard any seeds. You should have about 1 1/2 cups (375 mL) of raspberry purée. Stir in brandy, if using, and lemon juice. Set aside.
3. In a small heavy saucepan, bring the 2/3 cup (150 mL) cup sugar, 3 tbsp (45 mL) water and corn syrup to a boil over medium-high heat, swirling the pan occasionally to encourage even melting. Boil to the soft-ball stage (see tip, at left), about 4 minutes. Remove from heat.
4. Place egg whites and salt in the mixer bowl. Attach the whip and mixer bowl to the mixer. Set to Speed 4 and beat until foamy. Increase to Speed 8 and beat until stiff peaks form. Pour in hot syrup in a steady stream until incorporated. Continue to beat until bowl is cool to the touch, about 5 minutes. Using a large rubber spatula, gently fold into raspberry purée. Clean the mixer bowl and whip.
5. Place whipping cream in the mixer bowl. Attach the whip and mixer bowl to the mixer. Set to Speed 8 and beat until cream begins to thicken. Beat in the 1/4 cup (50 mL) of sugar until thick. Gently fold into the raspberry meringue.
6. Gently spoon into prepared dish and smooth top. Freeze for at least 6 hours or overnight. Carefully remove the collar and garnish with fresh raspberries, if using.

Serves 8

Blueberry Steamed Pudding

FLAT BEATER WIRE WHIP

- 6-cup (1.5 L) pudding mold or heatproof bowl, generously greased and sprinkled with granulated sugar
- Deep heavy pot or stock pan large enough to hold bowl with about 1½ inches (4 cm) on all sides, with rack to fit in bottom

1¼ cup	unbleached all-purpose flour	300 mL
1½ tsp	baking powder	7 mL
¾ tsp	salt	3 mL
1 cup	granulated sugar	250 mL
½ cup	unsalted butter, softened	125 mL
2	egg yolks	2
	Finely grated zest of 1 lemon	
1 cup	milk	250 mL
3	egg whites	3
2 cups	fresh blueberries	500 mL
1 tbsp	unbleached all-purpose flour	15 mL
	Sweetened Whipped Cream (see recipe, page 416) (optional)	

1. In a small bowl, whisk together the 1¼ cup (300 mL) flour, baking powder and salt.
2. Place sugar and butter in the mixer bowl. Attach the flat beater and mixer bowl to the mixer. Set to Speed 4 and beat until light and fluffy. Beat in egg yolks, one at a time, and lemon zest. Reduce speed to Stir and mix in flour mixture alternately with milk, making 3 additions of dry and 2 of wet. Transfer to a large bowl and clean the mixer bowl.
3. Place egg whites in the mixer bowl. Attach the whip and mixer bowl to the mixer. Set to Speed 4 and beat until foamy. Increase to Speed 8 and beat until soft peaks form.
4. Using a large rubber spatula, gently fold a quarter of the egg whites into the batter to lighten. Spoon this mixture over the remaining whites. Fold in lightly but quickly until mixture is just blended.
5. In a small bowl, toss blueberries with the 1 tbsp (15 mL) flour. Fold gently into the batter.
6. Gently spoon into prepared pudding mold. Cover with foil and secure tightly with kitchen string (or cover with a lid, if your mold has one). Place on a rack in pot. Add enough boiling water to pot to reach halfway up mold. Cover pot and steam pudding in simmering water, adding more boiling water if necessary, for 2 to 2½ hours, or until surface of pudding feels dry and firm. Transfer mold to a wire rack and let cool, uncovered, for 30 minutes. Loosen edges with a thin knife and invert onto a serving plate. Serve warm with whipped cream, if using.

Serves 4

Make ahead

Store wrapped in plastic wrap in the refrigerator for up to 2 days. Bring to room temperature before serving.

Chocolate-Pecan Steamed Pudding

FLAT BEATER WIRE WHIP

- 6-cup (1.5 L) pudding mold or heatproof bowl, generously greased and sprinkled with granulated sugar
- Deep heavy pot or stock pan large enough to hold bowl with about 1½ inches (4 cm) on all sides with rack to fit in bottom

6 oz	good-quality bittersweet chocolate, finely chopped	175 g
1 cup	pecans, toasted and chopped (see tip, page 361)	250 mL
¾ cup	granulated sugar, divided	175 mL
½ cup	unsalted butter, softened	125 mL
5	egg yolks	5
1 tsp	vanilla	5 mL
5	egg whites, at room temperature	5
¼ tsp	salt	1 mL
	French Vanilla Ice Cream (see recipe, page 391) or Sweetened Whipped Cream (see recipe, page 416)	

1. In a heatproof bowl set over a saucepan of hot, not boiling water, melt chocolate, stirring frequently until smooth. Let cool completely.
2. In a food processor, grind pecans with 2 tbsp (25 mL) of the sugar until as fine as possible without making nut butter, scraping inward occasionally.
3. Place ½ cup (125 mL) of the sugar and butter in the mixer bowl. Attach the flat beater and mixer bowl to the mixer. Set to Speed 4 and beat until light and fluffy. Beat in egg yolks, one at a time, and vanilla. Set to Stir and mix in melted chocolate and ground pecans until evenly incorporated. Transfer to a large bowl and clean the mixer bowl.
4. Place egg whites and salt in the mixer bowl. Attach the whip and mixer bowl to the mixer. Set to Speed 4 and beat until foamy. Increase to Speed 8 and beat until soft peaks form. Gradually beat in the remaining 2 tbsp (25 mL) sugar until stiff, glossy peaks form.
5. Using a large rubber spatula, gently fold a quarter of the egg whites into the batter to lighten. Spoon this mixture over the remaining whites. Fold in lightly but quickly until mixture is just blended.
6. Gently spoon into prepared pudding mold. Cover with foil and secure tightly with kitchen string (or cover with a lid, if your mold has one). Place on a rack in pot. Add enough boiling water to pot to reach halfway up mold. Cover pot and steam pudding in simmering water, adding more boiling water if necessary, until surface of pudding feels dry and firm, about 1 hour and 45 minutes. Transfer mold to a wire rack and let cool, uncovered, for 30 minutes. Loosen edges with a thin knife and invert onto a serving plate. Cut into wedges and serve warm with ice cream or whipped cream.

Serves 6 to 8

Make ahead

Can be prepared up to 1 hour ahead. Keep warm in covered pot of water, removed from heat.

Chocolate Chip–Almond Bread Pudding

WIRE WHIP

- Preheat oven to 375°F (190°C)
- 10-cup (2.5 L) baking dish, greased

5 oz	almond paste, crumbled	150 g
1 1/4 cups	granulated sugar, divided	300 mL
4	egg yolks	4
2 1/2 cups	homogenized (whole) milk	625 mL
1 tsp	vanilla	5 mL
4 cups	cubed day-old homestyle white bread (1/4-inch/0.5 cm cubes)	1 L
3/4 cup	semisweet chocolate chips	175 mL
4	egg whites, at room temperature	4
1/4 tsp	salt	1 mL
	French Vanilla Ice Cream (see recipe, page 391)	

Make ahead

Store wrapped in plastic wrap in the refrigerator for up to 2 days. Warm, covered with foil, in a 325°F (160°C) oven for 20 minutes

1. Place almond paste and 1 cup (250 mL) of the sugar in the mixer bowl. Attach the whip and mixer bowl to the mixer. Set to Speed 2 and beat until broken up. Increase to Speed 4 and beat in egg yolks, one at a time, until almond paste is broken into pea-sized pieces, about 3 minutes. Beat in milk and vanilla.
2. In a large bowl, combine bread and chocolate chips. Pour in almond mixture and let stand for 15 minutes, occasionally pushing bread down into custard, until liquid is absorbed. Clean the mixer bowl and whip.
3. Place egg whites and salt in the mixer bowl. Attach the whip and mixer bowl to the mixer. Set to Speed 4 and beat until foamy. Increase to Speed 8 and beat in the remaining 1/4 cup (50 mL) sugar, in 2 additions, until soft peaks form. Using a large rubber spatula, gently fold into the soaked bread cubes.
4. Spoon into prepared baking dish. Bake in middle of preheated oven until pudding is puffed and golden brown on top, about 50 minutes. Let cool slightly on a wire rack. Serve warm with ice cream.

Serves 6

Mango Raspberry Fool

FRUIT/VEGETABLE STRAINER
WIRE WHIP

4	mangoes, peeled and chopped	4
2/3 cup	granulated sugar	150 mL
1/4 cup	freshly squeezed lime juice	50 mL
1 tsp	unflavored gelatin	5 mL
1 tbsp	cold water	15 mL
1 1/2 cups	cold whipping (35%) cream	375 mL
1/4 cup	light rum (optional)	50 mL
1 1/2 cups	fresh raspberries	375 mL
	Additional fresh raspberries	

Make ahead

Store wrapped in plastic wrap in the refrigerator for up to 2 days.

1. Attach the fruit/vegetable strainer to the mixer. Set to Speed 4 and run mangoes through the strainer into a large bowl, with another bowl to catch the solids. Discard solids. You should have about 2 cups (500 mL) purée. Stir in sugar and lime juice.
2. In a small microwave-safe bowl, sprinkle gelatin over water and let soften for 5 minutes. Microwave on High for 10 seconds. Stir, then heat for 5 seconds. The gelatin should be melted. If it isn't, heat for 5 seconds more. Stir again and add to mango purée.
3. Place whipping cream in the mixer bowl. Attach the whip and mixer bowl to the mixer. Set to Speed 8 and beat until firm. Reduce speed to Stir and mix in rum, if using. Using a large rubber spatula, thoroughly fold in mango purée. Fold in raspberries and spoon into 6 serving dishes. Cover and refrigerate for at least 3 hours or overnight. Serve cold, garnished with raspberries.

Serves 6

Orange Sabayon with Fresh Berries

WIRE WHIP

4	egg yolks	4
3 tbsp	granulated sugar	45 mL
	Grated zest of 1 orange	
1⁄3 cup	freshly squeezed orange juice	75 mL
4 cups	berries, such as blueberries, strawberries, blackberries or raspberries	1 L

TIP
Use an instant-read thermometer to check the temperature of the egg yolk mixture. Food that contains eggs should be heated to at least 160°F (71°C) to ensure that any *Salmonella* bacteria present in the eggs are destroyed.

1. In the mixer bowl, whisk together egg yolks, sugar, and orange zest and juice. Set over a saucepan of simmering water, making sure the bottom of the bowl doesn't touch the water. Cook, whisking constantly, until mixture reaches 160°F (75°C). Continue to cook until thick and doubled in volume, about 5 minutes. Do not overheat or the egg yolks will scramble.
2. Attach the whip and mixer bowl to the mixer. Set to Speed 6 and beat until sabayon reaches room temperature, about 5 minutes. Spoon into 6 serving bowls, garnish with berries and serve.

Serves 6

Decadent Chocolate Mousse

ROTOR SLICER/SHREDDER
WIRE WHIP

- Pastry bag fitted with a ½-inch (1 cm) star tip (optional)

12 oz	bittersweet chocolate	375 mL
3	egg yolks	3
½ cup	homogenized (whole) milk	125 mL
¼ cup	granulated sugar, divided	50 mL
1 tsp	vanilla	5 mL
4	egg whites, at room temperature	4
Pinch	salt	Pinch
1 cup	cold whipping (35%) cream	250 mL
2 tbsp	confectioner's (icing) sugar, sifted	25 mL

This recipe contains raw egg whites. If the food safety of raw eggs is a concern for you, use pasteurized eggs. Many grocery stores now carry pasteurized eggs in their shells.

1. Attach the slicer/shredder, with the fine shredder, to the mixer. Set to Speed 4 and grate chocolate into a small bowl. Set ½ cup (125 mL) aside for garnish.
2. In a small heavy saucepan, whisk together egg yolks, milk and 2 tbsp (25 mL) of the sugar until smooth. Cook over medium-low heat, stirring, until mixture begins to thicken, about 7 minutes. (Do not let boil or the egg yolks will scramble) Remove from heat and whisk in remaining grated chocolate until smooth. Whisk in vanilla. Transfer to a large bowl and let cool to lukewarm.
3. Place egg whites and salt in the mixer bowl. Attach the whip and mixer bowl to the mixer. Set to Speed 4 and beat until foamy. Increase to Speed 8 and beat until soft peaks form. Gradually beat in the remaining 2 tbsp (25 mL) sugar until stiff, glossy peaks form. Using a large rubber spatula, gently fold into the chocolate mixture, in 3 additions. Clean the mixer bowl and whip.
4. Place whipping cream in the mixer bowl. Attach the whip and mixer bowl to the mixer. Set to Speed 8 and beat until firm. Gently fold half of the whipped cream into the mousse. Add confectioner's sugar to the remaining cream and beat for a moment to incorporate.
5. Spoon mousse into 6 goblets or a serving bowl. Spoon or pipe the sweetened whipped cream on top and sprinkle with the reserved grated chocolate. Cover tightly and refrigerate for 4 to 6 hours, or until cold and set.

Serves 6

Sunshine Lemon Mousse

WIRE WHIP

1	envelope (1/4 oz/7 g) unflavored gelatin	1
1/4 cup	cold water	50 mL
3	egg yolks	3
3/4 cup	granulated sugar, divided	175 mL
2 tsp	grated lemon zest	10 mL
1/3 cup	freshly squeezed lemon juice	75 mL
1 cup	cold whipping (35%) cream	250 mL
3	egg whites, at room temperature	3
Topping		
1/2 cup	cold whipping (35%) cream	125 mL
1 tsp	confectioner's (icing) sugar, sifted	5 mL
1	lemon, cut lengthwise into halves and thinly sliced (optional)	1

This recipe contains raw eggs. If the food safety of raw eggs is a concern for you, use pasteurized eggs. Many grocery stores now carry pasteurized eggs in their shells.

1. In a small microwave-safe bowl, sprinkle gelatin over water and let soften for 5 minutes. Microwave on High for 10 seconds. Stir, then heat for 5 seconds. The gelatin should be melted. If it isn't, heat for 5 seconds more. Stir again and set aside.
2. Place egg yolks and 1/2 cup (250 mL) of the sugar in the mixer bowl. Attach the whip and mixer bowl to the mixer. Set to Speed 6 and beat until thick and pale yellow. Reduce speed to Stir and mix in dissolved gelatin and lemon zest and juice until incorporated. Transfer to a large bowl. Clean the mixer bowl and whip.
3. Place whipping cream in the mixer bowl. Attach the whip and mixer bowl to the mixer. Set to Speed 8 and beat until firm. Using a large rubber spatula, gently fold into the yolk mixture. Clean the mixer bowl and whip.
4. Place egg whites in the mixer bowl. Attach the whip and mixer bowl to the mixer. Set to Speed 4 and beat until foamy. Increase to Speed 8 and beat until soft peaks form. Beat in the remaining 1/4 cup (50 mL) sugar, in 2 additions, and beat until stiff, glossy peaks form. Using a large rubber spatula, gently fold into yolk mixture until no trace of white remains.
5. Spoon mousse into 6 dessert dishes. Cover tightly and refrigerate for at least 3 hours or overnight.
6. *Prepare the topping:* Place whipping cream in the clean mixer bowl. Attach the whip and mixer bowl to the mixer. Set to Speed 8 and beat until it starts to thicken, then sprinkle with confectioner's sugar and beat until firm. Top each serving with a dollop of cream and a lemon slice, if using.

Serves 6

Easy Pumpkin Mousse

WIRE WHIP

1 1/2 cups	cold whipping (35%) cream	375 mL
1/2 cup	granulated sugar	125 mL
1	can (14 oz/398 mL) pumpkin purée (not pie filling)	1
1/4 cup	pure maple syrup	50 mL
1 tsp	ground cinnamon	5 mL
1/2 tsp	ground ginger	2 mL
1/4 tsp	ground cloves	1 mL
Pinch	salt	Pinch
3/4 cup	crushed gingersnap cookies	175 mL

1. Place whipping cream in the mixer bowl. Attach the whip and mixer bowl to the mixer. Set to Speed 8 and beat in sugar, in 3 additions, until firm. Remove the mixer bowl. Using a large rubber spatula, gently fold in pumpkin purée, maple syrup, cinnamon, ginger, cloves and salt until blended.
2. Spoon mousse into a serving bowl or individual serving bowls. Cover tightly and refrigerate for at least 2 hours, or until set, or for up to 24 hours. Serve cold, sprinkled with gingersnap crumbs.

Serves 4 to 6

Easy Apricot Sorbet

FRUIT/VEGETABLE STRAINER
ICE CREAM MAKER

2	cans (each 16 oz/500 mL) apricots in heavy syrup	2
1/4 cup	freshly squeezed lemon juice	50 mL

1. Attach the fruit/vegetable strainer to the mixer. Set to Speed 4 and run apricots and syrup through the strainer into a large bowl, with another bowl to catch the solids. Discard solids. Stir in lemon juice. Cover and refrigerate until chilled, for at least 3 hours or overnight.
2. Transfer to the ice cream maker and process as directed in manufacturer's instructions. When sorbet is icy and thick, transfer to an airtight container and freeze for at least 2 hours, until firm.

Serves 6

Make ahead

Can be prepared up to 1 day ahead. Keep frozen.

Pineapple Sorbet

ICE CREAM MAKER

1	very ripe pineapple, cored, peeled and eyes removed	1
1 cup	granulated sugar	250 mL
	Finely grated zest of 1 lime	
3 tbsp	freshly squeezed lime juice	45 mL

1. Place pineapple, 1 1/4 cups (300 mL) water, sugar and lime zest and juice in a blender and purée on high speed. Transfer to an airtight container and refrigerate until chilled, for at least 3 hours or overnight.
2. Transfer to the ice cream maker and process as directed in manufacturer's instructions. Transfer to an airtight container and freeze for at least 3 hours, until firm.

Serves 6

Make ahead

Can be prepared up to 3 days ahead. Keep frozen.

Orange Sherbet

CITRUS JUICER • ICE CREAM MAKER

8	oranges	8
8	sugar cubes	8
1	envelope (1⁄4 oz/7 g) unflavored gelatin	1
1 cup	granulated sugar	250 mL
2 cups	nonfat (skim) milk	500 mL

Make ahead

Can be prepared up to 3 days ahead. Keep frozen.

1. Rub the skin of the oranges with sugar cubes. (Be careful not to rub too deeply into the white pith or your sorbet will have a bitter edge to it.) The sugar cubes should turn bright orange and be completely saturated with orange oil from the skin. Set aside.
2. Attach the citrus juicer to the mixer and juice the oranges. You should have 2 cups (500 mL) orange juice.
3. Place juice and sugar cubes in a medium saucepan and sprinkle with gelatin. Let soften for 5 minutes. Add granulated sugar and heat over medium heat, stirring, until gelatin and sugar cubes have dissolved. (Do not let boil.) Remove from heat and add skim milk. (The mixture will look curdled.) Transfer to an airtight container and refrigerate until chilled, for at least 3 hours or overnight.
4. Transfer to the ice cream maker and process as directed in manufacturer's instructions. Transfer to an airtight container and freeze for at least 3 hours, until firm.

Makes 2 cups

Lemon Yogurt Sherbet

ICE CREAM MAKER

1 cup	granulated sugar	250 mL
2 cups	lower-fat plain yogurt	500 mL
	Finely grated zest of 2 lemons	
1/2 cup	freshly squeezed lemon juice	125 mL

Make ahead

Can be prepared up to 3 days ahead. Keep frozen.

1. In a medium saucepan, bring sugar and 1 cup (250 mL) water to a boil, stirring, over medium heat. Boil, stirring, until sugar dissolves. Reduce heat and simmer for 2 minutes. Let cool completely.
2. In a large bowl, combine syrup, yogurt and lemon zest and juice. Cover and refrigerate until chilled, for at least 3 hours or overnight.
3. Transfer to the ice cream maker and process as directed in manufacturer's instructions. Remove the dasher from the ice cream maker and scrape off any zest attached. Stir zest into the sherbet. Transfer to an airtight container and freeze for at least 3 hours, until firm.

Serves 6

French Vanilla Ice Cream

WIRE WHIP ◆ ICE CREAM MAKER

1	vanilla bean	1
1 ½ cups	whipping (35%) cream	375 mL
6	egg yolks	6
1 cup	granulated sugar	250 mL
¼ tsp	salt	1 mL
2 cups	homogenized (whole) milk	500 mL

Make ahead

Can be prepared up to 3 days ahead. Keep frozen.

TIP

Use an instant-read thermometer to check the temperature of the hot custard. It should reach 170°F (75°C) for the desired thickness.

1. Using a small, sharp knife, cut vanilla bean in half lengthwise. Using the knife tip, scrape the seeds from the pod.
2. In a heavy saucepan, bring whipping cream and vanilla bean pod halves and seeds to a simmer over medium-high heat. Remove from heat. Cover and let stand for 30 minutes to allow flavor to steep. Remove vanilla bean pods and bring back to a simmer.
3. Meanwhile, place egg yolks, sugar and salt in the mixer bowl. Attach the whip and mixer bowl to the mixer. Set to Speed 6 and beat until thick and pale yellow. Reduce to Speed 2 and gradually beat in hot cream in a thin, steady stream. Return to the saucepan and cook over medium-low heat, stirring slowly and continuously, until custard thickens and leaves a path on the back of a spoon when a finger is drawn across it, about 5 minutes. (Do not let boil or the eggs will scramble.) Remove from heat and stir in milk.
4. Push custard through a medium-mesh strainer into a large bowl. Cover and refrigerate until chilled, for at least 3 hours or overnight.
5. Transfer to the ice cream maker and process as directed in manufacturer's instructions. Transfer to an airtight container and freeze for at least 4 hours, until firm.

Serves 8

Philadelphia-Style Vanilla Ice Cream

ICE CREAM MAKER

3 cups	half-and-half (10%) cream	750 mL
2/3 cup	granulated sugar	150 mL
1 tbsp	vanilla	15 mL

Philadelphia-style ice cream is easy to make. It doesn't require any cooking, and contains no eggs. It's not as rich and creamy as the custard-based ice creams, but it's what many of us remember from our childhoods, when we ate it right out of the churners on hot summer days.

1. Place cream in a large bowl and gradually whisk in sugar until blended. Whisk in vanilla. Cover and refrigerate until chilled, for at least 3 hours or for up to 3 days.
2. Whisk mixture to blend, then transfer to the ice cream maker and process as directed in manufacturer's instructions. Serve immediately or transfer to an airtight container and freeze for at least 4 hours, until firm.

Serves 6 to 8

Make ahead

Can be prepared up to 3 days ahead. Keep frozen.

Chocolate Ice Cream

WIRE WHIP ◆ ICE CREAM MAKER

2 cups	half-and-half (10%) cream	500 mL
6	egg yolks	6
1 cup	granulated sugar	250 mL
1/4 tsp	salt	1 mL
8 oz	semisweet or bittersweet chocolate, chopped	250 g
2 cups	homogenized (whole) milk	500 mL

Make ahead

Can be prepared up to 3 days ahead. Keep frozen.

TIP

Use an instant-read thermometer to check the temperature of the hot custard. It should reach 170°F (75°C) for the desired thickness.

1. In a heavy saucepan, bring cream to a simmer over medium heat. Remove from heat.
2. Place egg yolks, sugar and salt in the mixer bowl. Attach the whip and mixer bowl to the mixer. Set to Speed 6 and beat until thick and pale yellow. Reduce to Speed 2 and gradually beat in hot cream in a thin, steady stream. Return to the saucepan and cook over medium-low heat, stirring slowly and continuously, until custard thickens and leaves a path on the back of a spoon when a finger is drawn across it, about 5 minutes. (Do not let boil or the eggs will scramble.) Remove from heat and stir in chocolate until melted. Stir in milk.
3. Push custard through a medium-mesh strainer into a large bowl. Cover and refrigerate until chilled, for at least 3 hours or overnight.
4. Transfer to the ice cream maker and process as directed in manufacturer's instructions. Transfer to an airtight container and freeze for at least 4 hours, until firm.

Serves 6 to 8

Chocolate Chip Ice Cream

ICE CREAM MAKER

1	recipe French Vanilla Ice Cream (page 391)	1
5 oz	semisweet chocolate, melted (see tip, page 337)	150 g

TIP
Drizzling melted chocolate into the ice cream as it's processing gives the best results, but if you find this method too awkward, you can stir in grated chocolate or mini chocolate chips once you've transferred the ice cream to a container.

1. Prepare French Vanilla Ice Cream through Step 4. Transfer to the ice cream maker and process as directed in manufacturer's instructions. When ice cream is almost set, carefully drizzle in spoonfuls of melted chocolate, avoiding the dasher. Transfer to an airtight container and freeze for at least 4 hours, until firm.

Serves 8

Variation

Mint Chocolate Chip Ice Cream: Add ½ tsp (2 mL) mint extract and 3 drops of green food coloring to the chilled custard base before processing in the ice cream maker.

Make ahead

Can be prepared up to 3 days ahead. Keep frozen.

Strawberry Ice Cream

ICE CREAM MAKER

1 1/2 cups	whipping (35%) cream	375 mL
4	egg yolks	4
3/4 cup	granulated sugar	175 mL
1	package (16 oz/454 g) frozen strawberries in syrup, thawed and chopped	1
1 tbsp	freshly squeezed lemon juice	15 mL
1 tsp	vanilla	5 mL
1 1/2 cup	homogenized (whole) milk	375 mL

Make ahead

Can be prepared up to 3 days ahead. Keep frozen.

TIP

Use an instant-read thermometer to check the temperature of the hot custard. It should reach 170°F (75°C) for the desired thickness.

1. In a medium saucepan, heat whipping cream over medium heat until steaming. Remove from heat.
2. Place egg yolks and sugar in the mixer bowl. Attach the whip and mixer bowl to the mixer. Set to Speed 6 and beat until thick and pale yellow. Reduce to Speed 2 and gradually beat in hot cream in a thin, steady stream. Return to the saucepan and cook over medium-low heat, stirring slowly and continuously, until custard thickens and leaves a path on the back of a spoon when a finger is drawn across it, about 5 minutes. (Do not let boil or the eggs will scramble.) Remove from heat and stir for 1 minute to cool slightly. Stir in strawberries, lemon juice and vanilla. Stir in milk. Transfer to an airtight container and refrigerate until chilled, for at least 3 hours or overnight.
3. Transfer to the ice cream maker and process as directed in manufacturer's instructions. Transfer to an airtight container and freeze for at least 4 hours, until firm.

Serves 8

Coconut Ice Cream

ICE CREAM MAKER

2 cups	homogenized (whole) milk	500 mL
1 1/2 cups	cream of coconut (sweetened coconut milk)	375 mL
1 tsp	rum (optional)	5 mL

TIP
Cream of coconut is often found near cocktail mixes in the grocery store.

1. In a large saucepan, heat milk over medium heat until steaming. Stir in coconut milk. Cover and refrigerate until chilled, for at least 3 hours or overnight.
2. Transfer to the ice cream maker and process as directed in manufacturer's instructions. Transfer to an airtight container and freeze for at least 4 hours, until firm.

Serves 6

Make ahead

Can be prepared up to 3 days ahead. Keep frozen.

Mocha Almond Ice Cream

WIRE WHIP • ICE CREAM MAKER

1	recipe Chocolate Ice Cream (page 393)	1
1 tbsp	instant espresso powder	15 mL
1 cup	almonds, toasted and chopped (see tip, page 361)	250 mL

1. Prepare Chocolate Ice Cream through Step 3, adding espresso powder with the chocolate. Transfer to the ice cream maker and process as directed in manufacturer's instructions. When ice cream is almost set, add almonds and finish processing. Transfer to an airtight container and freeze for at least 4 hours, until firm.

Serves 6 to 8

Make ahead

Can be prepared up to 3 days ahead. Keep frozen.

Cheesecake Blueberry White Chocolate Ice Cream

ICE CREAM MAKER

2 cups	homogenized (whole) milk	500 mL
1 cup	granulated sugar	250 mL
1 cup	whipping (35%) cream	250 mL
Pinch	salt	Pinch
1 tsp	vanilla	5 mL
8 oz	cream cheese, softened and cut into 8 pieces	250 g
6 oz	white chocolate, chopped	175 g
2 cups	fresh or frozen blueberries	500 mL

Make ahead

Can be prepared up to 1 week ahead. Keep frozen.

1. In a large saucepan, heat milk, sugar, whipping cream and salt over medium heat until sugar has dissolved. Remove from heat and stir in vanilla.
2. Place cream cheese and about 1 cup (250 mL) of the hot milk mixture in a blender and blend on high speed until smooth. Return to the saucepan and stir in remaining milk mixture. Transfer to an airtight container and refrigerate until chilled, for at least 6 hours or overnight.
3. Transfer to the ice cream maker and process as directed in manufacturer's instructions.
4. Meanwhile, in a microwave-safe bowl, microwave chocolate on Medium (50%) for 30 seconds. Stir for a few seconds to see if it is melted enough. If you must return it to the microwave, heat it in 10-second intervals, stirring in between.
5. When ice cream is the texture of soft-serve, stop the ice cream maker and remove the bowl from the mixer. Drizzle in melted chocolate, stirring with a rubber spatula. Stir in blueberries. Transfer to an airtight container and freeze for at least 4 hours, until firm.

Serves 8

Hazelnut Gelato

ICE CREAM MAKER

4 cups	half-and-half (10%) cream	1 L
1 cup	hazelnuts, finely ground	250 mL
Pinch	salt	Pinch
3	egg yolks	3
3/4 cup	granulated sugar	175 mL
1 tsp	vanilla	5 mL
1/2 tsp	almond extract	2 mL

Make ahead

Can be prepared up to 1 week ahead. Keep frozen.

TIP

Use an instant-read thermometer to check the temperature of the hot custard. It should reach 170°F (75°C) for the desired thickness.

1. In a large saucepan, heat cream, hazelnuts and salt, stirring, over medium heat until steaming, about 10 minutes. Remove from heat.
2. Place egg yolks and sugar in the mixer bowl. Attach the whip and mixer bowl to the mixer. Set to Speed 6 and beat until thick and pale yellow. Reduce to Speed 2 and gradually beat in hot cream mixture in a thin, steady stream. Return to the saucepan and cook over medium-low heat, stirring slowly and continuously, until custard thickens and leaves a path on the back of a spoon when a finger is drawn across it, about 5 minutes. (Do not let boil or the eggs will scramble.) Remove from heat and stir for 1 minute to cool slightly. Stir in vanilla and almond extract. Transfer to an airtight container and refrigerate until chilled, for at least 6 hours or overnight.
3. Transfer to the ice cream maker and process as directed in manufacturer's instructions. Serve immediately or transfer to an airtight container and freeze for at least 4 hours, until firm.

Serves 8

Condiments, Sauces and Extras

Homemade Mayonnaise

WIRE WHIP

2	egg yolks	2
1 tbsp	freshly squeezed lemon juice (approx.)	15 mL
1 tsp	Dijon mustard	5 mL
Pinch	cayenne pepper	Pinch
	Salt and freshly ground black pepper	
1 ½ cups	safflower oil	375 mL

Safflower oil is a light, mild-flavored oil that will not leave a strong taste.

TIP

It's very important to add oil very slowly, especially at first, or the mayonnaise will "break," which means it will look curdled and oily. If your mayonnaise does break, just pour the entire mixture into another bowl, add one more yolk to the mixer bowl and slowly reincorporate your broken mayonnaise.

1. Place egg yolks, lemon juice, mustard, cayenne, salt and pepper in the mixer bowl. Attach the whip and mixer bowl to the mixer. Set to Speed 4 and very slowly drizzle in oil until mixture is thick and emulsified (see tip, at left). Thin with a little more lemon juice, if necessary.

Makes about 1¾ cups (425 mL)

This recipe contains raw egg yolks. If the food safety of raw eggs is a concern for you, use pasteurized eggs. Many grocery stores now carry pasteurized eggs in their shells.

Homemade Wasabi Mayonnaise

WIRE WHIP

2	egg yolks	2
2 tbsp	wasabi paste	25 mL
1 tbsp	freshly squeezed lemon juice (approx.)	15 mL
Pinch	cayenne pepper	Pinch
	Salt and freshly ground black pepper	
1 1/2 cups	safflower oil	375 mL

Wasabi is a traditional accompaniment to sushi. We like to serve wasabi mayonnaise with grilled tuna or, better yet, tuna burgers.

1. Place egg yolks, wasabi paste, lemon juice, cayenne, salt and pepper in the mixer bowl. Attach the whip and mixer bowl to the mixer. Set to Speed 4 and very slowly drizzle in oil until mixture is thick and emulsified (see tip, page 400). Thin with a little more lemon juice, if necessary.

Makes about 1 3/4 cups (425 mL)

This recipe contains raw egg yolks. If the food safety of raw eggs is a concern for you, use pasteurized eggs. Many grocery stores now carry pasteurized eggs in their shells.

Garlic Aioli

WIRE WHIP

2	egg yolks	2
2	cloves garlic, finely minced	2
1 tbsp	freshly squeezed lemon juice (approx.)	15 mL
Pinch	cayenne pepper	Pinch
	Salt and freshly ground black pepper	
1 1/2 cups	extra-virgin olive oil	375 mL

Aioli is the Mediterranean version of our mayonnaise. It's made with olive oil instead of safflower or vegetable oil, so its flavor is stronger.

1. Place egg yolks, garlic, lemon juice, cayenne, salt and pepper in the mixer bowl. Attach the whip and mixer bowl to the mixer. Set to Speed 4 and very slowly drizzle in oil until mixture is thick and emulsified (see tip, page 400). Thin with a little more lemon juice, if necessary.

Makes about 1 3/4 cups (425 mL)

This recipe contains raw egg yolks. If the food safety of raw eggs is a concern for you, use pasteurized eggs. Many grocery stores now carry pasteurized eggs in their shells.

Roasted Red Pepper Aioli

WIRE WHIP

2	egg yolks	2
2	cloves garlic, finely minced	2
1⁄2 cup	roasted red peppers, peeled and finely chopped	125 mL
1 tbsp	freshly squeezed lemon juice (approx.)	15 mL
Pinch	cayenne pepper	Pinch
	Salt and freshly ground black pepper	
1 1⁄2 cups	olive oil	375 mL

TIP

To roast peppers, cut open and remove seeds and ribs. Lay flat on a baking sheet, skin side up. Place under the broiler, on the highest rack, about 4 inches (10 cm) from the element. Broil until skins have blackened. Transfer to a heatproof bowl, cover with plastic wrap and let steam for about 5 minutes to loosen skins. Peel skins from peppers.

1. Place egg yolks, garlic, red peppers, lemon juice, cayenne, salt and pepper in the mixer bowl. Attach the whip and mixer bowl to the mixer. Set to Speed 4 and very slowly drizzle in oil until mixture is thick and emulsified (see tip, page 400). Thin with a little more lemon juice, if necessary.

Makes about 2 cups (500 mL)

This recipe contains raw egg yolks. If the food safety of raw eggs is a concern for you, use pasteurized eggs. Many grocery stores now carry pasteurized eggs in their shells.

Basil Aioli

WIRE WHIP

2	egg yolks	2
1	clove garlic, finely minced	1
1⁄3 cup	finely chopped fresh basil	75 mL
1 tbsp	freshly squeezed lemon juice (approx.)	15 mL
Pinch	cayenne pepper	Pinch
	Salt and freshly ground black pepper	
1 1⁄2 cups	olive oil	375 mL

1. Place egg yolks, garlic, basil, lemon juice, cayenne, salt and pepper in the mixer bowl. Attach the whip and mixer bowl to the mixer. Set to Speed 4 and very slowly drizzle in oil until mixture is thick and emulsified (see tip, page 400). Thin with a little more lemon juice, if necessary.

Makes about 2 cups (500 mL)

This recipe contains raw egg yolks. If the food safety of raw eggs is a concern for you, use pasteurized eggs. Many grocery stores now carry pasteurized eggs in their shells.

Whipped Horseradish Cream

WIRE WHIP

1 cup	cold whipping (35%) cream	250 mL
1⁄4 cup	prepared horseradish	50 mL
2 tbsp	sour cream	25 mL
1 tsp	white wine vinegar	5 mL
	Salt and freshly ground black pepper	

Whipped horseradish cream is delicious on roast beef sandwiches, prime rib, hamburgers, steaks and salmon.

1. Place whipping cream in the mixer bowl. Attach the whip and mixer bowl to the mixer. Set to Speed 8 and beat until firm. Using a large rubber spatula, gently fold in horseradish, sour cream and vinegar. Season to taste with salt and pepper.

Makes 2 cups (500 mL)

Make ahead

Can be prepared up to 4 hours ahead. Cover and refrigerate.

Tomato Ketchup

FRUIT/VEGETABLE STRAINER

3	cloves garlic, chopped	3
1	can (28 oz/796 mL) whole tomatoes, with juices	1
2	cans (each 14½ oz/425 g) diced tomatoes with basil and garlic, with juices	2
2	cans (each 14½ oz/425 g) diced tomatoes with Italian herbs, with juices	2
2 cups	chopped onions	500 mL
⅔ cup	granulated sugar	150 mL
⅔ cup	cider vinegar	150 mL
1 tsp	dry mustard	5 mL
1 tsp	paprika	5 mL
¼ tsp	ground cloves	1 mL
¼ tsp	ground allspice	1 mL
¼ tsp	ground cinnamon	1 mL
¼ tsp	celery salt	1 mL
Pinch	cayenne pepper	Pinch
	Salt and freshly ground black pepper	

TIPS

If you can't find seasoned diced tomatoes, plain is fine.

There are about 1½ cups (375 mL) diced tomatoes in each 14½-oz (425 g) can.

1. In a large heavy pot, bring garlic, whole and diced tomatoes with juices and onions to a boil over medium heat. Reduce heat, cover and simmer for 45 to 50 minutes, or until onions are soft. Let cool slightly.
2. Attach the fruit/vegetable strainer to the mixer. Set to Speed 4 and run tomato mixture through the strainer into a large bowl, with another bowl to catch the solids. Add solids to the purée. You should have about 8 cups (2 L).
3. Return purée to clean pot and add sugar, vinegar, mustard, paprika, cloves, allspice, cinnamon, celery salt, cayenne pepper, 1 tsp (5 mL) salt and a pinch of black pepper. Bring to a simmer over medium heat, then reduce heat to maintain a gentle boil, stirring often to prevent scorching, until thick, about 2 hours. Taste and adjust seasoning as desired with salt and pepper.

Makes 4 cups (1 L)

Make ahead

Can be prepared up to 2 weeks ahead. Let cool, transfer to an airtight container and refrigerate. Tomato ketchup may also be canned as directed in your canning instruction manual.

Asian Cranberry Ketchup

FOOD GRINDER

1	bag (12 oz/375 g) fresh cranberries (3 cups/750 mL)	1
2	oranges, peeled and seeded	2
2 tbsp	chopped gingerroot	25 mL
1/2 cup	granulated sugar	125 mL
2 tbsp	liquid honey	25 mL
1 tsp	cider vinegar	5 mL
1 tsp	toasted sesame oil	5 mL
1/2 tsp	Asian chili paste	2 mL
1/2 tsp	salt	2 mL
Pinch	freshly ground black pepper	Pinch

Serve cranberry ketchup with grilled chicken, fish or pork. It is also delicious on turkey sandwiches.

1. Sort through cranberries, removing any soft or shriveled berries, and rinse well. Cut oranges into medium chunks.
2. Attach the food grinder, with the fine plate, to the mixer. Set to Speed 4 and run cranberries, oranges and ginger through the grinder into a bowl.
3. In a medium saucepan, bring ground cranberry mixture, sugar, honey and vinegar to a boil over medium heat. Reduce heat to low and simmer, stirring occasionally, until slightly thickened, about 20 minutes. Remove from heat and stir in sesame oil and chili paste. Season with salt and pepper.

Makes 3 cups (750 mL)

Make ahead

Can be prepared up to 1 month ahead. Let cool, transfer to an airtight container and refrigerate.

Backyard Barbecue Sauce

FOOD GRINDER

2 tbsp	olive oil	25 mL
1 cup	chopped onion	250 mL
3	cloves garlic, minced	3
2	cans (each 28 oz/796 mL) whole tomatoes, with juices	2
1/2 cup	ketchup (store-bought or see recipe, page 404)	125 mL
1/4 cup	cider vinegar	50 mL
1/4 cup	orange juice	50 mL
1/4 cup	soy sauce	50 mL
1/4 cup	fancy molasses	50 mL
2 tbsp	liquid honey	25 mL
1 tbsp	dry mustard	15 mL
1 tbsp	paprika	15 mL
1 tsp	salt	5 mL
1 tsp	ancho chili powder	5 mL
1 tsp	liquid smoke (optional)	5 mL
1/2 tsp	freshly ground black pepper	2 mL
1/2 tsp	dried thyme	2 mL
1/4 tsp	cayenne pepper	1 mL

This sauce is great on ribs, chicken and pork.

1. In a large skillet, heat oil over medium heat. Add onion and sauté until tender, about 3 minutes. Add garlic and sauté for 1 minute. Add tomatoes with juices and cook for 3 minutes to allow flavors to develop. Let cool for 10 minutes.
2. Remove whole tomatoes from the skillet. Attach the food grinder, with the fine plate, to the mixer. Set to Speed 4 and run tomatoes through the grinder into a bowl.
3. Return purée to the skillet and add ketchup, vinegar, orange juice, soy sauce, molasses, honey, mustard, paprika, salt, ancho chili powder, liquid smoke (if using), black pepper, thyme and cayenne pepper; bring to a boil over medium heat. Reduce heat to low so that sauce just simmers. Simmer, stirring occasionally, until sauce is reduced by half, about 3 hours. Taste and adjust seasoning as desired with salt and pepper.

Makes 2 cups (500 mL)

Make ahead

Store in an airtight container in the refrigerator for up to 2 weeks or in the freezer for up to 6 months.

Tomatillo Salsa

FRUIT/VEGETABLE STRAINER

- Preheat broiler
- Large baking sheet

2	serrano chilies, seeded	2
1 lb	tomatillos, husked and rinsed	500 g
1/2 cup	finely chopped white onion	125 mL
1	clove garlic, minced	1
1/2 cup	finely chopped fresh cilantro	125 mL
1/4 cup	water	50 mL
1 1/2 tbsp	freshly squeezed lime juice	22 mL
1/2 tsp	salt	2 mL
	Granulated sugar, if necessary	

TIPS

Tomatillos look like small green tomatoes with a papery husk on the outside. Once the husks are removed, they will be sticky and must be washed well before using. They are members of the nightshade family, as are tomatoes, potatoes, eggplants and peppers. Look for them in Latin American markets and some supermarkets.

Rinsing chopped onion takes away much of the unpleasant "bite" often associated with raw onion.

1. Place chilies and tomatillos on baking sheet and set under the broiler until darkly roasted, even blackened in spots. Let cool.
2. Attach the fruit/vegetable strainer to the mixer. Set to Speed 4 and run roasted tomatillos and chilies, including all the juices, through the strainer into a large bowl, with another bowl to catch the solids. Discard solids.
3. Place onion in a strainer and rinse under cold water. Shake to remove excess moisture. Stir onion, garlic, cilantro, water, lime juice and salt into the salsa. If too tart, season with a pinch of sugar.

Makes 2 cups (500 mL)

Make ahead

Prepare through Step 2, transfer to an airtight container and freeze for up to 2 months. Add remaining ingredients just before serving. Store salsa in an airtight container in the refrigerator for up to 3 days.

Chipotle Salsa

FRUIT/VEGETABLE STRAINER

3	large tomatoes, cored and chopped	3
1	clove garlic, minced	1
1	jalapeño pepper, seeded and minced	1
1/4 cup	chopped green onions	50 mL
3 tbsp	freshly squeezed lime juice	45 mL
2 tbsp	chopped canned chipotle peppers in adobo sauce	25 mL
1/2 tsp	ground cumin	2 mL
1/2 cup	chopped fresh cilantro	125 mL
	Salt and freshly ground black pepper	

Chipotle salsa is not just great with corn chips — try it on scrambled eggs or grilled chicken, beef or fish.

TIP

Because good-quality tomatoes aren't always available, you may wish to add more or less lime juice to taste. The salsa should have a tart edge to it.

1. In a medium bowl, combine tomatoes, garlic, jalapeño, green onions, lime juice, chipotle peppers and cumin.
2. Attach the fruit/vegetable strainer to the mixer. Set to Speed 4 and run tomato mixture through the strainer into a large bowl, with another bowl to catch the solids. Add solids to the purée. Run through the strainer again and add solids to the purée. Stir in cilantro and season to taste with salt and pepper.

Makes 3 cups (750 mL)

Make ahead

Can be prepared up to 4 days ahead. Cover and refrigerate.

Marinara Sauce

FRUIT/VEGETABLE STRAINER

3 tbsp	olive oil	45 mL
4	cloves garlic, minced	4
1	large onion, finely chopped	1
2	cans (each 28 oz/796 mL) crushed tomatoes (see tip, below)	2
2	small bay leaves	2
2 tsp	dried oregano	10 mL
	Salt and freshly ground black pepper	

Marinara sauce is probably the most common of the tomato sauces. Use it on pasta, meatballs — anytime you want a red Italian sauce.

TIP
Look for crushed tomatoes with tomato purée in the ingredient list. This type has a thicker texture and will give more body to your sauce.

1. In a large heavy saucepan, heat oil over medium heat. Add garlic and onion; sauté until onion begins to color, about 10 minutes. Add tomatoes, bay leaves and oregano; bring to a boil. Reduce heat, cover and simmer, stirring often, until flavors blend, about 30 minutes. Remove bay leaves.
2. Attach the fruit/vegetable strainer to the mixer. Set to Speed 4 and run sauce through the strainer into a large bowl, with another bowl to catch the solids. Run just the solids through once more. Discard solids.
3. Return sauce to the saucepan and bring to a simmer over medium heat. Season to taste with salt and pepper.

Makes about 6 cups (1.5 L)

Make ahead

Store in an airtight container in the refrigerator for up to 3 days or in the freezer for up to 2 months.

Bologneses Sauce (Ragu Bolognese)

FOOD GRINDER

1 lb	boneless veal shoulder	500 g
1 lb	boneless pork shoulder blade	500 g
8 oz	boneless beef chuck or cross rib	250 g
4 oz	pancetta	125 g
2 tbsp	extra-virgin olive oil	25 mL
2 tbsp	unsalted butter	25 mL
5	cloves garlic, sliced	5
4	stalks celery, finely chopped	4
2	onions, finely chopped	2
2	carrots, finely chopped	2
1 cup	milk	250 mL
2	cans (each 28 oz/796 mL) whole tomatoes, with juices	2
4 cups	chicken stock	1 L
1 cup	dry white wine	250 mL
	Salt and freshly ground black pepper	

Try this flavorful sauce with Basic Egg Pasta (see recipe, page 192) cut into fettuccine.

1. Cut veal, pork, beef and pancetta into 1-inch (2.5 cm) cubes. Place in a shallow container in the freezer for 30 minutes to facilitate grinding. Attach the food grinder, with the coarse plate, to the mixer. Set to Speed 4 and run meat through the grinder into a large bowl. Return to the freezer for 15 minutes. Run through the grinder again. Set aside.
2. In a large heavy saucepan, heat oil and butter over medium heat. Add garlic, celery, onions and carrots; sauté until onions are translucent, about 5 minutes. Increase heat to high and add ground meat; cook, stirring, for 15 to 20 minutes, or until no longer pink. Add milk; reduce heat and simmer, uncovered, until almost dry, about 10 minutes. Working with a few tomatoes at a time, crush with your hands and add to pot. Pour in juices and simmer for 15 minutes. Add stock and wine; increase heat to medium-high and bring to a boil. Reduce heat, and simmer, stirring occasionally, for 2 to 2½ hours, until flavors are developed and liquid has reduced to a sauce consistency. Season to taste with salt and pepper.

Makes 6½ cups (1.625 L)

Make ahead

Store in an airtight container in the refrigerator for up to 3 days or in the freezer for up to 2 months.

Savory Orange Sauce

CITRUS JUICER

4 to 6	thin-skinned Valencia or navel oranges	4 to 6
2	cloves garlic, minced	2
1 cup	chicken stock	250 mL
1/4 cup	liquid honey	50 mL
1/4 cup	cider vinegar	50 mL
2 tbsp	dry vermouth	25 mL
1 tbsp	Chinese plum sauce	15 mL
1 tbsp	soy sauce	15 mL
2 tsp	minced gingerroot	10 mL
1/2 tsp	Chinese chili sauce	2 mL
1/4 tsp	ground Szechuan peppers or freshly ground black pepper	1 mL

Use this sauce to glaze chicken, ribs, fish, duck and vegetables. It can also be used as a dipping sauce for chicken fingers, egg rolls and spring rolls.

1. Zest one of the oranges to get 1 tsp (5 mL) orange zest. Set aside.
2. Attach the citrus juicer to the mixer and juice enough oranges to make 1 cup (250 mL) juice.
3. In a large skillet, bring orange zest and juice, chicken stock, honey, vinegar, vermouth, plum sauce, soy sauce, ginger, chili sauce and Szechuan peppers to a boil over medium-high heat. Reduce heat to medium and boil gently until sauce is thickened and reduced to about 1/2 cup (125 mL), about 30 minutes.

Makes 1/2 cup (125 mL)

Make ahead

Can be prepared up to 1 week ahead. Let cool, transfer to an airtight container and refrigerate.

TIP

Szechuan peppers look like peppercorns, but they're really a mildly hot berry of the prickly ash tree. They're available in Asian markets and specialty stores.

Lemon Curd

CITRUS JUICER

3 to 5	lemons	3 to 5
1 ¼ cup	granulated sugar	300 mL
1 cup	unsalted butter, cut into pieces	250 mL
5	whole eggs	5
2	egg yolks	2

Use lemon curd as an accompaniment for biscuits, a filling for cakes and tarts, or a dessert sauce with pound cake.

TIPS

When adding the hot lemon mixture to the beaten eggs, be sure to add the liquid slowly and whisk rapidly or the eggs will scramble.

The lemon mixture may not seem very thick after cooking, but it will thicken further as it cools.

1. Zest the lemons to get 2 tbsp (25 mL) zest. Set aside.
2. Attach the citrus juicer to the mixer and juice enough lemons to make ¾ cup (175 mL) juice.
3. In a medium saucepan, bring lemon juice, sugar and butter to a boil over medium heat.
4. In a medium heatproof bowl, whisk together whole eggs and egg yolks. Slowly add lemon mixture in a steady stream, whisking rapidly. Return to the saucepan and cook over medium heat, stirring constantly, until mixture coats the back of a wooden spoon, about 5 minutes. (Do not let boil or the eggs will scramble.) Transfer to a clean heatproof bowl and add lemon zest. Stir for 1 minute to cool.

Makes 2½ cups (625 mL)

Make ahead

Can be prepared up to 3 days ahead. Cover and refrigerate.

Orange Curd

CITRUS JUICER

4 to 6	thin-skinned Valencia or navel oranges	4 to 6
1 cup	granulated sugar	250 mL
1/2 cup	unsalted butter, cut into pieces	125 mL
6	egg yolks	6
2	whole eggs	2

Use orange curd as a filling for cakes or as an accompaniment to pound cakes and biscuits.

TIPS

When adding the hot orange mixture to the beaten eggs, be sure to add the liquid slowly and whisk rapidly or the eggs will scramble.

The orange mixture may not seem very thick after cooking, but it will thicken further as it cools.

1. Zest the oranges to get 2 tbsp (25 mL) zest. Set aside.
2. Attach the citrus juicer to the mixer and juice enough oranges to make 1 cup (250 mL) juice.
3. In a medium saucepan, bring orange juice, sugar and butter to a boil over medium heat, stirring constantly.
4. In a large heatproof bowl, whisk together egg yolks and whole eggs. Slowly add orange mixture in a steady stream, whisking rapidly. Return to the saucepan and cook over medium heat, stirring constantly, until mixture coats the back of a wooden spoon, about 5 minutes. (Do not let boil or the eggs will scramble). Transfer to a clean heatproof bowl and add orange zest. Stir for 1 minute to cool.

Makes 2 cups (500 mL)

Make ahead

Can be prepared up to 2 days ahead. Cover and refrigerate.

Cinnamon Applesauce

FRUIT/VEGETABLE STRAINER

3 lbs	Crispin (Mutsu) or Braeburn apples, cored, peeled and cut into chunks	1.5 kg
1/2 cup	granulated sugar	125 mL
1/4 cup	apricot preserves	50 mL
1 tbsp	freshly squeezed lemon juice	15 mL
1/2 tsp	ground cinnamon	2 mL
1/2 tsp	vanilla	2 mL

TIPS

The apples you choose can make a huge difference in the texture and taste of the applesauce. Apples with a sweet-tart edge give a firmer texture and bigger flavor.

To save a step, you can leave the peels on the apples, but you may want to discard the solids after straining in that case.

If the applesauce isn't sweet enough for you, add 1 tbsp (15 mL) honey.

1. In a large saucepan, heat apples and sugar over medium heat, stirring, until apples begin to sizzle. Reduce heat and cook, stirring occasionally, until sugar has melted and apples give off water. (You are trying to cook the water out of the mixture and make it thick. Be careful not to let apples scorch on the bottom of the pan.) When mixture is thick, after about 30 minutes, add apricot preserves, lemon juice, cinnamon and vanilla. Cook, stirring, until mixture is thick again, about 5 minutes. Let cool for 5 minutes.
2. Attach the fruit/vegetable strainer to the mixer. Set to Speed 4 and run applesauce through the strainer into a large bowl, with another bowl to catch the solids. You may discard solids or incorporate them back into the applesauce. Run through the strainer again, and either discard or reincorporate solids. Serve warm or cold.

Makes 4 cups (1 L)

Make ahead

Store in an airtight container in the refrigerator for up to 2 days or in the freezer for up to 2 months.

Italian Meringue

WIRE WHIP

1 cup	granulated sugar	250 mL
1 tbsp	corn syrup	15 mL
4	egg whites	4
Pinch	salt	Pinch

Italian meringue is less likely to collapse or weep than traditional meringue.

TIPS

Syrup at the soft-ball stage measures between 234°F and 240°F (112°C and 115°C) on a candy thermometer. If you don't have a candy thermometer, drop 1/4 tsp (1 mL) of the syrup into very cold water. If it forms a soft ball that flattens of its own accord when removed, it is ready. If it doesn't, cook for another minute and try again.

Use meringue as a topping for cream pies. Spread it onto the pie with a rubber spatula or use a pastry bag with a 1/2-inch (1 cm) star tip to pipe rosettes of meringue over the pie, making sure the meringue touches the crust to prevent shrinking. Place pie under broiler until meringue is golden, or brown with a kitchen torch.

1. In a medium saucepan, bring sugar, 1/4 cup (50 mL) water and corn syrup to a boil over medium-high heat, swirling the pan occasionally to encourage even melting. Boil to the soft-ball stage (see tip, at left), about 4 minutes. Remove from heat.
2. Meanwhile, place egg whites and salt in the mixer bowl. Attach the whip and mixer bowl to the mixer. Set to Speed 4 and beat until foamy. Increase to Speed 8 and beat until firm peaks form. Reduce to Speed 8 and pour in hot syrup in a thin, steady stream until incorporated. Continue to beat until bowl is cool to the touch, about 5 minutes.

Makes 1 10-inch (25 cm) pie topping

Sweetened Whipped Cream (Crème Chantilly)

WIRE WHIP

1 cup	cold whipping (35%) cream	250 mL
2 tbsp	confectioner's (icing) sugar	25 mL
1/2 tsp	vanilla	2 mL

Whipped cream will keep for hours in the refrigerator, so go ahead and whip it up before company arrives. It will be ready and waiting for you when it's time for dessert.

1. Freeze the mixer bowl and whip for 5 minutes. Place whipping cream in the chilled mixer bowl and attach the whip and mixer bowl to the mixer. Set to Speed 6 and beat until cream begins to thicken. Increase to Speed 8 and beat in sugar and vanilla until cream is your desired texture: either softly billowing or firm enough to pipe in a pastry bag. (It takes about 20 seconds to beat from soft to firm, so watch carefully.) Cover and refrigerate for up to 2 hours. Use as a garnish.

Makes 2 cups (500 mL)

Homemade Vanilla Bean Marshmallows

WIRE WHIP

- 13- by 9-inch (3 L) metal baking pan, generously dusted with confectioner's (icing) sugar

2 1/2 tbsp	unflavored gelatin	32 mL
1/2 cup	cold water	125 mL
1 1/2 cups	granulated sugar	375 mL
1 cup	light corn syrup	250 mL
1/4 tsp	salt	1 mL
1	vanilla bean, split in half lengthwise	1
	Confectioner's (icing) sugar	

If you think marshmallows are just for kids, give these a try. This sophisticated version atop a cup of "fortified" hot chocolate will bring out your inner child.

TIP

Syrup at the firm-ball stage measures between 242°F and 248°F (116°C and 120°C) on a candy thermometer. If you don't have a candy thermometer, drop 1/4 tsp (1 mL) of the syrup into very cold water. If it forms a firm but pliable ball, it is ready. If it doesn't, cook for another minute and try again.

1. Combine gelatin and cold water in the mixer bowl. Let stand for 30 minutes.
2. In a heavy medium saucepan, heat granulated sugar, 1/2 cup (125 mL) water, corn syrup and salt over low heat. Using a small knife, scrape vanilla bean halves to remove seeds and add seeds and vanilla pod halves to the saucepan. Cook, stirring, until sugar has dissolved. Wash down sides of pan with a wet pastry brush to dissolve sugar crystals. Increase heat to high and bring syrup to a boil, swirling the pan occasionally to encourage even melting. Boil to the firm-ball stage (see tip, at left). Remove from heat and carefully remove vanilla bean pods.
3. Attach the whip and mixer bowl to the mixer. Set to Stir and slowly and carefully pour syrup into the softened gelatin in a thin, steady stream until incorporated. Increase to Speed 6 and beat until very thick and white and almost tripled in volume, about 15 minutes.
4. Pour into prepared pan and smooth top with moistened hands. Dust with confectioner's sugar. Let stand at room temperature overnight, uncovered, to dry out. Turn out onto a board and cut with a hot dry knife into 1 1/2-inch (4 cm) squares. Dust with confectioner's sugar.

Makes about 50 marshmallows

Make ahead

Store in an airtight container at room temperature for up to 2 weeks. Do not freeze.

Acknowledgments

We are most grateful to our families, especially our husbands, Rickey and David, who not only put up with the constant whirring of our mixers, but were also an endless source of inspiration and encouragement.

Thanks to all our friends, family, colleagues and culinary students who were willing to take on the task of testing more recipes than we can count. We would especially like to thank Nicole Anastas, Lisa Durkin, Julie Neri and Ann Norvell, for always being willing to test "just one more recipe."

We'd also like to thank Lisa Ekus and her staff at Lisa Ekus Public Relations for working so hard on our behalf; Bob Dees at Robert Rose for inspiring this book and trusting us to bring it to life; our editor, Sue Sumeraj, for her diligent work and careful eye; PageWave Graphics for putting it all together so beautifully; and KitchenAid Home Appliances for supplying us with mixers and all the attachments imaginable.

Library and Archives Canada Cataloguing in Publication

Deeds, Meredith
The mixer bible : over 300 recipes for your stand mixer / Meredith Deeds & Carla Snyder. — 2nd ed.

Includes index.
ISBN-13: 978-0-7788-0203-7.--ISBN-10: 0-7788-0203-5

1. Mixers (Cookery). I. Snyder, Carla II. Title.

TX840.M5D42 2008 641.5'89 C2008-902456-7

Index

A

B

C

D

H

I

K

L

M

N

O

P

Q

R

S

T

U

V

W

Y

Z